Rome and the Barbarians, 100 B.C.–A.D. 400

Ancient Society and History

Rome and the

THOMAS S. BURNS

Barbarians, 100 B.C.–A.D. 400

The Johns Hopkins University Press
Baltimore and London

Printed in the United States of America on acid-free paper
9 8 7 6 5 4 3 2 1

The Johns Hopkins University Press
2715 North Charles Street
Baltimore, Maryland 21218-4363
www.press.jhu.edu

Library of Congress Cataloging-in-Publication Data

Burns, Thomas S.
Rome and the Barbarians : 100 B.C.–A.D. 400 / Thomas S. Burns.
p. cm. — (Ancient society and history)
Includes bibliographical references and index.
ISBN 0-8018-7306-1 (alk. paper)
1. Rome—History—Republic, 265–30 B.C. 2. Rome—History—Empire, 30 B.C.–476 A.D. 3. Rome—Provinces—Administration. 4. Acculturation—Rome. I. Title. II. Series.
DG254.2 .B87 2003
303.48'2360397'09015—dc21
2002015858

A catalog record for this book is available from the British Library.

To My Departed Mentors
John F. Charles
Chester G. Starr
Edward A. Thompson
Sylvia L. Thrupp

Contents

Illustrations and Maps

Illustrations

Maps

Preface

This book began its long gestation when Eric Halpern, then with the Johns Hopkins University Press, asked me to write a book surveying Roman-barbarian relations. Little did I realize how difficult that task would be. I could not have completed the book were it not for the support of friends and colleagues and the patience and assistance of my wife, Carol. Among the former, are Prof. Dr. Helmut Bender, Universität Passau, with whom I have codirected excavations in Germany, including two seasons of work on a late Roman watchtower in Passau-Haibach, Germany (1978–79) and one campaign at the Celtic *oppidum* near Manching, Germany (under the overall supervision of F. Maier, Römisch-Germanische Kommission, 1985); and Prof. Dr. Zsolt Visy, Janus Pannonius University, Pécs, Hungary, with whom I codirected the excavations of a late Roman villa near Babarc, Hungary, in 1998. Prof. Dr. Bernhard Overbeck and Dr. Mechtild Overbeck of the Staatliche Münzsammlung München have given generously of their time and wisdom throughout the project. I owe a special thanks to Prof. Dr. Gunther Gottlieb, Universität Augsburg, for his encouragement over the years and especially while I was a visiting professor in his Lehrstuhl for the academic year 2000–2001. As the book was nearing its final form, five universities invited me to share the outlines of my synthesis: Michigan State University, Universität Heidelberg, Universität Potsdam, Universität Passau, and the Universität Augsburg. Closer to home, Prof. John W. Eadie has provided his insight on this project throughout. The Woodruff Library of Emory University and particularly reference librarian Eric R. Nitschke have worked closely with me over the years to create the type of research base that this project required. Over the past quarter of a century some three thousand students have taken my courses, and their footprints are on nearly every page. They have helped me to understand what level of detail is necessary and which explanations and analogies succeed. They have taught me that without adequate data and an engagement with the sources surveys become little more than just another textbook. My colleagues John Juricek and David Bright found time to read portions of the manuscript and offer their advice. To all these individuals and many more who have put up with my teaching, research, and writing over the years, I extend my most deeply felt appreciation.

Rome and the Barbarians, 100 B.C.–A.D. 400

One

Sometimes Bitter Friends

To invoke the phrase "Rome and the barbarians" is to open a Pandora's box of interpretation and suggestion: Rome, the city on the Tiber, the city of the Caesars, the holy City, the city of temples and churches, the quintessential symbol of urbanity on the one hand and of transcendent imagery on the other, juxtaposed with "barbarity," at once childlike in its simplicity yet unthinkingly violent, the annihilator of urban values, the handmaiden of the Apocalypse. As millions of us swell our already bloated cities, historical Rome floats before us as an earthly paradise. We, dismayed at the level of barbarity needed to survive in rush-hour traffic, hurry to embrace the illusion of Roma, home to functioning urban ideals. But on further inquiry she is revealed to wear many disguises: paymaster and jailer, mistress and mother, temptress and redeemer, to name but a few. So "Rome and the barbarians" conveys essential ambiguities that intrigue and hold our fascination. Finding historical realities within the subtext of our own presumptions is, moreover, an ever elusive task requiring an active engagement with the ancient sources at every level. Generalizations cannot but disappoint readers unless they are brought along on the road to discovery, until they see the flesh of history and not just its contours. Only then might they come away with a sense of the past that exists somewhere between the ancient sources and their own lives.

This book not only provides generalizations, it also takes pains to reveal the types of evidence upon which those statements are based and to illustrate with regionally and topically targeted narratives the great diversity that lies beneath the surface. In this manner each chapter explores a segment in the long relationship between Romans and "barbarians" and does so in an essentially chronological fashion. What changes took place did so at a snail's pace. The historical focus of each chapter is intended to reveal the special circumstances that created conditions necessary for change and to invite the reader to appreciate the various types of evidence available as well as to engage the concerns and priorities of the historical participants themselves. Thematic topics are set against the overall chronological framework throughout. This is a study of change and continuity in which the latter dwarfs the former.

One of the advantages of surveying more than half a millennium in one relatively slender volume is that often the significance of what took such a very long time to develop in historical time stands out much more clearly when viewed in the *longue durée.*[1] This gain is purchased at considerable expense, beginning with the fact that each chapter and many parts of each chapter might have been a fine subject for an entire book. What to include or exclude is, of course, always the author's greatest challenge, but in this case it has also provided some of the most interesting insights into my own approaches to synthesis. When faced with how to explain rather than just how to tell the story, what has worked in my classes over the past quarter of a century has informed my choice. My goal has been to write a history in such a way that students and their teachers will not just learn what scholars think happened and why but also experience a bit of the thrill of exploration. These readers should go away with a keener understanding of the minds and approaches of authors such as Julius Caesar, Augustus, and Ammianus Marcellinus, for example, but also of the ways in which numismatics, comparative methodology, and archaeology are changing the way we look at the ancient world and particularly at the evolving relationship between Rome and its barbarian neighbors. Other scholars working in the field should welcome many of the ideas expressed here, for we all are pruning vines in this vineyard and much found here is owed to them. As scholars we gain personal insight by agreeing and disagreeing with others, and my hope for this book is that it stimulates further discussion of major issues.

Another necessary cost of surveying so long an era is that mentally telescoping events is unavoidable. The result is that we tend to dramatize changes that were trivial and to accelerate changes that were glacial. When we note the limited cognizance and tortoise-like pace of change in the Roman-barbarian relationship among the participants themselves, we discover a historical manifestation of relativity. By the standards of the twenty-first century, obsessed with measuring change through the advancement of technology, when even nanoseconds seem to matter greatly, there were virtually no changes in Roman society worthy of comment. When the barbarians come up for literary discussion in ancient texts, they are accorded the same old rhetorical formulas that had worked among the Romans for centuries. The Romans used many types of literature as vehicles for self-analysis; others were more purely for entertainment. History and ethnography satisfied both needs, and their exposition remained essentially constant until Christianity took hold. Because the Romans were so content with these genres and their uses, they held fast to most of the traditional themes within each, including discussion of barbarians. Here too little changed despite the passing of centuries. Both historical and ethnographic works cast all barbarians as if they were like the famous sculpture of the "dying Gaul": mortally wounded, frozen in heroic anguish, timeless.

Ancient ethnographers, like ancient historians, employed a dichotomy between civilized and uncivilized, urban civilization and barbarians, as a basic tool in their analyses. Thus the literary record preserved in both genres reflects a consistent picture of barbarians as culturally inferior. No amount of direct contact seems to have mattered. An analogy might be drawn to a man looking at himself in the same mirror decade after decade. His face slowly ages, but the mirror remains unchanged. At first glance ancient ethnography seems to go beyond the ancient manuals and foreshadow modern

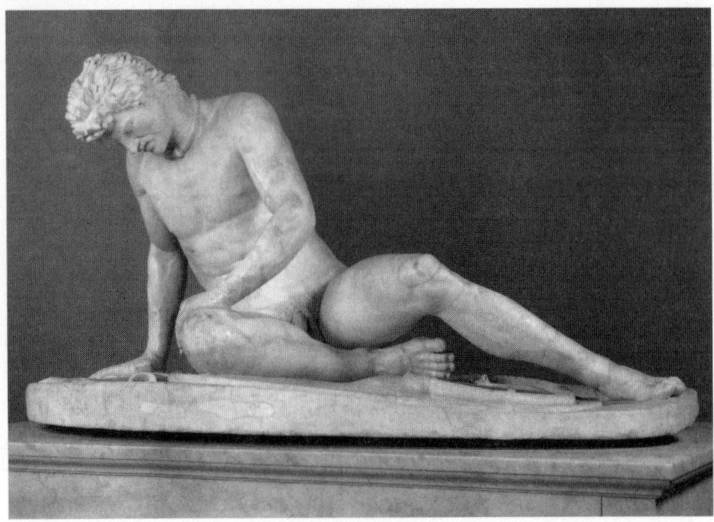

Dying Gaul from the Pergamon Altar. Roman copy of a bronze original dating ca. 230–220 B.C. Courtesy of Roma, Musei Capitolini, Archivio Fotografico.

anthropology, but that impression does a great disservice to today's social scientists.

The only complete ancient ethnography extant is Tacitus's treatise, the *Germania*, a work of vast importance in the ongoing redefinition of the German people from the time of its rediscovery shortly before the era of Martin Luther to the present, but one that is also quite typical of the ancient genre as a whole. Nor can it be readily established to what degree barbarian society changed as opposed to how much the perspective of the Roman observers changed. Tacitus and other Roman commentators analyzed barbarian societies by employing concepts and terminologies borrowed from their own history and the experience of Greek philosophers, particularly Aristotle. Their terminology and approach were in turn adopted by Western analysts in the late nineteenth century and form the language of what is often called Social Darwinism. A hierarchy and evolutionary teleology are implicit in this modern methodology as all societies naturally evolve from simple to complex or fail, but neither Tacitus nor any other Roman author described the process as inevitable or even preferable. The societies they depicted were essentially static until placed in contact with Rome.

All our sources of information, intentional and unintentional alike, suggest that the barbarians did most of the compromising in dealing with Rome and Mediterranean civilization. Roman influence upon the barbarians is evident with respect to material goods and political organization, for example, but Rome's inspiration was not nearly so transformative as it at first appears. If for comparison we use data from Roman rural areas, not just urban centers, then the differences between Roman society and that of the barbarians become far less notable. Were we to focus our attention on those areas within the empire bypassed by Roman urban and military culture, we would find fewer differences still. Unless the opinions expressed in our literary sources can be anchored in a more concrete framework, their independent contributions are best examined entirely within the context of ancient intellectual debate. Fortunately this Draconian solution is not usually necessary. There are checks upon ancient literary license, though none is perfect.

Archaeology provides us with a different window, one through which we can see change, but change appears here almost always as spread over a dismayingly lengthy period, typically at least several generations. By historical standards archaeology provides little in the way of chronological precision and is often without personality. Whereas an author steps out from every page of his text, finding individual motivation in the physical remains of an era is more often than not counterproductive; such impersonal data are best used in aggregate with the help of cold statistical analysis. Like ancient literary sources, modern archaeology, however, has tended to concentrate on urban sites and in that regard has strengthened the ancient bias towards towns. This is largely because modern urban building activities, particularly intense since World War II, have unearthed so much of the ancient substructures. Nonurban sites are much more difficult to finance, for there are rarely private contractors or local governments willing to share the costs of excavation in the countryside, whereas in the cities, once a cultural artifact is disclosed, they often have no choice but to excavate and record it. Such is now the law in most of Europe. Those nonurban sites receiving the most attention are Roman villas, which fed the urban centers and shared their values. Only very gradually has this bias been disclosed, and it has yet to be fully rectified.

When trying to balance impersonal physical data with what is often highly idiosyncratic literary evidence, there is a risk of going too far in one direction or the other. No source type offers a view free of distortion. The danger of using physical data without reference to the literary is that in so doing we jettison all constraints on theory. On the other hand, if we ignore the archaeological data there is a risk of accepting the Romans' view of themselves as history's principal actors, always performing on center stage in their own version of "Manifest Destiny." The literary sources reveal to us the conventional mental world of the upper classes, but we cannot accept their limits in historical explanation just as we do not write upon papyrus. When reading an author such as Julius Caesar, it is essential that we try to establish what he may have seen rather than merely accepting what he chose to record. Nonliterary material does that quite nicely. The literary trap is nonetheless not easily avoided, for the Romans are decidedly the best known of our protagonists. Somewhere between these extreme poles—one the wide-angle focus on generational change provided by archaeology, the other a close-up view through the eyes of great men—lies a more accurate historical reconstruction, one that this book seeks to capture. In order to keep the limitations of these types of evidence in mind, it is best to set them forth clearly and separately. Only after the various types of evidence have revealed their distinctive partial view is it appropriate to offer an overall causative analysis.

Although archaeological data and other unintentional evidence can go far in balancing the bias of the literary sources, neither physical data nor literary records really lessen the problem of time compression. Conceptualizing half a millennium may simply be impossible. Few factors appear to have been steadfast throughout these five centuries, but there were some. The chief among these is environmental conditions. Many of the most obvious differences between Romans and barbarians stemmed from differences in the environment, but not in the naive way that the ancient geographers and ethnographers thought. Europe has a great many climatic variations. Rivers and prevailing winds create numerous microclimates. The various Alpine ranges channel winds and weather in complex ways quite unlike the Rocky Mountains, which act as a general north-south barrier running the length of the North American continent. So too the effects of the Gulf Stream upon northern Europe are diffuse. The Mediterranean parts of the Roman Empire were wheat-producing and urban-centered. As the empire expanded into northernmost Gaul, Rome moved into a new environmental zone in which barley was the principal crop and large nucleated population centers were unknown. The transition from wheat to barley is not readily plotted on a map with a smooth line. The large number of rivers navigable by watercraft carrying modest loads, the diverse microclimates, and resulting crop patterns assured that pre-Roman Iron Age Europe would have many complex economic relationships. Roman expansion altered some of these preexisting patterns, but it did so neither immediately nor usually very thoroughly. These changes, when they did take place, did not necessarily move in the direction Romans wished, nor were they usually as profound as Roman authors imagined them to be.

Alongside these natural factors were four fundamental ancient assumptions about life that are quite different from modern views. These were the deeply entrenched notions that (1) an individual's character was established at birth; (2) society was fundamentally structured around patron-client relationships; (3) education involved a unilineal process in which rhetorical presentation was central; and (4) technology was essentially static. Perhaps the most foreign of these principles is the first. Simply put, many Romans believed that each individual had an indelible character at birth, which could rarely be changed and then only with great difficulty, although its true configuration might lie hidden for much of a person's life. Towards the end of one's life, senility and death intervene to cloud and finally to bring life to an end, but the essentials of one's character remain until death. Romans transferred much of their approach to individual character and their ideas on aging to their understanding of history. Like men, civilizations were born, passed through adolescence, matured, weakened, and died, but their defining characteristics remained until replaced by those of another civilization. Roman authors emphasized changing leadership rather than cultural or other types of collective change. A society's characteristics were like those of a single human being, irreducible and essentially unalterable. History was a moral template. Only force kept an individual's good character on track, or a bad one harnessed for good purpose, and so too a society. The goal of any people was the attainment and preservation of a healthy and mature society in which the society's defining values flourished. Romans understood themselves in relationship to others, for each was seen as a necessary force holding a joint world in equilibrium.

This line of reasoning helps explain why Roman authors so frequently resorted to migration theory—in essence, they replaced individual members of the cast—rather than analysis of subtle cultural developments involving complex changes among entire peoples. To hold Roman society on its predestined path against external pressure required constant vigilance and strict adherence to Roman traditions. This is not to say that there was no genuine movement of people, individuals and groups, in antiquity. The historical records cannot so easily be dismissed. Rather the point is that for ancient authors pressure from foreign invaders, migration, and the disasters that followed were irresistible explanations of events occurring within their own society. This psychology may also help account for the predominance of war within the literary genre of history, because war often quickly established the supremacy of one people over another and offered a convenient canvas upon which to display moral leadership. The other three basic assumptions are less subjective and so a bit easier to grasp, but their ramifications were hardly less important.

The second of these, the ubiquity of patron-client relationships, influenced virtually all personal, governmental, and international relationships throughout the entire period under investigation. Romans and barbarians shared this vision of how people should interact with one another as both individuals and groups, and everybody well understood the respective roles of patron and client and the webs of mutual obligation that united them. By the opening of the second century A.D. the empire's civilian government had emerged as a complex bureaucracy paralleling the imperial army, which had taken up positions in direct contact with the barbarians. The barbarian world, however, had not evolved complex administrative or social institutions nor would it ever, and so the empire quite naturally used its own institutions to dispense and manipulate imperial patronage among its barbarian neighbors as clients in a manner consistent with traditional practice. Thus the underlying patron-client mentality was alive and well beneath what appears in Roman records as a highly bureaucratized relationship.

The third assumption is that rhetorical training preserved style and the use of formulaic description, topoi, generation after generation. The rhetorical method encouraged the speaker or writer to engage the reader and lead him to a conclusion by surrounding the narrative with a familiar intellectual landscape, each image was to strike a resonance with the listener and urge him along the proper path. The creativity of the orator was in large part determined by the skill with which he manipulated these well-known portraits and set them to the pedagogic task at hand, not in his ability to manufacture new and more persuasive analogies, and certainly not in the verisimilitude of his examples. Such rhetorical methodology has all but disappeared from modern society.

Fourth, the technology available to alter the natural environment changed very little during the entire period of Roman history. Unchanging nature reinforced Roman society's inherent conservatism and understanding of history. Soon after conquest Romans extended the Mediterranean world's advanced hydrology, urban sanitation systems, and housing standards to the conquered; maximized the use of forced-air heating; and upgraded roadways for heavy military traffic. Further technological advance, however, was limited, and the minor advancements that did take place were more commonly the result of new circumstances arising along the frontiers than the further development of Mediterranean-based technology. Instead of being psychologically enthralled by the use of new devices and manufacturing techniques, Romans and non-Romans generally ignored what little technological change was taking place and preferred time-honored craftsmanship. Their favorite topics of discussion were family, warfare, moral leadership, and the gods.

Where we tend to see structural change and institutional evolution, they saw instead a chain of families. Thus the ancient sense of time itself was different than our own. During the fourth century Christianity both challenged and grafted itself onto this mind-set. Christians, taking over the Jewish prophetic tradition, ultimately established a new teleology and gave change over time direction by superimposing a beginning and an end, creation and salvation, upon ancient pagan tradition. The thorough Christianization of the empire had, however, scarcely begun by 400, and even then most people typically thought that change usually meant the loss of honor and with it cultural continuity. Even in the early fifth century, except for Christian moral perfection, change was something to be avoided. Societal change resulted from the imposition of one culture over another, one religion over another, or the will of one individual or family over another. In foreign affairs change was brought about by the conquest of one people by another. Romans saw themselves and their conquests as agents of positive change—bringing other peoples the rule of law, for example. While changing others for the better, they believed that they themselves were unchanged by the process. It might take a very long time for the culture of the conquered to come over to "the Roman way," but it was inevitable that it would, and at the end of the process Roman culture, that of the ancestors, would tower above all. Insuring Roman cultural continuity required strong leaders able to safeguard the Roman people, lest the tides of change imposed by them upon others reversed course. Good leaders demonstrated their personal merit and the health of Roman society under their tutelage through the celebration of victories over those outside it—that is, over the barbarians. Change could come about only if they let down their guard or failed in their task of keeping the outsiders at bay. A vision of barbarians forcing themselves into the Roman world was thus implicit in gauging the health of Roman society and the worthiness of its leaders.

Truly noble Roman leaders kept the currents of change moving in the right direction, that is, from barbarism towards the higher values of Roman civilization. Under their custodianship Rome prospered. They did so by manifesting traditional aristocratic virtues; foremost among these were manliness (*virtus*), respect for tradition and the gods (*pietas*), and clemency (*clementia*). At the center of each of these virtues stood the patron, that is, the father, the head of family, the head of government, acting as the defender, the link to the gods, and the stern but fair-minded judge. These concepts were not lost on the barbarians. Armed struggle against foreign aggressors most clearly tested one's manliness. The emperor Augustus appeared in art and literature manifesting these centrist ideals of Roman superiority at the dawn of the empire. He made them seem eternal and blessed by the gods. In Hades, Vergil's Aeneas, in one of the most famous passages in all Latin literature and one clearly addressed to Augustus, hears his father Anchises say of Rome's destiny:

> Others will cast more tenderly in bronze
> Their breathing figures, I can well believe,
> And bring more lifelike portraits out of marble;
> Argue more eloquently, use the pointer
> To trace the paths of heavens more accurately
> And more accurately foretell the rising stars.
> Roman, remember by your strength to rule
> Earth's people—for your arts are to be these:
> To pacify, to impose the rule of law,
> To spare the conquered, battle down the proud.[2]

The public display of these virtues was just as incumbent upon Augustus's successors as it had been to noble Romans long before Augustus took over the fortunes of the Julian family. The same values in their Christianized forms outlasted the empire. The Roman sense of destiny was an extension of overcoming historic challenges, learning from them, and building upon the successes of their ancestors.

The generation before Augustus witnessed the unbridled quest for personal supremacy between Pompey the Great and Julius Caesar. These megalomaniacs managed only to destroy the Roman Republic. As a part of this struggle for eminence, however, Caesar produced one of our most valuable firsthand accounts of foreign populations in the West, and, although it is largely lost, Pompey did likewise for the East. By the death of Augustus in A.D. 14 some aspects of aristocratic competition had been harnessed to the service of the state, and personal privilege had begun to give way to public responsibility. Peace demanded it so. Titus Livy's (ca. 60 B.C.–A.D. 17) great rhetorical history of Rome, written after Augustus's victory over Mark Antony at Actium in 31 B.C., argued that subjugating the individual's desires to the needs of the family and state was precisely the virtue that had made Rome great and could make it greater still. Before Livy, Julius Caesar and, a century and a quarter after Livy, Cornelius Tacitus struggled to plumb what this peculiar combination of personal dignity and Roman civic obligation meant for the destiny of their society. Each found a different answer. Caesar believed that the solution lay in the supremacy of one man over the senatorial elite. Tacitus placed the ruling class within a system directed by one man, the emperor. These changes reflected the progressive systematization of government and the concomitant need to realign personal ambition. The barbarians play a role in each of these discourses and not just as convenient protagonists. Both Caesar and Tacitus recognized that, for those whom Rome had "battled down," their sacrifice for the luster of Roman civilization was a heavy price. They were quite conscious of the fact that Roman expansion came at the cost of somebody else's freedom.

Such views of human relations precluded the idea that a healthy society might be multicultural. No Roman author celebrated diversity. Reality was contrary. Slowly but irresistibly the empire mixed peoples and cultures, and by the fifth century it was no longer just a mixing bowl but a melting pot, something that the city of Rome itself had long been. The world of Marius and Julius Caesar was not that of Diocletian and Constantine. The empire of the late Roman Republic was just then entering into a sustained relationship with barbarians north of the Alps, but by the reign of Constantine the Great, barbarians and Romans were locked in a daily symbiosis punctuated by sporadic outbursts of open warfare. There were always great regional and local distinctions, but there were also surprising similarities. What it meant to be Roman changed and, with it, what made non-Romans barbarians, but these transformations took centuries.

We presently stand so close to the end of the Cold War that we hardly seem able to convince ourselves that it is truly over, and in many places the end has exposed an unexpected fragility in the nation-state, leaving a void not yet filled. By Roman standards, the half century of global standoff between capitalism and communism is but the blink of an eye. Yet almost fifty years of so-called superpower confrontation clearly changed life on our planet without a single atomic cloud blotting out one human life. Surely the real fallout will be seen to have been in the areas of technological development, social-economic change, and political revolution and in subtle cultural forces so much a part of our daily life as now to be imperceptible. Vast sums of money, frightening percentages of the world's productivity, were transformed by this brief outbreak of military angst. Americans were told that they confronted an "evil empire." The Roman Empire lived with "barbarians," real and imagined, for ten times fifty years, and throughout most of those centuries it spent a high percentage of its wealth on military endeavors, also justified by claims of imminent barbarian threat.[3] By the end of the second century much wealth and technical competence had been transferred from the shores of the Mediterranean to the edges of the empire and beyond in order to contain the supposed barbarian threat.

Beginning around A.D. 240, Roman civil wars brought the periphery into the heart of the empire. Because there were never enough recruits to fill the ranks of all the competing armies, rival generals invited large numbers of barbarians to serve in or alongside Roman armies. When peace finally returned towards century's end, many barbarians were welcomed as permanent settlers in the empire. They took their newly found wealth with them wherever they ended up, some to the bypassed interiors of frontier provinces where they were established as farmer-soldiers; others took their pay to homes far beyond the Roman frontier. Regardless of the reason, these barbarians revitalized and changed the societies in which they lived, and in turn, were themselves changed. That emperors and generals preached that all this was done in the name of defense did not alter the nonmilitary impact of these developments, which went unnoticed in the literary record. Romans did not look at their investment in terms of technology and economics but rather as an extension of their own values and beliefs. The official line, unchanging from the republic through the empire, spoke only of the restoration of Roman power and the submission of barbarians to a higher culture. Always, Rome triumphed over the barbarians. Always, Rome came first.

Even the modest preeminence afforded to Rome by the word order in the book's title continues the long tradition of superimposing Roman upon barbarian. Turning the phrase around to read "Barbarians and Rome" does not liberate us from the walls of prejudice, for, regardless of the sequencing, in juxtaposing two we invariably simplify history into a Hegelian dichotomy of force and counterforce, a binary world, a "we versus them" scenario. In so doing we fall ready victims to the myopia of our Roman sources, whose approach is much the same, and through their eyes look outward from a secure center directly to a threatened periphery and overlook the mundane middle, where contrasts and compromise dominated the physical and psychological landscapes. Bipolarity depends upon the existence of monolithic poles, which never existed in antiquity among either Romans or barbarians. The only unity of vision was that conveyed in the Roman educational regime, which passed along centuries old literary traditions as if they were yesterday's observations. Barbarians were always and only the essential other, lumped together for ridicule or praise, all largely contrived for the moment, past or present. They were "outsiders" without whom there could be no insiders. The Roman world was incomprehensible without barbarians. Had barbarians not existed, Romans surely would have invented them as the Greeks did the Amazons, for to understand self Romans needed other. Non-Roman provincial populations were lost sight of in this conception of the world. These bypassed people were culturally still barbarians, and so we might call them "internal barbarians," to distinguish them from barbarians still dwelling outside. Beyond the barbarians lay emptiness and vast oceans.

Roman-barbarian interactions are not easily explored. In part this is because so much has been lost during the intervening centuries, but also because so much has been added. Much of the following discussion of Romans and barbarians takes place within three interlocking categories. First, "barbarians" figured prominently as cultural foils in ancient intellectual discourses about change and values. In fact, it is only within this intellectual sphere that the term barbarian was regularly used.

The second general area of Roman-barbarian interaction manifest in the sources lay in the policies and programs of leaders and governments. At no time, however, did Roman leaders create a barbarian policy. Rather, they shared a traditional Roman mind-set towards foreigners within which governments carried out restricted policies towards specific non-Roman groups just as patrons related to their clients within a recognized code of interpersonal relations. As Roman leaders, they had to appear to take action. This intellectual conservatism runs throughout all official announcements having to do with barbarians and is equally apparent in art and literature. When we find a Roman author employing the term barbarian, more often than not he is asking the reader to engage in a cultural exercise designed to culminate in yet another celebration of Roman superiority; however, if that author is describing specific actions for which he has detailed evidence, then he speaks of specific groups dwelling within the cultural category of barbarian and living apart from Romans. The specific barbarian peoples are then seen to act within the same traditional categories that emerge from official propaganda, although their actions are not usually portrayed in the same highly abbreviated form as was necessary on coins or public inscriptions. In ethnographic treatises specific barbarian groups were depicted as having special attributes of barbarism, so that taken as a whole each barbarian characteristic was separately delineated as well as integrated into the central dichotomy of barbarism and civilization.

Roman authors lived and wrote within the cultural parameters of the aristocratic elite to which they belonged and to which even the most hard-bitten soldier-emperors had to turn for political support. One result of this political symbiosis is the use of common themes and approaches in so much ancient historical writing and official propaganda. The nature of ancient historical writing, as we shall see, tended to assign barbarian groups levels of cohesion and permanence that they did not deserve. Barbarian peoples formed a single rhetorical image used to strike a symbolic resonance with the audience. Once coined, authors employed the same names for the same purposes generation after generation.

The third and most important way that we can still see barbarians and Romans interacting is on the personal level of normal exchange, with its hatreds, friendships, and mutual dependency. Romans and barbarians were rarely enemies. As in most long-term relationships, they were, however, sometimes bitter friends. Their interpersonal interactions are the most difficult to reconstruct and to do so requires careful attention to context, but they also afford us a more realistic view of the forces at work changing ancient society. Although this book approaches its subject from all three perspectives, absolute certitude remains beyond reach for each. In large part this uncertainly is the result of the opaque nature of the evidence, but it is also a reflection of the extraordinarily complex evolutions that were occurring among Romans and non-Romans simultaneously, region by region.

It is impossible to reduce the complex story of Romans and barbarians to a single concept or core element, but several themes stand out as especially important within the categories just noted. Perhaps foremost is the struggle of honor-based societies (Roman and barbarian) to accommodate an overwhelming military presence—that is, the Roman army as it emerged from the wars with Carthage and the struggles with the so-called Hellenistic monarchies. If we seek to define primary cause-and-effect for the outlines of the Roman-barbarian relationship, the Roman army will occupy center stage, and this stands out most sharply at moments of accelerated transition within the empire itself. As honor-based societies, Romans and their barbarian neighbors had well-understood mechanisms to preserve and restore dignity. Often these involved appropriate retribution against the party deemed responsible for the offense, but the party held accountable for the dishonor was rarely just the individual culpable for the transgression. Rather, people held responsible those whose authority over the perpetrator had lapsed. This could be his family (extended or nuclear), his village, or even an entire regional population.

Civil war was a curse among both Romans and barbarians. Typically Roman authors regarded their own civil wars as grave affairs while making light of the state of endemic petty warfare among the barbarians, when in fact both were much involved in the other's internal strife. Roman authors and the iconography of imperial victory employed a special vocabulary to distinguish civil war against other Romans and foreign wars, which included the revolt of conquered peoples under their native leaders. Only foreign wars could occasion the celebration of a triumph; there was no honor in slaying fellow Romans.[4] The careful attention Romans paid to these subtleties reflects the thin line that conceptually separated internal and external barbarians as well as the clear line that in the republic and early empire distinguished Romans from all others.

Violent exchanges among barbarians often took place far from Roman eyewitnesses and, as many Roman authors were well aware, were usually over long before Romans had any notion there had been a disturbance. As Roman clients those barbarians living nearer to Roman power were forced to limit their warfare or account to their Roman patron. Violence among the Romans themselves occupies a distressingly large portion of their historical records. It is readily overlooked, but Romans had their own principles of honor and dishonor, which had once upon a time been quite similar to those of the barbarians. By the end of the second century B.C. Rome had become an empire in all but name and was well advanced in the process of overlaying principles of state government and responsibility upon the familial customs of their less sophisticated ancestors; however, the outlines of those earlier traditions remained and helped narrow the conceptual gap between them and their barbarian neighbors. In the new state system Roman honor and dishonor were no less compelling than in the old, and redressing outrage was hardly less violent. Legionary might allowed Roman commanders to crush opposition and smash barbarian villages at will.

With the establishment of western provinces and the gradual shift to a system of preclusive defense based on the stationing of the army along the external administrative borders of the empire, the conditions were right for barbarians and Romans to carry on a sustained interaction. Violence within one society inevitably affected the other. One consistent result of this interaction was a new understanding of what constituted justice and appropriate retribution. Another was the clarification of appropriate action and responsibility between Rome and its foreign clients—that is, the barbarian regimes around the imperial periphery. When a client state stepped beyond these restraints, the legions redressed the imbalance. The army guaranteed and institutionalized the Roman code of honor and dealt out punishment to those who offended it, but the army was not always of one mind. A mutual concern for honor among barbarians and Romans was apparent in Gaul in the first century B.C. and in the frontier provinces of the next century and was still fundamental in the late empire of the third, fourth, and early fifth centuries; as the centuries faded into one another, however, barbarians and Romans also saw each other through different lenses.

All had to respond to the progressive institutionalization and urbanization of Roman society, to the forces unleashed on both by civil war, especially among the Romans, and to the gradual, sometimes imperceptible withering of distinctions between Roman and barbarian in the frontier provinces. Most important, both had to live with the Roman army and the tremendous concentration of resources and power that it represented. Although Roman legal and literary sources lead one to assume that the Roman frontier was based on exclusion, in reality Rome never had the manpower and resources that exclusion demanded. Permanent exclusion was never the goal. Rather, Roman efforts were directed towards controlling the process of inclusion, first among conquered provincials and then among those living beyond the frontiers who had proved worthy. Legal distinctions of status were used as rewards to encourage people along the path from non-Roman to citizen. In this regard the Roman frontier was more like that of the Spanish in Mexico and Latin America than the British in North America.[5] Roman conquests unleashed forces that no policies could control. Rome's legions shifted the social, political, and economic balance of the entire Mediterranean world. Although the supposed barbarian threat justified the maintenance of at least a quarter of a million men under arms, the army's demonstrable purpose was the protection and promotion of those Romans in power, that is, of their commanders-in-chief, the senatorial elite and later the emperors. Had Romans a longer-term perspective on their society, or had their historians been interested in structural analysis rather than moral criticism, they might have declared that it was no easier for them to live with their army than with the barbarians. Roman society, however, did find ways to coexist with its overwhelming military force and so did successive generations of barbarians.

Individuals and families, whether barbarian or Roman, were all dependent on the soil to some degree, and they all had to react on occasion to forces beyond the limits of their agrarian worlds. At one level anyone not a Roman was a barbarian, just as anyone not a Greek had been before Rome's rise to dominance. Yet among Roman authors as among those of classical Greece, there was much slippage in the usage of the term barbarian. Examples of ambiguity abound. The question of whether Persians were barbarians continued to be answered variously under the Romans as among the Greeks. What about the inhabitants of new provinces who were not citizens? What about immigrants? To identify "outsiders," one needs to define the insiders. Historians have long faced the problems deriving from ancient terminology. Edward Gibbon writing at the end of the eighteenth century distinguished Persians and "northern barbarians," although he still slid back from time to time into the habit of his sources by calling both barbarians. This book continues the tradition and concentrates almost exclusively on barbarians of the North, to use more of Gibbon's phraseology, but it is not restricted to those whom he or his sources called Germans.[6]

The rubric "German" never included all the barbarians in Europe. The non-Romanized populations of Britain, for example, were not Germanic peoples, nor were the Dacians, and neither was called such by the Romans. Most modern usage of the term German derives from classical philology of the eighteenth and nineteenth centuries that envisioned the Germanic language group as occupying a central branch of the Indo-European language tree. Another related branch was occupied by Celtic tongues such as

Gaelic. These linguistic theories were based on the study of surviving Celtic and Germanic languages, but there was always a problem with early Germanic because only fourth-century Gothic is extant as a written Germanic language prior to the ninth century. Concurrent with the creation of these linguistic theories, historians and politicians integrated them into their justifications and explanations of the rise of the nation-state, which is now again in question. One way out of this terminological conundrum might be to restrict our discussion to one term. In line with that reasoning, however, even if one were to narrow the topic to Roman-German relations as defined by the ancient authors themselves, one would scarcely avoid controversy and would incorrectly stress one component of ancient ethnographic discourse without really seeing the broader and richer historical panorama.

Seeking a specific ethnographic meaning in the terms "German," "Celt," or "barbarian" yields much the same result as forcing "Indian" into a precise descriptive category for all Native Americans. In both cases the terms reveal more about the dominant culture's preconceptions and inherited terminology than about those being described, but like "Indian" among European Americans, "German" or "Celt" conveyed a "something" that was recognizable and, most important, useful to Romans. Part of our task is to explore what that something was at differing moments in the long relationship. When groups such as Germans or Celts were subdivided into the numerous foreign *gentes* known to ancient Romans, or into "tribes" in the United States, the definition of the group by the dominant power external to it set parameters among the subordinate peoples. Dealing with the dominant power, in this case Rome, forced inferiors to create more effective internal organizations. Unless they were perceived as being able to assure their own compliance, there was no point in the dominant power making agreements with them. The dominant partner dictates the structures with which it will deal and usually establishes points of contact and standards of conduct. The greater the gap between dominant and inferior, the more disruptive these venues of interaction become. At some point the inferiors may seek to rekindle earlier cultural expressions in order to refashion their identity, but not always.

These patterns of dominant-inferior relations have appeared throughout world history, Roman, Mayan, Chinese, European, and American civilizations have all acted to transform their less developed neighbors.[7] In those cases in which an urbanized society abutted but did not conquer more primitive peoples, the result has been the gradual evolution of higher forms of political organization among the dominant society's neighbors towards urban standards.[8] In creating categories by which to discuss foreign peoples, the dominant society recognizes that the inferior has a certain level of independence from direct administration, but the dominant includes the inferior inside its active sphere of influence and orchestration. That is to say, the state system does not directly control the neighboring populations through taxation and the dispensation of justice, but it does attempt to control aspects of their political and military conduct and to prescribe certain types of interaction among the inferiors themselves. In the case of so-called Germanic populations, Roman influence increased as Celtic waned. Roman power was also more politically and militarily concentrated than the Celtic had been, and barbarian responses reflected that difference as well. No people in Europe remained totally unaffected by these processes, but a great many had no idea that they were being influenced.

Roman governments never expected all barbarian groups—or even all Celts or all Germans—to do anything. Rome did expect foreign *gentes* (tribes or bands) to relate to specific Roman interests near Roman settlements or those of other Roman allies. In other words, ancient Germans did not have to wait until the birth of scientific philology and the creation of a linguistic group or Lutheranism in the sixteenth century or German nationalism in the nineteenth to come into existence. Germans and Celts existed in the Roman mind as restricted categories of barbarians, but these were not operative conceptualizations upon which to base action. Barbarians, Celts, Germans, and other such terms were useful intellectual divisions of humankind, traditional to ancient ethnography and useful in describing the stages in complexity and cultural refinement leading to Mediterranean civilization, notably Roman. Because barbarian was the most general of all terms, applied to everybody not a Roman, it was the most commonly used but also the least useful for ancient ethnography. Varieties in life-styles among "Germans" and "Celts" were depicted as variations upon the general characteristics of the category. This tendency is clear in Julius Caesar's *Gallic War* and Tacitus's *Germania* (ca. A.D. 100), and was still viable when Ammianus Marcellinus wrote his history at the end of the fourth century A.D.

These same Roman authors also shared the desire to compartmentalize the cultural generality represented by barbarians into politically discrete units with which Roman governments interacted. So they speak both of Celts or Germans and of Arverni and Suebi. Once the name of a barbarian group entered the historical tradition, it became a part of the rhetorician's arsenal and was used over and over again, even if the group had disappeared. In this way Roman authors also manifested their common educational background, particularly their training in rhetoric, and their status as members of the ruling class. They also tended to use old names, both ethnographic and geographic, drawn from the literary tradition alongside novel entries, as if thereby to erect new honors upon the old. A leader mentioning a well-known barbarian group as having been reconquered by him connected himself thereby to the heroic standards of his predecessors. Triumphal processions visibly reminded Romans of the peoples and places their armies had conquered, and careful records of these were kept for generations.[9]

Roman administrative successes in the West often rested upon earlier Celtic organization, although Celtic societies were politically underdeveloped by Roman standards. Sometimes Rome erected forts, then towns, upon Celtic urban centers. Often urban colonies of legionary veterans were in the vanguard. Almost always Rome intervened in local politics, typically by favoring one family or faction over another. The Celtic world also reflected the underlying variations in European climate and topography with a brisk trade, which in its final stages utilized numerous local coinages. Yet the Celts were unable to surmount their topographic diversity with a centralized political system. To Celtic society Rome added standardization, broad political control, and easier access to markets and literary culture. Not all these advantages were immediately deemed attractive by the conquered, however. Rome accomplished much the same among the peoples beyond its frontiers without the burden of direct government. Because there was no precise division between the Celtic and non-Celtic peoples, there was no sharp demarcation in the patterns of interaction with Rome unless the Romans sought to create one. As far as Roman leaders were concerned, what worked among Celts should work among all northern barbarians, conquered or left free.

Overall, Celtic urban elites moved rapidly into imperial service whenever Rome decided to establish its governmental and military system in the area; however, when Roman centers were at a distance, change was slow. Everywhere local influence remained paramount. Celtic rural societies were less malleable, and where no or sparse Celtic urban structures existed at the time of Roman conquest, the overall pace of change lagged behind areas with preexisting urban cultures. This was true because Roman settlers neither cared to live at what they regarded as the rustic levels of rural society nor did they find much there that they needed or that could not be obtained more readily elsewhere. Urban culture was most convivial to Romans and their life-styles, and indigenous peoples related to Romans in towns or through networks of patronage radiating outward from them. These patterns are also visible in the so-called Germanic areas, which remained decidedly rural throughout the Roman era. Initially Rome had no reason to create different policies for the Germanic populations lying in a transitional zone adjacent to the Celtic heartland and beyond.

The fact that Rome shared so much with its northern neighbors was not a matter that the Romans themselves cared to note. Roman literature tends to make us to forget that most of the inhabitants of Europe, both inside and outside the imperial administrative system, were farmers and that even inside the empire a great many of these did not live in Roman-type villas. Most of Europe's agriculturists shared a common life-style and responded to local and regional markets, unless a peculiar circumstance such as a Roman camp or settlement opened up wider horizons and richer markets. This underlying sameness was overshadowed only by great exertion and only then after many generations had redirected the fiscal resources of the Mediterranean cities. In many areas that effort was transient.

Looked at from the perspective of the barbarians, the terms "German" and "Celt" in particular were terms that those being described very rarely if ever used among themselves. These and other terms were used by first Greek and then Latin authors to discuss various cultural gradients among those foreigners generally living to the north of the Mediterranean coastal cities begun as Greek colonies. The term German may have originated among certain Celts and, through their contacts, was transferred to the Greeks. Gradually as Rome became more and more deeply involved with creating and maintaining political, economic, and cultural interaction with its northern neighbors, more precise terms of identification largely superseded Celt and German in Roman usage. For a time Sueb was more popular than German, and later still Goth was commonly used as a generic label for a number of different barbarian groups. Celt and German never fell completely out of favor, although both terms were very rarely used by the opening of the fifth century. Even for so late a date, however, a few archaic examples can be found.

All such general terms had little practical application. The gradual replacement of general terminology by more specific names also corresponded to the increasingly cohesive nature of the groups that developed among barbarians along the frontiers, Germanic in speech or not. Many, perhaps all, of these regional and local groups of barbarians owed their existence to direct and indirect Roman influence. These developments took centuries, but the literary uses of "German" and of "barbarian" never lapsed entirely. Romans defined barbarians in fact and in myth but in divergent directions: in fact, as living in territorially recognizable groups; in myth, as constituting a cultural challenge to the urban civilization of the Mediterranean world. Beneath the standard rhetorical exercises Rome's interaction with the barbarians was complex and long-lasting, containing much give-and-take.

As decades turned into centuries, an intensification of the derogatory image of the barbarian among Roman intellectuals resulted from the fact that "barbarian" had slowly become largely synonymous with "soldier," with whom most authors had little social intercourse. The original distinction in the terms was all but lost by the end of the fifth century. Simultaneously "soldier" (*miles*) became a term denoting someone other than culturally Roman, at least as seen by the civilian aristocrats who saw themselves as being the quintessential "Romans."[10] Already by the middle of the third century soldiering was no longer a profession open to the senatorial aristocracy, and, in part because of this, there was a progressive isolation of the military profession, psychologically and spatially, from the civil administration. At the same time, recruitment into the army, particularly in the West, had already become largely a matter of enrolling young men from the neighborhood of the camps. Often these were the children of veterans, having reached age eighteen or slightly older. Young men living across the border in barbarian villages were also attracted to service in the Roman army when an opportunity arose. The division between the military and the civilian communities developed to the point that by the second half of the fourth century winners on these two career paths competed with one another for influence at court. But it was equally true that during this period of apparent competition, there was an increasingly significant level of intermarriage among the children of the civilian and military elites, as each sought insurance for its position.[11] Concomitant to this rivalry, new uses of old literary formulas appeared, so that by the late empire an apparently straightforward literary attack on barbarians could mask sharp civilian criticism of the Roman army and its commanders, even including the emperor himself. Such criticism was otherwise difficult to mount without grave risk.[12] The rhetorical imagery of crude but often noble barbarians was conventional and could be pressed to serve many purposes, ultimately with peculiar religious connotations as well. The empire was after all an absolutist state in which most avenues of political criticism open in a democracy were tightly sealed, and critics could steer clear of alienating the ruling regime by employing rhetorical circumlocution.

Those living in the indefinable middle, barbarian or Roman or neither, did not necessarily seek to lead their lives according to principles elucidated at the mythical hub to which all roads were said to lead. Nor did they care what senators or emperors thought of their petty decisions. Nor did they much frequent the great provincial cities in which Roman governors held sway, dispatching armies and tax collectors. And if they played literary games with rhetorical imagery, these games are lost, but very likely they had neither the education nor the desire to play them. This book unfolds as much as possible in ordinary neighborhoods, those overlooked arenas not bound to specific administrative theories, among common people for whom quiet accommodation rather than war was the rule. The book tries to ask their questions and to relate the grand themes to their lives by creating contexts that they might have understood. To illustrate their circumstances, materials have been selected from specific regions within a chronological and geographic framework. Even then the data often provide us with little more than informed vignettes. Wars happened, especially at moments of initial encounter, yet the din of battle soon subsided. Trade replaced plunder, and family life superseded rapine and pillaging.

As spectators in the last row of seats, we must strain to interpret the subtleties of plot and character unfolding on that far distant stage. Our visions blur; our imaginations fly. Even were we somehow transported into the front-row seats, more often than not there would be no action to see, only shadows and rumors speaking in whispers. Since when has humankind needed hard facts to make decisions? Romans and barbarians reacted to legends and hearsay as powerfully as to deeds and events. In an era without an independent news media, the only check on the distortions of aristocratic literature and governmental propaganda was common sense and personal observation. Like us, they were conditioned by preconceptions, and, again like us, they rarely saw the wholeness of the "others" in their lives. Nor did they understand the other's complex past and uncertain present. Politicians played upon their fears and built careers upon their strengths.

In every period women and men made daily decisions in keeping with the customs of their community as they considered anew life's little details. What are we to wear? What food is available in the market? Is today a feast day, a wedding day, or a day of mourning? Is a friend or relative in need of help? Foreign concepts and products might have figured into these choices in subtle ways. For example, wearing certain jewelry could send different messages to different groups—if, that is, there were alternatives. Working for the Romans might affect friendships and marriage patterns. Yet because of the fact that the essentials of life—food, housing, work, friends, family, and religion—changed so imperceptibly, very few individuals took notice. Private life remained private. Choices were limited both culturally and fiscally. This picture would be the same even had we barbarian accounts of their own societies, and these we do not have.

The adaptation of indigenous societies to Roman influence has long been called Romanization. Although the term and the concepts behind it are simplistic and one-sided, if not contrary to fact, it is so ubiquitous in modern literature that to avoid its use entirely would itself impose artificiality upon the discussion. The term is at best convenient, but when using it one must always keep in mind the complex circumstances surrounding it. It will appear very infrequently in this book, for the facts are clear. Cultural changes took place among all parties concerned, even though predominantly among the barbarians. From the beginning therefore what has for so long passed as Romanization was never the simple transference of Mediterranean values through Roman agents to nonurbanized populations in the interior. That is, it was not what Roman authors thought; there was no dominant "Roman way." As the simple bipolar concepts that gave it birth are abandoned in favor of a better understanding of the multifaceted, dynamic, and ubiquitous process of acculturation that was actually taking place, the term "Romanization" itself will have to find new meaning or be abandoned. Or to put it another way, real Romanization was a process by which barbarians, typically from societies with limited local diversity, adapted to the challenges of living near Romans and in, the process, left their own imprints upon Roman society. Reactions to this mutual exposure ranged widely. Most changes took place over generations, not years or even decades, and grandchildren responded to different Roman and barbarian worlds than those their elders had confronted. To some degree adaptation preceded direct contact, but once barbarians and Romans met regularly face to face, mutual change and understanding accelerated greatly.

In the western frontier provinces, the army was the primary agent for making the introductions, followed close behind by the support staffs of civilians, bureaucrats, and marketplaces. Everywhere religion helped anchor individuals in their communities: on the one hand, assisting the new to integrate themselves into the society of their new residence and vice versa; on the other hand, providing each family with a feeling that it still belonged to the old networks of family and village. As in most aspects of ancient life, religion operated at several levels, most notably public and private. Public religious observance united communities, whereas private provided for domestic continuity. There were occasional lapses in which archaic cultural styles, including religion, were briefly resurrected, thereby adding historical complexity to the witches' brew of ancient civilization. Even when an aspect of indigenous culture seems to have been completely replaced, the local usage of what had by then become a common Roman cultural artifact may still have differed from that of its original Roman archetype. The fact is that Romans did not force their culture upon native populations.

Rome's irresistible strength lay in organization, not cultural despotism. Roman urban centers lured men and women from the countryside, but it did not force them to stay. Wherever Roman power maintained fortifications, roads, and towns, the rural-urban dynamic took on new dimensions. The traditional Roman imperial frontiers—that is, the great river and wall systems—were developed relatively late and even then constituted only a rather restricted geographic zone where rural and urban values met. The rural inhabitants attracted to the cities and camps came from both sides of the frontiers. Although the militarized frontier was an extremely important area of Roman-barbarian interaction, it was by no means the exclusive area of their interactions. Romans and barbarians met inside the empire from early times, whether the latter were indigenous people or recent immigrants. The vast and complex American-Mexican relationship comes to mind as having many parallels. It too is essentially a riverine frontier with sizable sections of "wall" (fences and remote sensing devices), all quite porous, legally and otherwise. In the Roman-barbarian situation, and likewise in the American-Mexican, administrative frontiers were largely irrelevant to the cultural interactions transpiring among the respective populations. Ultimately the values of the barbarian-Roman frontier society, far more than the physical barriers thrown up to monitor human activities along their length, contributed mightily to the formation of a new set of values and traditions that gave rise to medieval civilization. Within early medieval societies we can discover many attributes of life on the Roman frontiers, a peculiar blend of rural and warlike traits, and can follow their transformation under the influence of formerly urban Christianity. However one understands frontiers in general and the Roman frontiers in particular, the sustained interaction of peoples of often different but usually converging backgrounds is what mattered, the give-and-take of daily affairs.

Until Roman power had reached an equilibrium between its capacity to administer and its universalist dreams—and some would argue that this never occurred—Roman power progressively distorted the human geography of Europe by incorporating barbarians within provinces and influencing, if not managing, the evolution of barbarian societies outside the provincial system. Once Rome made the decision to incorporate a new territory, the conclusion was usually quickly reached and, with but the exception of so-called free Germany and later the Hungarian Plain, successfully. Romans came to the bargaining table, so to speak, with limited goals. Perhaps their most concrete objective for a new province was the cessation of warfare. Barbarians enclosed within the new provinces became provincials—that is, those belonging to the provinces—but many of their patterns of life that long antedated Roman conquest, particularly their personal relationships, continued, and for several generations these personal associations supported much of the commerce and cultural exchange. So too trade continued with peoples farther removed from the Mediterranean world. The cultural adaptation within a Roman political context that characterized provincials went on beyond the confines of the provinces but without the concentration of opportunities present within them, but nevertheless the process was fundamentally the same regardless of the location. Romans welcomed non-Romans into their society as long as they acted in accordance to Roman manners. No Roman contemplated abandoning his own cultural paradigms.

No area of the empire was immune from change, but more often than not these changes were incremental rather than dramatic. Roman culture was never static, despite the extraordinary long-term regularity of its architecture and military systems, nor was it as homogenous as often portrayed. The Roman Empire was nonetheless far different because of its involvement with the barbarians from what it would have been without them. Among the most obvious differences is that without "the barbarian menace" it would have been quite difficult to justify the continued presence of so large a standing army on the frontier. Nor would the tremendous reallocation of economic resources from the Mediterranean provinces to those of the frontiers, which maintaining the army required, have taken place. Cultural influence was also very important.

Changes in civilization ultimately involve fundamental reorientations in culture across a wide range of human relationships. Among the cultural changes new senses of personal and collective identity are particularly significant. But attributing specific values to such nonquantifiables as culture and identity so as to assess their changes is a bit like creating an ice statue on a summer day. What it meant to be Roman is surprisingly difficult to ascertain. And if what it meant to be Roman can only be approximated, then understanding the sense of identity for anybody not Roman is clearly even more difficult. Ultimately what mattered was whether and to what extent barbarians and Romans could share mechanisms for creating and sustaining personal and group identities. Or, to put it another way, rather than focusing on "we versus they" by assuming mutually exclusive group membership among Romans and barbarians, it is more fruitful to see whether and when both barbarians and Romans were using identity in a common context.

Romans were obsessed with categorizing people, especially in terms having to do with status and legal rights. Rank and its display were equally important among the barbarians, and Roman authority catered to this need. Everybody within the empire had a host of identities and recourse to multiple identities increased the farther down the social-economic scale one lived, because those at the bottom had to resort to all possible entry points into the labor force in order just to survive. For Julius Caesar and his colleagues being a Roman of the senatorial class was sufficient. They did not have to note that they were born Romans, for everything about them said that. They preferred to underscore their superiority over the lesser orders of Roman society and over their rivals by noting the honors that had been accorded their fathers and grandfathers. They exuded privilege, but privilege had its costs. More was expected from those in higher categories, and more was offered them. Taxes were not uniformly imposed. Until late in the second century, citizens paid less, and those in Italy paid hardly at all. Even in the late empire, senatorial families were exempt from virtually all direct taxes and served the government at their own initiative. No matter where a Roman went, he carried his citizenship with him. Until the latter third century it was his most important identity.

Much of the oppressiveness of being so carefully anchored within categories of status was negated by another factor, mobility, both social and geographic. Men of ability in the provinces might expect that their careers would lead them into far-ranging imperial service. Soldiers moved about on assignment and rose in rank according to their merit and length of service. Important individuals in government and business traveled great distances, and even modestly wealthy men had business associates in distant ports. Geographic mobility among ancient Romans rivals that of all other ages up to the last half of the twentieth century. Even in the late empire, when the imperial edicts seem intended to restrict mobility in order to shore up the tax base, many men celebrated careers in which their professions had taken them from one end of the empire to the other. Women too, at least among the well to do, traveled regularly and broadly and not always with their spouses. Ordinary women worked in the trades and shops alongside their spouses. Soldiers were regularly transferred in the course of their careers, often over long distances, sometimes taking their families in tow.

Such population dynamics led to uniformity in some areas of life, such as commerce, public transport, defense, and governmental systems, yet also provided a never-ending variety of dress, diet, and spoken languages beneath the Greek and Latin of the professional classes. Punic was still widely spoken in the North African countryside in the fifth century, for example. Indeed, it is probable that few if any native tongues disappeared entirely under the emperors. Life in the empire exposed its members to a wide variety of people, languages, commodities, and traditions. The specific components varied from place to place. So calling the process whereby a native culture changed towards standards common among the Romans or vice versa begs the question: among which Romans? And, conversely, for which barbarians? Roman society assimilated barbarians—that is, non-Romans—both inside and outside the sphere of Roman administration in a host of ways depending upon the circumstances of the locale. While doing so, society too changed, but like all societal changes, these took place over many generations.

Conquered peoples did not automatically become citizens, not even after their territory became a province. Cicero and later authors occasionally referred to these peoples as provincials (*provinciales*), literally those belonging to the province, but this usage included both citizens and noncitizens without any distinction as to their legal status.[13] Another widely used term was foreigner (*peregrinus*). A *peregrinus* was originally any person not from Rome or a Roman colony, but by the end of the republic almost everybody in Italy had become a citizen. A *peregrinus* could not technically contract a legally valid marriage under the provisions of the Roman civil law without the special grant (*ius conubii*), but this was readily extended to new provincials. As a result of these grants to individuals and sometimes entire communities, marriages between citizens and noncitizens were common. Romans also recognized the legitimacy of marriage among foreigners dealing with Romans under the principles of the *ius gentium*.

In the period after the initial conquests a native to the province, if living in a Roman colony, might be a *peregrinus,* even though living on his ancestral lands. As such he would have been excluded from participation in local government. Noncitizen provincials (generally *provinciales* and legally *peregrini*) were removed from the ranks of barbarians by virtue of having acquired legal residence inside the empire, when Rome had conquered them and their territories and placed them under a provincial administration. They remained in this category until they became citizens or became residents in a town with legally recognized privileges just short of Roman citizenship, Latin status, which legally situated individuals between being a citizen and a *peregrinus.* The leaders of cities with Latin status were routinely granted full Roman citizenship in recognition for their service to the empire. During the first two centuries A.D., many *perigrini* achieved the citizenship in this way, either by direct imperial enrollment or when the legal status of their entire town was raised. Residence thus was a second category commonly used to identify persons.

Another was birth, both one's parents and place. In the Roman Republic citizens were identified by the traditional status of their families and accorded an appropriate place in the voting system of Roman tribes, centuries, and wards. In the course of the first two and a half centuries of the empire the legal status of most communities gradually moved upwards in rank. One's residence could change many times. Anybody wishing to live among the Romans had to know and note their citizenship, their lineage (often including its place of origin), and their habitual residence. Barbarians living in the empire were no different. They too needed to present themselves in a manner legally acceptable to the Romans.

Roman naming practices were quite distinctive, but barbarians need not have adopted them. They could certainly use their own personal names, but then what? Their village of birth would not do as a place of residence, because it had no place in the Roman legal schema. They might note their ancestry, but until late in the empire no Roman much cared about their bloodlines. Usually barbarians were "placed within the Roman system" by the use of a group name, for example, "Sarmatian," in place of the Roman name and location of citizenship. Thereby a barbarian immediately clarified his foreign origins within the accepted Roman practice and, having done so, could be welcomed as an outsider.

Marriage between citizens and noncitizens was forbidden by law, except for special provisions for soldiers whereby they were routinely allowed to contract such relationships and then legalize them after their discharge. In order to attract and retain soldiers, Roman law also recognized other privileges for soldiers regardless of family origin, especially in the area of testamentary process. Because soldiering was also of primary importance in the entire barbarian-Roman interaction, Roman recognition of the special personal needs and practices of its soldiers inevitably affected all parties, including barbarians and provincials. Native revolts were common occurrences in the decades immediately after conquest and the incorporation. These revolts were nasty business. To prevent them or at least restrict their scope required constant attention. Being a conquered people forced those subjected to balance new and traditional identities in a complex system not of their own devising.

When "provincials" rebelled, they were then again called by their traditional ethnic names by Roman authors, suggesting that by seeking to become outsiders they had once again become barbarians. After the Romans had crushed a native uprising and it was clear that the indigenous population had ceased to contemplate further rebellion, Roman authors once again referred to them as being from the province whence they or their ancestors had derived. Thus the act of rebellion carried the native from the company of provincials to that of barbarians. Culturally he had not much changed. Thus provincials who remained unacculturated to Roman values remained barbarians in all but name. They might be usefully called internal barbarians to distinguish them from those barbarians still unconquered but with whom they still shared a great deal. Rome never forced either provincials or barbarians to live in the Roman style, and so in the most remote areas of the empire nothing altered the lives of the indigenous population. The key factors were always proximity and access to Romans themselves. Within a few generations native rebellion ceased to be a major concern.

Noting the town of their birth and where their Roman citizenship was established, on the other hand, distinguished Romans. About a century after internal barbarians disappeared behind the facade of provincial status, the governance of the provinces shifted from being essentially an extension of military administration to a civilian system. Regular gubernatorial bureaucracies existed from about the reign of Hadrian (117–38). As the geographic and administrative definitions of the provinces sharpened, "barbarian" came to mean those living beyond the provinces. This geographic focus augmented the earlier cultural implications of "barbarity" until in late antiquity; *barbaricum,* the land of the barbarians, is used in literature and law to specify lands lying beyond Roman administrative control but nonetheless a part of the Roman world.[14] The dual existence of a finite sphere of governance and an infinite sphere of influence was a basic feature of the empire.

In an edict issued in A.D. 212, the emperor Caracalla extended citizenship to virtually the entire free population, the only exception being the most recently admitted barbarians. This edict set in train a series of terminological shifts in regard to identity. One was that henceforth the term *peregrini* (foreigner) was applied only to the barbarians, and mainly to those living outside the empire. Because by then revolts of native populations were matters of the distant past, his edict sharpened the legal demarcation between barbarians and Romans. Essentially it declared that citizens lived inside and barbarians outside the empire. The ambiguity of the non-Roman provincial population was eliminated. To that extent alone the status "barbarian" was made clear. Yet normal life on the frontiers was well advanced towards creating a single society. Being a Roman or barbarian was never quite as static as the legal sources make it seem. Even in the late empire, when "foreigner" was largely synonymous with "barbarian," as a term, "barbarian" never had a legal status as did "citizen." As citizenship waned as the primary Roman identification, the other forms of identity remained.

Most scholars would probably accept two basic requirements for establishing a personal identity: a self-declaration of belonging to a group and acceptance of that declaration by that group. If the declarer does not live up to whatever it is that the group accepting his declaration expects, then the members will typically withdraw their endorsement of the declaration and so end the effective affiliation. As a result, the declarer is forced into a set of defined actions and interactions.[15] These choices are, however, restricted by culture and circumstance. Nor is it to be expected that all choices are conscious acts or that one identity served for all occasions. Whenever we can see people seeking to identify themselves with or disassociate themselves from a group, we are on to something important because such choice carried risks as well as rewards. "Barbarian" was never an ethnographic term and was only rarely used by non-Romans to describe themselves. Among the few such cases is an undated inscription of a certain Murranus, who calls himself a barbarian but also notes that he was born in Pannonia. He was perhaps the son of newly admitted barbarian settlers, *dedidici,* or a member of a small group of bypassed people in the interior. Such isolated groups were regarded as "barbarians"—that is, outsiders—throughout Roman history.[16] In other words, very few claimed that he was a barbarian, the requisite self-declaration of personal identity. Nonetheless there were occasions when relating yourself to non-Roman traditions could be useful and be employed in a way that did not challenge the dominant culture. Other examples of individuals that come to mind are from the fifth century or later when reference to being a "barbarian" had lost much of its original meaning.

Of all the various types of identity traceable in the ancient sources, one has continued to hold primacy of place in current debate: ethnic identity. Although our current fascination with ethnicity in the ancient world may reflect issues inherent in our own society more than it does those of the ancients, there is no denying that ethnic identity was also important in Roman society, especially for non-Romans. Despite decades of discussion, however, there is today still little agreement as to what defines ethnicity even among living populations. It is now usually regarded as one of many attributes deeply embedded in most cultures and defined by them. In antiquity *ethnos* was a term borrowed into Latin from Greek that could be applied to any large group living together. An *ethnos* might be a band, a class, a tribe, a nation, and so on. Those constituting an *ethnos* in Roman eyes were supposed to manifest common cultural characteristics, but whether they actually did so is another question. The word was often used in conjunction with "barbarians," but it had many uses. Late Roman authors sometimes even lumped pagans or heathens together as a separate *ethnos* to distinguish them from Christians. Nobody seems to have used the term to describe their own large group affiliations, and so its use was limited to discussions of "others." The term was inherently vague and so had very restricted utility.

Men and women took over their practical identities, not merely their physical features, from their parents and neighbors. Unless confronted with either benefit or penalty, their traditional identities served them for a lifetime. Truly changing identity was rare and probably impossible, but rather than change one's identity, one could just add a new one. Whether attempting a complete change of identity or just expanding one's associational horizons, multiple incidents of the declaration of new identities should alert us to stress and sometimes crisis in society. For example, when an individual chose to proclaim his barbarian ancestry generations after his forebears had abandoned it, he had to have a reason. But finding out what that reason was in his individual case may lie beyond the scope of our records. If many people were doing likewise, however, then we are on more solid ground for speculation. Most strategies for personal and familial advancement must be seen to have operated in a village environment. If one left one's village or took on a new role within it—for example, by joining the following of some great war leader—then one might need to employ a new tactic in personal identity. But normally rural status changed little from generation to generation.

Romans had only infrequent contact with pastoralists and virtually none with true nomads until near the end of the fourth century. Yet, although they rarely mentioned it, they knew a great deal about life in the agrarian countryside. Progressive urbanization within the empire and along its frontiers meant that new opportunities challenged traditional rural life-styles. In this dynamic cosmopolitan setting, at some point, declaring a new identity, including an ethnic affiliation, might have strengthened one's career chances. For example, early in the empire being able to teach Greek could bring substantial rewards. Later a Roman soldier might stress his barbarian ancestry to gain admission to a higher social circle within the army or to further a marriage alliance with his commander's daughter. In any case it is the convergence with mutual and group self-interest that encourages an ethnic as any other declaration of individual identity.

An individual's declaration need not have been oral. People also made declarations of identity in their dress styles, in burial practice, in buildings and community layout—expressions that are often susceptible to archaeological inquiry. In both oral and material declarations a high degree of subtlety was possible, often essential, for there were always risks. Wearing a particular type of fibula—that is, a highly decorated and prominently worn safety pin—could proclaim one's status or membership in a wider group, just as wearing team colors at a sporting event does today, but there would have been contexts in which that identity would have been inappropriate. On most occasions people must have worn fibulae with little or no regard for making statements, but rather merely to hold their clothing together, which after all was a fibula's primary purpose. Just as religion had a public and private role, so too did identity. A Roman soldier could proudly wear the traditional armorial badges and yet still find a place for a small family heirloom; in fact, Roman military dress clearly encouraged such personalization.

For the sake of analysis, the roughly five centuries to be explored in this book are divided into three phases with two chapters devoted to topics within each. In reality each phase flowed seamlessly into the next, and the last phase is a very untidy straggler with threads still unraveling centuries later. The first phase is dominated by the expansion of Rome beyond the Mediterranean littoral. Around the end of the second century B.C., peoples known in Roman sources as the Cimbri and Teutones invaded Gaul and Italy. Their entry into the Mediterranean world left a permanent imprint upon Roman-barbarian relations and immediately became a standard historical theme. In the next generation Julius Caesar consolidated Roman power and his own career in Gaul. The second phase began as Augustus ushered in a long period of gradual institutionalization of Roman society. Along the Rhine the outward projection of Roman power ended when in A.D. 9 Arminius ambushed and defeated the Roman general Varus and with him three legions in the Teutoburg Forest, which is now securely located near Osnabrück, Germany.[17] These deaths of more than fifteen thousand men were said to have given Augustus nightmares for the rest of his life. Setbacks in the Carpathian basin preceded this great defeat by but a few years, and together they hastened the slowing of Roman expansion.

The second phase thus is one of consolidation and regularization with a few expansionary flourishes. Consolidation continued under succeeding emperors through the Severan dynasty (193–235) but with increasing difficulty. The second phase was also noteworthy for the shifting of most of Rome's military forces to the frontiers and the incomplete expansion of Roman administration into the Carpathian basin. The third, fourth, and early fifth centuries marked a third phase. This era witnessed transitions in a host of areas, and by its end the barbarian interaction with the empire had produced a unique composite frontier society, mutually interdependent and highly successful.

The major settlements of barbarians that took place from the early fifth century shifted the locus of the Roman-barbarian interaction by superimposing the frontier societies upon a still larger urban and traditional Roman hinterland. Increasingly thereafter Romans and barbarians had to respond to new political and religious forces inherently unlike those of earlier centuries. The many twisting paths leading each region into the Middle Ages began in earnest at this time: with the settlements, with the makeshift governments of the so-called barbarian kingdoms that willy-nilly exploited or rejected the traditions of Roman statecraft, and with the penetration of Christianity ever deeper into the fabric of society. When looked at from our vantage point, the opening of the fifth century was a staging point, not a chasm. The empire was poised to enter a new phase in its transformation but had yet to make the leap. In a sense, the ancient world stood ready for something but had not yet determined which road to take into that ill-defined future. In final analysis the story of Romans and barbarians is as complex as are we its storytellers, but unlike human life their history has neither a beginning nor an end. This study closes in the early fifth century, while acknowledging that many themes that developed earlier continued to evolve for centuries. From time to time the readers will be asked to look beyond the specific cases before them and to consider the long-term significance of the matters at hand. In a similar vein many times this can also be done by setting ancient issues in comparative contexts far removed from ancient Europe. Regardless of the technique, the goal of these excursions is always the same—to understand events by broadening our perspective.

Edward Gibbon wrote his classic work *The Decline and Fall of the Roman Empire* more than two centuries ago. It is often overlooked, however, that Gibbon, himself living in an age of empires, regarded Germanic barbarians and Romans as having a symbiotic relationship despite their wars. For Gibbon it was the Oriental world, particularly that of the Huns and Turks, that provided a polarity to ancient civilization, not the Germanic peoples. Virtually unnoticed in all the classical rhetoric—sources we share with Gibbon—each generation of barbarians and Romans had to work out a host of interconnections that involved some level of compromise. Temporary arrangements could easily become permanent. In the last century of the Roman Republic, where this book begins, most Roman relationships, both among themselves and with foreigners, were still essentially personal, great men knitting together their followers to pursue personal ambitions. Relationships among the barbarians were much the same, at least in Roman eyes. Romans saw themselves as the exclusive purveyors of a superior culture in transalpine Europe, but to others they were only the disseminators of their own values.

The last quarter of the second century B.C. marked a decisive turning point in Roman history. Up to then Romans had contented themselves with playing around the edges of their private sea, the Mare Nostrum, the Mediterranean. All of a sudden, however, they became embroiled with Parthians, Thracians, and, most important for our subject, Celts in Gaul. Soon Roman armies were marching against various peoples in Spain and Gaul, and those most remote opponents of all, Germans. Roman authors wrote of these encounters as if the further Romans forayed into worlds far distant, the more bellicose their adversaries became and the tests of Roman valor more rigorous. But surely had we the thoughts of barbarians pitting their swords against Roman steel, there would be a general agreement as to who were the most ferocious and aggressive people—the Romans. But then again Romans were hardly the first, and certainly not the last, lords of battle to see themselves as peacemakers. The stage is now set. Enter Marius, the Cimbri, and the Teutones and with them power, savagery, and fear.

Two

Recognition, Confrontation, and Coexistence

In 121 B.C. Rome successfully concluded its wars against a coalition of Gauls in the lower Rhone valley, led by the victorious Quintus Fabius Maximus, consul, and Gnaeus Domitius Ahenobarbus, consul from the preceding year and now proconsul of Rome. The conflict began after the Aedui in central Gaul had appealed for Roman support against the Arverni and their allies. The Roman victories had more than local significance because they secured the land link between Italy and Spain, which had become increasingly important after the defeat of Carthage in the Punic Wars. Rome had been at war in southern Gaul off and on for years, ostensibly because Marseilles (Massalia), a Roman ally, sought aid against the rising military power of several Celtic groups in its sphere of influence. Roman literary sources scarcely ever suggest an economic motive for Rome's expansion, perhaps because tradition maintained, against all evidence to the contrary, that the aristocracy was above such motivation. According to Roman sources, others—not the Romans—were expanding and invading, threatening friends of Rome. This chapter follows the expansion of Roman power into southern Gaul and then considers Rome's first encounter with people beyond the ken of the Mediterranean world. Because Romans regarded these new foreigners, the Cimbri and Teutones, in terms of migration as well as invasion, we also confront the issue of migration theory and its applicability to ancient history. The successes of the campaigns around Narbo placed Rome in a commanding position in southern Gaul, but they also enmeshed Rome much more deeply in Celtic political intrigue.

The last four years had been bloody as was graphically recalled by a silver coin struck in 116/115. On the obverse, a helmeted female personifying Roma as well as the legend ROMA, before her EX·S·C, "according to the decree of the Senate." On the reverse a Roman cavalryman holds the severed head of a Gaul.[1] Even after the victory of Roman arms much still needed to be done, but at least the fighting was over and the traditional machinery for assuring peace could roll forward. Domitius stayed in the area a year or two longer, busily directing pacification efforts, building roads, and locating the site for a Roman colony. He did not pause to celebrate his success with a triumphal procession in Rome until 120 or a year or two later. Only after heated debate did the Senate authorize the founding of the colony of Narbo Martius in 118 B.C., the first such colony in Gaul and only the second outside the Italian peninsula. Even so, the area centered on Narbo did not become a regular province until many years later.

Narbo, established some four kilometers from the nearest Celtic settlement, sat astride the juncture of the new road linking the valley of the Rhone to Spain and the ancient trade route that cut northeastwards through the central massif to Toulouse before descending with the Garonne River into the Bay of Biscay. This route had long been a conduit for people and merchandise moving between the Atlantic and Mediterranean. Marseilles had developed the overland route because it was cut off from the Atlantic trade by Carthage, which had long monopolized the coastal routes around Spain until its defeat by Rome in the Punic Wars (in 206). Despite Marseilles's economic dominance in southern Gaul, it had never pressed territorial designs, remaining content instead with Gallic recognition of its sphere of influence. The principal item sought from the Atlantic trade by those living along the Mediterranean was tin, an essential ingredient of bronze and found in abundance in Britain and Brittany. For tin as for any heavy trade item, waterborne

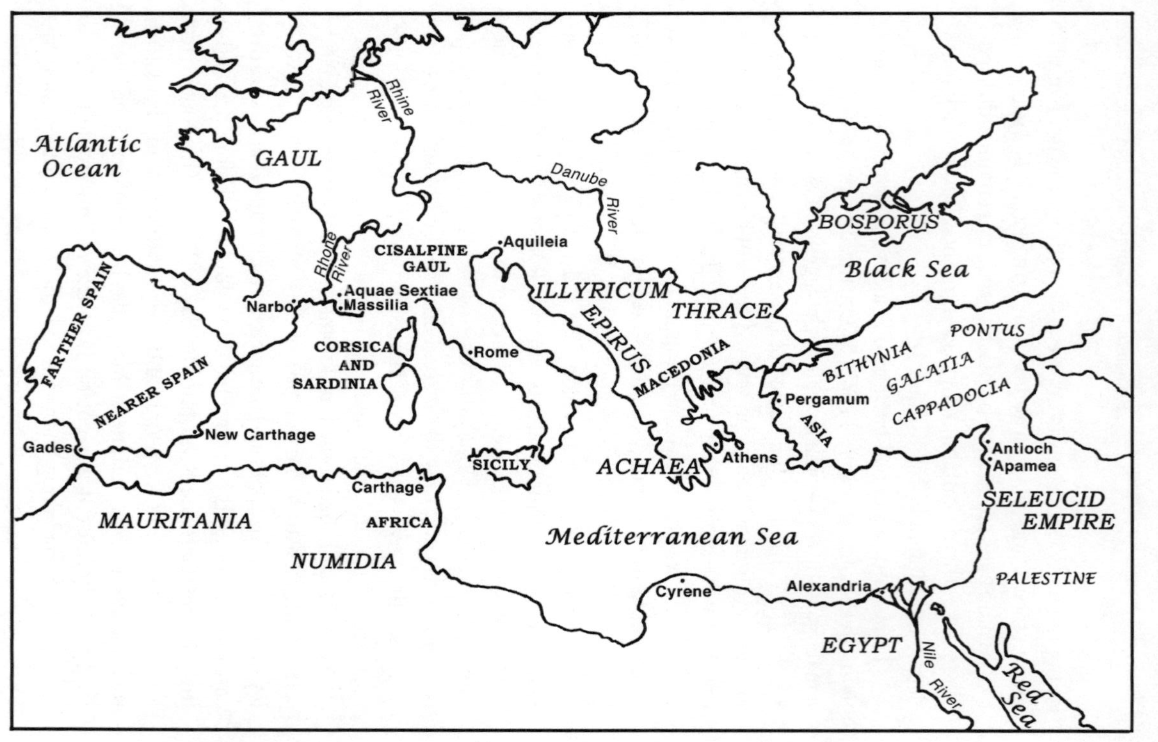

Atlantic Ocean
GAUL
Rhine River
Danube River
BOSPORUS
Black Sea
FARTHER SPAIN
NEARER SPAIN
Gades
New Carthage
Narbo
Rhone River
Aquae Sextiae
Massilia
CISALPINE GAUL
Aquileia
ILLYRICUM
THRACE
EPIRUS
MACEDONIA
PONTUS
BITHYNIA
GALATIA
CAPPADOCIA
Pergamum
ASIA
CORSICA AND SARDINIA
Rome
SICILY
ACHAEA
Athens
Antioch
Apamea
SELEUCID EMPIRE
Carthage
MAURITANIA
AFRICA
NUMIDIA
Mediterranean Sea
PALESTINE
Cyrene
Alexandria
EGYPT
Nile River
Red Sea

Denarius, silver, struck at Rome by moneyer M. Sergius Silus, ca. 116/115 B.C., giving his own name on the reverse and the helmeted bust of Roma on the obverse. Courtesy of the Staatliche Münzsammlung München.

commerce was much preferred, but lacking uninterrupted sea routes, the passes to the Garonne River were the next best route available to Massaliote merchants. Garonne-borne trade was still important even after the Punic Wars.[2]

Narbo's colonists, all Roman citizens of course, were situated to secure the road to Spain and generally protect Roman economic and political interests in the area. Foremost among Roman interests were those of the conquering generals, their families, and their supporters. Narbo's colonists, typically veterans of the recent campaign, were clients of the Fabii and Domitii. So too were the Allobroges (defeated by Fabius and Domitius in 122 B.C.) and the Arverni (121 B.C.). Now returned to their homes, these Gauls were expected to act as northern buffers to the colony and generally support Roman interests. Thus the basic assurance of peace in the area was not Roman arms but the mutual dependency of clients upon the same patrons. Recourse to arms meant that these personal bonds had failed. The Senate added to this personal dependency by tying itself and the Roman people to key Gallic communities. It

The Roman world in 133 B.C.

declared the Aedui *fratres consanguinque* (brothers and kinsmen) and so set out more clearly but within the same context Rome's special interests in Gaul. The language chosen had once upon a time been restricted to family.

This technique of bonding by extending personal relationships through corporate action was typical of senatorial policy towards barbarians. It might be extended to communities or to specific barbarian leaders. In essence and in language, the Senate accepted the role of patron; the Aedui, that of clients. Thereby both sought to secure a balance of power between themselves and the neighboring peoples in southern Gaul. In any dealings with Rome, the Aedui were expected to work through the patronage system of the Fabii and Domitii—or, in other words, what might look like institutional patronage between the Senate and the Aedui was actually still highly local and personal. Thus in southern Gaul as with all contemporary Roman conquests, Roman victories disproportionately favored the political agendas of the conquering generals and their allies in the Senate.[3] Southernmost Gaul thereby entered into a much closer relationship with Rome than before but, except for the colony of Narbo, remained outside direct Roman jurisdiction, bound only by clientage. To their senatorial peers and rivals, the Fabii and Domitii were overweening and threatened the political balance. Aborting their plans for a colony would check them, but despite prolonged haggling, stopping the establishment of Narbo proved beyond the power of the opposition. Apparently no thought was given to creating a regular province with a governor charged with its protection, for such an act would have involved much political compromise of the type that only crises brought about in Rome. The crisis that had provoked the creation of the colony had already passed.

Any time Rome established a colony, traditional patterns of trade and power shifted. This was true everywhere to some degree: in the former Hellenistic kingdoms of the eastern Mediterranean as well as in transalpine Europe. Everywhere some members of the indigenous population were better able to position themselves to take advantage of the new markets and broader political horizons than were others. Despite the cultural replication going on among the colonists as they tried to recreate as much of their former Italian-based life-styles as circumstances allowed, the vast majority of the indigenous population, even in the neighborhood of Roman settlements, went about its business as usual. What changed was that new, pro-Roman families were in the ascendance. Such families were also the first of the indigenous population to reflect Roman influence in their customs and careers. Such was the case among the Aedui and the other principal powers in southeastern Gaul, the Arverni and Allobroges. Here, as everywhere that colonies were established, the colonists expropriated the best lands in the area, but the new town and the supporting roads also created new marketing opportunities for local products and for natives to acquire items produced at shops far removed. Because the colonists were comparatively few in numbers, it was this secondary influence of colonization that created the economic quickening still visible in the archaeological record. The colonists and the indigenous elites together account for increases in the quantity of imported wares and expansions in settlement size, but what began in the colony and among native elites spread only very gradually to neighboring settlements. In the area around Narbo and Marseilles economic change was a continuation and intensification of the slow Greco-Roman penetration into preexisting economic and cultural spheres that had been going on for almost half a millennium by this time. Unlike in the lands to the north, where very few Celtic centers became important Roman towns, in southern Gaul the reverse was true.

Southern Gaul was definitely not a newcomer to cultural exchange with advanced Mediterranean societies. The Rhone valley and coastal Gaul had long been on the periphery of the Greek world, tied to it through trade with Marseilles, founded as a Greek colony ca. 600 B.C.[4] As early as the fifth century Greek ceramics and bronzes were important prestige items in Celtic communities in contact with coastal trade centers such as Marseilles, particularly along the riverine trade routes to the Atlantic, the Garonne route and those branching off the Rhone River itself and employing the Seine and the Loire. This trade never completely drove out products of local manufacture. After Roman conquest and the establishment of colonists at Narbo, there was a notable increase in imported products of Italian manufacture, because some of the colonist's needs initially could be met only by imports, but this appetite was soon satiated by local production of items made in Roman styles. Some of these locally made goods were direct copies, but others were improved versions, designed to accommodate the special needs of natives who wished to use Roman-style wares for their own purposes. Certain native dishes, for example, might require special utensils or cooking vessels. Even those items made in a purely Roman style can occasionally reveal complex and enduring changes in native culture.

Wine production, for example, was crucial to the Roman table and cult practice and required special drinking and sacrificial vessels. According to tradition, always with the Romans came vines and drinking vessels; one just "could not" sip wine from a water jug without appearing to be a country bumpkin. When Roman wine paraphernalia turns up in a Celtic context, as happens early on in southern Gaul, this probably reveals more than just that the family enjoyed wine. The vast quantities of wine amphorae, for example, have raised the possibility that perhaps the Gauls not only imbibed but used wine in religious observance in some way, perhaps inspired by Roman example. Within a few generations Roman imports gave way almost completely to large-scale local imitations and adaptations. Other markets also competed locally for the high-end trade, but near Narbo, as around all colonies, goods traditional to the locale continued to find customers, particularly among the rural populations. Ceramics of Roman style but Gallic manufacture ultimately rivaled and even surpassed Italian-made products, particularly in the trade in fine tableware. Conversely in southern Gaul, typically Roman household items were adapted for local uses in diet and ritual, often with highly original and lasting results.

Although the presence of Roman residents in southern Gaul only minimally and slowly changed people's daily lives—patterns already tightly intertwined with the Mediterranean world—and although the Senate did not see fit to create the province of Gallia Narbonensis for almost two decades, the establishment Narbo signaled a permanent and immediate change in the political life of southern Gaul as Roman and pro-Roman families took over the reins of power. In this, too, the experience around Narbo mirrored that of areas caught in the wake of Roman conquests elsewhere and foreshadowed the experiences of barbarians interacting with Rome for centuries to come. Despite or perhaps because of these political changes, some Celts in the area were still restless even after fifteen years of having Romans for neighbors and demonstrated their irritation by revolt. Native revolts were always crushed with vigor, and the rebels punished in the most memorable manner. The colonists were "Roman" by citizenship and membership in one of the Roman "tribes" that legally bound each adult male Roman to his city, but what Romans meant by the terms Celts or Gauls is more difficult to discern.[5]

The so-called Gallic tribes were among the westernmost of the Celtic peoples, whose general culture stretched from what is now Ireland eastward as far as central Turkey. Greek authors spoke of Celts, whereas most Roman authors spoke of Gauls (Galli in Latin), even though describing one and the same people.[6] Modern scholars prefer Celt, largely because it is not related to a single geographic area. Rather, it denotes an overall cultural pattern, the boundaries of which are still much disputed. There is a general but not universal practice in American English of using the adjective Gallic rather than Gaulic. Celtic peoples had lived in much of Gaul for many centuries before Roman involvement there. Had they created and preserved a common history, it would have stretched back to era of Rome's own mythical foundation, that is, into the eighth century B.C. Celts had served in the armies of Alexander the Great, some returning veterans apparently carrying their pay home to Gaul. This would explain the numerous Alexander types on early Celtic coinages. Most Celts had long ago achieved a high level of local and regional economic consolidation, although they never shared much politically. Surely no one ever even contemplated a Celtic empire.

In Rome a narrow ruling class operated in the name of a common polity, the Senate and the People of Rome. Yet its members competed among themselves over a very broad geographic playing field. In foreign competition as in the debates in the Senate, the goal of the senatorial class was the extension and maintenance of family power. No Celtic people, even at the time of the foundation of Narbo, could boast of a comparable governmental system. Some communities did dominate others in their region, but their influence was typically limited to a river drainage or a transportation corridor. No group claimed anything on a grander scale. The idea of a united Celtic Gaul was completely foreign. Territorial control as usual reflected political power. Aside from lacking a common political structure, the Celtic peoples of late Iron Age Europe communicated and traded over long distances by rivers, across the English Channel, and along roads in the interior.[7] Celts loosely shared a common language that probably merged with German where these languages were both spoken, areas such as along both banks of the lower Rhine. Everywhere regional trade was broadly based. Celtic agricultural production included a wide variety of vegetables, barley, and, in the more temperate areas, several strains of wheat. Animal husbandry was also very important with pigs and cattle being the most common domesticated livestock, followed by goats.

Some Celtic trade items, like certain refined materials from the Mediterranean, traveled great distances. On most Celtic sites the large quantity of Roman goods suggests that there was a regular market for them. By the second century the concentrations of lavish imported goods no longer distinguished the graves of the elites, who were employing other means to set themselves apart. For example, if we may extrapolate from objects found in cult centers, there were many opportunities to display prominence during the performance of public religious rituals. Highly refined and systematized production of iron products increased rapidly on Celtic sites throughout the second century B.C. and is a very important and distinguishing feature of this era. Celtic iron implements made their way far beyond their areas of manufacture in central and southern Gaul into northern and rural areas where no iron ore existed and ironworking was quite limited. Roman traders also purchased Celtic ironware for resale. Certain types of fine pottery, such as graphite wares, and, from the later half of the first century, finely painted pottery, were also traded across Celtic Europe. So too a few objects of personal attire, such as certain distinctive styles of fibulae and belthooks, as well as peculiar glass bracelets, were popular among the Celtic inhabitants of much of late Iron Age Europe.

By the establishment of Narbo trimetallic Celtic coinage was in use for trade in most southern areas. Although only minted at the major centers, the widespread presence of bronze coins is a sure indication that a full monetary system, not merely one used for prestige items, was current.[8] Statistical analysis of those coins struck just before the Roman conquest has revealed that by then Celtic monetary weights were based on Roman standards, thus making the two systems interchangeable.[9] Like many fortified settlements, some open settlements also struck their own coins. Also, during this last phase before Roman conquest, writing in Greek characters was spreading among the elites at a few sites, particularly in eastern Gaul.[10] From the second century silver and bronze coins were struck in small enough values and large enough numbers for daily use. Although a concentrated settlement pattern emerged relatively quickly and then spread over a wide area (often it seems by bringing together the populations of earlier open settlements from the surrounding countryside), small undefended settlements and isolated farmsteads continued to be ubiquitous. Many of the finest examples of Celtic crafts circulated far beyond the lands of their origins. They were particularly popular in what would today be northern Germany and the Low Countries, where fortified settlements did not exist nor did comparable population and manufacturing centers.

Even this very brief initial survey concerning the Celtic world probably contains more information about its inhabitants than that possessed by the average person in Rome, whose opinions would have been more often than not based on secondhand information. Those caring to delve into the subject more deeply would have been exposed to a mishmash of information assembled over the centuries and passed on as the last word. Romans inherited Greek literary traditions regarding the Celts and made them their own. The great explorer Pythias (ca. 325 B.C.), the historian Polybius (ca. 200–118), and the ethnographer Posidonius (ca. 135–51) were particularly important. Posidonius may have visited Marseilles and

Celtic areas along the Mediterranean coast of Spain. His work and that of Pythias are extant only as quoted by other authors, but they greatly influenced all future historians, ethnographers, and geographers writing on the Celts and the early Germans, beginning with Julius Caesar. Even these Greek authors did not rely exclusively on contemporary knowledge. Instead they filtered earlier Greek myths about Celts through the prisms of their own desires, but, as we shall see in the next chapter, even firsthand knowledge is not unbiased. In this tradition Celts were regarded as excessive in their personal habits and in cult practice. Some of these literary opinions are testable against the archaeological record; many are not. Of the former, archaeology has tended to refute at least as many as it has confirmed.[11] From the founding of Narbo increasing numbers of Gauls, appropriately humbled in the name of Rome, worked with Romans as individuals or in small groups through patron-client networks.

Clientage was an honorable and ubiquitous relationship. Clients were not slaves, just as barbarians were not inherently enemies. In Roman law the client was regarded as under the guardianship (*tutela*) of the patron and could expect fair and often special treatment so long as he the client acted his part appropriately. Patrons protected, supported, nourished, and judged; clients displayed *obsequium et reverentia* (obedience and reverence) and supported their patron in all ways. Such bilateral networks had evolved everywhere—among Celts, Romans, and others—largely out of the needs of agrarian societies faced with perpetual uncertainty. Without institutionalized credit instruments families regularly responded to bad harvests by turning to those with greater resources. They had no choice. A dead ox could not be revived, only replaced. That or a similar catastrophe had to be addressed at once, not after the next harvest. Without an ox, without seed, came starvation—the old and the very young were the first to go.

A successful appeal for help to your family's traditional patron might be sealed at this time by pledging a share of the next crop or even by entrusting a child to him as a servant or slave. Many centuries later these practices were still accepted. With regard to the latter practice, there was a general understanding, ultimately made a law, that children thus "sold into slavery" could be repurchased by their parents for the original sale price. Even this law misses the point, however. By "giving" an extra mouth to feed to his patron during a famine, the client may have been able to keep others in his family alive. The gift of life to your child, even if as a slave in the patron's household, was priceless in another sense: when under the best of circumstances such a child came back home, the parents would feel an obligation to their patron far beyond the weight of a few coins.

You turned to the family patron because you knew that if it were even barely possible for him to help, he would, for he too was obliged by tradition. He was expected to live up to his role as patron in an honorable fashion unless in so doing it placed his own family at risk. The next bad harvest or unexpected death was never far off. In the seamless world of ancient farmers these obligations flowed back and forth across what we today would regard as separate spheres of life and comprehension—those categories into which we have learned to compartmentalize our lives—so that in the course of countless generations patronage relationships took on very complex religious, political, military, and social dimensions. From our perspective, that of *homo economicus,* the need for economic support during years of bad harvests or unexpected deaths of man and beasts should have been repaid in kind or cash, once and for all. Through the eyes of ancient farmers, rich and poor, however, this was hardly the case. Obligatory reciprocity was not a matter of economic quid pro quo, but rather a subtle merging of all aspects of life into a perceptional hierarchy of human relationships.

A client would include the household gods of his family's patron among those of his own family, fight alongside his patron in battle, join with other clients in supporting their patron's political aspirations, and just lend a hand when needed. He need not be ordered to do these things. Nor should he have any other relationship that might interfere with that owed to his patron. The original cause of these obligations was irrelevant, lost in the twilight of custom. Patronage was a matter of family and as such generational, virtually timeless. In the case of the Roman senatorial elites, by the founding of Narbo these various threads of patronage served to support their political careers at Rome itself. International clients, obviously connected to only the most powerful Roman families, were integrated into the web as if they lived next door. Here too, however, interaction was seamless, a combination of social deference, religious fraternity, and political subservience. The great Roman families exerted their power over priestships, dress styles, foreign contacts, and, most important for them, public office. They too were linked in complex bonds of patronage among themselves. Celtic elites played similar roles among their own people.

Portraying elite status through conspicuous consumption and/or public ritual is still alive and well in our own society with imported ceramic wares now replaced by expensive automobiles, edible delicacies, our own peculiar dress fashions, and the image of the town mayor chatting with the striking garbage collectors on the front page of the local newspaper. Principal Gallic families showed off and maintained their status with Roman products, although not always using these items in a Roman way. Hard to obtain items, in this context, had heightened value. Once the item is readily available and at an acceptable price—for example, Roman jewelry—it loses its role in defining upper-class membership. Political or religious office was a high-status symbol, and one that did not necessarily leave any archaeological trace. There was no need to announce with special dress the routine holding of office by members of an established elite, for everybody was already quite aware of their status and need not be reminded in so open a manner. Underscoring status by visual display was more important to those new to political power. Roman intervention gave new families a chance to rise politically, and such families chose to adopt or adapt Roman styles of dress and consumption. Adopting items from Roman sources of supply might not only play up to a sense of self-importance and please Roman visitors by suggesting shared values, but also remind locals that whatever fruits of Roman contact were important to them, they were brought about through or because of the new elites within their community. In eras of especially rapid change—often the time when new elites emerge—there is also more frequently a special need to flaunt family wealth by discarding it in public burial rituals. The new elite family thereby demonstrates that it can provide for departed members and also has the power to renew the treasure so that those still living can lead. Because so much of the archaeological material relating to personal and family beliefs derives from burials, it is important to recall that funerary practices are at least as much for the living as the dead.

If a hypothetical Roman visitor came from Italy or one of the older provinces of the Mediterranean, he may have been astonished to see how some of the symbolism that he associated with Roman religion and daily life had found new uses among the Gauls.[12] Rather than seeking to change the culture consciously, Romans sought privileged access to markets and control over any alliances among their Gallic clients. In no case did Rome attempt to convert subjects to new religious beliefs, for example, and as a result traditional cult practice lasted very long. Replacement was simply not the way clients honored the gods of their patrons; rather they added the patron's gods to those of their own household. They worshiped them together. There was no rush to the Roman gods at the expense of the traditional cults, especially in rural areas far removed from the urbanization process that so powerfully abetted cultural change towards Roman standards. Among those closest to Roman centers, the native elites added the new gods to their own by combining their worship and their names. These compound names are ubiquitous examples of religious observance in such areas and sometimes lasted for many generations before giving way to a purely Roman name, but by then local practice had altered the relationship with that god. The "new, purely Roman" deity had succeeded by providing for peculiarly local needs.

Ancient polytheism, whether barbarian or Roman, was a very flexible and socially sensitive combination of beliefs and observances, and it does barbarian religion a great injustice to state, as Tacitus did, that native cults absorbed Roman deities and worshiped their own gods in Roman style, *imitatio Romano.* Ancient religion mirrored ancient society, and one society could not merely graft another's gods upon its own. Celts worshiped anthropomorphic deities, or at least our Roman authors thought that they did. They understood them within the context in which they themselves lived, that is, primarily in terms of patrons and clients, honor and dishonor. Using two names simultaneously—that of the native god and that of the Roman—or interchangeably did not alter the fundamental beliefs and obligations between man and the deity and therefore is not imitation. This process of expanding divine patronage by association was ubiquitous in the ancient world and did not carry the imperialistic overtones that Tacitus placed upon his northern barbarians for doing the same thing. For example, in various eastern cities the Egyptian goddess Isis was associated with the Greek goddess Kore, and so on. The client offered specified service—that is, ritual and sacrifice—and the gods were expected to respond, as good patrons should by recognizing and evaluating the petition.

Abandoning a patron was extremely dishonorable, and so was the reverse. In the world of divine patronage, the gods were thought to live up to their part of the bargain, generation after generation, provided the client demonstrated proper *obsequium and reverentia.* Many gods were needed because no one expected each god to show concern for each and every care. Worshipers had recourse to a divine network and interlocking patronage, just as they had in their daily lives. The ancient gods themselves—that is, when we can catch a glimpse of them in myth—also lived in a world of patronage with much bargaining, posturing, and display before decisions were taken and, usually even then, with much effort being made not to offend another god by inappropriate conduct. The gods were honorable among themselves. Men were to be honorable among each other and show respect to their gods. Both barbarians and Romans well understood these relationships with the divine.

The complex hierarchy of Greco-Roman gods was a manifestation and parallel expression of early social and political differentiation in Greece and Italy. That the barbarian gods about whom we know so much less are not so prescribed reflects the more amorphous nature of barbarian societies just as clearly. To change religion was at least as risky as abandoning your patronage network; for without either, you and your family were adrift. Patronage was so intractable because it existed on so many levels and effectively provided the support necessary for all participants. The worship of the old gods who had for so long concerned themselves with things beyond your immediate family was the business of the established order, the leading families, or more rarely, as with some Celts, special priests trained to represent the entire community. Just as the Roman conquerors did not annihilate the leading families of the conquered but rather gradually moved them into Roman society, they did not interfere with the spiritual patronage of the conquered either. Exceptions occurred only when Roman political or military considerations demanded intervention, but even then replacing a family that had opposed Rome was much easier than eradicating a religion. Other than extirpating Druids in Gaul, whose political and military roles were deemed a major threat, the Romans never took the radical step of suppressing a native cult. Much later on Christians fell into the same category of political dissenters as had the Druids, but unlike the political activism of the Druids, that of the early Christians was never sufficient to inspire a truly intense and sustained persecution. Early Christians were nonetheless at pains to demonstrate their support of Roman secular authority.

The pagan gods were inextricably tied to the social and cultural environment of agrarian populations, and these communities were very conservative. Whichever new god took over an old paternal obligation to his clients, that god had to produce results over time. All the while the old god would lurk in the shadows, ready to take up the task again. Perhaps he was remembered by name, perhaps merely by a single attribute now associated with the new god, such as a peculiar headdress, an object held in his hand, or a sacred grove or outcropping of rock. Gods worked over the course of generations. When new gods took on old tasks, in the process they were themselves made new. Even when the new god seems to have completely triumphed, now called by only a Roman name, his or her relationship to the worshiper still might reflect the original god in the manner in which the ritual was performed and in the expectations of the celebrant. This was not imitation but a natural extension of patronage networks just as that which followed upon Roman conquest in the social and political domains. Although we cannot often penetrate the realms of barbarian religions, as long as we keep patronage and honor in mind we will not wander far off the mark, and in that way these religions shared much with those of the Romans themselves.

There is a tendency, greatly furthered by the modern film industry, to regard Rome as having been infinitely rich, but in fact Rome had to solve governmental problems with an economy of means. Recourse to military coercion was not only costly and unpredictable but went against the entire ethos of the patron-client relationship that was at the heart of social and political intercourse. Even a successful war might lead to a return to less secure and predictable barbarian leadership rather than the reverse. The use of military force was rare in Gaul as everywhere. As far as Roman sources permit us to see, no major social or political systematic change took place in Gaul because of the initial Roman conquests. Warfare had to cease, but otherwise Romans were quite content with the status quo. They moved in and went about their lives as much as possible as they always had. Although Rome moved quickly to replace rebellious ruling families, Gallic political organization, religion, and economic systems remained. In selecting new rulers the aristocrats of the Roman Republic were highly skilled, as were, for that matter, the emperors later on. They regarded their actions as quite natural, just a part of normal life among themselves and their clients.[13]

Holding office was the principal honor of Roman aristocratic life. It was conducted on a finely appointed stage with the actors moving at a prescribed pace. Officeholders were accorded special though not elaborate dress and ritualized opportunities to display their dignity and authority. Their comings and goings were announced to bystanders. Republican officeholders were never paid and had no official staff. They governed provinces largely out of their own pockets, taking with them a few administrators from their estates (some free, some slave), sons, and the sons of friends, relatives, and political allies needing the experience. This meant that, like the lowly colonists, they too were dependent on local support. Roman dependence on indigenous leadership inexorably led Romans to seek understandings with newly conquered barbarians around shared aspirations and values. The greatest Roman families moved about the Mediterranean, going from the house of one client to that of another. In turn these clients were provided for if they ventured to Rome or elsewhere within their patrons' web of influence. The penetration of Roman values often moved laterally across class lines through contacts and example—religious, social, and ultimately political—into the ranks of the conquered peoples. This remained true for centuries. Republican government rested firmly on the shoulders of Roman patrons with their vast reach.

In Gaul, even in southern Gaul, Roman patrons focused much of their attention on building their personal clientage in neighboring Gallic communities. Rome offered native elite families powerful support among their own people and supported their control over regional life to a degree never possible before Roman intervention. Progressively during the second century B.C., as judged by buried artifacts and a very few notices in Roman literature, Gauls almost everywhere were governed by elite families, which were bonded together through marriage and service within the community and region. The degree of authority that these elites exercised over their clients is largely unknown before the middle of the first century B.C., when the extant writing of Julius Caesar lifts the veil slightly.[14] The fact that since about the beginning of the second century many Celtic communities, once open and small, had become defended and much larger, suggests the presence of elites with increased power to demand service and obedience. In this regard Celtic elite formation followed the same path that the Romans themselves had taken long before and by now took for granted. In an abstract form this pattern had become a part of the standard evolutionary sequence for Greco-Roman historians and ethnographers, and so appears more natural and structured in our sources than in reality it was.

For elite Gallic families deft use of Roman contacts could turn handsome profits. Those opposing Roman expansion suffered accordingly. For Livy writing under Augustus, such highly personalized approaches to politics, often based on family connections, distinguished Romans from the citizens of the Hellenistic world. In the East government seemed to Livy highly impersonal and therefore less dependable. Just how such Roman favoritism proceeded and affected Gallic and later other barbarian societies overall remains a matter of intense debate nurtured by the paucity of data and the abundance of modern theories of historical causation. One thing is clear: Rome regularly saw to the replacement of one individual (and implicitly one set of familial alliances) by another more favorable to Roman interest. To cite a single example, shortly before the arrival of Fabius in the area of what would become Narbo (ca. 120 B.C.), Rome had forced the defeated Gallic king Toutomotulus to flee to the Salluvii, but they could not risk Roman ire. He next sought refuge with the Allobroges, who as a result soon became the focal point of Roman attention. In his place the Romans supported his rival, Crato, whose followers, some nine hundred according to our Roman source, were spared the punishments meted out to those who had followed Toutomotulus into war—that is, enslavement, death, or, like their leader, exile.[15]

Our attention so far in this chapter has been focused on Narbo, but we need to recall that Rome, led by a shrinking number of families, was at this time pursuing many other adventures simultaneously. In part this was because of the competition for power among the narrowing Roman elite itself, which demanded the perpetual expansion of clientage and the economic and political power that those clients represented. The second century witnessed most Roman energy focused on the eastern Mediterranean, where great fortunes and unprecedented power were still to be had. In order to win support among the senatorial class for these escapades, it was necessary to justify them by an appeal to the safety of Rome and its citizens. The purported threat could be piracy, slave revolts, or foreign aggressors impinging upon Romans or their allies. It would be disingenuous to dismiss all claims to have acted in self-defense of Roman vital interests as lies, but as Roman armies ventured farther and farther afield, real threats to Rome receded with them. In contrast, Gaul was only episodically a matter of interest. Let us take another look at the Celts in Gaul through the window provided us by nonliterary material.

By the end of the second century B.C. most people in Gaul with whom Romans had dealings, a minority of the Celtic population, lived in large nucleated settlements, *oppida*. These were walled communities containing from three thousand to five thousand inhabitants. Such large populations supported some full-time craftsmen, but many items, even simple iron products such as nails, could have been produced by less skilled, part-time laborers. The origins of the great enclosures, so vast as to be indefensible except against the relatively small forces of another *oppidum,* may lie in the needs of the new elites that came to power during civil wars. Warfare required many things that *oppida* could provide: large recruitment bases, plentiful and secure food supplies, and especially large quantities of iron weapons. The apparent safety of the great walls isolated farmers and craftsmen from the surrounding countryside and placed them rather securely under the protection and leadership of the new elites. Metalworkers particularly flourished in this new environment, making weapons and various prestige goods for their patrons. All these Celtic communities produced their pottery on wheels and shared a small range of decorative styles; they were especially fond of graphite ware. *Oppida* do not seem to have had community centers except in those in the southernmost districts where Mediterranean urban standards had made an impression. Yet they were effective market centers for regional trade and focal points for people living nearby in undefended villages and farmsteads. Some craftsmen from the *oppida* probably traveled well beyond their walls. One might have found, for example, blacksmiths from an *oppidum* in the surrounding villages peddling their wares, repairing broken metal tools, looking for clients. By the end of the second century most *oppida* had advanced money economies, and increasingly their populations had enclosed very large areas with stout earth-filled defenses. The enclosed space was considerably more than that required for habitation and industry.

An *oppidum* near Manching in Bavaria can illustrate. Here the nine hectares, approximately twenty-two acres,[16] opened by excavation is but a small fraction of the total area enclosed within its defensive walls, which ran almost seven kilometers. These walls incorporated an extensive settlement area with workshops and housing as well as a large area of pasturage. The various locations of special usage shifted over the course of the site's existence. Most of the enclosed area remained dedicated to gardening and livestock.[17] As judged from the few *oppida* sites excavated sufficiently to hazard a guess, industry was dispersed around the inhabited zones, sometimes with smithing nearer the gates or water sources, probably as a precaution in case of fire. We need not rely on the spade of the archaeologist alone for the construction of *oppida* walls. In the case of these massive defenses, we have the corroborative testimony of a contemporary faced with attacking them, Julius Caesar. His description of these *murus gallicus* (Gallic walls) with their carefully boxed and linked sections of cut timber, stone, and turf stacked to the required height, leaves little to the imagination.[18]

About the time of the establishment of *oppida,* burial practices changed from inhumation to cremation. Whatever its cause, it has had a negative effect on several aspects of modern inquiry. For example, so long as archaeologists had whole bodies laid out in their best dress, they were able to reconstruct status, gender, age, and so on. This is rarely the case with cremation burials, although on occasion grave goods are added to the burials alongside the vessel containing ashes. Even so, it is clear that by the early second century elites were no longer wearing special dress. The ritual life of the Celts also entered a new phase, one in which the elites could better reinforce their public roles. Not until shortly before the general collapse of *oppida* beyond the Rhine and Danube (ca. 100–80 B.C.) do we find a return to the long-lost tradition of elites using conspicuous adornment, especially with rare foreign goods, to announce their status. This resurgence of conspicuous consumption may indicate that new families had come to power as a warrior elite. An alternative explanation is that these men had also grown rich by dominating trade with the Romans to the south, perhaps including the trade in slaves, who would have certainly been more numerous in a warlike environment. Slaves best did many tasks. As for the importance of slaves and the slave trade among the Celts of the second century, there are no data upon which to even hazard a guess.

Oppida were confined to Celtic peoples living in the more temperate climatic zones in which traditionally mixed agriculture of wheat and barley predominated. *Oppida* stretched roughly in a broad arch from the Garonne River valley north to the English

Channel, then eastwards as far as Cologne, including the valleys of the Moselle and Main Rivers but not the lower portions of the Rhine, then eastwards up the drainage systems along both sides of the Rhine and the Danube almost as far as Budapest. Farther to the east fortification size diminished markedly, suggesting that they were used essentially as bastions for emergency defense rather than as enclosed townships like *oppida.* These eastern sites shared very little with those farther west. There were very few *oppida* in Britain, only one enclosing more than thirty hectares. *Oppida* did not extend onto the north European plain or into mountainous regions of the Alps They existed but only briefly across the Harz Mountains and in the upper valleys of the Elbe and Oder Rivers. Spain had its own type of defended site peculiar to the peninsula. The style developed too late to affect Celtic populations in Italy that had already fallen under Roman control.[19] It is worth stressing that this band of *oppida* settlements included both sides of the middle and upper Rhine and the upper Danube. The number of Celtic sites so far identified as *oppida* varies according to the criteria applied, ranging from two or three dozen to more than two hundred. Even in areas with many *oppida* the majority of Celts still lived in open settlements.

At most locations in the second century the defensive walls and the area needed for basic domestic life within the *oppida* had to coexist with increasing demands for space from traders, craftsmen, and livestock. Because pigs require much less space to roam for food than cattle, even the smallest had plenty of room for pigs. The smaller *oppida,* however, had to supplement their supplies of beef by imports from the countryside. In southernmost Gaul, much of it taken into the province of Gallia Narbonensis, many of the public structures inside the *oppida* were built in stone and set along streets laid out in a grid pattern. These features doubtless reflect the influence of Greco-Roman concepts of town planning, but they also added to their personal prestige of the families that built them. North of the Roman province, *oppida* were frequently very large, their walls and settlement areas on average larger than those to their south but without the stone embellishments. One of the largest of all *oppida* and one of the most extensively excavated is Manching.

Manching lay alongside the Paar River near its confluence with the Danube in southern Germany, and this proximity to the Danube mirrored that of most other major *oppida.* In the second half of the second century these settlements reached scales that required water transport for the importation of iron ore and perhaps even for the vast amounts of firewood and charcoal needed in the smelting process. Skilled loggers must have harvested all the large trees for many miles to provide for the kilns, smelters, and domestic needs. Felling trees was also a first step in land clearance. Largely on the basis of Julius Caesar's accounts, it is thought that warfare among *oppida* created regional power centers with one *oppidum* in ascendancy over several others nearby. The very length of the typical *oppidum*'s circuit walls made them very difficult to defend with their available populations. The defenders would have had to choose which section was about to receive an assault and concentrate their manpower there. As in the great siege of Constantinople in 1453, the day that the inhabitants guessed wrong was their last day of freedom. So long as the attackers were just from another *oppidum,* however, the numbers would have been about equal and so rushing about from point of attack to point of attack might have been quite enough. On the other hand, despite or perhaps because of the massive size of the fortifications, the odds favored any attacker with sufficient numbers to assault several sections of the wall simultaneously.

Our Roman sources would have us believe that Romans brought civilization to Gaul, but they certainly did not. They did, however, bring order and ultimately peace, but first they brought war.[20] Nor should we forget that Rome did not expand into all areas of the *oppida* settlements, most notably not beyond the Rhine and Danube except in their uppermost reaches, and in those areas *oppida* had ceased to exist long before Roman armies had set foot there. Clearly in many ways Celtic civilization was economically sophisticated and technologically on a par with that of the Romans. Such complexity was lost on Roman commentators, who usually lumped all Celtic peoples together, calling them Gauls. A few Roman authors, nonetheless, knew better than to press generalizations too far.[21] Roman traders would have known the Celts much better, but their insights seem to have provided only a dim awareness within the literary circles.

How long Rome could have allowed southern Gaul to remain dependent upon the patronage of the original conquerors, their heirs, and their colonists is a question made moot by the career of Gaius Marius and the disruptions caused to Roman interests in Gaul by the arrival of peoples new to the Romans, the Cimbri and Teutones. Although both names are perhaps Celtic or made Celtic,[22] no Roman seems to have regarded these newcomers as in any sense related to those Gallic peoples with whom Rome had had long-established relations. The Cimbri and Teutones were outsiders to the Roman world and so had to be fitted into Roman concepts of human geography. As early as the voyages of the Greek Pythias, that is, around the time of Alexander the Great, ancient geographers had located the Teutones on the southern coast of the North Sea, that is, to the northeast of the Gauls and north of the Scythians. The Romans merged the latter two groups into one people, the Gallo- or Celto-Scythians. These Celto-Scythians were believed to occupy an area from Gaul to above the Black Sea. Like most peoples in ancient ethnography, Roman authors divided them into smaller groups, each exhibiting some peculiarity.[23]

Political unity did not figure into ancient classifications of such large assemblages as Celto-Scythians, and, of course, none existed. Ancient ethnographers were primarily interested in cultural characteristics, and these in turn were regarded as having resulted from natural factors, such as climate, closeness to the Ocean or major river systems, and other large topographic features. Scythians were well known to Romans from Greek accounts, most notably that of the fifth-century historian Herodotus. "Scythians" were the archetypal barbarians in Greek sources, their name often being used indiscriminately.[24] According to Roman tradition the Cimbri and Teutones were as different from other contemporary barbarians as was the geography whence they came. They were compared with the Gauls who had sacked Rome in 390 (387) B.C. The very mention of these Gauls had the same effect as bringing up Pearl Harbor in discussions of Cold War American defense budgets. How the Cimbri and Teutones largely took over the old Gallic role as Rome's archetypal aggressor is wrapped up in the career of one man—Gaius Marius.

Marius was an outsider to the system, a man without family links to the roots of power, by wealth probably several notches below the top of his order, an obscure equestrian needing a patron. The army offered about the only chance for him to move up, but for a man without connections progress on that career path was slow. He became a military tribune (a junior officer) only in 124 B.C. after many years of military service. He had begun his long career in the army at least a decade before this in Numidia, where he was attached to the command of Cornelius Scipio Aemilianus Africanus. While Quintus Fabius Maximus was concluding the war against the Allobroges near the future site of Narbo, Marius was in Rome preparing to launch a political career. In 119 he was elected a tribune of the plebs. At this time many equestrians including Marius were finding support from the Metelli family, from whom Marius later broke ranks while in Africa. Equestrians of even the highest income levels could not play senatorial politics without the aid of the truly great families such as the Metelli.

These families maintained their political alliances over generations through marriage and adoption. Their bloodlines were limited to the uppermost members of the senatorial class and all but closed to outsiders. For example, the previously mentioned Cornelius Scipio Aemilianus, an early patron to Marius, was himself the second son of Lucius Aemilianus Paullus and was adopted by Publius Cornelius Scipio, son of the hero of the Hannibalic War. Paullus's first son was also put out to adoption—to Quintus Fabius Maximus, consul and a founder of Narbo. Marius could not compete in such circles. To succeed in this high-stakes game, Marius needed great victories and for that he had to have worthy enemies. First Jugurtha, king of the Numidians, and then the Cimbri and Teutones became appropriate protagonists. In point of fact, Metellus had already twice defeated Jugurtha when Marius took over command, and the barbarians to the north had proved themselves rather stumbling invaders. Unraveling the details of Marius's career is a real problem for historians. There are no firsthand accounts of

Marius, not one, and so too all that we know about the Cimbri and Teutones from literary sources is what later generations felt that they could use to entertain or edify their readers, and even this seems to have had its origins in the literary and patronage circles surrounding Marius.[25] As the first to build a career upon victories over northern barbarians, Marius and his barbarian antagonists figured in virtually all subsequent efforts by generals and even emperors who followed his path.

Towards the end of his long career Marius lost the support of his young protégé, Cornelius Sulla Felix, commonly known as Sulla. The Senate split into two factions supporting either Marius or Sulla, as their rivalry threatened to spill over into civil war. Marius emerged as the leader of the *populares,* and Sulla stood as the champion of the *optimates.* Ostensibly the *populares* were senators who cooperated for the good of the people in contrast to their opposition, the *optimates,* who saw themselves as the aristocratic guarantors of traditional values. In reality neither faction was rigidly characterized by its title as much as by its allegiance to self-interest. Their rivalry also colored all records surviving to be used by later commentators. More to the point still, these accounts were typically used by the subsequent generation to defend or attack Julius Caesar, who claimed a spot among the heirs of Marius through his avowed concern for the commoners of Rome. Thus with the rise of Marius it was necessary for aristocratic families to choose sides, for or against somebody more powerful than they, and this remained the case until Augustus eliminated the old factions all together. First it was Marius or Sulla, then Pompey the Great or Julius Caesar. Like the newspapers in nineteenth-century America, Roman family archives—an important source for generations of historians such as Livy—made their loyalties clear. For them, their involvement with or opposition to Marius was the culmination of their family's political history. Many of their careers bore the imprint of his blessing or disfavor. We know them because of the fact that their family records caught the attention of later historians. With the possible exception of Tiberius Gracchus, Marius was the first Roman about whom neutrality was impossible. Unfortunately for the Roman Republic, he had many worthy successors with similarly polarizing personalities. Given the partisan taint of our literary sources, it is impossible to see the Cimbri and Teutones for what they were.

The most readily demonstrable contribution of the Cimbri and Teutones to Roman history was as a justification of Marius's monopoly of power from 107 until their defeat and subjugation in 102 and 101. Our sources do reveal something else of broader importance: the Roman penchant for using foreign dangers to justify internal innovation. Aulus Gellius in his *Attic Nights* (composed ca. 180 A.D.) toyed with a recollection, perhaps recalled from his reading of a source now lost or from his notes to a professor's lecture in Athens, that Marius's lowering of the property qualifications for recruitment into the legions was because of the Cimbri. On further reflection Gellius decided that he had better take the account in Sallust as his best source, so he assigned this innovation instead to the pressures of the Jugurthian Wars.[26] These fragmentary and distant recollections about the Cimbri, the Teutones, and their various allies illuminate a complex conceptual relationship with barbarian populations of the Alpine and central European areas that had little to do with specific events. Independently they offer no support to an investigation of what it meant to be a northern barbarian. Nonetheless Roman politicians' playing upon Roman fears of invasion was an important part of the barbarian-Roman relationship and may have been mirrored among the barbarians.

Appealing to the Gallic sack quickly became a standard feature in the discussion of foreign policy and was never forgotten. The Cimbri and Teutones, their numbers surely far less than Plutarch's exaggerated report of 300,000 men but ultimately sufficient to defeat three consular armies, were usually remembered in the context of the fourth-century sack of Rome.[27] As such they were regarded as an elemental threat to the Roman way of life. Long after their pacification, their names continue to exert this effect. So we often read the names Cimbri and Teutones alongside that of "the Gauls" or in place of them. Even in the age of Augustus, when stories of Rome's past were reduced to moralistic vignettes used to exemplify basic Roman virtues, the legend of Cimbri and Teutones was still current. Upon the sacrifice of fellow citizens and under stern and compelling leadership, Romans built a stronger state. The vast majority of authors mentioning Marius, the Cimbri, and the Teutones wrote after Augustus. In this context the Gallic sack of Rome and the struggle against the Cimbri and Teutones were but two of many tales of noble individuals sacrificing self and family. Augustus's contemporary Livy recalls a detail about the Gallic sack of Rome that no ancient source associated with Marius and the Cimbri mentioned; they should have. According to this story the Gauls took the city but not the citadel, where Marcus Manlius and a small band of defenders held on. Shortly thereafter, Manlius became haughty, opposed the legitimate government, and was thrown into prison. When he attempted to make himself king, he was tried, convicted, and executed on the very Capitol that he had helped save.[28] The obvious moral lesson of the Manlius story seems to have failed to impress Marius and his supporters.

By his death in 86 at age seventy-one, Marius had held seven consulships and had celebrated numerous triumphs, but none of more lasting fame than those over the Teutones and Ambrones (102) at Aix-en-Provence, ancient Aquae Sextiae, and the Cimbri (101) at Vercellae in northern Italy about one hundred kilometers west of Milan.[29] Marius and his legions could claim to have blunted a giant pincer movement designed to envelop Rome and its allies. He and his supporters exaggerated and manipulated their victories for political advantage, but they did not make up the invasion or the invaders. The defeated were dispersed; some ended up in Gaul, others returned beyond the Rhine. Julius Caesar passed on to his readers a claim made by the Aducatuci that they were descended from the Cimbri and Teutones. If so, their ancestors would have settled near modern Tongres. Similarly two later inscriptions found on Roman votive statuettes, one discovered in Roman territory along the Main River and another in Baden near Heidelberg, proclaim that the dedicators were themselves Cimbri.[30]

Tacitus reports that some were still dwelling in northernmost Jutland as late as A.D. 100, but that they had lost much of their former power. But Tacitus could not just leave it at that, because the Cimbri held pride of place as the forefathers of all Germans in their long struggle for liberty against the willfulness of the empire.

The theme of liberty and the costs of its preservation are dominant literary motifs in Tacitus's politico-cultural discussion of barbarians and Romans. He used it whether he was addressing matters concerning the Germans or the Britons. Both settings allowed him to explore the contributions of Roman culture and the meaning of empire. In his *Germania,* Tacitus gave the Cimbri undeserved credit for building the circuit walls of *oppida,* which were still visible to him on both banks of the Rhine, and which in reality had nothing to do with the Cimbri. He went on to declare that by measuring the walls of their great encampments one could get a sense of the Cimbri's formidable numbers, technical sophistication, and "the greatness of their trek." Thus he holds the honor of being "the first survey archaeologist." Britain was all but conquered; Germany remained free.[31] Clearly by the end of the first century A.D., the Cimbri had entered into legend, and as with all legends, this one could serve many causes. The first such cause was of a different sort, but one also based on legends. By manipulating legend and fact, Marius achieved a career without precedent. Who were these barbarians who were so fearsome that Romans repeatedly called upon Marius to lead them, and why were they suddenly appearing on Rome's distant frontiers?

A case can and will be made that at least originally the barbarians invading Gaul and elsewhere under Marius—their numbers never really known yet wildly reported—were seeking to serve as Celtic mercenaries. We would be ill advised to accept at face value any ethnic identity as recorded in Roman sources. Plutarch, like Tacitus writing around A.D. 100, although assigning motives to these invaders, better captures what Cimbri and Teutones came to symbolize—destruction, slaughter, and rapine, the opposite of things Roman:

> For three hundred thousand armed fighting men were advancing, and much larger hordes of women and children were said to accompany them, in quest of land to support so vast a multitude, and of cities in which to settle and live, just as the Gauls before them, as they learned, had wrested the best part of Italy from the Tyrrhenians and now occupied it. They themselves, indeed, had not had intercourse with other peoples, and had traversed a great stretch of country, so that it could

> not be ascertained what people it was nor whence they had set out, thus to descend upon Gaul and Italy like a cloud. The most prevalent conjecture was that they were some of the German peoples which extended as far as the northern ocean, a conjecture based on their great stature, their light-blue eyes, and the fact that the Germans call robbers Cimbri.[32]

Plutarch's invaders were pure barbarians, untouched by foreign influence. That they came to take over the land is made manifest by showing them as having their families in tow. This is the standard stuff of ancient ethnography and historical causation. The farther removed the barbarian, the more strikingly different were his physical and personal characteristics from those of the citizens of the Mediterranean cities. These "German peoples," living at the end of the world, as far away as one could imagine, beyond all contact with other humans, were therefore according to ancient ethnography taller, fairer, more lawless, and so more truly wild, than those closer to the Mediterranean and anybody else living in between. Other typical "barbarian virtues" included the purity of their marriages, the closeness of their family bonds, simple dress, a life close to nature, loyalty to leaders, and so on, qualities that ancient ethnographers believed their own urban life-styles placed at risk. In order to raise the specter of the potential replacement of one set of cultural values by another, many ancient authors augmented their portraits of invasion with signs of migration, that is, by reports of families accompanying their warriors. That these barbarians wished to live in cities, according to Plutarch, is a remarkable shading of the narrative even by the standards of ancient ethnography.

Plutarch's near contemporary Lucius Florus explained their departure from their coastal homelands on "the farthest parts of Gaul" as the result of a dramatic rise in ocean levels there, but for him too they were drifters seeking land to settle. Climatic change was another explanation featured in ancient ethnography and history and so is immediately suspect: oceans may rise but not just locally. Like Plutarch's story of their lust for land, Florus's account of their seeking settlement is a traditional but not necessarily false characterization. There is no way for us to know the truth, but there is equally no doubt that a desire for land had become a part of the standard literary topos for barbarians. Florus rhetorically has the invaders ask the Senate of "the people of Mars"—that is, of course, the Romans themselves, the warrior race—for land in return for unrestricted armed service on Rome's behalf.[33] Because these particular barbarians were being described as at war with Rome, Plutarch need not extol any virtues that went along with their barbarity other than their ferocity. Tacitus is more fulsome in his praise of Germanic virtues in his purely ethnographic treatise, the *Germania* but, like the biographer Plutarch, much less so when writing about specific wars against Rome.[34] What was said of the Cimbri was also told of the Teutones and their allies and virtually every barbarian people found in Roman literature.

As early as 113 B.C., according to Appian writing more than two centuries later, some Teutones stumbled into Noricum. This was the first time that Romans had even heard of these people. The Teutones were completely ignorant of Roman involvement in the area. When they learned of them, they quickly apologized for their attacks and moved off towards Gaul. Consul Papirius Carbo, who apparently feared that they were headed for Italy, ambushed them only to come within a hair of losing his life in a debacle that left many of his men dead. Appian points out that at this time the Teutones had no desire to move southwards into Italy, despite Carbo's fears and actions. Cimbri were reported in western Illyricum (approximately Croatia today) at this same time.[35] In 109 B.C. some Cimbri, Teutones, and Tigurini petitioned the consul Marcus Junius Silanus, then in southern Gaul, to grant them lands for settlement in return for their military alliance. When he refused, they defeated his and the next two armies sent against them.[36]

In 107 these same Tigurini, a subgroup of the Celtic Helvetians, perhaps not eager to get too far from home, killed the consul Lucius Cassius Longinus and held hostage many of his men.[37] The incident seems to have become a matter of pride for all Helvetii, for they recalled it to Julius Caesar half a century later, but perhaps Caesar put the recollection into their mouths for his own purposes.[38] In the same year Marius was elected consul for the first time. The client system that had been established by Quintus Fabius Maximus and Gnaeus Domitius Ahenobarbus began to disintegrate as the Celtic Tectosages rose and took Toulouse. The year 106 was a disaster with a reported eighty thousand Roman legionnaires slain fighting the Cimbri near Oranges. Like all strength estimates in ancient texts, these cannot be confirmed and were doubtless greatly exaggerated to enhance their effect upon the reader. Only in 104 did Marius's legate Sulla capture Copillus, the leader of the Tectosages, and restore the status quo ante around Narbo.[39]

The struggle against the Cimbri and Teutones culminated in 102–101, when within a year Marius and his generals defeated the Teutones and Ambrones in Gaul, and the Cimbri in Italy. The Romans reportedly fielded an army of fifty-five thousand against the Cimbri.[40] Florus passes on the story of a certain Teutoboduus, who fled the battlefield near Aix-en-Provence only to be captured by some Sequanni and handed over to the Romans. Subsequently he was paraded in Marius's triumphal procession. Naturally Florus tells us that this Teutoboduus was no ordinary man, literally larger than life. Standing head and shoulders above the others in the triumph, he was known to have been able to "vault over four to six horses." The same author, joined by Plutarch, also records that the Cimbri lost their king, Boiorix, in battle the following year on the Raudian Plain near Vercellae, where sixty-five thousand of his men fell.[41]

The distances over difficult terrain that these allegedly massive groups of invaders traveled defy explanation. There was no coordinated planning among the various barbarian groups, no pincer attack on Rome. There was no single leader and perhaps hardly any leaders at all. The kings' names are suspect: Teutoboduus, perhaps "warleader of the Teutons." The name is a compound of two common Celtic elements and seems more a title than a name. Boii were traditionally Celts of the Po Valley, where they lived as early as the opening of the fourth century. Later Caesar reported some living in Gaul and opposing him, but naturally Caesar also notes that in short order he defeated and settled them among his allies the Aedui.[42] The Boii in Italy were infamous in Roman eyes: not only had their ancestors sacked Rome, but they were also remembered for having gone over to Hannibal as he descended the Alps. Even more, they had dishonored the Roman people in their treatment of the slain consul-elect Lucius Postumius during that war: they reportedly gilded his skull and use it as a cup to hold libations at religious festivals.[43] Rome punished the Boii mercilessly after Hannibal returned to Carthage, and they were never heard of in Italy again. Romans likely to read Caesar, Livy, or other late republican authors may have been familiar with Celtic dialects; some had personal business contacts in Gaul or had served there in the army on campaign. To these and later Romans the name Boii was synonymous with savagery, which is precisely why reference to it worked, and rhetorically trained men of Roman letters pulled it from their quiver of topoi for the next half millennium.

Thus the death of Boiorix, a name perhaps invented merely to convey the impression of the "king of savages" now humbled, also could not but have recalled the earlier and still most painful episodes in Roman history associated with Gauls. Marius is portrayed in our sources as settling all these accounts. By parading their leaders in his triumphal procession, as was Roman custom, he gave visual assurance to the populace that there would be no recurrence of this transgression. In this very personal way, the people saw that Roman honor had been restored. This carefully contrived imagery would have been lost if instead of personifying the restoration of Roman honor in the person of a humbled "king," a motley band of pathetic barbarians had been herded around the triumphal circuit. The reason such pageantry worked was that it struck a resonance with the populace through rekindling and immediately allaying their fears of another Gallic sack of Rome. Marius was not the last Roman politician to play the Gallic sack and Cimbri-Teutones cards.

Marius's stratagems—tricks revealing Roman mental superiority—are the stock-in-trade of another literary genre, military handbooks or manuals. Perhaps the best examples of these are the works of Frontinus. Frontinus's *Stratagems,* composed ca. A.D. 90 contains five vignettes about Marius. The stories, and they seem hardly more than that, told to us by Plutarch, Florus, and especially Frontinus cannot be pressed. Can anybody really believe the legend of Marius testing Gallic loyalty at the start of his campaign against the Cimbri by sending one sealed letter inside another with orders not to open them and then personally showing up to check whether anybody had? Then you might believe that he did it twice, once to the Gauls (potentially in league with the Cimbri) and once to the Ligurians (just possibly soft on the Teutones). So says Frontinus anyway.[44] These later Roman authors were having some fun surely, but they provide us with scarcely any hard data about barbarians. Shortly after Marius's victories and at his urging, the Senate created a new province, Gallia Narbonensis, to protect Roman interests. By the mid-90s regular gubernatorial selections for the province were routine, but the full elaboration of a Roman administration and defensive policy for Narbonensis had to await Julius Caesar and another Gallic threat. Creating a regular province centered on Narbo made Rome's position there more formal perhaps, but it also accelerated the shift of patronage away from the families of the founding generals to the Senate as a body. There Marius's will prevailed.[45]

Not to belittle the Teutones and the Cimbri, their suffering, or that which the well-attested fact of invasion caused, particularly in Gaul, the truth is that these events were never simply told and probably never completely understood. The Romans themselves had at best an incomplete picture of events beyond the Alps, particularly beyond the Danube, so contemporary Romans had to make sense of the fragmentary news that reached them through their own filters, specifically those provided them by Marius, his supporters, or his detractors. Although by 102 Marius, four times consul, had already transformed power among the Roman people through his triumphs and his extraordinary patronage, he was never content. Nor could he have been, and that is one of the few facts beyond dispute. Marius rose to power over his supporters and later rivals, the Metelli faction, by his generalship. He changed the fighting order of the Roman legion, giving it greater flexibility and staying power, by continuing the evolution of the cohort as the core unit within the legion—something Gellius had thought to connect to the wars against the Cimbri before changing his mind in favor of the Jugurthian Wars.

Marius also paid greater attention to equipping both infantry and cavalry properly. Perhaps most significant Marius opened the profession of soldiering to the poorest Romans (the *proletarii*), with one result being that conscription became less common and instead volunteers filled the ranks. These new recruits were professionals in all but name. Their goals were personal and economic, and their loyalty to those who led them, intense. Marius's popularity among the army and lower orders of citizenry allowed him to push aside much of the traditional aristocratic opposition, but he needed victories to sustain his image and underwrite the costs of his patronage. In the latter half of the second century prior to Marius, Roman armies had suffered numerous defeats, including several recent ones against the northern barbarians, but Marius approached these setbacks as opportunities. His victories restored Roman pride and sense of security. In return his supporters were extolled with public honors and recorded his name in their family archives as a great benefactor. Wrapped in the cloak of Marius, the Cimbri and Teutones had entered Roman politics and Roman history almost as phantoms.

Let us briefly explore the archaeological record of the late Iron Age and especially of the *oppida* beyond the Rhine and Danube for the decades surrounding the so-called invasions of the Cimbri and Teutones. Perhaps in this way we can illuminate, if ever so dimly, the shadows their legends cast and get a first impression of how migration theory played out among Roman authors. The locations of Roman battles with the Cimbri, Teutones, and their allies leave little doubt that they must have passed by Gallic *oppida* and very near if not through the area of *oppida* in what would today be Bavaria and Baden in southern Germany, but the health of these eastern settlements at this time is far from certain. Once again much of what follows depends on a very few sites, all only partially excavated because of their vastness despite great effort. Any attempt at general synthesis therefore risks pushing interpretations of specific sites beyond what their data suggest, just as does extrapolating from the few literary allusions, but to some extent every source type helps control the others.

Excavations of Celtic sites in what is today southern Germany, particularly the *oppidum* of Manching, which has already figured prominently in this chapter, and recently also that of Kelheim, have revealed that sometime between roughly between 120 and 50 B.C. *oppida* ceased to exist in the region. Roman sources provide us with two violent interruptions of normal Celtic life during this period: the first is that of the invasion of the Cimbri and Teutones; the second, the Gallic wars conducted by Julius Caesar (58–50 B.C.). The temptation to link the demise of *oppida* in this region to one or the other or both of these historically attested events has not always been resisted. Of the two sets of actors, at least the Cimbri and Teutones probably passed through the area, whereas Caesar never came close. As Julius Caesar campaigned in Gaul (58–50 B.C.), conducting lengthy sieges of *oppida,* he did not know that there ever had been *oppida* beyond the Rhine and upper Danube. Still less could he have known that this civilization was dead, the great sites virtually abandoned.[46] Although when and why this disintegration began is still unclear, signs of market disruption, settlement shrinkage, and changes in customs suggest that something was changing at the heart of these particular communities in the course of the two or three generations before Caesar.

As a result of particularly intense archaeological efforts, it now seems clear that by around 60 B.C. Manching was deserted or all but. Greater precision is beyond reach. Some scholars argue for a cessation of settlement there not later than 80 B.C. Others, basing their opinions on new studies of coins found on site suggest that the actual end came just after Caesar's Gallic wars. Other *oppida* had a similar devolution, although not necessarily the same absolute chronology as at Manching. In archaeological terms this is the transition from the La Tène (or Celtic) Phase C, the high point of *oppida,* and Phase D1, the archaeological levels marking the end of *oppida* settlement. For some non-*oppida* sites, D1 is followed by Phase D2, post-*oppida* pre-Roman conquest. Many *oppida* have no D2 phase, for they had already been abandoned by this time and remained unoccupied. Because assigning calendar dates to the current relative chronologies offered at most sites has proved extremely difficult, there is great risk in generalizing about circumstances that may have affected more than one site, but to avoid the effort entirely is to give up the search for cause-and-effect relationships. The dating at most sites is sufficiently secure to set forth in outline the physical landscape during the time that the Cimbri and Teutones were Roman concerns.[47]

For the sake of argument, it does not seem unreasonable to suggest from the archaeological materials that the cessation of occupation at Manching and elsewhere in this region was due to some type of turmoil lasting for at least one generation, and probably longer. Abandonment of these sites thus began around the opening of the first century B.C., or slightly earlier in some cases. The *oppida* do not seem to have been destroyed in a cataclysmic event such as a battle or natural phenomenon, nor did they all collapse at one time.[48] Manching apparently had a significant armed struggle about 120 or slightly earlier but survived as an *oppidum* for at least five decades and probably in a diminished manner for a while longer. Concurrently the *oppidum* at nearby Kelheim, perhaps a dependency of Manching but itself a major *oppidum,* was also deserted and not destroyed. Other *oppida* in the region were abandoned by 80 B.C. In any case, it is clear that none ended because of an attack by Cimbri or their associates, and that ripples from Caesar's wars hardly mattered to the population.

An attractive theory is that the *oppida* destroyed one another in a series of hegemonic struggles such as we see a half century or so later in Gaul in the opening book of Caesar's narrative. Just as the origins of the great walls may lie in the needs of new elites that came to power during civil wars, so too their abandonment may mark the demise of the ruling elite and, with it, the culture that supported it. At some point the competition for power may have so shaken the authority of the leading families and their religious and ideological underpinnings that in this one area *oppida* civilization, in effect, imploded. Elsewhere Caesar cut this scenario, always possible given the highly competitive nature of Celtic elite families, short. The Cimbri and Teutones may fit obliquely into this scenario, perhaps as recruits drawn into Celtic civil wars. They may also have profited as recruiters themselves from the societal self-questioning that these wars may have produced.

Several facts are worth recalling in this context. There was no such thing as a unified Celtic civilization. When it came to political and military power, whatever was going on in Bavaria need not have had any parallel in Gaul. Although Caesar's account opens with some of the *oppida* in Gaul at war over regional hegemony, there is no hint that Gallic *oppida* were on the edge of a general disillusion. Nor is there any indication whatsoever that the basic ethos of living in these large manufacturing and marketing centers was questioned in Gaul. Instead, in Gaul there was a heated realignment of allies and aristocratic families. This process had reached a level of regional warfare, in which a few principal *oppida* were struggling for interregional supremacy. Onto this stage strode Caesar, who quickly became the major player. If one seeks a Roman-type explanation for the abandonment of the *oppida* in southern Germany, then an invasion would have to be considered as the primary cause. Following this line of reasoning, the invasion would have to have been that of the Cimbri and Teutones, because the Romans knew no other. Indeed, if you really believed that the Cimbri and their allies could field an army of 300,000, then indeed they could have engulfed even the largest *oppidum*. But because no Roman seems to have been aware of the events in southern Germany, no such explanation was offered.

The gradual denouement of *oppida* in the area of southern Germany does not correlate with the type of invasions attested to in the literature for the Cimbri and Teutones. Moreover, the archaeological data assembled from the areas most likely to have produced "invaders" strongly suggest that anybody coming from those areas would have been very hard-pressed to besiege *oppida*. Most modern archaeologists have wisely avoided the problems associated with Cimbri and Teutones or any other historically attested people. Instead of attaching these historical names to artifacts, as was once so commonly done, they have generally agreed to call the aggregation of late Iron Age archaeological materials found along the southern coast of the Baltic Sea from Jutland (where Tacitus believe the Cimbri still lived) eastwards along the north German plain (where some ancient ethnographers had situated the Teutones) the Jastorf complex.[49] The Jastorf archaeological complex is characterized by pottery made without turning on a wheel that is colored but left without designs. Other common characteristics included locally made metal tools, rare use of iron, no indigenous coins and few imported ones. At the time of the historical Cimbri and Teutones (ca. 100 B.C.), these northern settlements were largely unfortified and many hardly even nucleated. Most of the population lived in dispersed farmsteads with a central building shared by humans and livestock.[50]

In Jutland some evidence suggests that at about this time new families were asserting their hegemony over their village communities, stepping out from the norm and building simple enclosures at a time when there is also evidence of increasing amounts of imported prestige items, mainly Celtic, in elite burials. Some scholars have suggested that this social differentiation represents an early phase of the evolution of war bands, which, they believe, emerged as a result of an intensification of internal conflict. Some materials buried in bogs and elsewhere at this time also suggest a kind of tribute system, in which underlings gave gifts to the elite farmers. The dislocations caused by these alleged local power struggles might help account for the willingness of elements of the population to depart for lands elsewhere. Even if true, however, this cannot account for the type of invasions recorded in the historical sources.[51]

Everything considered, Tacitus was inadvertently and then only partially correct about the Cimbri and Teutones, when he concluded that the once mighty Cimbri had built the *oppida* and only after their defeat had they fallen from their former glory. In reality, he accepted a false premise about the Cimbri in 100 B.C., that is, that they had been like the Celts of the south but had fallen upon hard times. The cost of their freedom after defeat was poverty, but they remained the current generation of the brave warrior race of old. What Tacitus could not understand was that they had always lived this simple life. The reports of Tiberius's fleet for A.D. 5 upon which Tacitus apparently based his opinions were accurate, but he could not unravel the myths created two centuries earlier. In A.D. 5 as in 100 B.C. these people lived in basically the same way as did all those peoples beyond the European *oppida* zone regardless of whether their farms were in Jutland, the north German plain, or the valleys of the Elbe and Oder. They all lived in scarcely defended villages and hamlets and would have had no experience whatsoever in siege warfare.[52] Some may have found employment as mercenaries fighting for one *oppidum* or another.

Any attempt by such people to besiege *oppida* would have ended in failure; at any rate, no *oppidum* can be shown to have succumbed to assault and rapid destruction. It must be said, however, that because of the immense length of the walls of most *oppida* and the limited time and money available, no circuit walls have been excavated in their entirety. A sudden breach by attackers coming from an unexpected direction could have spelled disaster, but then there should be other indications of a sudden and violent end. There are not. People living in the northern communities—as revealed by excavation, not those misidentified as the builders of *oppida*—would have not been able to destroy the *oppida* had they wanted to do so. Even the historically attested Cimbri and Teutones did not assault walled towns. That said, if any invader appeared, the inhabitants would surely have sought protection behind their still functional walls or at least have cannibalized parts of them in order to throw up a refuge. No temporary defensive measures for this late period have come to light. The *oppida* walls were not destroyed, indeed they were indestructible. Other explanations must be sought for these problems in *oppida* civilization. Let us look beyond warfare, for *oppida* were much more than just their circuit walls.

The desertion of site after Celtic site in this region must have some sort of ideological explanation as well as that of a hegemonic reversal. Perhaps there was a widespread doubt in the existing norms and values of society, such as a rejection of the claims to leadership made by long dominant families and of the means these families used to project their status. In this atmosphere elite dress and the role of the leadership in religious observance may have come under scrutiny. The dominance of one family or community over the local landscape and its inhabitants had long found expression in ritual. The great walls were not the only public constructions. Another common one was the peculiar rectangular enclosures, the scene of cult rituals, situated outside the walls of the *oppida*. All public building projects were occasions to remind the community of the peculiar combination of secular and divine powers at work there. If buildings were to last, they required the blessing of the gods. Walls and sacred precincts required sacrifice, sometimes of humans but more often of animals, in order to empower them. Iron tools were buried in both as well, thereby somehow affirming that their use and manufacturing was in accordance to the will of the gods. Celtic and early Germanic gods, at least as seen in their distant echoes left in early medieval sagas, combined the forces of creation and destruction, support and denial, that produced among other things a lingering sense that secular leadership could be, perhaps should be, a necessary link between humans and the divine.[53] Leadership among the gods and men was in keeping with eternal forces of nature, and men had to revere these powers through sacrifice. Walls meant to defend against attack by men were intertwined in this blend of secular and divine power with sacred springs, grottoes, and other natural anomalies.

Homes, shrines, and even walls might have to be rededicated or abandoned if this network of dependence between leaders, followers, and divine sanctions was placed in doubt. Theories connecting the abandonment of walls and religious enclosures to defensive needs alone are at best incomplete explanations, and furthermore associating either their building, rebuilding, or abandonment with specific historical invaders is more than dubious. It is surely wrong. At Kelheim, for example, the area of the rectangular enclosure, although the structure itself had fallen into disrepair, was still used for ritual purposes even after the *oppidum* was no longer occupied. At Kelheim seven infants were buried there in the period just after the *oppidum*'s abandonment.[54]

It is possible that Roman intervention in Gaul in the late second century precipitated a ripple effect extending far beyond its point of origin, and that somehow this disturbance set off a hegemonic shift within *oppida* as far away as the valley of the upper Danube and beyond. Despite its attractiveness, this particular version of the domino theory remains unproven and is probably unprovable. At the very least the explanation is decidedly Romanocentric.

With the collapse came an abandonment not only of the *oppida* but also many of the styles of personal ornament and domestic items that had characterized the inhabitants. But was this due to the arrival of new elements of the population or a change in values among the indigenous population? Peoples living in the same areas in the first three quarters of the first century—that is, on both sides of the time of probable abandonment—continued to import Roman items, but they were also attracted to styles of personal ornament and domestic wares previously found only in the region of the Elbe and Oder Rivers. Although people in the post-*oppida* period were indeed somewhat attracted to the decorative styles and objects normally associated with the Jastorf complex, more often than not they used them in ways familiar to their own culture, that is, to support life-styles and customs similar to those formerly associated with the *oppida.* Thus we have evidence of modest changes in tastes but none for the presence of a new people. Certainly there is not even a hint of the arrival of any major new component of the population. There are, however, strong indications of a general upheaval and of people being resettled. Perhaps as the dominance of the elites waned, their tastes and values, which ran towards imported Roman wares, were also questioned. In such circumstances new material influences, styles not previously associated with the former elites, could have made headway.

Whatever the causes of stress within the *oppida* beyond the Rhine, the change from a society accustomed to living in large, interconnected, and economically advanced settlements to ones completely without such centers must have created substantial disruptions and dislocations. Those previously engaged in the market economy would have been progressively displaced and consequently would have had to find land to farm, but good land was limited and long held by others.[55] Any restructuring of alliances between and within *oppida* would have affected somebody. The reversion to open-settlement living probably occurred over generations and produced its own dynamics including a steady problem of displaced persons. If Cimbri and Teutones were in any way connected to the transformations among the *oppida* communities east of the Rhine, it may have been because some Celts from Bavaria and Gaul threw in their lots with them and so swelled their ranks. A few Cimbri and Teutones may even have sought to become mercenaries with the Celts, as they may have with the Romans, if, that is, we can put any credence in the stories told by Florus. For the sake of argument a much more radical theory might be constructed in which no emigrations from the north took place at all.

Might there be something in Plutarch's attempt at linguistic derivation—another common feature of ancient ethnography, by the way—that "Cimbri" meant simply "robbers" among the Germans? A few freebooters—and nobody coming from the north or east would likely have been regarded as more by the civilized Celts of the south—might well have received offers from Celtic communities in the early stages of a traumatic transformation. Indeed, if taken literally, to call such men "outlaws" to *oppida* civilization would have been quite natural. However that may be, the terms Cimbri and Teutones seem to have or share Celtic roots. Restructuring *oppida* alliances surely left many former insiders as outsiders. Julius Caesar is the first Latin author known to employ systematically the term "German" for barbarians, and there is no reason to think that anybody around 100 B.C. would have done so. "Cimbri" in particular could have been a Celtic name widely applied to brigands and not reserved for those of the far north at all. There could have been many Cimbri. Such is the state of our records that almost anything seems possible—anything, that is, except the traditional story of massive and well-led groups of invaders threatening Rome and its allies. That these "bandits" ultimately found homes in Gaul and had some success there in recruiting more supporters underscores that, whatever language and cultural differences existed between the newcomers and the native Celts, they were not barriers, a point that comparative linguistics supports.[56] The chief problem with completely rejecting any involvement of "Cimbri" from Jutland and others from the northern coastal zone is that it requires us to abandon completely the ancient ethnographic tradition, including even what appears to have been an eyewitness action report made by the commander of a Roman fleet. It is this last conjecture, as implicitly suggested by Tacitus, that offers the strongest support for those theories that assign at least some real northerners to the role of combatants. From the Romans' point of view these people, about whom they had no previous knowledge, were invaders from beyond their world. Literally, of course, they were "barbarians." Later historians and ethnographers manipulated and retold their story to the point that it is now largely lost beyond retrieval. Marius, not knowing much and probably caring less about either the causes of these invasions or the backgrounds of the invaders, took advantage of their presence to further his career. Romans were still very much a Mediterranean people.

The theory that has been advanced in this chapter as the most likely is that the material influence of Jastorf slowly expanded into an area in which *oppida* were already in a state of heightened turmoil from unknown but sui generis causes. In their efforts to restore order and to achieve a new local hegemony, the leaders of some or all *oppida* in southern Germany turned to mercenary recruitment in an effort to upset the balance of power that was perpetuating endemic warfare. By necessity they turned outside the *oppida* zone itself because the men within it were already committed to one side or another. This combative climate attracted the attention of young men seeking profit through arms. Rather than one or two large groups of people migrating many hundred kilometers over exceedingly rugged terrain—and that is precisely the view given in the ancient sources—it seems much more likely that the Romans first confronted numerous groups calling themselves or being identified first by the Celts and then later by the Romans with the same two or three names, which are themselves Celtic or derivative of Celtic terms. These various groups consolidated briefly when Roman legions approached. Chronologically their appearance in the historical records seems to coincide with an early, but not the first, stage of the disruption of *oppida* settlements east of the Rhine. This seems to have occurred at least two generations before their general collapse.

Furthermore, this theory suggests that the stories surrounding the Cimbri and Teutones represent how the Romans understood and wished to portray one part of these events, the plight of unemployed mercenaries perhaps accompanied by others dispossessed by the upheavals in the Celtic world. These bands caused much destruction among undefended communities. Romans fought and under Marius decisively defeated these forces, which then sought and received permission to settle among various Celts; a few drifted back to the farms they had left behind.

If this scenario approaches historical reality, then it foreshadows the circumstances surrounding Roman involvement in Gaul under Julius Caesar by half a century. The *oppida* in southern Germany were more likely to have first turned to "Germanic" sources of recruits simply because of proximity and necessity. By ca. 120 B.C. they were also fragile internally. Of the underlying circumstances for these events, Romans knew nothing and so we know extremely little. Roman authors filled the explanatory void with traditional explanations drawn from the deep reservoir of ancient ethnography. Roman influence, particularly through trade, quite likely played a part in these events, but the archaeological data suggest only a very subtle one. The Cimbri and Teutones were fundamentally a Celtic problem.

Over the past quarter century there has been a general retreat from migration theory across all fields of history. There are usually better explanations for major historical changes, just as the preceding discussion has tried to suggest for the "invasions and migrations" of the Cimbri and Teutones.[57] Even when there seems to be adequate proof that some sort of intrusion occurred, as in the case surveyed in this chapter, there is no reason to blame the invader for more than the deaths incurred in battle. Internecine warfare, on the other hand, has afflicted many civilizations, and has proved capable of rather quickly returning urban life-styles to their agrarian roots. European scholars invented modern migration theory in the nineteenth century and have been particularly slow to abandon it, perhaps because of the fact that it is so deeply rooted in the literary legacy of antiquity and is a part of the national myths of both France and Germany.

Two completely non-Mediterranean examples, also once thought to reflect migration or invasion, may serve as a concluding reminder of how perilous such interpretations are. In North America the highly complex Mississippian culture, commonly called the Mound Builders, was dispersed over hundreds of miles with sites as distant from each other as Cahokia in Illinois and Etowah in Georgia, but it largely disappeared within two centuries without a hint of a single adversary. For the Mississippians there was no identifiable natural disaster, no systematic burning, no mass graves, only some indications of a general breakdown in the political and social order as seen in the short intervals between rebuilding phases at sites such as Cahokia. Common ideologies and ceremonials gave way to a fragmented world in which solutions to living together in very large numbers—Cahokia had at least 10,000 inhabitants—were irrelevant.[58] Similarly, Classic Mayan civilization with its divine kings and literary records collapsed within a century. Most sites peaked around 750, and almost all were abandoned within but fifty years (ca. A.D. 840–90). Victims of internecine warfare, they gave up their god-kings and, with them, the organizing principle of their civilization.[59]

Parallels to the collapse of *oppida* sites are readily apparent in each of these examples, but as always it would be very risky to press a detailed comparison and draw hard conclusions from analogies. The circumstances may have been quite different. The examples from the Americas do, however, oblige us to consider explanations other than external invasions by foreign people or their products. They also caution us not to underestimate the possibility of a major paradigm shift among the population, especially among the elites. Finally, of all those peoples involved with the Cimbri and Teutones, none was changed more than the Romans themselves. Marius and his contemporaries, in responding to and redefining the "barbarian threat," shifted the political balance of power in Rome and in Italy and tilted the focus of Roman attention westwards.

Three

Through Caesar's Eyes

Julius Caesar begins his commentaries on the Gallic war with one of the most familiar passages in all ancient literature: "Gallia est omnis divisa in partes tres, quarum unam incolunt Belgae, aliam Aquitani, tertiam qui ipsorum lingua Celtae, nostra Galli appellantur" (Gaul is one, divided into three parts: the Belgae inhabiting one, the Aquitani another, and those who in their own language are called Celts, in Latin called Galli, living in the third). Yet despite its familiarity, let us not be deceived by its apparent simplicity. From our perspective we might say all Gaul remaining outside Roman jurisdiction in 58 B.C. was so divided, but the rhetorical effect would be the same. Gaul is one entity. Thus at the outset Caesar prepared his readers for a major struggle, one that would conclude in total victory in Gaul, all Gaul. How Romans understood this passage and many others at the time of publication is important, but their reception is cloaked in the mysteries of the manuscript itself. Caesar the author, the general, the politician, the explorer, is everywhere present in the text that has come down to us. In this chapter, it is through his eyes, and through classical literature in general, that we view the barbarian.

The technique of composition of the *Gallic War* remains unknown. It seems likely that the first seven books, all those written by Caesar himself, of "commentaries" on his campaigns in Gaul were published together as a volume not long after the events described in book 7 (ca. 50 B.C.). The "book," as here in "book 7," was the ancient equivalent of a modern chapter and was a unit physically created by combining sections, ancient "chapters," written on standardized lengths of papyrus and read as a scroll. Caesar seems to have based these books on the notes that he made for his annual reports to a not universally grateful Senate. In some respects each book still reveals the gradual growth of his knowledge about Gaul, but the high degree of coherence both in terms of the details of the narrative and also of the overall literary effect attests to careful editing and revision. We are left to debate just how much of the original epistularies remain in the polished product, but it is impossible to believe that Caesar wrote what we have without detailed notes. The personal and group names, the dates and times, and the detailed military information all attest to the use of extensive notes, probably those kept for his original reports to the Senate.

Many of the different readings of the text relate to the irresolvable problem of the degree to which Caesar edited and revised his manuscript. If you assume that there is a close correlation to his annual reports, then we the readers of the book can still share some of the excitement and concerns of those who heard read the yearly reports in the Senate. From the beginning they would have wondered just how long this campaign would last. The senators knew Julius Caesar was not a man to settle for half a loaf, but they also knew that they had not authorized an open-ended campaign. In fact, we can read much of the *Gallic War* as a justification to the Senate for expanding the war farther and farther into Gaul and further and further from the original and restricted senatorial charge. The Senate had instructed him as governor to take measures appropriate to the defense of the province of Gallia Narbonensis. To construe that this order authorized military campaigns all the way to and then beyond the English Channel required creative interpretation. On the other hand, if the *Gallic War* contains very little of the original reports, we can know next to nothing of either the original material or of the thoughts of the Senate upon first learning of the events described. In that case, the manuscript would have always been read just as we read it today, as a story of conquest and adventure, of grand accomplishments by the foremost Roman. In 50 B.C., Caesar was also restless, a man still not satisfied with himself.

In truth, internal evidence regarding the composition of the *Gallic War* seems to point in both directions: sometimes carefully following earlier notes, including even the original justifications, but at other times departing from the original purposes entirely and becoming a much richer and more broadly based story of cultures in conflict.[1] Especially in the first book, Caesar is at pains to justify his expansion of the campaign, and this concern runs throughout the first six books, but is of diminishing significance. Nonetheless, the opening sentence quoted here and, more important for the theme of Rome and the barbarians, Caesar's discussion of barbarians and their affairs with Rome are carefully executed, often with a degree of wisdom and knowledge that reflects years of experience. Careful elucidation, however, does not necessarily mean studied objectivity.

As a book it remains a very good read. The depictions of bravery and self-sacrifice rank among the most moving Latin ever written—straightforward, sparsely constructed, powerful. The great battle at Alesia in book 7 (52 B.C.) ranks as one of the finest battle narratives of all time. It is an exciting story, filled with compassionate accounts of heroism on both sides, splendid tactical detail, and a stunning conclusion in which besiegers and the besieged reverse roles. Vercingetorix, the Celtic commander, is Caesar's equal, a brilliant tactician, personally brave and revered by his men, but his fate is to be led through the streets of Rome as part of the booty displayed in Caesar's triumphal procession, after which he was probably sacrificed to the gods. Knowing the suffering and grand finale, we realize that the unity of Gaul forecast in the opening lines was artificial, used for its rhetorical effect of planting an idea in the reader's mind. Caesar casts it aside almost as soon as it has left his pen. His second sentence notes that the various Celtic peoples had different languages, institutions, and laws. We are left to ponder if there is anything at all that they had in common other than neighborhood.

Although Caesar wants us to begin thinking about a united Gaul at the outset of the narrative, he himself did not face the issue of one Gaul, one nation, until after five books and five years. Caesar's tripartite division of Gaul mirrored his campaigns. The peoples living in the three parts did not come together, even within their respective regions, until after six years of being defeated piecemeal. Then and only then did the peoples of Gaul revolt in unison against their common oppressor, Rome, choosing Vercingetorix to lead them. Julius Caesar also alerts his readers at once that his goal is to put Gaul in order, all of it, no matter how long it might take and thereby permanently secure Rome's northern flank. What he never mentions was his abiding personal need for command, without which he would have had his career suspended by hostile legal action from the opposition. He did not wish to face his political opponents "unarmed," so to speak.

Caesar was in good company in publicizing his success. His erstwhile ally Pompey the Great, with a following of writers and friends was filling the libraries and even the streets with accounts of victories. Costly public inscriptions applauded his triumphs and the enormous material rewards that had accrued thereby to the Roman people.[2] The Roman world had never before witnessed two men of such wealth and power. With Caesar and Pompey we have entered the final decades of the Roman Republic, when competing careers, armies, and conquests doomed it to civil war, and those within striking distance of its armies, to defeat and submission. There was nothing that Caesar would not sacrifice in his vainglorious bid for power and prestige. This striving required honors equal or greater than those of Pompey and everybody else. Complete verisimilitude was never even considered.

Accepting the fact that Caesar had powerful literary and political motives in writing the *Gallic War,* motives that we must keep in mind, he nonetheless and indisputably provides us with our first and most extensive eyewitness account of how Romans, Celts, and Germans interacted on a sustained basis. It is also a peculiarly Roman narrative: the story of a great man and the children of great men leading thousands of extraordinarily disciplined, loyal, and brave Roman citizen soldiers to victory. His personal bravery and that of his troops—and they were *his*—are beyond question. The story revolves around them. The Senate, invisible but never forgotten, was—a crucial fact requiring some effort on our part to keep in view—Caesar's personal focus of attention. Back in Rome he was a patron of the patron class, paving the way for their careers and those of their families, and to his soldiers he was paymaster and the protector of their lives and interests. The *Gallic War* is not history as we know it to be. The author addresses his Roman audience in ways they understood. His success as a rhetorician was so great that Cicero felt the need to challenge his style. Caesar was not even trained as a historian as Romans understood the craft. Sallust was the great historian of his generation, not Caesar. Just as we cannot expect medieval monks to abjure the principles of hagiography and write matter-of-factly about the saints, we cannot hold Caesar accountable for being a rhetorician rather than what we regard as a truth-telling historian. Neither the monk nor Caesar lied in the eyes of their contemporaries; each represents his age and its subtle uses of literature to communicate with a contemporary audience.

At the end of the campaign, Caesar's veterans like those of Pompey depended on their general to force a reluctant Senate to reward their service to the state. Patronage everywhere shaped the world of Julius Caesar. If there was one constant in the *Gallic War* and in Roman society as a whole, from beginning to end, it was patronage. Caesar's barbarians fitted in nicely; they were there to be conquered and then civilized through Roman patronage administered by Caesar, his heirs, and a grateful Senate. Not that much had changed since Marius. There were still no governmental institutions in the Roman Republic as we understand the term except perhaps the Senate, but it was hardly comparable with any institutional government we see around us today. Although we might be tempted to regard the army as an institution because, since Marius, it had become largely professionalized under the command of an ever smaller set of great men and had a tough cadre of veterans moving up established grades of rank, it was conceptually still very personal. The army was not yet a standing force; there was no regular pay, no permanent camps, not even in the most exposed provinces.

In theory the Senate still authorized the consuls to raise and train legions for each specific campaign. Upon their victorious return the

Senate rewarded them only if forced to do so by their former commander. As the campaigns lasted longer and longer and took place ever farther from Italian shores, fewer Romans sought to leave their families and occupations for a bloody vacation fighting some foreign war. Increasingly, soldiers of one campaign signed on for the next. During the first century B.C. the disbandment of a general's legions became a recurring crisis. While in the provinces and even more at the head of their legions, the aristocrat generals had no institutional restraints on their conduct except for another recurring event, the virtually automatic court cases resulting from charges of misconduct lodged in the Senate by their opponents.

The first five books of the *Gallic War* constitute a chronological narrative of events, starting in 58 B.C. and going through 54 B.C., year by year. About a third of book 6 (chapters 11–28 out of 44) is an ethnographic discourse on the attributes of the Celts and Germans. In this section Caesar follows the tradition of Greek and earlier Roman ethnographers and departs from anything likely to have been in the original campaign reports. By breaking away from the standard narrative in the middle of a chapter, in the middle of a campaign, Caesar creates a rhetorical pause, a moment that allows, virtually forces, the reader to reflect upon what has gone before. Book 6 also sets the stage for Caesar's departure for Rome at the end of year, 53 B.C. At that moment all Gaul has apparently been subdued and the Germans driven deep into the impenetrable forests beyond the Rhine. This is, however, a false dawn.

Book 7 tells of the final struggle, at least as far as Caesar himself was concerned. Vercingetorix, raised to virtual kingship over the Gauls, unites a prostrate people. These Gauls are worthy adversaries for Rome, culture against culture, just as Vercingetorix is for Caesar, leader to leader. On reflection the reader now fully comprehends that throughout the *Gallic War* Caesar has defined the Celts as lying culturally and spatially between the Romans and the Germans. He has driven the Germans back into their forests but, in so doing, has created a united Gaul that now must be brought to heel. His ethnography, not just the ethnographic treatise within book 6 but as developed throughout, justifies his policy. Finally there is book 8, unique in its own right as an independent narrative. Composed by Aulus Hirtius, who completed the conquests while Caesar waged politics in Italy (51–50 B.C.), its motives were more complex than just to finish the story, for within months of Hirtius's campaigns, Julius Caesar ordered his tenth legion to cross the Rubicon. At their head he marched into immortality.

Caesar waits only to the third sentence of his first book (58 B.C.) before confirming for his readers the traditional Greco-Roman belief that contact with Mediterranean civilization, even if only through its manufactured products, led to effeminacy and weakness, as contrasted with the warlike valor of those farther removed. Because the Belgae were farthest away and therefore less influenced by Roman wares, they were purest in virtue. For Caesar this distance, combined with the Belgae's close proximity and daily confrontations with the Germans, both offensively and defensively, had made them the bravest of the Gauls. This view of social evolution as a result of cultural contagion reflects traditional Roman ideas, but not necessarily Caesar's own observation. Following this approach, even if we have no reason to question Caesar's facts, it is always prudent to be skeptical of his theories of causation, especially when these explanations are generic. Such surgery on the text is, however, rarely easy to accomplish, because Caesar selected so many of his "facts" precisely to illustrate his causative analysis. His evidence simply cannot always be dissected. The complexity of Caesar the author does not stop here. Not only did he purposefully edit his narrative for its literary and political effect, his education greatly influenced his causative structure, as did his rarely acknowledged position as explorer. Like all explorers, Caesar saw what he had trained his eyes to see, and like so many others in self-imposed exile in "the wilderness," at some point his desire to go home outweighed his need to stay.[3] With these precautions in mind, let us look at Rome and the barbarians through Caesar's eyes.

People were on the move. Whole regions were in turmoil, notably what is now western Switzerland under the Helvetians. Hemmed in by the Jura Mountains to the west and the Rhine River to their north, they were, according to Caesar, spoiling for a fight that would release their burgeoning population from the constraints imposed by geography. They chose to attack the Sequanni to the west rather than the Germans beyond the Rhine because the former's lands were thought better able to support them. Here again Caesar introduces us to a standard Greco-Roman principle of historical causation: population pressure leading to forced migration. This does not necessarily mean that the events recorded did not happen, just that they may not have happened for the reasons given or in the manner described. An attack of Helvetians against the Sequanni seems clear enough, but overpopulation is a too convenient explanation, one often disguising political forces not well understood by our ancient authors. Telling of women and children struggling to preserve kith and kin is the conventional way ancient authors described a migration. Until very recently any ancient reference to families in flight, wagons piled with personal belongings and supplies, was thought to be the surest proof of a migration, but as our knowledge of the topoi of ancient ethnography and history increases, our suspicions mount.

The Helvetians according to Caesar lived in twelve *oppida,* four hundred villages, and numerous structures not associated with either. There is no reason to doubt this depiction, for it corresponds well with what we know from excavations. These numbers regarding settlements play no role in supporting the overpopulation explanation; no figures for population are even presented. Nonetheless, the number and types of living units rather nicely illustrate the nature and scale of Helvetian society, which, although large, is not atypical. All people did not live in defended centers, *oppida,* for many continued to reside in villages scattered about.[4] The rest of the story is not as compelling. The Helvetians are said to have burned everything—every domicile, every outbuilding—so that no one would turn back from the trek and abandon the mission.[5] Although this area was not brought into the empire until the time of Augustus, Romans had long had dealings with the Helvetians and so knew them and their neighbors rather well. The account of their unity of purpose is something that the Roman reader would surely have praised, reminding them perhaps of the celebration of Roman deaths during the Gallic sack of Rome three centuries be-

Caesar in Gaul

fore. Following the Helvetians' example, their allies burned all their communities and packed up their food and belongings.

As the story of forced migration and invasion opens, nearby foreigners are in conflict. A cultural threat to Italy looms. For Roman political authority the core problem was that the Helvetians and their allies sought to cross Roman territory in order to attack the Sequanni, one of whose most prominent families was tied to Rome by formal friendship. So without Roman authorization, the migration began, a classic search for "living space," an ancient theory of historical causation that much later would provide a historical and philosophical justification for imperialism and bloodshed in the nineteenth and twentieth centuries. One important aspect of the confrontation is manifest. The struggle pitted Celt against Celt. Population pressure is not a very plausible explanation, and Caesar himself provides a better one. The scope of the resulting upheaval points to a guiding hand, a strong political force. Caesar notes as a parallel factor to population pressure the desire of Orgetorix, the noblest and richest man among the Helvetians, to assert his kingship over the Helvetians against their customs. Here Caesar seems on to something, at least something that he surely would have understood, and it is on this personal level that Roman interests were more genuinely at stake and where its policies must share the responsibility.

"Friends of the Roman People" were clients of the Senate itself.[6] Neither the Senate in its role as patron nor the individuals or sometimes entire communities in their positions as the clients owed the other specific support. The bond of friendship (*amicitia*) was nonetheless a reciprocal obligation; it was an inside track to diplomatic support, favorable trade, and hospitality for visiting friends. In the case of diplomatic friendship the bond was particularly strong between the client and the senator or his family who sponsored the enabling legislation in the Senate. In the case under discussion, the friend had been Catamantaloedes, king of the Sequanni for many years and father of Casticus, whom the Helvetian leader Orgetorix urged to seize the kingship for himself. Elsewhere Orgetorix urged Dumnorix to take power among the Aedui, and together these three would "conquer all Gaul." Both Orgetorix and Dumnorix had sizable groups of armed retainers squiring them about. They were very wealthy men. Dumnorix had gotten rich farming the taxes of his people, outbidding or intimidating all competition.[7] Among the Celts, clients were expected never to desert their patrons, not even in the direst circumstances. Later Vercingetorix rose to power by first rallying his family and its clients, then by appealing to the common cause of resisting Roman oppression.[8]

The Aedui were the major regional power in central Gaul even before the establishment of Narbo. They were separated from the Sequanni by the Rhone River and were routinely "hailed as brothers and kinsmen" by the Senate. Such regional groupings as the Aedui and Sequanni were called in Latin *civitates.* Each *civitas* had a primary *oppidum,* or fortified settlement, and for the Aedui that was Bibracte (Mont Beuvray), one of the most extensively studied of all

Celtic sites.[9] Not unlike other great *oppida* in size and economic orientation, Bibracte may have contained within its walls five hundred acres of land, much of it set aside for gardens and livestock. The relationship of the Aedui to the Roman Senate is an example of community-to-community friendship. King Catamantaloedes is an example of an individual bound to the Senate as a whole. There are three other cases of such friendship in the *Gallic War,* but the relationship was privileged and, as such, rare. While not exactly a buffer zone of special relationships, the small circle of friends was one of Rome's earliest political responses to its barbarian neighbors. These friends were in a sense ears, allowing the Senate to monitor events far from Roman soil. Maintaining such "buffers" fit in nicely with concepts of patronage. The Senate operated almost as a family council in which all members could speak, although some had greater weight when it came time to make decisions. From their chamber in the Forum, they oversaw a familial empire, which like patronage itself was conceptually expandable almost indefinitely. The identity of one of their friends may surprise us, the leader of the Germans, Ariovistus, whose sponsor had been Caesar himself. Ariovistus, in a familiar gesture, received gifts from the Senate, but, as Caesar well knew, these friendships were often skin deep.[10] Even after the empire became highly institutionalized, barbarian buffer states were orchestrated in a manner reminiscent of the last decades of the republic. In every case, however, Roman influence was very far from control.

From Caesar's perspective in 58 B.C., it seemed that sooner rather than later somebody would unify Gaul and mount a major challenge to Roman control in the south. Most of the principals were officially "allies"—that is, those who held a special relationship to Rome. That they may have learned the game from their chief patron goes unstated in the *Gallic War.* Caesar's Aedui, Sequanni, and Helvetii lived in urban settings. Caesar described their towns (*oppida*) and regional communities (*civitates*) as run by magistrates operating under the rule of law. Within these *oppida* the most distinguished and wealthiest families met in senates, and their actions were empowered by assemblies. The assemblies, at least in cases like the Aedui, who were the pivotal group in Caesar's strategy and so figure prominently in all aspects of the narrative, elected an annual magistrate with regal powers. In the case of a disputed election, the priests decided. One person alone from each family could have the honor of holding office, and only after he had died could another member of the family achieve the distinction. In this way no family was allowed to build extraordinary power through public office.[11] The citizen paid taxes to the state. A few made great profits off the many. All this seems very Roman. These three Celtic peoples had long had contact with Roman traders and were much influenced by Rome. Nonetheless, it is important to keep in mind that Caesar routinely saw features of Celtic life through its parallels or lack thereof to Roman customs. Even as he moved far away from these southern allies, he always believed that there were Roman supporters just waiting for a chance to rally to his banners. In this he was often not far off the mark, but not because of the intrinsic values of Roman culture. Caesar does not seem to understand that he and Rome were being used just as they were using the Celts.

For Caesar, Celtic community assemblies were local equivalents of the Roman assemblies, and local senates were parallel to the Senate in Rome but with correspondingly lesser dignities. These social aggregates, he reports, were of great antiquity among them, sufficiently ancient as to authorize the quasi governments so created to act on behalf of their people. The many parallels to Rome are obvious, inescapable, too close perhaps. The use of Roman terminology was natural. Latin was after all Caesar's language and that of his audience. Teachers have always resorted to literal translation and comparability when explaining foreign concepts, often at the expense of accuracy. Parliament, parlement, and congress tend to become synonymous; the distinction between presidents and prime ministers tends to disappear. Within the *Gallic War,* the Celts of southern Gaul were regarded much as Romans, and excavation has confirmed a high level of Roman influence among them. This is most obvious in the layout of their towns, their displays of wealth in their daily lives, and in their coinage. The suffix "rix," Latin *rex,* in Orgeto*rix* and Dumno*rix,* as elsewhere among the Gauls, reflects the fact that a few families within each community, *civitas,* had a tradition, perhaps only of a generation duration, of primacy. In his dealings with Celts, Caesar works through these families. Orgetorix was both the most noble and the wealthiest of the Helvetii.

As Caesar moved northwards, he left lands comparable with Italy for areas of sparser rural settlement and quite different lifestyles. Perhaps the Roman reader was also meant to lament the political division and factionalization of his own society, *stasis* in Latin, that occurred whenever the peaceful mechanisms for resolving political crisis proved inadequate. The reader would likely note that the present time was such a time. Surely, however, any Roman reading the *Gallic War* would come away thinking that the communities Caesar described were quite comparable with his own. He would understand that the Celts in southern Gaul were a sophisticated people with legitimate political institutions and with concepts of justice and procedure comparable with those of the Romans themselves, if somewhat less sophisticated. In the case of the Helvetii, Orgetorix and his three co-conspirators challenged this legitimacy with their personal power and almost destroyed their people as a result. Unlike Roman leaders, in Caesar's eyes, these had rejected the rule of law and the customs of their ancestors. Caesar could have learned a personal lesson here had he been able to distance himself from his own program, but there is, of course, no such self-analysis. Nonetheless, it is important to note that "barbarians" will always play roles in Roman literature when Roman writers wrestle with the legitimacy of power. Stories recalled from Caesar formed a necessary backdrop in this dialogue even when the empire itself was only a memory. At the opening of the fifth century A.D., when barbarian Roman generals were commonplace and governmental agents were ubiquitous, men were still debating the basis of legitimacy of the rule of few over many. These narratives still framed their arguments in republican ideals of the state as a collection of individuals and families in which ruler and ruled held common rights.

Celtic noble families were allied across territorial boundaries by conspicuous largess and marriage, as the case of the Aeduan Dumnorix and others demonstrate. Dumnorix was well known for his generosity among the Sequanni, and his marriage to Orgetorix's daughter had placed him in good stead there. When the Sequanni and Helvetii agreed to a peaceful passage of Helvetii through Sequanni territory (to enable the Helvetii to attack the Aedui in support of Dumnorix's bid for power), the Sequanni and Helvetii exchanged hostages.[12] Hostage exchange was a standard part of Roman and Celtic societies. Hostages were treated well and returned. The late twentieth-century examples of hostage treatment are irrelevant to the ancient experience; our barbarities were unthinkable. The exchange of hostages overlapped with various other social customs, such as tutelage when the hostages were children and guest friendship when adults. All these practices are rather common elements of patronage systems and were another of the basic similarities between barbarians and Romans that allowed them to understand and influence each other. Hostages were always exchanged among social equals, elites to elites. To become a hostage was to play an honored role. By unilaterally giving hostages the client placed his supporters and often members of his family literally and symbolically in the hands of his conqueror or new patron. Conversely in accepting hostages the receiver acknowledged a reciprocal relationship in which, although noted as the superior, he nonetheless had obligations of prescribed conduct. Such unilateral exchanges underscored Caesar's superiority in Gaul.

Territorial boundaries separating one Celtic *civitas* from another were clear to Caesar, but in reality what appears in the *Gallic War* as fixed geographic zones peopled by distinct peoples and bounded by rivers and mountain ranges was quite fluid. Caesar described this world at a single moment frozen in time, but the forces about to change it were equally clear. The elites in the South were culturally international. Their power defined the areas ruled from the major *oppida,* and their political successes and failures determined the equilibrium within and among communities. In the Celtic *civitates* neighboring the Roman province, the ranking of elite families was quite complex, and Orgetorix and Dumnorix were attempting to reshuffle the cards.[13] Elites such as Orgetorix had about them numerous retainers, armed supporters who could be counted on to come to their aid in war and in the community court of justice. Orgetorix had some 10,000, so at least says Caesar. He could also enroll his numerous clients and debtors, two groups distinct from his *familia* of armed men.[14] Even after Orgetorix committed suicide, the Helvetii continued with their preparations and war, so he alone had not completely defined their policies. Some *civitates* had two or more *oppida* within them; others only one. The Helvetii apparently had twelve. Kinship ties secured the lesser *oppida* within the *civitas* to the dominant families at the main stronghold.[15]

At the point that Caesar entered the fray, the southern Celtic world was in the early stages of a major realignment of political boundaries that Rome saw as a threat to regional stability and so as something it needed to resist. Now with Caesar and for the next five centuries, Rome's constant goal in its dealings with barbarians was stability and control, not instability with its resultant unpredictability. The problem was not in the goal itself, but in the fact that the political structures among the barbarians, especially those without any urban experience, were inherently incapable of accepting external direction. Such direction they did accept was almost entirely personal and familial.

After the conclusion of the Helvetian campaign Caesar recounts obtaining a Helvetian document written in Greek characters and listing those who had joined in the Helvetian exodus: a total of 263,000 Helvetians, 36,000 Tulingi, 14,000 Latobrigi, 23,000 Raurici, and 32,000 Boii; 92,000 were armed men out of a combined 368,000 people, precisely 1 out of 4. "Written in Greek characters" must mean that the Celtic language and numbers were written in Greek letters, much as we use Latin script to write English. Surely the Helvetians did not use the Greek language, and even after the Greek was transliterated Caesar would have had to have a translator, just as he often used an interpreter in his personal dealings with them. Caesar himself used Greek letters and other tricks on occasion to encode his communications with Romans and interpreted the Celtic usage in the same context as hidden messages.[16] The number of initial participants is extraordinarily high, if true, but the convenient ratio of fighting men to the general population arouses suspicion. A guess on somebody's part? The census that he ordered upon their return home produced but 110,000—more likely, but not to be taken as more than a rough estimate. A quarter of a million casualties is beyond belief as are many of Caesar's other estimates of populations.[17] None of these figures can be taken at face value.

The forced return of the Helvetian survivors had another purpose, however. The story of their return to their homelands, appropriately humbled by Roman arms, closes the cover on the theme of a population-induced migration. The staggering losses effectively reduced the population of each participating community to a size supportable by its former boundaries. Orgetorix unexpectedly committed suicide. Thus the underlying causes of the Helvetian war have been addressed in ways that the ancient reader would have readily understood. The return of a supportable population to its homeland, where the returnees had to rebuild their houses and barns, not only reestablishes the antebellum diplomatic system, but precludes anybody then or now from validating the entire migration thesis; Romans, however, were predisposed by their culture and education to accept it.

Roman interests among the barbarians from the era of the late republic on were to define obligations at the least cost to Rome and to maintain them for as long as possible. This meant territorializing these relationships whenever possible, so that a native government could be held accountable for the actions of all those living within a region. The territorial approach was especially needed because there was so much fluidity in social bonds and internal barbarian politics, not because everybody was peripatetic. When and if this policy towards the barbarians failed, another and permanent solution was to extend provincial status to the area. Provincialization required a much greater commitment of resources, usually including colonies of veterans, new road systems, and the building of urban amenities that were the hallmarks of Roman civilization. Thus Roman power gave incentives to those indigenous leaders who could deliver accountability. We should not read this to say that Celtic *oppida* were monarchical or that Roman policy favored monarchies among the barbarians. Just the reverse was true. Rather than favoring monarchy, like the Roman Republic itself, the politics of the *oppida* were in the hands of a few families. Romans led by their greatest families had long ago shed the monarchs in favor of oligarchy. Unlike the Roman oligarchy, whose core elite was restricted to a very few families who prided themselves on their great antiquity and regular office holding, the current Celtic elites were rather new to the game—a bit like Caesar himself. Caesar, of course, was not "a new man," a *homo novus,* but his claim to traditional family greatness was more useful for its propaganda potential than real. Caesar did not have to stretch himself to understand his opponents.

The Aedui were unable to withstand the Helvetian onslaught and appealed to Caesar. Reminding him of their special relationship to the Roman people, the Aeduan spokesman painted a gruesome picture of the cost of defeat: towns looted and their survivors sold into slavery.[18] What then would the Helvetian conquers have done with their new slaves? Sold them? To whom, to Romans? Or kept them to pay tribute from their farms and industries? These are ponderable but unanswerable questions upon which rests much of the current theoretical debate surrounding barbarian societies. To what degree were barbarian communities dependent on slavery for either their own productivity or for the foreign exchange necessary to maintain their domestic life-styles? There is ample evidence for slavery among the Celts and later among the Germans, but all ancient societies used human chattels and so this is hardly surprising.[19] Romans purchased slaves whenever and wherever opportunities arose. Their own wars were the major supplier of new material and recent events in the Near East, where Pompey rolled over his opponents, and Caesar's own successes in Spain had brought large numbers of slaves to market. Roman slavery was never entirely self-sustaining. Field slaves were not allowed conjugal relationships, and the manumission of domestic slaves and their children was decried as too commonplace by imperial lawmakers, although their declamations do not necessarily make it so.

What was the regular source of so many slaves, generation after generation? As aggravating as it is important to admit, we do not know the answer to this and even more fundamental questions. We do not know how many slaves were in the empire at any time, or accurately how common it was to own a slave. We have no demographic statistics other than a few census data counting Roman citizens during the republic, and these may not be what they seem.

We have no idea about whether slave owning fluctuated. Virtually nothing is recorded from the provinces until after the provincials had adopted Roman inscribed funerary monuments. We do know some superficialities: that large numbers of prisoners of war were sold at auction, that the price went down substantially when a large influx came to market after a major victory, that ancient technical manuals took slavery for granted, and so on. Like any commodity, slaves were cheaper nearer their point of production. At the end of the fourth century, the Roman senator Symmachus wrote a friend in Trier asking him to purchase some slaves there because they were cheaper on the Mosel than in Rome. Rather than organize the transport of slaves to market, the army sold them to middlemen.

All sources suggest that slave labor was absolutely essential in dangerous or noxious trades and for large-scale manufacture. Fullers, for example, used slaves to stomp soiled fabric in vats of urine to speed the cleansing action of uric acid. Agriculture used slaves in a variety of tasks ranging from wine production, with slaves used much as did fullers, to gangs working in the fields, to running the olive presses in the workshops of the villas. Shifts of carefully supervised slaves were set to the task of striking and engraving coins in Roman mints. Towns throughout the Mediterranean world were fearfully aware of the fact that slaves were numerous and often went about their master's (and their own) business largely unsupervised. Certain quarters in the larger towns had reputations of being frequented by slaves and lower-class workers. Intermarriage between free, freed, and slave was common enough to require regulation by imperial legislation. We should not be far off if we assumed that nearly all small businessmen owned slaves, but that nearer the bottom of the social ladder slaves and freemen often found themselves working and resting side by side. Gauls owned slaves.[20]

Inscriptions, particularly from the first and second centuries A.D., offer direct testimony that foreigners composed a large percentage of slaves and took their master's name upon gaining their freedom. Roman merchants would doubtless have been happy to purchase any newly enslaved barbarian. Merchants were round about, providing Caesar with information, pursuing their own interests, arranging for Caesar to buy provisions, and occasionally buying war captives after a battle.[21] In a theory reminiscent of what may have been the case with the slave trade along the eighteenth-century African Ivory Coast, Rome's barbarian elites, profiting from the slave trade, transformed their own societies by their efforts to secure supplies of their raw material. Still following this theoretical line of reasoning, once Roman control of Gaul pretty much ended civil war and restricted foreign adventure, Gallic elites had an ever harder time obtaining the human raw material in the traditional manner and had to resort to new techniques of procurement of this and other trade items necessary to maintain their social dominance. If this model is applied to the imperial period, it might explain some of the endemic war apparent among the so-called free Germans—that is those permanently beyond the direct reach of imperial government. Thus the great frequency of interbarbarian warfare might be seen as a result of new men vying for control of the lucrative war-making and slave-producing capacities of their people.[22]

Elegant as such theories are, all that is safe to say is that slaves were a standard and necessary commodity and remained so throughout antiquity regardless of which area one examines. There were many reasons for endemic petty warfare among the barbarians, and, as we explore in subsequent chapters, economic motivation was probably a tertiary cause behind political and social factors. The tendency lately is to reject the most expansive extensions of such theories while acknowledging that slavery was a normal part of trade between Romans and barbarians. This more subdued influence is also in line with current understanding of the effects produced by the slave trade in Sierra Leone, where it is now clear that tribal and intertribal warfare had been endemic long before the European slavers arrived in force. Trade in nonperishable commodities between West African and Europe, as much earlier trade between Romans and barbarians, had also a long history prior to European expansion.

The hard evidence needed to press analogies to the African slave trade in the Roman-barbarian context remains elusive. A few studies have tabulated Roman handcuffs and chains in museum collections and have attempted to assess the trade from that perspective, but this approach too is limited by a general lack of comparative data, making any conclusions only suggestive of the need for further work. From the late republic through Trajan's conquest of the Dacians at the opening of the second century, foreign wars probably accounted for the necessary replacement of slaves. During these two centuries Roman expansion was unrelenting. Augustus may have suggested to his heir Tiberius a curtailment in the extension of imperial dominion, but Augustus's own acquisitions had added more lands to Roman dominion than any predecessor had. Tiberius could follow his advice, because by then he had already established himself as the greatest general of his generation. Julius Caesar, great but not the undisputed greatest general of his age, at least not yet, saw no end of either expansion or cheap slaves.

Caesar accepted the request of the Aedui for aid, defeated the Helvetii, and secured the Aeduan government and attached it to Rome. This course of action was followed throughout his campaigns as each step justified the next, ultimately propelling him across the Rhine and the English Channel. What is clear from the outset is that Romans had already reached a modus operandi in dealing with barbarian communities—be they Celtic, Germanic, Dacian, or other—before Caesar ever entered Gaul. Romans sought out those who could make and keep commitments, the men in charge. If nobody stood to claim leadership, Caesar found someone who could be prompted. Roman power in that community would flow through that man and his family, theirs to use to enhance their position in society as they saw fit.

Romans did not press their own standards of conduct among barbarians, only between barbarians and Romans. This was already true in 121 B.C., when Quintus Fabius Maximus and Gnaeus Domitius Ahenobarbus conquered the territory that would become the province of Gallia Narbonensis. There is nothing peculiarly Roman in seeking to deal with those who can deliver the desired product, be it gold, grain, or military assistance. What is, however, very Roman is that the Roman commanders used their own aristocratic values to select those with whom they did business. Romans manipulated existing aristocratic rivalries to align them with Roman goals.

Perhaps Roman merchants earlier dealt directly with the producers in the various *oppida,* but their transactions could be easily taxed. Men like Dumnorix and Orgetorix were wealthy and famous for their largess. They were neither merchants nor craftsmen. Caesar notes only their wealth and influence and that they were noble. Caesar often notes that certain *civitates* were rich, producing large quantities of grain, but he never depicted them as the centers for metallurgy and manufacturing that they were. Roman aristocrats were not supposed to be interested in industrial capacities.

Caesar did not inquire as to how Celtic aristocrats extracted revenue. The existence of a wealthy class, a complex monetary system linked by weights of metals to the Roman standard, and imported items from the South all point to taxes in some form. Perhaps these taxes were shares of the harvest, a tariff on manufactured goods, fees for access to towns, or social dues at special occasions. Caesar's class prided itself on not doing manual work, and its members rarely spoke in detail about their own finances. Among the Romans only the supremely rich and those unfortunate senators, whose property fell below the standard for qualification, were odd enough to find their fortunes debated in the public arena. Caesar comments upon the techniques that worked to achieve his priorities in Gaul, and they were the same as those he deployed at home. Patronage grew upon itself. The patron's power was enhanced whenever a client's family rose in rank because of his influence and assistance. Similarly it fell when he turned his attention elsewhere.

That Caesar could turn the tables on his Gallic clients with a nod must have given hope to those momentarily out of favor as well as sending a clear message to those in power, reminding them of the cost of betraying his trust. Finding fissures among Celtic elites was easy. Once found, Caesar used his resources to exploit them, but in this he was not alone. Celtic leaders also knew how to play the game. Orgetorix did it, and so too did the German Ariovistus. As a soldier and politician Julius Caesar did not particularly care what went on inside the walls of the *oppida* that did not affect their ability to resist his will. He recorded what concerned him, even when that was not necessarily well understood. He was primarily interested in military necessities: the number of soldiers available to the enemy, keeping roads open, arranging for the transport for his army. He was also keen to know the political processes of his opponents, how they could and could not respond, and so how he should conduct his own agenda. Caesar was much concerned with securing supplies for his men and winter quarters. His men had weapons; they needed food and shelter. He did, however, realize that each *oppidum* contained everything necessary to conduct a war. Whether he needed it or not, his opponents could not be allowed unfettered access to such depots.[23]

His marches and negotiations necessarily revealed much else both by their inclusion and omission. Celtic ships are reported as being particularly good in shallow waters because of their flat keels, but their tall prows and sterns made them also fit for rough seas.[24] He could hardy have missed seeing Celtic religious centers nearby the *oppida*, but because they usually posed no military threat, being undefended despite their terminus walls, he passes them in literary silence. Celts dressed so differently that their soldiers could be distinguished at great distances.[25] That he took mountains of booty would be unknown were it not for Suetonius and others, but this is not because of his sense of modesty or fair play. The great bounty just had no significance to his daily operations or to the geopolitical rationale he wished to impart to his readers. Celtic society, not just the reporting of its final years of freedom, had long been influenced by Roman economic and cultural contacts, but now it was molded by specific choices made by Roman leaders. When Caesar was in Gaul, his priorities eclipsed all others.

Once more embroiled in Gaul, Caesar now carried Rome deep into the midst of a realignment of Gallic society that had been going on for at least half a century. By the middle of the first century the rivalry had been reduced to the confrontation of two groups (*factiones*): the Aedui in the center and the Arverni in the south-central, just north of the Roman province. Each had the support of its clients (*clientes*). The direct antagonists in central Gaul were the Sequanni and the Aedui, but the Sequanni were unequal to the task and long ago had sought the help of the Arverni, living to their southwest. In many respects southern Gaul for Caesar was much the same as it had been for Fabius and Domitius sixty years before.

New families had come to the fore, some allies had shifted allegiance as a result of Roman intervention, but the principals had remained the same. Rome's special relationship with the Aedui meant that for the Arverni and their clients there was little likelihood of finding Roman sympathy. Bracketing border peoples by striking special friendships with those living to their rear—as seen from the Roman perspective—had the effect of isolating Rome's potential enemies, but maintaining working friendships with people at once removed from direct contact was difficult. Seen from the Aedui's point of view, the special relationship with Rome carried with it an invitation to expand their own power, which they did. It also created a need to maintain the status quo among the members of their own alliance and the families that led them, and this was difficult. Increasingly they also had to dance to Caesar's tune, their magistrates working as he wished.[26]

When the Sequanni could no longer withstand the Aedui, they had appealed to the Germans under Ariovistus for aid. The Romans were not to be trusted. Some goodly number of Germans heeded the call, but Caesar's tens of thousands is surely a rhetorical exaggeration. Victory over the Aedui did not take long to accomplish. The victorious Germans, mercenaries of the Sequanni, are reported to have quickly resolved to stay, demanding and receiving a third of the best lands—that is, the arable lands—of their employers. Not long afterwards, they demanded that another third be evacuated. Thus, despite their victory over the Aedui, the Sequanni were crushed by the demands of their allies. They could give up a third but not two-thirds.[27] Roman testamentary law gives us a hint at how agrarian societies managed the division of property. The largest portion of extant Roman law concerns property and its transfer, and within this corpus it is clear that these procedures evolved for centuries. Many early principles survived only as theoretical norms, but they did so for centuries. Any attempt to summarize such a complex mass can merely suggest general features; there were always innumerable special circumstances. In general, property at death fell into thirds with one-third to the children, one-third to the wife, and the remaining third available for any other disposition, almost as if the family reserved a third as a cushion against hard times. Later the Christian Church brought these same norms into the canon law. Ariovistus's demand for a third was painful but not impossible; two-thirds meant starvation. To accept such a major agrarian transformation as giving up a third of the best lands attests to a strong political establishment among the Sequanni.

The Aeduan leader Diviciacus had once stood before the Senate appealing for aid by invoking the special relationship and calling upon his patrons for protection. Now he appealed to Caesar. In casting the appeal as a request made directly to him, Caesar seizes the opportunity to contrast himself and Rome, both good patrons, to Ariovistus, the invited guest who demands the table at which he sits. Through the speech of Diviciacus, Caesar paints Ariovistus in the darkest hues—a dishonorable man, a man who abuses hostages, a barbarian, irascible and cruel, his demands unbearable. Diviciacus goes on to foretell the price Rome will pay if it stands idly by while Ariovistus has his way with the Aedui and the Sequanni—massive flight by the Celts and a tidal wave of immigration by savage Germans even more uncontrollable than the Cimbri and Teutones before them. Soon all Gaul would be in German hands, leaving Rome without the comfortable relationship of the Celtic groups with whom it had fashioned a degree of political stability. Italy itself would sooner or later be at risk again, if not from a Germanic menace, then from Celts fleeing their homelands in droves.[28]

Caesar draws upon the "Cimbri and Teutones" on five occasions in the *Gallic War.* On each occasion he strikes a symbolic resonance with his audience. With just the simple coupling of these two names, he evokes a complex but predictable response, not of fear but of unpreparedness. The listener knows what is implied and what the speaker wants to be done without recourse to elucidation or justification. Immediate action is required. The Roman People are at risk; the ship of state wallows in harms way. In a complex role reversal, Caesar draws a last time upon the image of the Cimbri and Teutones near the end of book 7, almost in conclusion. This time it is a Celtic chief who recalls their invasion. He reminds those being besieged at Alesia by Caesar's legions of how their ancestors had held out against the assaults of the Cimbri, terrible though they were, until they abandoned their attacks and left Gaul—leaving the

Gauls still in possession of their "rights, laws, lands, and freedom." The Romans, he says, are far worse: they conquer and enslave and do not leave. They make a land of free men into a province of slaves; they replace native laws and customs with their own.[29] The speech by a Celt makes "Cimbri and Teutones" polite equivalents of "predators." The message of Rome's greatness is not lost on the reader. Rome is great because, although the equal of the greatest savages in valor and ferocity, it has something no barbarian society could muster: the staying power of civilization. In the *Gallic War* as in subsequent Roman literature, barbarian societies are ephemeral. Individuals and groups come and go. Their contribution was limited to their presence; they forced others to react.[30]

Ariovistus, however, was not just another feckless barbarian; for the Senate and the consul for 59 B.C., Julius Caesar himself had recognized him as *rex atque amicus,* "king and friend."[31] So Caesar as governor of the Roman province, charged with its protection and that of the friends of the Senate, in other words maintaining the fragile balance of forces in the area, was at an impasse. One friend was attacking another friend. This ran diametrically counter to the goals of Roman diplomacy. He requested a face-to-face meeting with Ariovistus to avoid war. How had Rome come to this standoff? Most likely the Senate (through Caesar) trying to bracket the Helvetii, as it had done with the Aedui behind the Arverni, had concluded a "friendship" with Ariovistus. This would place Ariovistus and his Suebi somewhere just north of the Rhine, across the river from the Helvetii in what today would be southern Bavaria, in the area that had about a half century before Caesar's invasion of Gaul ceased to be organized around *oppida.* Another fact pointing to a Bavarian homeland for Ariovistus is that one of his two wives was Norican, the people then living in southern Bavaria and upper Austria and who will become the native population of the Roman province named after them under Augustus.[32]

Caesar demanded that Ariovistus halt all further German migration, although those already present in Gaul could remain. He also insisted on the return of Aeduan hostages taken by his German followers and his Sequanni clients. For his acceptance of these terms, the Senate would again recognize him as "friend" of the Roman people and bestow upon him the favors and kindness due a friend. If he chose to reject Caesar's terms, war would follow. Ariovistus refused and gave what is for Caesar an unusually candid explanation. Of course, speeches like numbers of participants were fictional parts of the genre, tools of the rhetorician's trade, so Ariovistus does not really speak to us but rather Caesar does through another voice. Caesar's Ariovistus declares that the Aedui had made war and lost, thereby rendering their status as friends of Rome irrelevant. They now paid tribute to Ariovistus, not Caesar, and to guarantee that payment he announced that he would keep their hostages. He saw no reason that the exercise of Roman rights should have priority over his ability to further his own. His view was that he had left home and family in response to pleas from the Gauls and had arrived before the Romans. Gaul was his territory, his province, not Rome's. Friendship with the Roman people should be an honor, an elevation, not a burden. Somebody was going to conquer Gaul, either Caesar or he himself, and the victor would dictate the terms to the conquered. Defiance.

Caesar countered the "first come, first to conquer" claim by asserting that the Senate had long ago, that is ca. 121 B.C., decided that Gaul would remain free, thereby serving as a buffer to the Roman province to the south. So with Ariovistus, Caesar claimed that Roman alone had long ago determined Gaul's unique status: Caesar, the just statesman, or Ariovistus, the barbarian conqueror, on the one hand; on the other, Germanic society, "uncivilized" in the literal sense of people without cities, or Roman civilization, based on the rule of law, the capstone of civility.[33] In between and at stake was the world of the Celts.[34] In this dialogue Caesar also makes clear to his primary readership, his senatorial colleagues, that he understood their policy and was trying to carry it out even under these very difficult circumstances. The Gallic buffer between Rome and barbarism was destined to disappear. The level of freedom accorded to the friends in the first actions of the Senate had been too great. Caesar would improve upon it by establishing tighter controls, less freedom in exchange for greater stability. What Caesar and his colleagues in the Senate meant by "control," however, was the extension of patronage networks, certainly not bureaucratic systems or political accountability. Romans governed newly conquered provinces as they did Italy and Rome itself.

Caesar like all other provincial governors during the republic had no staff. Like many governors of important provinces, Caesar had a *quaestor*—the lowest-level state officer—attached to him by the Senate. Marcus Licinius Crassus, son of Caesar's consular colleague and sometimes ally by the same name, was Caesar's *quaestor* in 54. He found himself in overall command of logistics and as general of one legion while on campaign. In addition to their elected assistant, the *quaestor,* governors were allowed to nominate a small number of legates (*legati*) from among the younger members of the senatorial class. Caesar had ten, a relatively large number because of the war. In peaceful provinces legates assisted with the legal and administrative tasks, but in Gaul Caesar's legates were his direct subordinates in command, often commanding an entire legion. So Publicus Licinius Crassus, the younger brother of the *quaestor,* was at first the principal cavalry officer and then a legate. He served with great distinction in a number of difficult assignments, often with little or no supervision from his commander-in-chief. With such minuscule staffs Roman governors waged war or governed their provinces. By modern analogy, they "supervised" rather than governed, because of their dependence on local elites to do most of the "governing." Not until the second quarter of the second century A.D., did governors have professional staffs in residence in most provinces.

At the conclusion of the Helvetian campaign Caesar gave his consent to a meeting of *totius Galliae,* literally of "all the Gauls." This first such occasion seems to have included only those Gauls involved in the most recent struggle and who were still in camp at its conclusion. Gallic councils subsequently were summoned by Caesar from time to time and served him as a means to test the loyalty of his clients and integrate them into his plans. The attendees were the leaders (*principes*) of each community, or at least those leaders loyal to Caesar. Such men and their families would be the first to profit from Roman peace. Henceforth, their positions within Gaul were secured and enhanced by their connections with Rome, and such visible honor carried with it many local rewards. It is important to reiterate that Rome and the barbarians were honor-based societies. Individual Romans and barbarians were supposed to act in accordance with accepted norms of behavior, and for the elites the highest honors were those which demonstrated the public's faith in the individual and his family to protect and further society's interests. Those with honor had the respect of their peers and inferiors; they were the patrons. Political power among the Celts had never been of long duration, perhaps because of societal prohibitions such as the "one magistrate per family" rule among the Aedui, perhaps because of internal competition among those like Orgetorix, the Helvetian, who believed that their wealth entitled them to more.

For whatever reason, the *Gallic War* often mentions more than one notable family living in a specific *oppidum*. This plurality of honor holders allowed Caesar to support rivals to power, as his needs demanded, without ever running out of candidates of sufficient quality to assume successfully the leadership of their communities. Roman administration offered these families numerous outlets for their energies and talents. No longer would their quests for honor need to be focused on the small world of their own local community. Their connections to other families, trade links (often a seamless extension of gift-giving customs and often far distant in range), and personal experience would all be essential to the success of Roman government in Gaul, especially in its first centuries. Gallic councils were an early phase in the political and social evolution of Gallo-Roman society. Through them Caesar set about knitting together a provincial-wide network of native integration and cooperation among the new elites and with their governor.

Once begun, the idea of assembling the leadership of Gaul or relevant portions of it found other proponents, in particular Vercingetorix, who summoned his allies to a general council at Bibracte during his great war against Caesar.[35] Thus Caesar expounded and promoted a sense of Gaul as a community of elites, and it is unlikely that such a group had previously existed. His desire for accountability superseded their parochialisms. Not even the Aedui were unqualified in their enthusiasm for greater Roman presence, which they and others saw, at least according to Caesar, as a threat to their liberty.[36] Previously Celtic alliances, strengthened through marriage and gift exchange, had at best linked a few great families into regional confederacies and had made only limited progress in linking regional into supraregional alliances. With the raising of rebellion under Vercingetorix in 52 B.C., Roman encouragement of Gallic unity helped create a unified enemy. This would not be the last time that, by seeking clear avenues of control over barbarian societies, Roman policy led to the establishment of higher levels of political and military cooperation among them. Paradoxically Rome thereby receded from its goal of keeping barbarians regionally divided while individually accountable.

Caesar concluded the Helvetian campaigns by accepting the surrender of the defeated. The Latin here is significant in that it would recur over and over again in connection with the barbarians: *traditis in deditionem accepit,* he accepted them into the power of Rome. Within the empire those who had surrendered, had "given up," were henceforth restricted legally, almost as if they were placed in tutelage to the Roman state. They were free but not allowed to dispose of property by testament or become citizens. These restrictions were of no importance to the surrendering Helvetians, but the language used to describe their status opens another window onto the Roman attitude towards barbarians. The category was also used for manumitted slaves in republican times, freedmen, who although free usually remained dependent upon the estate of their former masters. Barbarians were equal to Romans only so long as they were free. In their freedom they lived as unfettered children with many of the same virtues and vices. Once defeated they had to be assigned a Roman legal category and schooled in the ways of Rome. Inevitably, given the difficulty Romans had formulating personal change and maturation, this status stayed with them.

The concept of *deditii* (literally those who had "surrendered") remained a commonplace way to describe the act by which barbarians were allowed to settle inside the empire for the remainder of Roman history. The explicit psychological and cultural inferiority that the term itself graphically conveys remained and was rendered iconographically by depictions of kneeling or prostrate barbarians at the foot of a Roman general or trophy. Among the most beautiful examples of the theme is a silver denarius struck for Julius Cae-

Denarius, silver, struck in Gaul by Julius Caesar, ca. 48–47 B.C. Obverse: head of Venus, patron to the Julian family. Reverse: A bound Gaul with characteristic shield and trumpet beneath a trophy. Courtesy of the Staatliche Münzsammlung München.

sar himself, significantly also the earliest example of a coin struck with the name of the consul then in office. Venus, the patron deity of the Julian family, graces the obverse. On the reverse, a bound Gallic warrior is seated before a stylized Roman trophy composed of captured Gallic arms (note the characteristic shield and war trumpet), his hair standing almost straight out in a wild and typically "barbarian" fashion. The captive's head is held between the letters CAE and SAR, leaving no doubt as to who is responsible for his submission to Roman authority.[37] Triumphal arches, columns and column bases, medallions, and countless coin issues, all depicting barbarians in acts of submission, attest to one of the longest-lasting artistic conventions in Roman art.

In the case of the Helvetians, Caesar commanded the defeated forces to go home, replant their fields, and rebuild the houses and farm buildings, which they had put to the torch just months ago. He also allowed the Aedui to settle some Boii, notable among the Celts for their prowess, along their borders, providing them with farmland sufficient for their needs and shortly also legal rights as if they were Aedui.[38] Mentioning the Boii would have dramatically enhanced the passage's rhetorical effect by directly connecting his pacification of the Helvetians to Marius's and, before him, Scipio's victories. His remedy of finding the Boii a permanent legal status among the Aedui is another instance of Romans dealing with barbarians by an extension of Roman customs. Romans included foreigners by defining a place for them in Roman law; so too did the Aedui, at least here in Caesar's account.

The war cost Ariovistus both wives, one daughter dead, and the other captured. Caesar notes with pride that he was able to rescue Gaius Valerius Procillus, a leading Roman from the province, from captivity. Caesar adds that Procillus had personally witnessed German women deciding whether he should be burned alive by casting lots day after day. Clearly his luck held. Equally Caesar had perfectly balanced the need for caution—detouring around areas where ambush was likely—and the need for haste to free his friend and the other captives held by the *barbarians.* This incident is but one of many unverifiable observations of Celtic and Germanic societies in the *Gallic War,* including in both the so-called historical narrative and the ethnographic treatise of book 6. Another example—this one reportedly took place in front of Caesar himself—involves the German forces opposing him deployed for battle "by nation," *generatimque constituerunt,* with each group separated slightly from the next and wagons drawn up on the wings, where sat their women. The spacing vanished at the onset of battle.

On the field before the battle opened Caesar made out Harudes, Marcomanni, Triboces, Vangiones, Nemetes, Sedusii, and Suebi.[39] How he knew that these were among the units gathered together under Ariovistus he does not say, but because the deployments were so important to him as commander, we probably should give him greater credence here. Could he, however, have truly heard women beseeching their men "not to allow us to become Roman slaves" over the rising shouts of battle? Could he have understood them had they yelled to him at arm's length? What should we make of such details, particularly when they do not relate to military necessity? Is Caesar just embellishing an already good story with colorful anecdotes and rhetorical flourishes? Does it matter that preexisting Greek ethnographers and historians had used much the same material for generations before Caesar? That some unknowable part of his literary education had included a careful reading of the Stoic philosopher and ethnographer Posidonius on Celts and other barbarians?

Caesar's fellow senators brought much sophistication to their reading. They too had read or been influenced by Greek ethnographers and the travel reports of legendary explorers as far back at least as Herodotus, but especially those spinning out from the world of Alexander the Great and the Hellenistic monarchies. The general characteristics of barbarian societies were commonplace in these stories, as routine as characters in modern science fiction novels and inspired by many of the same needs. Today's students of antiquity, particularly the late empire, are initially rather shocked that respected authors so routinely took entire passages from their sources. We call it plagiarism. Yet, among ancient authors, reciting verbatim from an older source gave your own work added respectability. We do not possess the earlier literary sources available to Caesar on Celts and Germans—notably not his near contemporary Posidonius (ca. 135–51 B.C.)—in sufficient detail to render a verdict as too how much and from whom Caesar borrowed. Nonetheless we cannot help but be very suspicious.

Posidonius was one of the most famous Stoic philosophers of his age and, like Cicero, a moralist who believed that history was shaped by moral action, the result of individual and collective character.[40] In his *History* Posidonius apparently saw a need to write chapters on Celtic and then Germanic customs in order to provide an ethnographic background for Fabius Maximus's campaigns around Marseilles and the campaigns to save Italy conducted by Marius, to whom Posidonius served as ambassador from Apamea. Bits and pieces of these ethnographic accounts appeared elsewhere in his corpus as well as in his historical work.[41] For him events illustrated the moral qualities of the actors. The footprints of Posidonius and the moralist tradition are sufficiently visible in the *Gallic War* as to reach a conclusion that may surprise some. Romans were eager to learn more about their new adversaries, whom they could no longer relegate to the margins of myth, but they sought this knowledge within their own intellectual context.

Caesar need not have been concerned to establish the accuracy of most of the details he included about Celts, Germans, or other barbarians in his commentaries. Because Posidonius and his intellectual forebears had already established barbarian moral qualities, the point was to reveal how these characteristics manifested themselves and so shaped Gaul. Against them he pitted those of exemplary Romans and his own. Perhaps the various groups of barbarians and their leaders did have these stereotypical attributes, perhaps not. The testimony of Caesar just does not prove the affirmative. The supposed eyewitnesses' testimonies certainly lend a personal touch and add human interest, but they also support the author's verisimilitude among his contemporaries by providing them with validation of the received literary tradition. This is what his readers expected, and this is what they found. When he speaks as an eyewitness himself, Caesar intentionally lifts elements, which his primary readers and we understand as mere tropes, onto a higher level. The effect is to confirm further our image of him as a truthful reporter. He becomes believable by personally meeting our expectations. His story of "Procillus and the lots" was just such a tale, and so too was the one in which he himself reports having seen German women urging on their men with reminders of the bondage that would surely follow upon their defeat. His readers, on finding these vignettes, doubtless smiled an approving literary grin, marveled at his rhetorical skill, and read on, more intent than ever upon the real story: the shifts in Roman external policies set in course while Caesar was in Gaul and the transformation within Caesar himself from difficult colleague into a Titan of his age.

What if Caesar had indeed seen hundreds of German women sitting on their wagons, surrounded by crying fear-struck children, but instead of shouting at their menfolk, these women were reading a papyrus roll? Would he have reported it? Surely not. Hundreds of quietly reading barbarian women would have seriously disrupted the narrative. Such a totally unexpected element would have demanded a substantial explanation and, more important, would have seriously detracted from the basic subtext of the entire work, the cultural imperative of the war. He was a stylist giving his readers what they wanted, not a field anthropologist writing for *National Geographic Magazine*. Each book of the *Gallic War* has a formulaic framework. New threats need immediate attention before they grow into catastrophes, and the preparations required to meet them demand the support of reluctant allies. There is a breakdown of diplomacy; next, battle commences with victory because of Roman bravery; then the legions must be assigned to winter quarters; finally events await the next year while Caesar tends to other business. This cadence cloaks his political message. All his commentaries, not just those concerning Gaul, reveal Caesar extending and perfecting Roman policies and Roman dominance. Scenes such as that of a barbarian female fearing enslavement, or of sparing the conquered, or of a bound captive kneeling before a Roman trophy on a coin reverse all reveal Caesar being attentive to Roman interests. In such depictions he manifests the traditional aristocratic virtues. These attributes—clemency, military prowess, piety—reveal the same stern but fair image that in theory characterized the republican patron class and that Augustus would soon transpose into the public arena.

Caesar had no desire for Romans to live with and learn from barbarians. On the contrary, he sought to buffer Romans geographically and culturally from them. Romans could learn more and better things from fictional barbarians with their simple virtues than from flesh-and-blood barbarians. The details about barbarians that Caesar provides his readers were created, as were the speeches and the apparently statistical material, to support his overall theme of a clash of cultures, which if left unchecked would bring the Romans into direct contact with the most primitive forces in Europe. He waged his Gallic war to defeat and deflect that catastrophe before it threatened Romans at home. Romans thought that history taught clear lessons, among them that, when barbarians were close by, Rome suffered invasion, devastation, and civil unrest. Romans did not fear defeat—they always came out on top in the end—but rather they dreaded the collapse of ordered life that so often accompanied foreign invasion.

In telling of disaster averted, Caesar also articulated a general Roman sense of social evolution. Accordingly societies developed by building on households and kindreds, which were regarded as the most elemental units of society. The next level was reached by uniting kindreds into tribes, then tribes into a people, and finally a people into a state with the inhabitants living under public officials, rather than monarchs, and ruled by law. Rome stood at the apex of state development. Barbarians with their peculiar values could alter Roman life, dragging it down from its lofty level of civility. Caesar's depiction of Ariovistus proclaims that a noble savage could rise up and destroy civilization. Like Vercingetorix in book 7, Ariovistus is especially dangerous to Rome, because he combined the simple virtues of the warrior with a personal knowledge of how Roman society worked.

Despite rejecting many of the colorful anecdotes in the *Gallic War* as examples of literary technique and evolutionary theory, there is still much to learn from Caesar about the barbarians and about Romans. And this is true, in spite of the fact that his comments about Roman politics and warfare, those about individual heroism and the legions, even his tightly focused style, all served to praise himself and, by so doing, denigrate his opponents. Always there is a pattern of presentation overlaid with details, many of which cannot be verified. Stories of crusty centurions emboldening their men to face the charge might just as well be literary fabrications. Like the women casting lots, they etch a visual image in our minds. The valor of the Roman soldier on campaign, together with the tidbits about barbarians, justifies Caesar's war. Rather than query his narrative about specific features of Celt or German, however, it is better to concentrate on his depictions of the general features of barbarian societies, for which we might find either confirmation or at least the essential physical context from the archaeological record. Many subjective features of Caesar's account nicely illustrate how Romans regarded and dealt with barbarians. Examples include the extension and manipulation of patronage networks, the relative civility and political sophistication of life in Celtic *oppida* in southern Gaul, the contemporary state of aristocratic rivalries, and the speed and direction that Roman influence penetrated the barbarian world. Reporting aspects of barbarian societies such as these did not color the narrative so much as inform it. They related directly to the ways in which Caesar conducted his campaigns.

Caesar also allows us to understand better some of the ethnographic terminology in our sources. For him the Germans were a people, as were the Gauls or, using our nomenclature, the Celts.

They were primarily organized "by nation," whereas the Celtic society was centered on *oppida* and *civitas,* town and community. Competing confederacies dominated the South, but even in Brittany, Celts had *oppida,* the Sotiates there but one.[42] Or to put it in comparative terms, the Germans were more primitive, in the sense of being less socially differentiated and with less nucleated settlements, than the Celts, who were in turn more primitive than the Romans.

Rome did not seek acculturation with the barbarians in any context. Roman jurisprudence maintained that no foreign people was worthy of Roman rights. They provided only a meager legal framework to carry on normal relations, the *ius gentium,* which was based on the absolute separation of Romans and barbarians. The *ius gentium* allowed foreigners to conduct transactions and fix contracts while in Roman territory. Otherwise it did not play any noticeable role along the frontiers. Roman jurists usually discussed the *ius gentium* in the context of natural law, the *ius naturale,* and both remained primarily in the realm of theory.[43] There would be no bilateral exchange as far as Roman law was concerned. Romans, like Caesar, thought that, although some barbarian virtues were exemplary in their simplicity, the superb qualities manifested by individual barbarians were, more than not, offset by the refinements of Roman life. Single Roman soldiers might be only the equals of barbarians, but when fighting as a legion, barbarians could never match their power. Organization was Rome's greatest virtue. Caesar used the commentaries on his campaigns to illustrate the value of discipline and sacrifice of the individual for the group in a way quite characteristic of the Roman mentality. The theme runs through virtually all Roman literature of the era: Cicero, Sallust, Livy, Vergil, and a host of others. Romans sought to harness barbarism for the good of civilization, of humanity. Thus Caesar, like so many of his peers, was a moralist, and his wars against the barbarians afforded him an opportunity to rekindle, and possibly even reshape, Roman pride and sense of purpose.

Rumors of a conspiracy among the Belgae to launch a preemptive attack on the Roman legions called Caesar north. As his army neared the lowermost Rhine, urban institutions familiar in the

South waned and faded into a world of village and hamlet. Families along the Rhine shared their world with those on the other side, thereby complicating Caesar's use of the river as a boundary between Germans and Celts that he had posited during his previous campaigning season. Caesar does not abandon the Rhine as a cultural boundary in book 2, but his comments make the border appear porous. Just as "all Gaul" had no unity, so neither did Belgica. The Remi, for example, immediately sent two of their leading citizens to pledge their loyalty to Caesar. All the other Belgae, they said, were conspiring against him. These same ambassadors revealed to Caesar the tradition that the ancestors of most Belgic peoples had once been Germans, having crossed the Rhine some generations ago because of the fertile soils to be found there. Their remembrance had it that, once across, they had easily driven out the Gauls, that is the Celts, living there. These new masters of the northern Gaul were so fearsome that even the "Cimbri and Teutones" had not ventured to attack them.[44] Thus from the outset Caesar establishes that many of the Belgae were actually Germans in Gaul, or rather Celto-Germanic, but at this point he does not say whether he thinks this still had significance.

The Suessiones, the Remi's neighbors, had recently been under the power of Diviciacus, a man bearing the same name as the leading man of the Aedui. The Remi claimed that the dominion of King Diviciacus extended over "all of Gaul" and Britain. Twelve *oppida* made up the core of the Suessiones. Like a great many Celtic *civitates,* that of the Suessiones gave its name to a modern city by virtue of its Latinized form as a provincial capital, in this case the city of Soissons, and elsewhere the Remi, modern Reims, the Treveri, modern Trier (Trèves), the Aedui, modern Autun, and so on. The Roman towns by these names were in the vicinity but not necessarily on the same sites, primarily because of the fact that Celtic defensive needs were superseded by Roman economic requirements for trade and manufacture. As far as the Remi were concerned the Nervii, who lived farthest away from them, were the fiercest of the Belgae. Like all Gauls, their battle cry was frightening to hear. Looking at them through Roman eyes, the Nervii were farther from the Remi, who were beyond the Celts, who were beyond the province and Roman law and government. In all, some dozen Belgic tribes had risen against Rome, but not the Remi and not the Treveri. The latter had allied themselves with Rome the previous year during Caesar's war against Ariovistus and the Suebi, many thousands of whom, the Treveri had claimed, were now trying to cross the Rhine into their lands.[45] As before Caesar had to defend his allies, Rome's new clients. The rest of the Belgae lost no time in attacking Bibrax, a major *oppidum* of the Remi and one whose location has yet to be securely established.

The social and political life of the Remi was similar to that of the Aedui and others to the south: *oppida,* villages and hamlets organized into *civitates* (communities) with annual officeholders selected from among members of the most noble and esteemed families. Chief officers[46] were responsible to the people, who held jurisdiction over them.[47] The elites could turn out a great many friends and relatives to support their leading members. They also shared their leader's fate, if he were forced into exile. Without them a leader was severely crippled among his people.[48] When Caesar and the Romans stepped into this world, they found that in each community some of the leading families were always in exile awaiting their turn to take power. Such exiled groups provided a ready-made rallying point for the opposition within the community. They challenged or rejected Caesar's initiatives accordingly. Each community had boundaries recognized by the other *civitates,* but these former territorial divisions were being challenged across much of Gaul.

Caesar continued the Roman policy of influencing the internal balance in Celtic society. Once the *civitates* were conquered he was able to force the elevation of his major local supporters. Sometimes Caesar's candidates received a very hostile reception. Those with Roman backing proved to be much more difficult for their traditional opponents to oust.[49] In general the relatively amorphous paternalism with which Caesar was quite familiar prevailed among the Belgae. Like the Celts to the south, they were familiar with elementary siege tactics, including the use of a *testudo* or tortoise shell of shields held edge to edge on all sides and over the heads as a defense against things shot or hurled down from the walls. Caesar attributed their knowledge of siege tactics to their observation of Romans and to captured Roman soldiers rather than giving them any credit for independent invention.[50] The war with the Belgae hinged on supplies. When those of the Belgae ran low and Caesar's did not, the former's alliance dissolved, leaving each member group to face the Romans alone, a routine repeated many times in the *Gallic War.* Supplying his force in Gaul led Caesar to secure the Great St. Bernard pass through the Alps, thereby providing traders with greater security and fewer tolls.[51] Political and military organization and the Roman's tenacity in war wore down the barbarians and splintered their efforts at creating a unified front. Once again the women and children demand our pity. The leaders of the conspiracy are reported to have fled to Britain. Caesar took a reported six hundred hostages.[52] With the main war over and the campaigning season still young, Caesar, the explorer, took the opportunity to push his army into the lands of the Nervii near the mouth of the Rhine. As he moved up to the Rhine, he began to see firsthand the limits of *oppida* civilization and the melting away of cultural differences.

The Nervii, the most distant of the Gallic peoples from the Roman province, offered Caesar a truly determined foe. Standing on the bodies of their fallen, they matched the Romans blow for blow. Only the arrival of the Tenth Legion, Caesar's most trusted, saved the day and turned fate against the Nervii. None but pitiful women, children, and old Nervian men remained alive to sue for peace. Their stalwart defense won for the sorry remnant the right to keep their lands and *oppida* under Roman protection. Just as victory was being celebrated, allies of the Nervii arrived, the Aduatuci. The newly arrived warriors mocked the short legionaries, but the runty Romans deployed siegecraft that seemed to the Gauls to have been god-sent.[53] The assault teams took the town by storm. Battering rams crushed the gates. Caesar initially offered the Aduatuci security under Roman protection if they lay down their arms in surrender, but they attacked him from their stronghold again during the night. His clemency rejected, Caesar sold the entire population into slavery.[54] What can we see in this narrative?

Unfortunately once again the most interesting vignettes are unverifiable and clearly relate to the moral structure of his work. In Caesar's telling, the farther from civilization one gets the more striking are the differences between the populations living there and the Romans. This is made clear in the story of the diminutive Romans employing advanced technology to overcome their inferior stature. The notice of women and helpless noncombatants taking the lead after their protectors have fallen in battle illustrates another standard aspect of "barbarians," strong, capable women, of the highest moral virtue. That the Belgae shared siege techniques with the Celts to the south and the Romans resulted from the fact that there were *oppida* in their *civitates,* which demanded knowledge of how to besiege them. But also by his treatment of the Belgae, Caesar makes it clear that the presence of *oppida*—not ethnicity, as we would understand the term—is for him a defining characteristic of Celtic civilization. Belgae and Germans living here shared many common ancestors, and Caesar knows this, despite the story of the Germans taking over the lands of the Celts in Gaul and driving them out. The Nervii were doubly warlike because of the great distance separating them from Mediterranean civilization and because of their proximity to the Germanic menace. They were so tough that they had successfully harassed the rear guard of that icon of savagery, the "Cimbri and Teutones," and lived now with their descendants, side by side. The presence of merchants eager to purchase war prizes, particularly slaves, is amply demonstrated after Caesar's second defeat of the Nervii. The discussion of the Belgae is more interesting conceptually, less clear-cut, less political than that of the southern Gauls. Here Caesar is forced to look beyond simple ethnographic lore. Fighting in the coastal area near Boulogne, the enemy fades into the countryside, a world of farmsteads and villages, with no *oppida* into which to retreat.[55]

In 55 B.C. Caesar continued his northern campaign, symbolically bridging the Rhine to carry the conflict into the lands of the Suebi. He does not seem to have learned much about these barbarians during his brief foray, but his description instead extrapolates standard ethnographic tradition to fit the type of inhabitant his reader might have anticipated encountering in these remote and exotic places. The Suebi are reported to have no private land and to be seminomadic, never occupying the same place longer than a year. Their diet was composed almost exclusively of milk products and cattle. From childhood, Caesar continues, boys grow into men, men of immense stature, unschooled, wild. Suebi wore little other than skins even in the coldest climes. They rode to battle but dismounted to fight. Foreign merchants were restricted to purchasing their war booty. Imports were rare, of wine never because it was believed to strip men of their manliness. These savages forced other, weaker Germans to cross the Rhine into Gaul. These refugees included the Usipetes, recently subdued by Caesar and now under his protection.[56] Only the Germans living along the Rhine, such as the Ubii, lived in fortified centers, not the Suebi.[57]

The Suebi cared next to nothing about the outside world, except to raid and plunder it. Their isolation was complete even from other Germanic groups, such as the Cherusci, who maintained an unoccupied buffer between themselves and the Suebi.[58] Remote, ferocious in battle, every man a warrior, every woman pure. No wonder that these images were championed by those seeking a German past since at least the era of the Protestant Reformation, but could they have been true? Only in a world of myth. People living in this area were certainly not seminomadic, but to quibble over details is to miss the point of the narrative. The Suebi were for Caesar the purest antithesis of the Romans, and therefore played a leading role in his drama of clashing cultures. They are cast as *the* true barbarians. In reality the Suebi as seen in the *Gallic War* were not simple rustics. They were usually mercenaries and as such, dependable servants of their Celtic or Roman masters. By 52 B.C. Caesar kept a unit of four hundred German cavalry with him. The Suebi had no common cause.[59]

In contrast, the Gauls were "news hounds," cornering any passing merchant and pumping him for information. Throughout his Gallic war merchants provided Caesar and sometimes his enemies with valuable information. After Caesar had subdued an area, Roman merchants established permanent residence among the Gauls. This trade must have been very lucrative because one of those Romans then in residence was of equestrian rank.[60] At the juncture of the Meuse and Waal Rivers lay an island inhabited by the Batavians. The various inhabitants of the islands at the estuary of the Rhine were particularly barbaric (*barbarisque*), some thought to live on fish and bird eggs.[61] Obviously few of these stories can be confirmed, and many are such childish fictions as to be laughable, at least from our perspective. Tangible imports or their lack, villages and farmsteads, types of fortifications, and some aspects of diet have left traces in the archaeological record. On the other hand, cold climates, nothing but skins for clothing, complete freedom from discipline, and peculiar diets without grains are all standard elements of the ancient ethnographer's inventory of traits.

Caesar declares that a migration of Suebi had begun, forcing others to abandon their homes and scurry westwards. Only one tribe, the Ubii, asks Caesar for friendship and provides him support.[62] All others, thousands upon thousands are caught up in the early stages of invasion. Taking the offensive in such a way that it leaves an indelible impression is the best deployment of Roman power. The more quickly it moves, the more impressive the victories that follow. When the Ubii offer boats, they are rejected as unworthy of a conquering army. Caesar wanted to make a more lasting impression than slipping across the Rhine in borrowed boats would leave, but he had no intention of staying or of conducting a major campaign. So to demonstrate Roman power and cultural superiority, Caesar orders a bridge built and then launches a scorched-earth attack cross the Rhine before withdrawing. No lives are lost, but villages and anything else man-made is put to the torch. The Suebi and their allies flee into the immensity of the forest, hiding their valuables and disappearing. In his description of the Suebi we are told that all able-bodied men responded to the call to arms, settlements were abandoned, valuables hidden away.[63]

Only in theory did all Romans flock to the standards in Caesar's day. His army was professional in all but name. At the core of Caesar's legions was a cadre of battle-hardened centurions, who had risen through the ranks in the course of years of campaigning.[64] His readers could not have overlooked the literary contrast between culturally and politically inferior barbarians and Roman strength.

Caesar offered total war as the ancients understood it, but nothing much really came from this. It is intended as another lesson from ethnography for his readers, as a reaffirmation of Roman superiority over the barbarians, and not coincidentally as a reminder to the Senate of his personal prowess. Caesar "showed the flag" and returned to Gaul. Before the year was out he was on the coast of Britain.

While not officially recognizing that the Rhine marked the limit of the Roman power, Caesar plants the idea through a speech delivered by the Suebi, in which the Germans accord Rome the west bank but lay claim to all lands to the east of it as their own.[65] Were it not for the fact that soon thereafter Caesar withdrew from beyond the Rhine and invaded Britain, we might say that he had found in the limits of Gaul the limits of empire. Well, not really. His two forays to Britain proved much more difficult than he anticipated, a very near thing indeed. Although he claimed it as conquered, Britain remained beyond Roman control for almost a century. Most important for us, we see over and over that Julius Caesar did not think in terms of a limit to empire. For him there could be no geographic limit to the networks of patronage defining and channeling Roman power. Writing years after the events, he takes the opportunity to prepare the reader for a closure of his Gallic war. To do this he will return in book 7 to the theme of "all Gaul" and declare a complete victory over it, but he had not yet humbled all "the Gauls," for some had fled to safety in Britain.

The two British campaigns (55–54 B.C.) were sideshows to his main efforts and proved costly in time and resources. Caesar's depiction of the Celts of Britain makes it clear that they share many but not all the characteristics of the Belgae. Most significant perhaps, in Britain as in Gaul elite families had established themselves at the head of the various *civitates*. The elites fought on foot, but they arrived in battle on chariots—a peculiarly British fashion it seems. As in the case of Gaul, families were more important than were their individual members. Caesar's invasions again united a formerly disunited society under a single commander, in this case Cassivellaunus.[66] Caesar explained the British connection to Gaul as he had done that of the Belgic relationship to the Germans, through former warfare. For him, the British comprised two elements: the indigenous population and those families whose ancestors had been Belgae, originally raiders but now turned settlers. This was probably how the natives themselves explained their history, in terms of war and migrations. The island was already famous for its mineral wealth, especially tin. Caesar confirms this to his readers in his general description of the riches and life-styles of the British and how they resemble those in Gaul. He also notes that they used both bronze and gold coins and iron bars of a standard weight. Although Caesar still uses *oppida* when speaking of Celtic settlements in Britain, he is careful to point out that there were major differences between them and those in Gaul. The former was defended only by site selection, the latter by extraordinarily stout walls.[67]

The clash of cultures runs throughout the *Gallic War*, so that when the reader arrives at Caesar's ethnographic excursus on the Celts and the Germans in book 6 there are few surprises. The treatise on the customs is both a standard ethnographic exercise and an opportunity for the author to provide a more coherent cultural background to his political agenda. The stress throughout is on their differences.[68] Because it contains supposedly cultural material, it is impossible to verify, or for that matter deny, a great many of the comments. His earlier portrayal of the Gauls as being rent by factions is given a historical analysis up to the time of Caesar's arrival, at which point the Aedui and Remi have risen to preeminence in their respective areas. But Caesar prefers to treat general culture rather than political events in this section. All Gauls share a bifurcated social system in which the masses of poor are in debt bondage to the rich. They are, according to Caesar, in servitude. The ruling class is similarly divided into two: Druids and knights.[69] The Druids formed the priestly class, supervising public and private ritual, and being the chief judicial arbiters for all crimes, inheritance, and boundary disputes. One Druid is higher than all others. The knights are leaders in war, which Caesar points out was endemic before his arrival. Because the military levy is based upon family and clientage, the knights with the greatest followings are the most powerful. Little else was worth mentioning about them, perhaps because so much attention had already been paid to warfare and clientage. Neither the term Druid nor knight is otherwise mentioned in the *Gallic War.*[70]

Caesar's only extensive discussion of Celtic cultural practice concerns the role of the Druids in religious ritual. Caesar makes a distinction between Druids and the masses over which they preside. All Druids are exempt from war and any tribute levied to support war. Their records and instructions are kept secret by using Greek characters but not their most sacred teachings. These are passed down orally from generation to generation. Their central spiritual belief, which they try to teach to initiates, is the transmigration of souls from one to another, thereby negating death through the spiritual regeneration of self. They are also keen on astrology. Those truly seeking training in Druidism should go to Britain, whence, legends told, it had come to Gaul in the distant past. The Druids are treated almost as if they constituted a mystery cult similar to that of Isis, then quite popular in Italy. It is Celtic public rituals that Caesar finds most troubling. His Druid priests, while teaching about an imperishable soul, also preside over all public sacrifice and some personal healing rituals. Criminals were routinely used as sacrificial victims, and when these were unavailable, innocents were slaughtered for the gods instead. Victims were sometimes hung in wicker baskets and burned alive. Surprisingly he does not mention cutting off and displaying heads, something that he must have read about in Posidonius and which has been abundantly confirmed archaeologically, not only for heads but other body parts such as femur bones. The remains of children have likewise been discovered in gateways, bogs, and sacred sites across Celtic Europe. Although ritual human sacrifice was part of Rome's own historical tradition, albeit one not invoked for centuries, now the Romans had advanced beyond such practice.

The Celtic gods demanded "A life for a life." These bloodthirsty gods are otherwise described as being very comparable to the Roman gods, so much so that Caesar uses the names of the Latin gods to describe them. Their principal functions are also very Roman. He reports having seen many statues of Mercury, worshiped as the god of travel and commerce. Next after Mercury comes Apollo, the healer; Mars, god of war; Jupiter, the ruler of Heaven; and Minerva, goddess of the arts and crafts. Beneath this anthropomorphic pantheon, lies Dis, the common father and god of darkness, god of the underworld, who has led the Celts to calculate time by nights rather than days. The Romanization of some of aspects of religion among those Celts having most contact with Romans is very likely. The process went on for centuries after the conquests here and elsewhere and may have been incomplete even when Christianity replaced paganism, but Roman religion itself was highly syncretistic, regardless of the names associated with specific deities.[71] Caesar omits religion in the rest of his ethnographic description of Celtic customs and stresses family matters such as public rights of manhood and the irresistible power of the *paterfamilias,* the male head of household. Among the Romans themselves the power of the *paterfamilias* was no longer absolute except in the arcane sense that it was the first of the Laws of the Twelve Tables, which every child learned by heart and was still in theory valid.

The Germans were different. First, they had no Druids. Their gods are not presented with the names and functions of current Roman gods, but as older forms of earth deities, Sol, Vulcan, Luna (Sun, Fire, and Moon). They were supremely hunters and warriors, annually on the move, with no time for sowing and harvesting. Wealth was spread evenly among the population. Each community dwelled in the center of a man-made wilderness created to separate those within society from contact with their neighbors. Young men proved their manhood by crossing this no-man's-land to raid. Chiefs were selected to lead for but one campaign. There were no permanent client followings to draw up as a personal army. The leading men were not officers but primarily judges chosen for their wisdom. Those Gauls who once upon a time had crossed to the east of the Rhine in search of land became Germans in customs and shared their relative poverty and diet. They grew to be the same kind of men. In contrast those Gauls who lived nearest Roman territory learned to love imported wares and became weak—permanently conquered, never conquerors. Caesar was most loquacious about the endless Hercynian Forest, which dominated life for the Germans and the exotic animals living within it. The Germans had learned to live in the forest, take advantage of its resources, but no Roman army could hope to survive there for long.

In these two brief descriptions, Caesar confirms the underlying cultural suppositions in the rest of the *Gallic War.* The Gauls stand developmentally halfway between Rome and the Germans, between civilization and savagery. Just before launching into his narrative on the Hercynian Forest, Caesar acknowledges that he has read Eratosthenes and other Greek geographers.[72] But his debt to earlier work is not usually noted. A basic ethnographic assumption is manifest: the farther away from the Mediterranean world in travel time, the more primitive the society. The products of the Mediterranean were regarded as a cancer to virility. They lured men and women from a life of simple virtues that nurtured family honor, the basis of all ancient society. Social complexity arose as greed destroyed innate equality. The process was inescapable and irreversible. Cultural purity could only be preserved by extreme isolation. To return to the world of exotic men and animals was to abandon civilization, but that was not the goal of ancient ethnography. Rather the point was to frame questions by comparison while entertaining the reader. Ethnographers, like historians, were moralists. They invited the world of fantasy to challenge reality much as good science fiction does. Perhaps Caesar's contemporaries in the Senate would have appreciated the colorful descriptions of the unbridled power of the *paterfamilias* among the Celts or even the scenes of human sacrifice.

Except for the most obvious cases, such as the complete social egalitarianism among the Germans, upon which the career of Ariovistus and modern anthropological studies cast justifiable doubt, it is virtually impossible to verify or discredit Caesar. The fact is that foreign observers, even well-informed ones, often misinterpret what they see. They errantly relate it to their own society, they simplify it, they denigrate it, but Caesar is not an observer of culture so much as he is a politician and general justifying his decisions through the devices of contemporary literature. Book 5 had opened with Caesar returning to Britain. In book 6 we learn that Britain was the home of Druidism, thereby underscoring the need for him to have waged two campaigns there. The description of impenetrable and inhospitable forests—foreboding to Romans at least—beyond the Rhine sanctions Caesar's limited campaigns there in book 4. The systematic cultural portraits in book 6 unite the strands depicting barbarians that run throughout the *Gallic War* and put them into a more memorable form. By the end of book 6 we have returned to the war.

Unfortunately his swift conquest of Gaul left many loose ends, and the carefully constructed alliance system broke down. While he was in Britain in 54 B.C., the Belgae revolted and this carried on into 53. In 52 all Gaul came together, but not under Rome, rather under the greatest Celtic hero in recorded history, Vercingetorix. Caesar develops his character to personify complex issues involving Gaul, Rome, and Caesar, just as he did for Ariovistus. Even Rome's most trusted friends, the Aedui, now rose in rebellion, but on the field of honor each individual *civitas* fought as a unit in the battle line; one even refused that and waged its own war against Rome.[73] Nonetheless, they all raised their voice in opposition to Rome; Gaul had become the political and military entity that it had never been. The campaign against Vercingetorix had to end not merely in victory but in triumph, the consummate defeat of the enemy for which a Roman general might be accorded the highest honor, a public triumphal procession through the most sacred precincts of Rome.

A man of worth and a society that mattered shared one thing, *libertas* (freedom), the right to choose their own course. For Julius Caesar and his fellow senators, *libertas* included their right to pursue their public careers. For a slave, it meant to shed his bondage. Romans fought and justified war in terms of it. Men were expected to die to protect it. One man's or society's *libertas* sometimes interfered with that of another. Romans understood their obligations and freedoms, so when Caesar depicted the general Gallic revolt in 52 B.C. as a matter of *libertas* for the Gauls, his readers felt their plight. They knew what inspired Vercingetorix and his people. Caesar sets out a dilemma. A Roman would die to regain his honor, his *libertas,* and so would a Gaul. The Gauls must loose their *libertas* to preserve that of the Romans; Gallic honor must be trampled, their leaders humbled.[74] To this clash of *libertas,* there was no obvious solution. Caesar suggests that as subjects the conquered will live in peace, but we must wait for Tacitus to provide a clear justification for submission, spoken once again through the voice of a defeated barbarian, but to that we come in the next chapter.[75] Despite the frequency of warfare in the late Roman Republic, war was conceptually a spiritually troubling event to Romans. The gods still weighed its justice.

Caesar left Gaul before its conquest was truly complete and without much in the way of a transitional government. The events leading up to the clash at Alesia had at least identified and concentrated his opponents, and these he had eliminated or forgiven. In each Gallic *civitas* the leading elements all professed their loyalty and became his clients and secondarily Rome's subjects. With but few modifications the Gallic *civitates* remained as before. The great remained great. The lives of most of the population were still fixed on their particular *oppidum*. The Aedui and Arverni were still favored *civitates*. Caesar left no apparent provincial organization to cloud the importance of his patronage. This was completely in accordance with his vision of how the empire should interact with barbarians, conquered or unconquered. Caesar continued the practice of colonization that he had begun while in Spain, but he was certainly not an innovator in this. Colonization had played a key role in Roman expansion as it spread out over the Italian peninsula in the previous centuries. The mechanisms for establishing colonies were time-honored and were essentially civilian in origin. Recent military expansion had left its mark, and in the late republic colonization more often than not meant settling the veterans of recent campaigns. Caesar established a few such military colonies in Gaul, but they were peripheral to the traditional government of the *civitates*.[76] No matter where these veteran-colonists were, however, their presence lured recruits from among the indigenous warrior class. This state of affairs characterized Gaul until the reorganizations begun by Augustus in 27 B.C. that created three provinces from "all Gaul" beyond Narbonensis: the province of Belgica still corresponded rather closely to the lands of the Belgae; Lugdunensis was a much foreshortened remnant of the former "Celtic" zone; and finally there was Aquitania, which as a province expanded considerably northwards from the territories of the Aquitainians, who had fought Julius Caesar. Within each province Augustus reorganized the boundaries of the *civitates* to eliminate the old concentrations of power and to serve better as administrative regions. Augustus also greatly improved the major roads and generally set about creating the conditions under which Gauls became Romans in the course of the next three generations. Although often artificial, the *civitates* created by Augustus in Gaul and elsewhere survived with little modification throughout Roman history. They will be explored as a setting for acculturation in the subsequent two chapters, especially Chapter 5, which focuses on a different geographic area, the middle Danube.

Of all the Roman authors to treat the theme of "Rome and the barbarians," Caesar is far and away the most exciting. Moreover, his impressions of the physical features of barbarian Europe have been proved generally accurate, though often incomplete. Despite his desire to declare the Rhine as a cultural boundary, his narrative reveals a transition zone in which life-styles and peoples merged around shared topographic features—for example, along the lower Rhine. Along the middle Rhine the cultural cleavage between civility and barbarism, as seen in the difference between life in *oppida* or their absence, was sharper in 50 B.C. than if Marius had crossed the Rhine. Heavily fortified *oppida* were quite rare beyond the Rhine in Caesar's day, because they had been abandoned for unknown reasons about half a century before. He knew next to nothing of Germanic society and its cultures. His depictions of them were based on his own firsthand contact, limited in time and reduced by the disappearance of the inhabitants. In addition to his own impressions, he had rumor and tips from traders, but mostly he told the same stories that ethnographers had told for generations. The complete rhetorical product was a compelling justification of his policies. "German" meant something for Caesar but it was not an ethnographic term as we would understand it today. Simply put, Germans were not Celts. He had conquered the latter; the former remained outside the Roman domain, within reach and under its influence, revealed to his critics as too primitive to be worth the sacrifice needed to subdue them.[77]

In Roman Gaul *oppida* were made obsolete, for now Roman legions monopolized violence. As always, colonies were little Romes with their senates and urban magistrates, their tastes in food and decorum. Their values and needs gradually changed Gaul as they did elsewhere in the West. Colonies and other new towns, many peopled by the inhabitants of former *oppida* or their descendants, prospered. There was a period of transition as Celtic forms of leadership gave way to developing forms of Roman administration. Little by little Roman religion was grafted on to and in some cases replaced that of the indigenous populations, but, especially in the countryside, this process was of very long duration. It was most rapid where Rome concentrated its economic and human resources, near military camps and colonies, and among those for whom presenting a Roman appearance mattered most. The hinterlands lagged far behind, content with the traditions of their ancestors.

Rome had no policy to coerce cultural compliance or uniformity in Gaul. Caesar had no intention to stay around long enough to learn from or even interact with the barbarians that he had defeated. His goal had been to create and then conquer a cultural and geographic buffer and then move on to greater conquests elsewhere. At no point in the narrative of his campaign did Caesar believe that the ultimate triumph of Roman civilization was in doubt. In Caesar's mind the preexisting cultural and economic interactions between Rome and its barbarian neighbors hardly mattered. He left Gaul as quickly as possible; the barbarian menace had been quelled, its force harnessed to propel Caesar to new heights. The generations that followed him had other goals.

After the death of Julius Caesar anybody seeking to present himself as an authority on barbarians found it was mandatory to read Caesar. Pliny the Elder, Strabo, Plutarch, Tacitus, Cassius Dio, to name but the most prominent, knew their Caesar. Strabo in particular acknowledged his debt to the master in regards to the barbarians. Even including Tacitus, who may have grown up on the Rhine, none added much depth to his descriptions. Pliny the Elder, who died in the eruption of Mount Vesuvius in A.D. 79, was in position to draw upon his own observations, because he spent time along the Rhine and traveled about Gaul, but his work on the Germans has not survived. As his *Natural History,* however, reveals, Pliny had an encyclopedist's thirst for knowledge and a bibliophile's approach to discovering it. Many have long seen Pliny's work on the Germans as lying behind Tacitus's *Germania,* not that this hypothesis greatly lessens the difficulty of understanding either.

For most members of the Roman upper class, real barbarians were irrelevant. If they were in command of a legion, barbarians were objects of booty, their submission a testament to their conqueror's valor. If they found themselves writing a treatise or giving an oration, then barbarians were a generic literary vehicle for social commentary: invariably they lived in cold climates and wore little. Nonetheless, their marriages were rock solid, with the women sometimes acting more manly than their mates. These stereotypic barbarians were always pastoral and never had their own money. In fact, they are often depicted as not even interested in the precious metals from which coins might be struck or deals concluded. Their diets too reflected their climate and were heavy on dairy products and meat. These tired accounts are sparsely sprinkled with details, which sometimes can be checked against the surviving archaeological data, but attitudes and social customs rarely leave physical records. In general old stereotypes were embellished rather than corrected by successive tellers. The mark of a serious and scholarly commentator was the addition of a few current observations to the ethnographic tradition.

The archaeological record is more valuable than Caesar on barbarian ethnography. Rather than exploring more fully the Romanization of Gaul and Roman influence along the Rhine, let us shift the investigation eastwards to the Carpathian Basin and the Danube, to what is primarily Hungary and Serbia today, ancient Pannonia.[78] By changing the geographic focus, general features of the interaction between barbarians and Romans can stand out in sharper relief.

Four

The Early Empire and the Barbarians: An Overview

Caius Julius Caesar Octavianus, better known as Augustus, moved the Roman world away from the closely knit aristocratic world of the republic towards a vastly more complex empire. The goal of this chapter is the reverse of the one that goes before. There we entered into the mind of the greatest Roman of his generation to explore how barbarians were treated in classical literature. Beneath the stereotype of the noble savage was a world dominated by patronage. For men like Julius Caesar, it was primarily through the relationship between patron and client that cultural values were exchanged. Caesar regarded it as quite natural that every Celtic community had a few families vying for political power and that one or more would come forward seeking his aid. Their existence and submission confirmed Roman cultural superiority and provided a convenient justification for Roman involvement whenever necessary.

Just as patronage could be extended almost indefinitely, so too could the empire itself, but there were zones of greater and lesser control. The source of patronage in international affairs was Rome itself, but as embodied in the Roman senatorial aristocracy individually and collectively. At the heart of the web of patronage was

Italy, next came the provinces, next the client states, and finally a receding world of irregular contact and acquaintance. Yet all were aspects of one vision. The provinces themselves were held together by personal and familial links to the few Romans present, but especially to the family of the conquering general who had first established the network of dependency and obligation that defined the provincial hierarchy. Although the importance of patronage would never lapse in Roman society or in its foreign relations, its role was gradually augmented by a standing army and later by a regular civil administration. This evolution was gradual, but much of it took place in the course of about three-quarters of a century (ca. 75–150).

This chapter surveys how changes within the newly created Roman Empire altered its relationship with the barbarians during what is called the Principate after the governmental spirit inaugurated by Augustus. A case is made that there was little fundamental difference between the initial Roman involvement with conquered peoples within the new provinces and those remaining outside the Roman administrative system. Although the forces at work were essentially the same, the differences sharpened as more and more Roman effort and population were focused on the external borders. Moreover, the barbarians were only one factor, and often a secondary one at that, in the emperor's decisions to place their armies where they would be both far from Rome and from each other. In some provinces the shift of emphasis to the frontiers took place even before some interior areas of the provinces themselves had felt much Roman influence, at least not as judged from the material records of domiciles and ceramics. Peoples living in particularly difficult terrain, such as in mountainous areas far from rivers, were bypassed. In several cases such pockets remained as semi-frontier areas within the empire. Seutonius writing at the end of the first century A.D. says of Augustus that he had seen little difference between client states and the empire itself, treating all with equanimity.[1] Contemporary usage of the term *peregrini*, foreigners, captures some of this same indifference. Anybody not a Roman citizen could be called a *peregrinus*, whether he lived in a Roman province or beyond.

One first-century and two second-century developments were crucial in changing this: (1) Augustus's stationing in the provinces a large standing army, which he created from the armed forces available after his defeat of Mark Antony at Actium in 31 B.C., (2) the second-century development of a professional administrative staff in the provinces; and (3) also in the second century, an intensification of the shift in the pattern of governmental investment in infrastructure to the edges of the provinces, that is, to what are often, although inaccurately, called the imperial frontiers. In some areas this shift began under the Flavian emperors (A.D. 69–96), in others it took place not before the great efforts of the emperor Hadrian (A.D. 117–38). Of these three developments, the final one was decisive because it concentrated the economic, political, and military resources of the Mediterranean world at the doorstep of those barbarians remaining beyond direct Roman administration.

The result was a network of flourishing urban centers dependent upon the transference of wealth and technology from the Mediterranean world. Regardless of their size, these nucleated communities attracted the rural populations in their areas, and people awakened to the opportunities of the new markets. This pattern is apparent wherever we look in the western frontier provinces and to a lesser extent in the East as well. It was only a matter of time before the often sparsely populated lands beyond the frontiers similarly flourished and for much the same reasons as did the rural areas within the provinces. The barbarians were after all part of the rural population in the frontier areas, separated from Roman markets by an administrative frontier but linked to it by safely traveled river arteries. Sooner or later those rural populations that had access to these markets took advantage of them.

In the core provinces of the Mediterranean, well-established urban foundations had proved to be the key element in transferring values from Romans to non-Romans and vice versa. In sharp contrast, in the frontier provinces the army first dominated the interaction and only later was joined by a parallel civilian government. These Roman institutions acted much as had former individual patrons when dealing with the barbarians beyond the frontiers. Without Roman towns and camps, no towns developed within the provinces, let alone outside them. The barbarian world stayed securely within the domain of patronage. This said, it is important to note that within the provinces civilian communities quickly sprang up to take advantage of the markets provided by the garrisons. The composite effect of this development was that during most of the Principate the frontier areas were characterized by a blend of Roman civilian and military influences. In some places urban centers had to be built on bare earth, but this was generally not the case because of the presence of Celtic *oppida* and other proto-urban settlements in many of the conquered areas. The defensive considerations that had prompted the building of many *oppida* were no longer so important after Roman conquest, for from now on defense was an exclusively Roman concern. Sometimes *oppida* could be reorganized or even resettled with Roman colonists; at other times all that remained of the original *oppidum* was its name now applied to a new administrative unit, the *civitas*.

The fabric of economic and personal interactions, which had always made *oppida* regional centers, continued under Roman aegis. These *civitates* were usually modified and often more than once. When the initial *civitas* was established, it always included people not originally associated with the particular pre-Roman *oppidum*. The *civitas* was subsequently altered according to Roman military needs and subsequent urban expansion. Soon after the conquest former *civitas* communities were placed under Roman military supervision but often without regard to their original territorial configurations. Typically they retained their old names. Actual governance was still carried on by the native aristocracy, having been pruned of notable Roman opponents. Although in their reconstituted form the *civitates* survived for a very long time, municipal development during the second century eclipsed their significance. Clearly they remained as religious organizations charged with cult observances, but they had entered a long twilight.

Roman authority was always concerned to clarify the administrative borders of these new communities. Once it became clear that former defensive considerations were no longer their concern, the indigenous populations gravitated to more commercially advantageous locations along transportation corridors or near Roman military posts or colonies. That this took as long as it did may attest to the importance of religious sites associated with former settlements, but of this little more can be said. Frontier provinces were often created as governmental capstones through which elite Romans, with the considerable assistance of native aristocrats, administered discrete territories through staffs originally attached to legions. The senior military commander governed the province in which his army was stationed. The commander governed as an imperial legate and built his government around his legionary staff. These "borrowed personnel" were very few in number and were augmented by the domestic staff, typically freedmen and slaves, belonging to the legate himself. A civilian governed provinces without regular army units, but in most cases these men had previous military experience. The most important civilian provinces were plums, their governorships handed out to them by the emperor as rewards for a lifetime of service. These men usually had vast military experience, including long service as legates, before being appointed. Without exception, the frontier provinces were governed by the commanders of their legions.

A legate served at the discretion of the emperor, not for a fixed term. When he left his post, he took his staff with him. Only gradually did this change. By the second quarter of the second century a core of gubernatorial specialists stayed in place to continue the government under the new appointee, but there was never a decree mandating a permanent staff for all provinces. Beyond the military camps, whole areas of the provinces remained much as they had been for generations—rural, isolated, and administered as *civitates* by local elites. Lacking independent and adequate staffs, the quality of the governor's personal leadership was crucial. Any bad qualities he possessed were magnified by the dependence of the provincials on his favor.

Because the governor had virtually no Roman staff, he depended on the existing Romanophile elites to do much of the governing for him outside the capital. This was not a straightforward task, for those he aimed to use aimed to use him. In order to maintain their own positions, the pro-Roman elites did the bidding of the governor and used their favored status to augment and maintain their positions over rivals. This is a good example of how patronage continued at the heart of governance, even though technically political and administrative officeholders administered the provinces. Perhaps even more than the Romans, the indigenous elites wanted to maintain the status quo. A reasonably well documented case involving a Roman governor, his indigenous supporters, and their potential rivals is that of Pontius Pilate and the trial of Jesus. Pilate's venality is clear even from non-Christian sources, but the biblical narratives are hardly straightforward.

The governor's command of all military units in his province underscored his exclusive right to use armed force. To challenge his monopoly meant rebellion or civil war. Taking up arms always led to terrible death tolls for the rebels. The defeated British followers of Boudicea were crucified for mile after mile, their bodies left to rot, carrion, unburied if not unmourned reminders of the price of armed resistance. The besieged Jewish rebels took their own lives, when it became obvious that the Romans were about to break into their redoubt at Massada. Had they been captured, crucifixion awaited them too.[2] Only gradually, very gradually, did Roman habits penetrate the countryside and thereby realign or replace traditional familial governance. Customs such as patron-client relationships predated Roman conquest and remained at the core of life. Republican leaders like Pompey and Caesar had bequeathed a vast array of client kingdoms, but by the end of the first century A.D. almost all these republican client kingdoms had been absorbed into the empire as provinces. By the middle of the second century, the provinces had become functioning territorial units of government, and beyond them stretched the world of the barbarians. Yet Roman appreciation of their own territoriality was slow in emerging even after it became clear that expansion into vast stretches of nonurbanized areas was not worth its cost. Nor did the end of client kingdoms inside the empire lead to an end of their utility outside. As life in the provinces evolved along Italian lines, their governors manipulated their external neighbors into new client kingdoms.

Our traditional sense of "frontier" is a reflection of our own concern with regulating political borders between organized states. This conceptualization is undergoing major rethinking in much of the world, as is our understanding of premodern frontiers. Even in modern situations, however, political boundaries rarely correspond to cultural distinctions. An example of this would be the border between Mexico and the United States. Here the political border runs through an increasingly common economic and cultural zone, the edges of which are indistinct. In this case, as in the ancient Roman, family and friendship circles influence and preserve culture more effectively than political systems can. Additionally, Americans rather commonly use the term "frontier" in the sense of the edge of civilization, specifically the "American frontier" with the native populations or the "frontiers of outer space," where no human civilization yet exists. None of these common definitions of frontier fits the actualities of Roman-barbarian interactions.

Because patronage was the earliest and most enduring relationship among Romans and between Rome and the barbarians, all Roman clients would have been included to some degree as being "within" the empire. Just as clients within Roman society, barbarian clients were a part of their patrons' "family," a recognized part of their inner world. Thus conceptually Romans would have set their frontiers at the limits of the diplomatic network held together by personal and political clientage, which in fact had no limits. This conceptual rather than geographic boundary, beyond which there were no clients, would have been impossible to locate on a map precisely because patronage itself was regarded as essentially personal rather than territorial. Roman authors, guided perhaps by their earlier Greek models, very rarely speak of taking territory; rather they tell of Romans conquering other peoples. At all times the Roman frontiers of patronage would have extended well beyond the area that Rome directly administered, over peoples and their leaders as far as the Roman political classes had contacts.

Vergil captures this sense of unbounded empire in the first book of his *Aeneid,* when Jupiter speaks to the Romans though an address to Aeneas: "To this [empire] I set neither material nor temporal bounds: I give you empire without end." Into this empire wandered Aeneas with his father Anchises, but as his followers the Roman people filled the areas given them by the gods to administer, their imprint grew deeper in some areas than in others.[3] A visual analogy would be something like the complex swirling and shading that takes place as two rivers, whose waters are decidedly different in color, merge. The blending sometimes takes hundreds of meters and varies from moment to moment with the currents and the winds. As long as we understand the Roman frontier in this manner, then it is useful to employ the Latin term for boundary, *limes,* when referring to the line of fortifications that ran just behind the natural or man-made feature demarcating the end of Roman legal jurisdiction and to reserve "frontier" for the much more fluid sphere of interaction. Recourse to this more descriptive terminology becomes increasingly important in the course of the first two centuries after Augustus as boundaries are made more visible because of administrative development.

During this period the Roman-barbarian relationship went from preconquest influence to the postconquest incorporation of selected barbarians into the fabric of the empire. Those barbarians remaining outside witnessed the systemization of Roman clientage over and among them. At no time was there a plan outlining a barbarian policy, but nonetheless there was an enduring mind-set within which governors made decisions. Several features stand out. First, Rome consistently sought to territorialize barbarian groups within recognized boundaries: as *civitates* within the provinces and as *gentes* for those beyond. From the Roman perspective both internal and external barbarians needed to be grouped together under governmental organizations competent to yield predictable results, even when this meant redrawing ethnic and geographic boundaries. Roman success at manipulation manifested itself much earlier among those within the provinces than those remaining outside, but those barbarians external to the provincial system responded nonetheless.

Second, Rome had relatively simple goals. A major one was fiscal accountability; another was political compliance. Provincials paid taxes; barbarians offered tribute. Those in or near provincial towns made their payments to the town, whereas those living in decidedly rural areas paid the tax farmers (*publicani*), who bid for the rights to collect in these areas. Even this apparent simplicity is deceptive because the type and rate of taxes owed depended on one's citizenship status. Citizenship in turn varied according to the status of the town itself. Like so much else, the early empire lacked a cohesive and uniform tax system, and this amorphousness diffused group interactions. External barbarians were expected to pay tribute, but this could have been seen as a way to defray the costs of their defense in case of attack from a third party as well as making a symbolic and psychological statement.

Third, if any group of barbarians resorted to armed conflict against Rome, the Roman response was equally consistent. Time after time Roman armies faced down the opposition, no matter how long that took, and reorganized Roman supervision accordingly. Finally, Roman actions began with the minimum level of intervention and personnel costs and escalated only when circumstances so required. No effort was made to press all barbarians into a common mold. Or, to put the matter somewhat differently, the Roman government did not engage in social engineering among the barbarians. Intervention in their political life was another matter and one in which the Roman authorities were keenly interested, because stable and friendly regimes could best guarantee peaceful intercourse.

In some areas from the late first century, but in most only from the early second, clients beyond the borders were forced to deal with the results of a major shift in Roman investment as successive emperors oversaw the building of a series of fortifications and roads along the borders directly opposite lands occupied by barbarians. In the case of the middle Danube, the area singled-out in the next chapter for illustrative detail, this meant on the opposite riverbank. This was not true of the lower Danube. Once Trajan (A.D. 98–117) had conquered the Dacians and had created a new province from their territory, corresponding rather closely to modern Romania, Roman efforts were concentrated there, not along the Danube far to the south. The provinces south of the Danube remained fertile military recruiting grounds for relatively impoverished youths. The new Trajanic borders north of the Danube consisted of the arch of the Carpathian Mountains, the Pathisus (Tizsa) River, and a line of fortifications roughly at the edge of the Roman piedmont towards the Black Sea. Farther east stretched the plains.[4] Because of the topography these borders were hardly comparable to the great rivers and walls common elsewhere. This redeployment of civilian and military resources to the administrative borders set up a controlled and sustainable interaction between barbarians and Romans that could not have occurred without preceding and corresponding changes within both societies. Except for Trajan's efforts to recruit settlers for Roman Dacia, the government did very little to encourage civilians moving into newly conquered areas.

The standard way that the government encouraged settlement was by establishing veteran colonies, the last of which were undertaken to accommodate Trajan's returning soldiers. Because all citizens of a *colonia* were Roman, they provided a convenient recruitment base for the legions. Trajan apparently appreciated this fact and made sure that the number of *colonia* equaled that of the legions.[5] Veteran colonies led the way in building a Roman cultural base in the provinces. Retiring auxiliaries gradually raised the number of citizens in the neighborhoods of their camps, which were often established to supervise the locals in their *civitates,* which in turn provided recruits for the local military units. The sparse Roman presence in the newly won territories meant that the indigenous society's pre-Roman networks and life-styles took many decades—and, in the most remote parts of the provinces, centuries—before they responded to the Roman presence. The remaining barbarians, that is, those left outside the provincial system—the internal barbarians having been made into provincials by their conquest, submission, and absorption—were everywhere encouraged to have regular contact across monitored frontiers.

Our shift eastwards into central Europe, the Balkans, and Carpathian Basin is not only geographic but specifically historical. It was here that Augustus directed his personal attention throughout much of his reign and where the empire regularly faced its greatest challenges. This remained so throughout the Principate and for centuries thereafter. It may be debated whether Rome had a clear plan of territorial expansion and acquisition elsewhere, but it certainly did regarding the Balkans and the Danube River basin. Because of the peculiar central European geography, barbarians here were under exceptional stress. In part this was a result of Rome's successful efforts in establishing its control of the Danube and the Balkan peninsula. Equally important, however, it was a consequence of Rome's ultimate failure to control ingress and egress into the area from the north. Wars marked the local failures of clientage, both Roman and barbarian. Overshadowing Roman actions was the nature of the territory itself, for nowhere else in Europe is there such striking topographic and cultural variation. No one system of government was ever extended over this diversity. Even if Rome had tried to have a general policy governing relations with barbarians, no detailed framework could possibly have united the peoples of the Balkans, a land of mountains and valleys cut by countless streams and with few large areas of flat land. Some sections along the Danube and the great Hungarian Plain, the westernmost extension of the great steppes of southern Russia, were exceptions.

The life-styles of the northern and eastern plains were completely different than those of the Mediterranean world and were at least as old. Peoples long present in the Carpathian Basin, such as Sarmatians (Iazyges), Dacians, and various Celts, contributed to the cultural complexity confronting other barbarians and Rome itself. Contours and shades of policy were visible everywhere. There were subtle differences even among neighboring frontier provinces along the Rhine as well as the Danube.[6] Despite differences caused by preexisting societies in some areas, notably north of the lower Danube, a general homogeneity eventually manifested itself along the entire course of the frontiers in Europe. This was a result of the long-term application of the Roman military and civil systems, but this consistency was not apparent until towards the end of the second century, and in some areas not until even later. The reason for this cultural uniformity among the Roman populations of the frontier areas is not hard to find. By initially recruiting new soldiers in one area and then shifting them to opposite ends of the empire, the Roman army in particular served as a giant mixing bowl in which cultural diversity was submerged under the general forms of military life.

At the theoretical level Romans sought to conceptualize barbarians as topographically discrete political units, defined by natural features such as rivers and organized in varying degrees by personal rather than institutional bonds. This tendency was already apparent with Julius Caesar. On the ground, barbarian societies rarely reflected the tidy compartmentalization of Roman intellectuals and administrators. Rather, they were locked into an infinite series of personal, familial, and small community adjustments necessary to deal with each other and the Mediterranean world. In a sense, barbarian societies were microcosms of the empire in that they too lacked coherent boundaries within which their leaders exercised exclusive jurisdiction and influence. As the Roman Empire itself became more and more a managed society, it had more and more difficulty understanding the limits of this earlier type of sociopolitical organization still current among its neighbors. The Principate spanned approximately two centuries. In the newly created frontier provinces these were centuries of intense development and change. While the city of Rome itself underwent an unparalleled provincialization during these years, the frontier provinces underwent comparable change in the opposite direction, dominated by urban centers, transportation systems, and fiscal redistribution. Beneath the placid surface that so attracted the attention both of Aelius Aristides writing in 143 and Edward Gibbon sixteen centuries later lay a churning prosperous society busily carving in stone enduring hallmarks of its vitality. In the frontier provinces the pace of change was particularly keen in the second century and reached a plateau towards its end. No two generations of barbarians experienced exactly the same Roman Empire, nor did Romans discover the same barbarians living along their borders, as had their forefathers.

Two Roman institutions were paramount in affecting the Roman-barbarian relationship throughout these centuries: the army and urban centers. This continued to be true long after the Principate had become only a convenient political memory for those living in the much more autocratic world of the late empire. The imperial army served as a means through which a host of cultural values were transported and transformed for the frontier environment, as well as being a military strike force. The army was not merely there to defend provincials in case of attack, or to crush insurrections. More fundamentally it was integral to the governance of the provinces themselves, and its loyalty to the emperor remained vital to imperial stability.

There should be no doubt, however, that the Roman army was itself transformed by its new mission as a standing army poised first to suppress and then later to further an atmosphere favorable to the development of civilian values. The former—suppressing revolts—meant taking measures to reimpose Roman control over the newly conquered or recently incorporated, that is, over the internal barbarians. The latter mission—protecting civilian centers—meant warding off raids into the provinces by external aggressors. More important than armed conflict, Roman soldiers and former soldiers transformed the frontier provinces generation after generation as they themselves changed from foreigners to natives, and those natives became Romans. As far as the lives of barbarians were concerned the nonmilitant aspects of the army were of much more lasting importance than the destruction it wrought on the rare occasions of its deployment against them.

Augustus and his successors should not be given credit for what the army ultimately did as a cultural force in the course of the next four centuries. Barbarians played no role in the formation of the Principate other than as one of many vehicles used in propaganda to announce the new golden age. They did not threaten the empire; civil war did. Internal warfare had to be stopped, and the concentration of military power that had made it so destructive eliminated. With the civil wars at an end, there were many pressing problems, chief among them were: (1) what to do with so many troops and (2) how to retain senatorial involvement in government without generating new contenders for ultimate political power. The two were linked, for political success in the late republic rested upon the command of armies. The first problem Augustus solved just as he stated in his *Res gestae:* he discharged tens of thousands of soldiers with bonuses and settled them in veteran colonies.[7] The second required much more finesse, but part of its solution too involved the army.

What Augustus chose not to mention in the *Res gestae* was his operational division of the provinces into those with troops and those without and the functional relationship between them. He controlled the imperial provinces, that is, those with all significant troop concentrations, through the appointment of legates; the other provinces remained as always, governed by those elected in the Senate, but now with his advice and consent. The senatorial provinces were surrounded by the imperial, and by shifting the army to these areas Augustus and Tiberius also removed the training grounds for young aristocrats from the seats of power in Rome. A noble youth still needed military experience and henceforth that was to be achieved as imperial officers rather than, as was still true under Julius Caesar, alongside individual generals obliged only to their own political factions. Augustus did not move against the class from which he himself had come. Rather, he placed himself at the helm of its career development process. Some aristocrats took a while to learn the rules of the new game.

The *Res gestae* reflects Augustus's wish that he be remembered to have done all things in order to defend and reward the Roman people, particularly the senatorial class, but this was a charade. In reality he could and did manipulate the governorships of any province that he wished without consultation with the Senate. Senatorial provinces were transferred to overt imperial control, but the reverse never occurred. The reason for garrisoning a large army in the frontier provinces was to be understood from his repeated reference in the *Res gestae* and on other public monuments to victories over barbarians. The armies were there to protect Romans and Roman possessions, and this after all was the only justification for armed might remaining. There could be no glory, no celebration of triumphs otherwise. No public recourse could be made to the need to suppress provincials or to guard against usurpation. On the other hand, not a single barbarian group stood marshaled along the frontiers waiting to invade. The only barbarians likely to feel the sharp edge of Roman steel were the internal barbarians.

The subtle distinction is lost in the rhetoric of the *Res gestae* as in all other contemporary documents, but as the internal threats waned in importance, the emphasis on barbarians was clarified. The "barbarian threat" shifted without any barbarians having moved. Within the imperial provinces the auxiliary units assured daily peace, and the legions stood in reserve. Because from early on Roman practice recruited auxiliary units in one area and assigned them elsewhere, the provincials in one frontier province were policed by those of another. In the early Principate the location of the auxiliary camps often resembled a fishnet thrown over the province, whereas each legion was concentrated as a unit. The siting of the legionary fortresses whenever possible on the coast or navigable rivers both assured economical supply and rapid mobility to trouble spots elsewhere than their province. The role of the auxiliaries was bolstered by veteran colonies, which continued the important provincial roles that they had played under the republic. During the early Principate external barbarians rarely figured into these calculations. Augustus's subtle handling of his provincial reforms was but a part of his overall military and political program. To the extent that it had anything directly to do with barbarians, it was as a program for pacifying the internal rather than defending against the external.

Augustus institutionalized the army and opened up its ranks to non-Romans for the first time. Augustus's new army followed a calendar of religious festivals honoring the imperial cult and the emperor's care for his troops. Later emperors added many new days of feasting so as to include themselves in Augustus's divine status among the soldiery. The effect was especially significant among the auxiliaries, who had no choice but to participate in regular Roman religious ritual.[8] Augustus clarified lines of promotion within the ranks; soldiers in this new standing army never again had to worry whether a jealous clique within the Senate would delay their pay and retirement bonuses. The total number of men under arms when Augustus defeated Antony at the battle of Actium (31 B.C.) was soon halved.[9] At its maximum strength under Augustus the army numbered twenty-eight legions, but the three legions lost with Varus in the Teutoburg Forest (A.D. 9) were not replaced. Thus when Augustus died in A.D. 14, his successor Tiberius commanded twenty-five legions, or approximately 150,000 men. In addition to the legions, Augustus bequeathed a parallel force of auxiliary units approximately equal in combined troop strength to that of the legions, for a total of 300,000 men under arms. Over the next two centuries the number of legions increased, but only gradually and in response to specific needs. For example, Marcus Aurelius (161–80) raised two new legions and Septimius Severus (193–211) three, all five for wars in the East. These legions, as in theory all others, were raised in Italy, but until Septimius none was stationed there in peacetime.

The rough numerical balance between legionnaires and auxiliaries, an unintended legacy of Augustus, also changed in favor the latter. Smaller deployments were more flexible, first in policing occupied territory and then in countering the small raids by external barbarians that characterized so much of the military activity of the Roman army during the second century. The use of auxiliaries as a permanent part of the imperial army was a natural development from the armies of the republic. Farther back than the Romans had records, Romans had fought alongside their allies: first the Latin city-states to the south and gradually allies from all of Italy. It was and remains good policy to involve allies in one's foreign wars, for it is not only cheaper but achieves much goodwill among the leaders. Thus at a critical moment in his civil war against Mark Antony, Augustus could extend what was originally a military oath of allegiance to all Italy (*totia Italia*) as a single unit. As Roman republican armies had become more professional in the sense of established ranks and routine reenlistment, so too had the allied components.

Such a mixed fighting arrangement inherently fused the combatants into a single force and thereby strengthened the political and social ties of the member states to one another. Conversely, whatever tactical advantages one contributing state had were soon honed to equal perfection by all. This parity could make for a very prolonged and bitter struggle in the case of a civil war among allies, as happened during the Social War, so-called after the Latin word for allies, *socii,* that racked Italy early in the reign of Sulla. Although Augustus's move to create a regular system of auxiliaries had a long evolution behind it, its subsequent development was even more striking. Ultimately internal barbarians were completely merged into the essential fabric of the empire, and this stemmed largely from their participation in the auxiliary forces and in the towns that grew up nearby to their camps. Roman employment of internal barbarians found a parallel beyond the empire's administrative boundaries as Augustus and his successors created and recreated systems of alliance, established regular trading relationships, intervened in barbarian internal politics, and selectively admitted barbarian groups into the provinces. All of these peoples were in some sense part of the Roman Empire. By the end of the Principate (ca. A.D. 240) Rome had created a new and ubiquitous paradigm: The Empire. Insiders and outsiders shared in its centrality and eternity.

If the size of the Roman army relative to the civilian population is compared with the peacetime armies of modern states, the result is a striking testament to the Roman commitment of resources. Despite the rather primitive fiscal instruments available to the Romans, the entrenched reluctance of the elites to pay or allow their dependents to pay taxes, the political risks of having a standing army, and the limited surpluses being produced by its primary economic activity (agriculture), Rome maintained a force ratio of 1 soldier to every 250 to 300 civilians and perhaps as high as 1 to 150 by the opening of the third century. Although certainly too widely dispersed and too cumbersome to assemble normally for large operations, maintaining such a huge army was unprecedented, and it was always the largest item in the imperial budget.[10] As a result of its fiscal needs and a pattern of deployment that placed it far from Mediterranean resources, the army's requirements gradually transformed Roman government and traditional values, but these facts were scarcely apparent until many decades after the death of Augustus. As far as the barbarians were concerned, enlistment in the army, whether as a legionnaire or an auxiliary, was a very honorable and attractive career option, so much so that Roman authorities could be quite selective in whom they accepted into service. Although the tradition that citizens had a responsibility to serve in the army never completely died, volunteers mostly filled the ranks. Emperors resorted to drafting civilians only in the most dire circumstances. Those entering military service as young men of eighteen to twenty could have looked forward to living out their enlistment, at which time they would have been around forty years of age. With another decade or more of life still to live, and a substantial nest egg saved, they were likely to play an important role in their new communities. Various emperors, particularly Septimius Severus and his son Caracalla, made regular efforts to raise the pay of their soldiers and thereby to keep the profession competitive in the job market.

The combined force of legionnaires and auxiliaries was successful in every respect. The empire did not erupt in a major civil war again until A.D. 68, the year of the four emperors, but there were numerous native revolts: in Pannonia, roughly former Yugoslavia and Hungary (A.D. 6), Gaul (the last in A.D. 21), Britain (A.D. 60), Palestine, modern Israel (A.D. 68–70) and again in the second century (A.D. 131–34). In these native rebellions and in campaigns to expand the empire, the imperial army served its commander-in-chief, the emperor, loyally. Of these armed conflicts few ended in failure, the notable exception being Augustus's move to create a province between the Rhine and Elbe Rivers and then ultimately overland down to the middle Danube. Until the reign of Hadrian (A.D. 117–38) most soldiers would have served well within the provinces as an army of occupation rather than as a frontier force poised to ward off an external threat. Even after the redeployment of the army to the frontiers the most likely incursion was that of a few raiders trying to carry off a little booty, perhaps to prove themselves brave back home. An inscription is one of the clearest records of the rationale for the deployment of the Roman army in the late Principate, that is, to oppose "furtive crossings of the river [Danube] by robbers." This is particularly apparent in the section of the Danube known as the Iron Gates, but ultimately a similar density of small fortifications stood along numerous sections of the river.[11]

The dispersal of the army achieved one of its most important goals. From the reign of Vespasian, who began the systematic redeployment of the army to the peripheries in key areas, there were no military challenges to the reigning emperor from the frontier armies. The civil wars that brought Vespasian to power were not repeated until the third century. The four contenders for emperorship in A.D. 68–69 were the last to fight a civil war with legionnaires re-

THE ROMAN EMPIRE
AT THE DEATH
OF AUGUSTUS
Germania
Belgica
Lugdunensis
Aquitania
Raetia
Noricum
Alpes Poeninae
Alpes Cottiae
Alpes
Maritimae
NARBONENSIS
Lusitania
Tarraconensis
BAETICA
SARDINIA-CORSICA
Pannonia
Illyricum
Moesia
Thrace
MACEDONIA
ACHAEA
SICILIA
Mauretania
Africa
Nova
AFRICA
BITHYNIA
Pontus
Galatia
Cappadocia
ASIA
Lyconia
Pamphylia
Cilicia
Lycia
Syria
CRETA
CYPRUS
Palestine
CYRENAICA
Egypt
Germania = Imperial Province
AFRICA = Senatorial Province
Mauritania = Client Kingdom
0
500
1000 km

cruited almost entirely from Italy and auxiliaries from the provinces. This was certainly not, however, the last time that Roman civil war affected the barbarians. Throughout the empire's history the odds were that if you fell in battle it would be against a rebel rather than an invader, but most soldiers either retired or died of natural causes. Major campaigns were rare, but on them the auxiliaries and the legionnaires fought as one army, with similar but not identical equipment and common tactics. The legions deployed in larger units and carried slightly heavier equipment, and they excelled in technical warfare, particularly in the conduct of siege operations in which complex equipment and highly trained personnel were needed. Although legions could deploy small cavalry formations, such lightly protected combatants found their home in the auxiliary. There were other special units of auxiliary recruited from among native peoples of the empire with peculiar expertise, such as slingers. These special units were also unusual in that they were the first to recruit men from outside the empire, that is to say, barbarians. The most famous such unit was the imperial guard itself.[12]

Roman soldiers regardless of their deployment needed supplies and benefits, and they did so year in and year out. Augustus endowed a special treasury to provide for their needs, and ordered that it be supplemented by a 5 percent inheritance tax paid by all Roman citizens. This fiscal reform resolved one of the most intractable issues in late republican politics and allowed for the complete professionalization and deployment of the empire's military forces in the provinces. Augustus also saw the need to have a standing garrison in Rome under his direct command, the imperial guard. Terms of recruitment into and service within the various armed forces were different from the outset. Legionnaires served for twenty years, auxiliaries for twenty-five and for somewhat less pay, but the most significant difference was in status. Legionnaires generally had to be citizens at the time of their enrollment, whereas auxiliaries became citizens upon the completion of their term of

The Roman Empire at the death of Augustus

service. Legions had to be commanded by a man of senatorial rank. By contrast, for many decades some auxiliary units were commanded by their own native leaders, while others were under Roman officers of equestrian rank.[13]

Auxiliaries were typically recruited from among the provincials, often in newly acquired territory and probably through the implementation of forced conscription from the recently conquered peoples. There was, however, no barrier to a recruit coming from completely outside the administrative system, as the early recruitment of Germanic soldiers into various auxiliary units attests. Recourse to outsiders, however, progressed inversely to the success of the civilian development within the empire, and it remained relatively unimportant until the civil wars of the third century. The auxiliary forces included units of cavalry (*alae*) and infantry (*cohortes*). Even late in the first century, there were few units stationed along the external provincial boundaries. Where possible a natural topographic feature, usually a river, served as a border indicating the limit of Roman jurisdiction. In a few areas the terrain was so rugged that precise borders, especially between provinces, were never important nor was the assignment of garrisons to these remote regions. In others the topography was so gentle that it was essentially porous to traffic. Such areas had to be carefully monitored.

A major source of auxiliaries under Augustus was Gaul, where the sons and grandsons of former enemies redirected their ancestors' military traditions to Roman needs. After a few generations, however, Gauls progressively showed less and less interest in the army as a career. Nonetheless, there were individual recruits from Gaul. Some continued to show up in legions in North Africa and Spain throughout the first century, while others joined local auxiliary forces regardless of the original ethnic composition of these units. In many cases there seems to have been an interim between conquest and the organization of auxiliary garrisons. During this period local militias from the indigenous populations under their own native leaders kept the peace. But this relative laxity ended in A.D. 69, when various Batavians under Iulius Civilis rose in revolt. Following the suppression of this revolt, militia units were absorbed into an expanded auxiliary system with all units commanded by a

Roman of equestrian rank. The defeated Batavians provided several units to the auxiliary, and they carried their ethnic name as a part of their unit identification to their new duty assignments in Britain and the Balkans. Those in Britain support Agricola's pacification efforts there.

The assignment of newly raised units elsewhere was standard practice, although hardly popular with the men. In the West, to hazard a generalization, there was some effort made to raise replacements in or near the original areas from which the unit had been constituted. The ties that some men maintained with their families and friends back home may have aided this. New arrivals from their former homelands would, for a time at least, have also facilitated unit coherence.[14] Such recruitment was often impractical from the beginning because of the scarcity of men in the original area or the difficulty in getting them to their comrades far distant. By the opening of the second century, most retirees were replaced by locals from the area of the camps, and this trend came to dominate recruitment henceforth. A successful career meant making it to the centurionate, and that meant being regularly posted to different units in the course of your career. Even a soldier whose military career had not been so bright would have acquired numerous marketable skills while laboring in various tasks of construction and supply, and this independence of the military grew steadily. Major engineering projects always required at least military engineers and usually specialized work details assigned from the regular units. Such work also provided jobs for civilian laborers in the vicinity, both citizens and barbarians, upon whose resources the army and the closely related civil government depended for routine maintenance of the infrastructure.

As long as militias were commanded by their native leaders, the men needed little or no Latin, but once they were placed under Roman commanders they had the same need for Latin as the legionnaires. Roman recruiters could afford to be selective, because they needed only about six thousand new legionnaires and a comparable number for the auxiliaries each year. Legionnaires had to pass a rigorous physical examination and had to know enough Latin so as to understand their commanders. The standards for the auxiliaries were less stringent.[15] It seems that some recruitment areas were preferred, whereas others were avoided, apparently until their inhabitants had proved themselves trustworthy.[16] As Roman citizenship spread among the native populations more and more, recruiters for the auxiliary enlisted citizens, perhaps by offering them the same pay and status as legionnaires. The less developed areas, typically those bypassed by major Roman roads and urban development, long remained fertile grounds for Roman recruiters once their pacification could be taken for granted. The interior of the Balkans was such an area and within it especially Thrace,[17] but little by little everywhere the most important group was the sons of veterans who had grown up in sight of the camps and understood the military career as insiders. As external barbarians became more familiar with the life of the camps, they too sought careers in the Roman army.

The role of the auxiliaries in the process of Romanization cannot be overemphasized. Roman citizenship was a privilege and very difficult to obtain. Service as an auxiliary was the surest way for an individual to secure the citizenship, and statistically it was the most significant factor in expanding the citizenry. Otherwise citizenship status was usually a matter of residence in a Roman town—that is, in a *colonia,* originally established as a colony to settle veterans and other citizens, or as a *municipia* with its important Roman elements of the population, especially merchants, and with its second-echelon urban status (legally, Latin rights). Rarely an individual was granted citizenship for other than military service, for this was carefully reserved for members of the native aristocracy. Auxiliary service was much the best of these alternatives. Annually, as individual auxiliaries reached retirement, they were honored by their commanders before the unit, awarded their discharge, and enrolled as Roman citizens, unless they already held the honor.

Citizens in the early empire were distinguished by their Roman trinomial name, which every new citizen needed to have. Often they took the name of their commanding officer, the governor, or the emperor, whomever it seems they believed responsible for their good fortune to have survived to retirement. Their certificate of service (*diploma*) or grave inscription might also indicate their original name with an ethnic affiliation often standing in place of the traditional Roman town of origin because many of these men had not been born in towns or necessarily within the empire. Those veterans of the auxiliaries who had joined as citizens kept their own throughout. Comparing the numbers of those assuming new names with those already having a Roman one provides some indication of the evolution of auxiliary recruitment as well as the expansion of the citizenry in the areas of the camps over the course of the first two centuries A.D.

Whether most newcomers held on to their birth names was up to them as was the choice and use of a cognomen that revealed an ethnic connection—until, that is a noncitizen soldier retired and had to choose a trinomial Roman name. Otherwise freedom of choice had always been true except for slaves. Slaves were occasionally named for their geographic origin as well as their ethnic group, and this practice continued through the fourth century—for example, Suebus Germanus or the twelve-year-old boy Gaepidius Theodorus remembered by his mother, a domestic slave.[18] Roman soldiers taking up with Germanic women could produce complex naming patterns. An inscription from Virunum, capital of Noricum, probably dating to the later part of the second century records the death of one Vibennius Primitius, whose mother was Quintilla Peucina. The name Peucina suggests that she was from the Peucini, the people of Peuce, and that she used this identity as her nickname. Her daughter, Vibennius's sister, was Auicia, similarly not Latin in origin and perhaps Germanic. The father was Primitius, probably a Roman soldier, whose consort went by the fittingly Roman name Quintilla but was apparently known in the family as Peucina.[19] In a different context, a son might wish to recall his father, who had gone by an ethnic name, and thereby link himself to this ancestral group as well.[20] If your Germanic parents gave you a Latin birth name, occasions such as their funerary monument might be an appropriate place to note an old tribal identification in the place where more Latinized Romans might have chosen a place of birth. In such cases we would otherwise never suspect Germanic parentage.[21]

By the end of the second century many auxiliary units were

drawing their recruits overwhelmingly from among local citizens. This useful source of information ends rapidly after the extension of citizenship by Caracalla in A.D. 212. The commanding officer handed each new veteran a certificate, a small scroll recording his Roman name and declaring him to be a citizen, in front of the assembled unit. Bronze plaques with the same information as on the scrolls were kept on display in the unit, and the names of the veterans were incised on the registry of citizens in Rome itself. In times of extreme emergency recourse still had to be made to conscription and then even slaves were enrolled, especially it seems among the auxiliaries, yet these occasions were truly exceptional. Roman leaders were extremely reluctant to turn to slaves, and even when they did recruit them, they may have manumitted them first.[22]

We can still see some of these men proudly holding their discharge certificates on grave monuments across the empire. In theory a citizen could join an auxiliary unit, but there would have been no point in sacrificing pay and especially status in doing so. As long as there were vacancies in a legion, they would have directed themselves there, but already by the middle of the second century there was a flow of citizens into the auxiliary units as well. This was a result of the fact that by then a high percentage, perhaps the majority of recruits, were the sons of veterans. These young men may have wished to join their fathers' former units even though they were auxiliary. Their fathers had probably retired near their last duty station as citizens, moving directly into positions of honor and responsibility.[23] Their sons too would have been citizens, even if born before their father's retirement. One of the most attractive features of auxiliary service was that upon retirement, the soldier's domestic partner became his legal wife and their children became citizens. Distinctions between auxiliary and legionnaire, and between legally recognized domestic partners and wives, disappeared with the third-century legislation extending citizenship.

On the other hand, all barbarians were noncitizens and so were potential recruits for the auxiliaries. The fact that few noncitizens came from outside the provinces in the early empire is probably due to their lack of proximity to the Roman garrisons rather than the result of any policy. As provincial governments evolved largely out of the army command system, and then later in parallel to the army, their need for territorial definition created a geographic distinction between barbarians and nonbarbarian, noncitizen provincials that seems implicit in the literary sources at our disposal. Just as in the case of Caesar's commentaries, our literary sources for the Principate manipulate "barbarian" within accepted traditions as was determined by the genre in which their authors chose to work. In the provinces, Roman governors established and maintained foci—concentrations of Roman citizens and development—often intruding upon preexisting patterns of exchange, indigenous material culture, and native religion. The support given these centers made them irrepressible agents of change, but, in changing others, they were themselves changed. The Roman army often led the way, both the relatively small auxiliary units, which secured the infrastructure of the new territories, and the concentrated fighting and economic power of the legions. Although the Roman army was remarkably standardized, there was room for local variance even within it. For example, the god Jupiter was portrayed as a mounted horseman only in the German provinces (Germania Superior, Inferior, and Raetia). Except in rare cases, no such dynamic foci of Roman influence existed beyond the immediate area of the *limes* itself. This made for a much slower adaptation to Roman culture among the external barbarians than among those elements of the provincial population in close contact with Roman military and administrative centers.

Legionary camps were vast, self-sufficient communities housing over five thousand men with granaries, carefully engineered latrines, a hospital, barracks, a large house for the commander, and a headquarters building. The headquarters structure housed the cult shrine of the emperor, the treasury, and an audience hall where court-martials took place. Nearby was that sine qua non of Roman civility, a bath. The baths depended upon a supply of firewood, which had to be seasoned, often within the bath complex itself, to assure maximum dryness and a minimum of soot. The result of all this building and maintenance was a widening belt of deforestation, which as it grew beyond the immediate area of the camp served also to expand the area of arable land.[24]

There was extremely little variation in the original layouts of the legionary camps, and their outlines held throughout the camps' long occupancies, despite the gradual accumulation of local features, until the major reorganizations of the army during the fourth century. A sleepwalker recently arrived from afar would have been able to navigate his way from his barracks to the hospital without difficulty, whether in Gaul, Spain, or Syria. Similar architectural regularity prevailed among the far more numerous auxiliary camps, which usually housed five hundred men and sometimes up to one thousand, in scaled down versions of the legionary facilities. At some camps this insistence on regularity could have led to some rather comical scenes, which of course no records mention. Take the second-century auxiliary fortress at Abusina (Eining in Bavaria), for example. There the carefully built north gate opened directly into a ravine, a drop of many meters; the unwary would suffer a similar fate at Intercisa (Dunaújváros) in Hungary. Naturally these gates were rarely, if ever, opened. They were built nonetheless. In the early empire the auxiliary camps were established to monitor the population and protect important transportation points such as bridges, roads, and ferry crossings, and so were distributed over the province. Roman towns like Roman camps were laid out in a grid system whenever possible, but for towns this plan sometimes had to accommodate preexisting construction features, particularly when built over Celtic or Dacian centers.

As you entered a Roman town you likely passed by rows of personal monuments to the departed ancestors buried there, those closest to the street rising highest. They catch your attention with images of the deceased or ornately carved mythical figures and floral decoration. On almost every monument there is an inscription. The streets are at right angles and the main ones are paved with cut stone; livestock is not free to roam, and the dominant smells are those of men and women working in shops. Most people are wearing clothing made from professionally woven fabric. Public spaces display stone statues of the emperor, and temples dot the landscape. People gather at the public fountains to chat and draw fresh water for the day. Learning to navigate in a Roman town largely depended on recalling the location of these public areas. Within a short time after the conquest of a new territory, a few such urban centers rapidly took shape, thereby changing the lives and patterns of commerce of everybody throughout the region.

There is no sign, however, that there was much actual migration to towns from the rural areas, and town size grew slowly. Other than the initial settlement of veterans in colonies, the Roman government did nothing to encourage Romans to leave Italy or the Mediterranean provinces. A town adjacent to a legionary campus had *collegia* of citizens dedicated to supporting its legion that could be counted on to guide local youth into military service. Rather than luring farmers from Italy, provincial towns attracted members of the indigenous ruling elites, and these helped them dominate local and then regional markets by employing local craftsmen to produce for Roman tastes and by drawing upon their family and client networks in the countryside. The influence of Roman building styles drifted into the countryside and in some areas beyond the frontiers, where stone dwellings were becoming more common by the second half of the century, at least among the Marcomanni.[25]

The cumulative effect that these carefully controlled urban spaces had upon barbarians, whether as rustic provincials or as visitors from beyond the empire, must have been dramatic. One need not stretch the imagination to see how the net result of plan and decoration served to indoctrinate newcomers into the ideology of the governing classes. Visitors and recent immigrants had little choice but to react to the recurring images of order and authority all around them without necessarily agreeing with specific rulers or policies. The consistency of imperial ideology as conveyed through architecture, public inscriptions, and coins would have acted to precondition conquered populations to accept the normal demands of local tax collectors, customs officers, and governmental administrators, in much the same way that modern advertising affects our own choice of products. Various written materials on public display, ranging from official pronouncements to the private eulogies on grave stele, also brought home to the observer the need to read Latin or, in the eastern Balkans, Greek.

Everywhere, starting with their purses, were reminders of local and imperial patronage. Every coin from a western mint broadcast the likeness of the emperor or a member of his family. The cities of the eastern provinces continued striking their own bronze coins—the currency of daily commerce—until that privilege was withdrawn during the third century. Yet even in the East silver and gold bore the imperial portrait, each a not too subtle reminder of the economic prosperity brought about by the policies of the supreme patron, the emperor. The standardization of Roman coinage and its convertibility within the trimetallic system were first implemented by Augustus with the approval of the Senate, as the SC (*Senatus Consulto*) on bronze coins attested throughout Roman history. The uniformity of coinage, particularly in the West, underscored the permanency of Roman rule both to those within and beyond the provinces.[26] Official statues of the emperor adorned public space, so that even the illiterate would feel his radiance. There was an obvious lack of enthusiasm in some communities for imperial statuary—for example, imperial busts with a hollowed-out space to insert the reigning emperor's head, which were cost-effective although aesthetically inept. Passersby took the imperial office for granted.

If war came, the concentration of population and matériel in towns gave Roman authorities an important advantage over their barbarian opponents, just as these same urban resources presented an irresistible cultural force in peacetime. Neither the towns nor the camps had very stout defensive walls, because it was assumed that military intelligence would allow the Roman forces to sally forth and confront any enemy on chosen ground, hopefully on barbarian ground. By centering their taxation upon towns, first in the Mediterranean provinces, and spending the revenues primarily upon the army, which in turn was itself a prime consumer of urban manufactured goods, the emperors nourished the recirculation of wealth that was a major source of imperial economic strength. Just as the army funneled recruits into new cultural encounters, so towns did for those in the countryside. Almost everywhere camps spurred urban development nearby. Roads linked all.

In contrast to Roman towns, native centers in pre-Roman Europe, except for the southern fringes of Celtic *oppida* civilization, consisted of a single street winding its way between two poorly defined rows of houses. There were no politically charged symbols, nothing that would pass as a public square, no statues, except for personal votive offerings to the gods. Even these were modest, often made of wood, and were most frequently used in or near cult centers lying some distance outside the settlements. In the lands remaining beyond Roman control, this life-style never changed regardless whether inside the provinces or in the lands beyond. Towards the end of their independence from Roman rule the greatest of the indigenous Celtic proto-urban centers manifested signs of direct Roman craftsmanship or minimally, Roman influence. But even on the eve of conquest there were no public inscriptions, and most communities lacked public buildings and a central public focus. Excavators mostly discover disturbances in the soil—postholes, garbage pits, burials, and the like—and the small items of everyday life.

Occasionally graves offer better insights into the changes going on among the living and provide us with some early indications of the directions and depth of Roman influence. Signs of animal husbandry abound, making it likely that livestock ran freely in most hamlets and villages, squealing pigs and chickens everywhere underfoot. Barnyard odors would have permeated everything and everybody. The fears among the conquered populations immediately following their military defeat were short-lived but genuine. The Roman historian Tacitus, writing at the end of the first century of his father-in-law Agricola, one of the greatest generals of his age, had little difficulty putting their foreboding into words through the voice of the defeated British chief, Calgacus: "Robbers of the world, having by their universal plunder exhausted the land, they rifle the deep. If the enemy be rich, they are rapacious; if he be poor, they lust for dominion; neither the east nor the west has been able to satisfy them. Alone among men they covet with equal eagerness poverty and riches. To robbery, slaughter, plunder, they give the lying name of empire; they make a solitude and call it peace."[27]

Tacitus was only slightly less compelling, but much less rhetorical, when he outlined the fruits that Rome extended to the conquered: foremost was peace, which brought with it access to the international community through Latin, public monuments, urban refinements, and usually dependable government. A sign of their acceptance for Tacitus was their abandonment of their native dress—at least among the ruling classes—in favor of Roman fashions, love of the baths and Roman cuisine, and their eagerness to learn Latin.[28] The physical legacy of this process can still be traced in the archaeological record and mirrors that already discussed for southern Gaul. What Tacitus does not say is that these transformations usually took generations to be complete, that there were many halfway measures along the way, and that none of them was required for admission. Tacitus, like many Roman authors, is morally ambivalent towards the suffering of non-Romans experiencing Roman conquest. In much the same way, Vergil had expressed no sorrow for the death of Turnus at the hands of Aeneas. In Roman literature, the price of Roman destiny was barbarian suffering: Roman honor rested upon barbarian submission to the Roman will. The inevitability of one was confirmed by the loss of freedom by the other. In this nothing had changed since Julius Caesar had invented dialogues on freedom and honor for Ariovistus and Vercingetorix. The Roman literary world could not accept otherwise, nor could it acknowledge that the alleged cornucopia of the empire seduced only some. Once again the literary tradition diverges from the historical. In fact, some of the conquered—either because they were isolated from Roman influences or because their identities depended upon resistance to Roman values—did not go over to Rome, and they were free to so choose.

About the only change that Rome insisted upon was political and military subordination. The conquered could not maintain an independent political system, violate Roman law, or raise arms against Rome, but otherwise they were free to pursue their customs. Indeed, Roman law guaranteed their rights to do so. In their recent past, able-bodied men were expected to rush to defend their villages from attack, but after the conquests the imperial government held a monopoly on the use of violence. Roman authorities moved swiftly whenever possible to disarm the new provincials, sometimes causing much unrest in so doing.[29] Roman citizens went about their lives unarmed and untrained in their use. After a decade or two, sometimes a while longer, the imperial army was unchallenged within the provinces. The old displays of prowess that continued to characterize and limit barbarian warfare had no place within the empire. Traditional religions were safe so long as they could accommodate appropriate honors paid to the emperor. Native languages remained viable, although generally unrecorded, throughout the imperial centuries. In an obvious rhetorical flourish Tacitus notes how soon men clamored to wear the toga, meaning that they sought the citizenship, but none was forced to abandon their dress codes in its favor. An immediate result of Roman conquest was that the recently purged barbarian elites were strengthened. Preexisting family networks were routinely tapped by all parties in antiquity, and it would seem that in many cases leading Celtic families redoubled their efforts within and beyond the new Roman provinces, particularly in regard to trade, by capitalizing on their influential positions inside the empire. Many of these twists and turns are demonstrable in the provinces as well as from the areas left outside direct Roman jurisdiction by charting the distribution of Roman goods in the archaeological record. Modern theoretical explanations, however, vary considerably. The full import of what the speech of Calgacus only hints at is that for the old governing classes they could continue to play politics in the wings much as they long had, while they adjusted to the new game played by Roman rules and for Roman rewards. The ordinary conquered barbarians had fewer choices but even less compulsion. Those who now faced Rome not as their master but as their neighbor had different choices.

Rome continued to admit carefully selected barbarians into its territory, a process begun much earlier and nicely illustrated for us by the actions of Julius Caesar in Gaul. These admissions were completely at the discretion of the emperor, but they were a regular process along the frontiers. Just as when an auxiliary soldier received the citizenship, external barbarians were rewarded for good service. Barbarian groups surely realized that by upholding their treaties, serving as allies, welcoming Roman recruiters, and supporting their native leaders whom Rome placed over them, they in all likelihood greatly increased their chances of being allowed to settle in the empire. Sometimes their admission was a part of a Roman effort to reorganize the client system along the frontiers. At other times, the timing of barbarian admissions was linked to the emperor's need to manifest the traditional virtues of Roman rule. No barbarians forced their admission upon an unwilling Roman government.

Augustus admitted groups of barbarians into the empire almost as soon as he decided to follow in his father's footsteps. As early as 38 B.C. Augustus, acting through his chief lieutenant Marcus Agrippa, granted the request of the Ubii to shift their settlements to the left side of the Rhine, where they were allowed to remain together under their traditional leaders. In 8 B.C. another major admission of barbarians took place on the Rhine when perhaps tens of thousands, recognized by Rome as being from two groups, the Suebi and Sugambri, were resettled. Shortly thereafter another major resettlement took place along the Danube in present-day Bulgaria, this time of certain Dacians. The Ubii, Suebi, and Sugambri were groups well known to Caesar. The Ubii were peculiar in that they had so clearly manifested the blending of cultural characteristics along the Rhine downstream from its confluence with the Mosel, where they lived in *oppida.* Both Sugambri and Ubii had by this time lived peacefully as Rome's neighbors for half a century. Such long-docile barbarians were scarcely ever denied permission to settle inside the empire.

In fact, given the nature of Roman literary genres, which would have turned almost any Roman invitation into a barbarian request, it is likely that even as early as Augustus, Rome encouraged such resettlement as a solution to various economic and recruitment factors no longer to be ascertained. For generation after generation, Roman literary texts, inscriptions, and coinage consistently repeated images of humbled and dejected barbarians, grasping the knees of their conquerors. Normally they did this in the presence of the insignia of the Roman army, and just as often reference is made to whole families seeking and being admitted. By such traditional testament, Roman leaders announced to their own people that all was well along the frontiers. The honor of Rome stood radiant within their virtuous—in the Roman sense of the term—

hands. We are left to wonder how those living out their lives in the provinces received such declarations.[30]

The creation of such barbarian enclaves took place throughout Roman history and seems to have accelerated after the Roman army moved to the frontiers,[31] but there was no period in which emperors and their provincial governors did not extol their own eminence by acclaiming their admission of barbarians. Such a reception of barbarians by Plautius Silvanus, governor of Moesia under Nero, is known from an inscription set up to honor his accomplishments. This document demonstrates that admissions could be handled at the provincial level as early as the first century. Not only did Silvanus extol the fact that he had received whole families from those living across the Danube, a rather common declaration, but he stressed that he had even extended the client network to include peoples hitherto unknown.[32] His efforts to remind his audience that he had both continued policy and extended it to new peoples were already a time-honored tradition, so there is little novelty in his inscription except that an announcement of such expansions of foreign clientage was typically an imperial prerogative, as Silvanus well knew. Like the Greeks before them, Romans first ruled people; then they dealt with land. Land without people was of no concern, and the proven way to rule people was through patron-client relationships, which, although they clearly conveyed superiority and inferiority, nonetheless were honorable and reciprocal. Thus ceremonially defeated barbarians, once received into the empire or accepted as foreign allies, replaced their subjection with obligation.

One of the most attractive career paths for any newly "humbled and received barbarian" was to fight for Rome as an auxiliary soldier, where coincidentally he would have no choice but to learn to live like a Roman. At this early stage Roman commanders concentrated their efforts at pacification upon individuals and small groups. Their wisdom in doing so reflects the realities of most barbarian societies at this time. Few if any had durable political systems that could galvanize actions requiring a leader to organize beyond the local level. The Marcomanni, for example, were too amorphous for Roman commanders to try to deploy them against others even after their long involvement with Rome. The Roman objective was to keep barbarians in place, relatively peaceful, and under leaders who could guarantee compliance to the obligations set forth by their treaties made with Rome. Naturally enough, Roman diplomacy took the form of a patron dealing with clients, but with one noteworthy difference from the days of the republic.

In the frontier provinces Roman commanders-governors progressively acted as their positions as imperial legates suggested. They acted in the place of the emperor, not so much as individuals but as officials, albeit without adequate staffing other than the personnel whom they could detach from the army. These military governors sought to play the role of a counterweight that could swing the balance of power among local populations by quiet manipulation and occasional armed intervention. In these dealings the emperorship replaced the Senate as the corporate entity to which *obsequium et reverentia* were due. Obligations owed to men like Julius Caesar in the previous century were no longer appropriate, although it is likely that few barbarians understood such abstract concepts as loyalty to the office rather than to the officeholder and his family.

Being servants of the imperial family, albeit very rich ones, was not an easy transition for Roman aristocrats to make, but learn it they did. By the middle of the first century A.D., Roman commanders were rotated through commands of escalating importance and opportunity in a relatively systematic way. They did not spend their careers in one province. The paths of career advancement became more sharply defined over time. The division between senatorial and imperial provinces was one of the consequences of Augustus taking on proconsular *imperium* in 27 B.C. and thereby accepting the command of all provinces in which legions were billeted through his delegates (*legati*). During most of the Principate a man of military merit, usually proven on the field of valor, shifted back and forth from civil honors—that is, traditional office as prescribed by the senatorial *cursus honorum,* to military commands in the imperial provinces. Normally he would command the same legion for several years before taking over as governor somewhere else. Some never made the transition.

Eventually those provinces with one legion were under a military governor of praetorian rank, and those provinces in which two or more legions were stationed received a man of consular rank. Thus at the official public level the perpetuation of an intertwined civil and military was assured. Election to the praetorship and consulship was still accomplished in the Senate, although the emperor could and did intervene whenever he felt it necessary to appoint somebody to command who had not yet held the appropriate senatorial offices. This submergence of the civilian under the military was the image of government that all barbarians, internal or external, witnessed, so that during the Principate there was not a single source of Roman influence, although the military was primary.

Tacitus, himself a senator, reveals to us how an illustrious man such as his father-in-law Agricola could pursue an honorable career even in the service of an unworthy emperor such as Domitian. Just as the Stoic philosopher-emperor Marcus Aurelius (A.D. 161–80) would write three generations later, Tacitus (ca. A.D. 100) teaches that one must accept his lot, do the best with what fate bestows upon you. Do not seek power beyond your station. Despite the accolades shed upon its subject, the *Agricola* leaves the reader with a bitter taste because of Tacitus's inability to accept that Domitian had never made Agricola governor of the lucrative senatorial consular province of Asia. Asia was the obvious capstone for the glorious career of a man who had successfully commanded four Roman legions and restored Roman governance to Britain. Agricola, who had accomplished so much, particularly in Britain, and who had never challenged the imperial right to rule, was never accorded the ultimate acknowledgment by his emperor. In the grand sweep of imperial government even great men were subordinate to the demands of state, rapidly replaced by others willing to shoulder their tasks. Similarly, first-century barbarian leaders such as Calgacus and Maroboduus were transitory figures. For them too a door to imperial service stood open, although it was not as wide as for Agricola. It read "soldier." Both the extent of the individual sublimation and the opportunities that it opened up for individuals, barbarian or Roman, had yet to be worked out when Mark Antony and Octavian struggled for hegemony. The army of the Principate began only after their civil war had ended. This new force was never intended solely as an army of occupation and defense, for it existed at least as much to support the emperor's domestic persona.

In the defeat and subjugation of barbarians, real or exaggerated, the Roman government justified itself in the eyes of its own citizens. Indeed, from the time of Augustus, victory over the barbarians was a principal standard against which emperors and therefore governments were evaluated. Augustus himself was able to survive defeat at the Teutoburg Forest, but it is no wonder that the legend of his being awakened by a recurring nightmare, screaming "Varus, Varus, give me back my legions," found sympathetic readers throughout much of Roman history. Emperors did not have to always win battles, but they could not lose wars. Nor could they lose control of their army to rivals. In A.D. 17, eight years after the disaster in the Teutoburg Forest, the heir apparent Germanicus restored Roman pride by returning the last of the legionary standards lost by Varus, but the loss of what had almost become a province remained a bitter memory.[33] Despite the permanent loss of Germania, emperors of the Principate perpetuated an aurora of invincibility against barbarians, and celebrating victories over barbarians was an essential part of defining successful emperorship, just as it had played a central role in defining individual greatness in the republic among the elite families.[34]

Augustus himself spent little time in fighting barbarians, but took credit for their submission nonetheless. Like his father Julius Caesar, Augustus was proud to be honored as *pater patriae,* father of his country, which traditionally had acknowledged one's paternal-like protection of and generosity to the people.[35] Such an honor itself reflects the mentality of Romans towards barbarians. There were many threats to the Roman people, but none so reliable as the barbarian, ever ready to undermine the Roman state through invasion. Real victory could only be claimed over outsiders. Tiberius had already fought his battles against barbarians before succeeding Augustus on the throne, and so he never again had to take to the field. His successor Gaius (Caligula, A.D. 37–41) conducted no campaigns worthy of the name but took appropriate credit nonetheless.[36] Claudius fell into the conquest of Britain when his tinkering with the Caesarian client system there came to naught. Thus even before the death of the last Julio-Claudian emperor, Nero in A.D. 68, barbarians had been reduced to a single uniform element in early imperial iconography and probably in popular psychology. They were all the same, homogenized, because their presence served one purpose—the demonstration of imperial *virtus*. Otherwise they were either conquered and thus submissive or lived far away in lands scarcely realized and even more poorly understood. The inevitable result of the Roman political need for validation by victory reached dizzying heights of self-aggrandizement in the third century, when actual victories were rare. But this tendency is already apparent in the first emperors.

Augustus was able to build on his legacy as the son of the conqueror of Gaul to earn his fame as the third founder of Rome. The "barbarians" again provided their assistance and in the process began to lose their individuality, at least in propaganda. Men like Pompey and Julius Caesar had emphasized their personal triumphs over barbarians in very specific and highly personal ways. There are no dialogues in the literature for Augustus like those between Caesar and Ariovistus and Vercingetorix, for there is no attempt to fashion a similarly personal counterpoise between himself and barbarian leaders. Instead Augustus preferred to list masses of barbarians conquered and to connect himself with the legends of earlier saviors of the city through complex allusions to the Boii and Cimbri. Combined, the literary and nonliterary materials relating to Augustus reveal an important psychological evolution within the political leadership in keeping with the transition from the late republic to the early empire—the public reduction of traditional aristocratic virtues to a set of iconographically manageable and simplistic entities. Victory over barbarians was one of these entities. By the end of his dynasty, taking the field against real barbarians was no longer required. "The barbarians" were, of course, not uniform. Not even the northern barbarians could so easily be poured into one mold, but the subtle differences in their material goods, domestic economies, and political leadership appear to have been largely irrelevant to Romans, at least to their government.

In justifying its source, imperial propaganda portrayed all barbarians within a very few fixed categories of representation. For example, regardless of whether they lived along the Danube or the Rhine, or were highly urbanized opponents in the East, barbarians were always depicted on Roman coins and public monuments in postures of submission, typically lying on the ground or kneeling, bound and with their weapons hung as a trophy or symbolically broken and lying on the ground around them.[37] Portraying victory over barbarians could be still further simplified to include only the captured weapons without a single human form being presented.[38] In noting Roman victories, barbarian figures lost their humanity even when visually depicted, because they were often used to personify the territories conquered rather than the specific peoples defeated. This emphasis on territory rather than subjects became apparent towards the end of the *Gallic War* as Julius Caesar sought to limit his campaigns and return home. By creating a workable cultural definition for "Germans" and simultaneously fixing their abode as beyond the Rhine, Caesar had linked two aspects of barbarian to a single geographic zone, which did not in fact exist. The early empire took up where Caesar had left off.

Augustan and early imperial iconography reveals a host of such groups of non-Romans (that is, barbarians) similar at least iconographically to Caesar's Germans. These barbarians lived in lands on the edges of the empire. In addition to the Germans there were Dacians, Parthians, Nabateans, and many others. The level of political development of these peoples was irrelevant to inclusion in this category or to the nature of their depiction. "Germans" had no political, economic, or military unity. In other words, "Germans" did not exist as a people, but already "they" had been made into a rhetorical subcategory within "barbarians," and, like the others, they were accorded a general geographic location. But during the first century that territory had been greatly expanded intellectually from the Rhinish confines developed by Caesar for the Suebi and their clients into a vast cultural and demographic assemblage bordering Roman lands throughout central Europe. In contrast to the vaguely defined barbarian "Germans" stood the barbarian Parthians, who were highly sophisticated culturally and politically, and who were serious competitors to the Roman Empire in the East. All were barbarians. So, for example, a coin of Domitian celebrates his victories over the Germans as GERMANIA CAPTA, Germany taken, and one of Marcus Aurelius celebrating a victory in an entirely different region shows a captive German on the reverse and recalls GERMANIA SVBACTA, Germany subdued, not Germans conquered.[39] Roman numismatic practice thus articulated general barbarian territories and personified them in a highly standardized way. This custom of ignoring the specific groups against whom battles were really waged in favor of generic proclamations of victory began with Augustus.

These standard images also reveal the convergence of land and people—territory and personalities—that is at the core of most human societies, including Roman. Ruling people through personal links such as clientage had considerable positive features, which were never entirely abandoned. There were real limits to how much control the new governing class could exert through such means because of the fact that the preexisting alliances upon which they were based were hopelessly complex. Being based upon family marriage patterns going back generations, they were slow to change and even slower to expand. Most of these familial alliances in pre-Roman times were quite limited geographically, although some elite families traded and occasionally intermarried with families far afield. With the very slender administrative means available to the early emperors, it was probably inevitable that the empire moved from ruling diverse people to governing territories.

In stressing that ultimate allegiance was owed to the officers of the state over and above individual and family, the government was merely institutionalizing and extending to the provinces what was in Roman opinion one of the central characteristics of a healthy society. Roman government, however, long remained highly personal even at the very top despite the rhetoric and institutional claims; emperors spent much of their time hearing and responding to petitions from individuals, including delegations from foreign states, and various interest groups in the cities of the empire. Ruling people was challenging, yet governing the land too had restrictions determined by the people who lived there. Provinces were Rome's administrative solution inside the empire; creating and supporting client states to rule specified territories was the Roman response to government beyond the provinces. There was not much difference between how foreign and domestic business was conducted at court. As in the iconography, when, dealing with barbarians, the land and the people who lived on it were ultimately inseparable.

Because every person in the empire carried coins, everyone held cognitive cues revealing barbarians living all around them. Thus while imperial iconography emphasized the general quality of victory, it indirectly served as an intellectual device for ordering the world into large geographic blocks populated by Romans at the center and surrounded by barbarians. Or to look at it another way, "the empire without end" was nonetheless developing a sense of bounded self-interest. The point here is that coins and monuments, although dealing with fictive units of barbarian life, including hypothetical aggregates such as German—nevertheless manifested the same tendency to territorialize barbarians that we see most clearly in contemporary written sources, particularly in Tacitus's *Germania.*

Tacitus created a cultural subtext that linked the hypothetical category, the territory of the Germans, to various military opponents thought to be living there or to have lived there. His treatise combines literary traditions of ethnography and geography, many already old in the day of Julius Caesar, with insights that may have been based on the experience of his contemporaries and perhaps even his own.[40] In the *Germania* each barbarian group has its home territory where it manifests in its own peculiar way "Germanic characteristics." Those living nearest Rome were more dependent, less purely barbarian, in contrast to those who were still isolated from foreign contact. According to Tacitus two types of leadership were present among all Germans: leadership in war (that of the duke, *duces*) and sacral leadership bridging man and the gods (the leadership of kings, *reges*). The *duces* were chosen because of their prowess in battle; *reges* because of their blood.[41]

In the detailed discussion that follows his survey of general Germanic qualities, Tacitus makes it clear that only military leadership had survived among those closest to Rome and that only those farthest away were still ruled purely by sacral kings. In between were gradients of leadership as in all else. In each geographic area the barbarians living there had something to distinguish them: weaponry, subtle and not so subtle religious differences, mannerisms, and so on. Rome gets credit or blame for transforming barbarian purity into militant clientage and cultural dependence among those closest to its borders and weakening the vigor of those farther away in direct relationship to distance and contact. Under such influence, sacral kingship had given way almost everywhere. For example, "The Marcomanni and the Quadi retained kings [*reges*] of their own race down to our time—the noble houses of Maroboduus and Tudrus: now they submit to foreign kings also; but the force and power of the kings rest on the influence of Rome. Occasionally they are assisted by our armed intervention: more often by subsidies, out of which they get as much help."[42] Directly behind these Roman pawns lived people influenced indirectly but nonetheless significantly, real Germans by language and culture and "non-Germans" alike. Among the latter were the Cotini, who were said to speak a Gallic tongue and to be working iron mines, much to the discredit of their claims to be real Germans, who in their purest form had no concept of monetary exchange. Near the Cotini were the Osi, who spoke Pannonian. Both were weak, paying tribute to Sarmatians and Quadi.[43] Truth or fiction?

The *Germania* is foremost an ethnographic treatise, secondly a didactic device, and only marginally historical. Nonetheless, Tacitus's descriptions of the empire's immediate neighbors are better informed than his fanciful stories of those living in the interior. Whether any barbarians lived under purely sacral kings is an open question, but there can be no doubt that there was a belief among Celts and Germans that once upon a time such kings existed. It was thus up to the war kings who followed them to rekindle their divinely sanctioned leadership and in so doing unite their extended people once again. So ran myth and so sought kings. A constant interplay existed on either side of reality: a mythical divine kingship in the past and the goal to revive it in the future. Indeed, it is not hard to find historical examples of barbarians trying to move beyond being war leaders, the man of the hour so to speak. The first step was creating a dynasty, and the next and far more challenging was for subsequent generations to secure as their birthright the mythical position of the sacral kings without necessarily abandoning the position of chief warlord. The tension between myth and real life was an especially significant and creative element among the so-called barbarian kingdoms, which succeeded to power during the fifth century A.D., but it can be seen from time to time much earlier.[44]

When combined, the extant literary, monumental, and numismatic data reveal that the Romans gradually and unconsciously superimposed a territorial understanding of empire upon the earlier one achieved by the extension of patronage circles, and in this way the concepts of barbarian and Roman were themselves changed. What is so surprising to modern readers is how Roman authors placed legend and reality side by side with so little concern to distinguish between them. Only conquest produced real knowledge of the barbarian world, but then it ceased to be barbarian. Thus conceptually the barbarians were forever retreating from Roman understanding. They occupied the land between the unknown and known. External to these administrative boundaries Roman rule remained as always, gray and paternal, but eternal and infinite nonetheless.

Provinces were the territories accorded governors to administer for the Roman people, and in that sense they were geographically fixed. The creation and perpetuation of culturally and spatially prescribed barbarians in vaguely understood areas bounding the empire occurred as Rome first organized and defended its provinces beyond the Mediterranean littoral. Because this also preceded by at least a century the development of provincial bureaucracies, one result was that the Roman government was able to define levels of dominance in terms of territory while continuing to conduct daily intercourse with various barbarians according to the well-trodden pathways linking patrons and clients. This twofold awareness of barbarians is hardly surprising. Ancients were used to bracketing their world with a characteristic result being that there were often two places bearing the same name, one east the other west, one north and the other south, as the great circular world of myth doubled back on itself. When ancient explorers and settlers traveled to distant spots, they named the new physical landscapes in keeping with mythical nomenclature. Thus, for example, there were two Iberias: one Iberia in the area of the modern Republic of Georgia, the other being the more familiar Iberian peninsula. But rather than bound the known world in the sense of closing it off, the territorialization of barbarians created an intellectual membrane within which lay Roman society and culture. Like all membranes this one was porous and transparent. Beyond it lived barbarians, each academically assigned to a region of the world at large with its features leaving each group different than the others.

By the end of the first century A.D. this membrane began to stiffen as troop concentrations and colonies were established in some areas: for example, along parts of the Rhine, particularly at Cologne (Colonia Agrippinensis, founded in A.D. 50 under Claudius and named in honor of his wife) and between the upper Rhine and Danube Rivers where Domitian sought to rationalize the frontier. The Flavian dynasty, particularly Domitian, also engaged Roman troops along the lower and middle Danube in what amounted to an opening skirmish against the Dacians. Little by little what had been merely a psychological segregation became a physical demarcation, but real hostilities between external barbarians and Roman armies in the North did not begin in earnest until Trajan (A.D. 98–117) attacked the Dacians with the full weight of Roman might. Trajan, the great warrior-emperor, also forced the Parthians out of the Tigris-Euphrates River valley.

Along with expanded military operations, the Principate witnessed the emergence of policies towards the various barbarians beyond its borders that were predicated upon more stable barbarian governments exercising prescribed power over territories sanctioned by Rome. Rome expected more, and barbarian leaders stepped forward who took on these obligations. This Roman effort to territorialize its barbarian client states emerged concurrently with the evolution of provincial governments within the empire (that is, ca. A.D. 75 to 125) and is another indication of the interdependence of Roman internal development and its external relationships. The redeployment of a great many units along the administrative borders is generally associated with the emperor

Hadrian, who also encouraged the urbanization of native centers in the provinces by granting them the status of *muncipia* and their leaders citizenship. Rather than the architect of a new policy, however, Hadrian completed developments begun under his predecessors. In some cases his commanders merely replaced earlier wooden constructions with stone. This work was hardly in response to a general threat of invasion because no such universal opponent ever existed. In the most crucial zones Hadrian continued the redeployments begun under the Flavian emperors and Trajan.

Hadrian recognized that the provinces were integral parts of the empire and that the welfare of the provinces depended on the native aristocracies being completely integrated into provincial government. The provincials were no longer content to occupy the battlegrounds where Roman legions could fight barbarians. Simply put, there was a mutual acceptance that the frontier provinces were no longer expendable in the defense of Italy and the Mediterranean provinces. The evolution of provinces into effective units of Roman civilization had taken place almost everywhere by his reign, so a change in governmental policy was long overdue. No other development rivals the movement of the armies to the frontiers in significance to barbarian-Roman relations. Marcus Aurelius spent most of his reign engaged in northern Pannonia, where barbarian wars took a heavy toll upon provincials and barbarians alike, trying without success to expand the empire still further.

Concurrent with the development of a provincial awareness of being as Roman as those living in Italy, a new level of political organization emerged among those barbarians most directly associated with the empire and perhaps even among some of those farther removed. The enhanced organizational capabilities of those barbarians closest to the empire took the form of more tenacious and protracted warfare along the frontiers as some barbarian societies came together under stronger leaders. Sometimes, although not nearly as frequently as we have traditionally assumed, these two evolutionary paths crossed violently. When, for example, the evolution of more stable leadership among a barbarian group such as the Marcomanni culminated in the creation of a hostile power, otherwise peaceful coexistence dissolved into warfare.

As the career of Decebalus, the leader of the Dacians who opposed Domitian and Trajan, indicates, a new level of cohesion existed among this barbarian people, but this was not the first time. The Dacians were united for at least one generation as early as the time of Julius Caesar. Even among the highly sophisticated and partially urbanized Dacians, however, achieving political unity depended on a single war leader. Rome provided such men with a very notable enemy against which to rally their people. In fact, "the people," be they Dacians or some other, were precisely those who rallied to the leader and his war. One way to go beyond this limited allegiance, if one survived, was to exploit myth and the ideals of sacral kingship. With the wars of Marcus Aurelius (161–80), there can be no question that a new and powerful regional force had emerged for a second time in the area of today's Vienna, the Marcomanni. The name itself—meaning warriors inhabiting the borderlands—attests to a military confederation opposite Roman soil. In this case, as in that of the Dacians, barbarians put aside their local antagonisms and came together under a war leader to resist Rome. Armed conflict invariably ended with a reaffirmation of Roman organizational and tactical superiority and the elimination of the offending leader and his family. By replacing the chief and his heirs, Rome nullified any attempt to build a lasting kingship among that people for at least a generation. Fortunately these outbreaks of violence were rare.

Far removed from direct contact with Romans, barbarian societies in the hinterlands of eastern Europe were also being influenced by the expanding Roman infrastructure along the frontiers. The archaeological data suggest a gradually increasing concentration of wealth in the hands of fewer families and the use of Roman import items to display power relationships among the military-political elites. These artifacts could have been acquired through trade in which prestige rather than monetary value determined worth as well as through diplomatic contact. A few local residents may have served in the Roman army. In some places the normal longhouse, combining space for animals and humans under one roof, increased in area, perhaps suggesting a corresponding increase in family size and a growth of population. Settlement size also in-

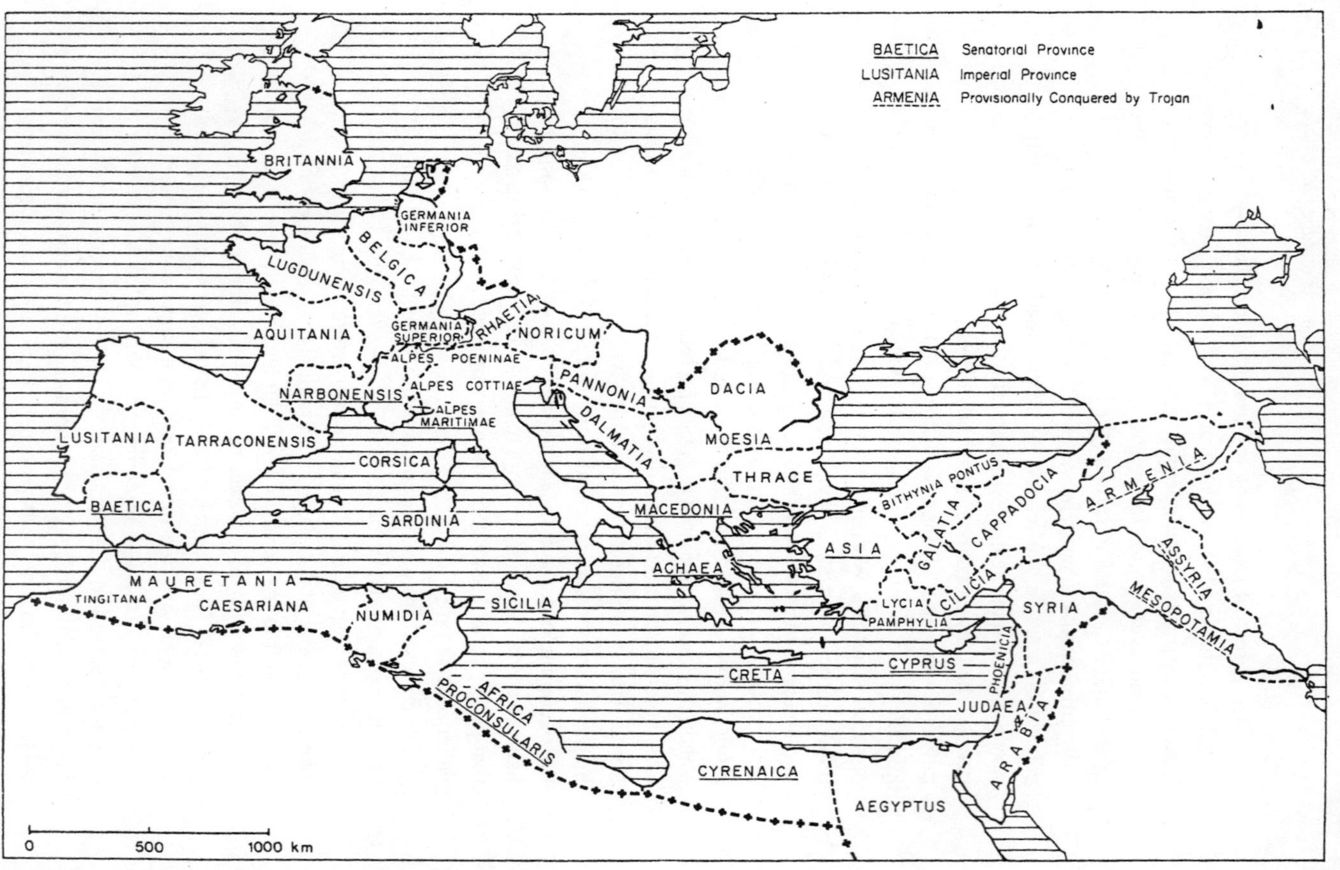

BAETICA Senatorial Province
LUSITANIA Imperial Province
ARMENIA Provisionally Conquered by Trojan
BRITANNIA
GERMANIA INFERIOR
BELGICA
LUGDUNENSIS
AQUITANIA
GERMANIA SUPERIOR
RHAETIA
NORICUM
ALPES POENINAE
ALPES COTTIAE
ALPES MARITIMAE
NARBONENSIS
PANNONIA
DALMATIA
DACIA
MOESIA
THRACE
LUSITANIA
TARRACONENSIS
CORSICA
BAETICA
SARDINIA
MACEDONIA
ACHAEA
ASIA
BITHYNIA PONTUS
GALATIA
CAPPADOCIA
ARMENIA
ASSYRIA
MESOPOTAMIA
LYCIA
PAMPHYLIA
CILICIA
SYRIA
PHOENICIA
CYPRUS
CRETA
JUDAEA
ARABIA
MAURETANIA
TINGITANA
CAESARIANA
NUMIDIA
SICILIA
AFRICA PROCONSULARIS
CYRENAICA
AEGYPTUS
0
500
1000 km

creased and forested areas declined, as more intensive agriculture became more common. These changes may have resulted from the local accumulation of wealth and power, as witnessed by the distribution of buried goods of Roman origin. In other areas, however, these trends had begun as early as the second century B.C., long before Roman involvement. The general increase in concentrations of wealth during the first two centuries of the Principate may point to the emergence of hereditary leadership, because the graves of young men often contain items of prestige beyond their ability to acquire without the assistance of well-placed elders. Dramatic development of hierarchical social systems based upon war cannot, however, be documented before the third century or even later in many areas beyond the imperial frontiers.[45]

Subsequent to Hadrian's efforts to align the military frontier with the areas administered by the provincial government, life in and around the army camps lapped over the rivers or artificial barriers separating Romans and barbarians. The extension of Roman camps and towns and the building of bridgeheads across from them on the opposite side of the *limes* greatly influenced the tenor of life for all concerned, regardless of which side one lived on. A magnet ran through the frontier zone, attracting people and products from all directions.

Shortly after Trajan's incorporation of Dacia and much of the Euphrates River valley, Roman policy shifted. In the course of his long reign Hadrian continued the Flavian redeployment of troops from the interior of the provinces to their frontiers with the barbarians. This had begun in the area between the upper Rhine and Danube Rivers half a century before. This forward troop emplacement created a fundamentally different environment, one in which barbarians could work for wages and trade directly in Roman markets. As more and more found jobs near Roman camps, the relative economic importance of long-distance trade, which included slaves

The Roman Empire at the end of the second century. Courtesy of the University of California Press, from Paul Petit, *Pax Romana*, translated by James Willis (Berkeley and Los Angeles, 1976).

and other high-value commodities such as certain minerals and amber, decreased substantially, but the trade itself remained. The elaborate Hadrianic frontiers monitored egress and entry of men and commodities, including slaves. Henceforth when barbarians seeking trade, work, or plunder crossed the Danube or the Rhine, or passed through a guarded gate in Hadrian's Wall, or walked along the even longer wall between Mainz on the Rhine and the upper Danube near Regensburg, or rested their caravans along the boundary between arable land and the Sahara Desert, they viewed the same Roman presence—the Roman army and its supporting civilian infrastructure. Whereas earlier only provincials, "internal barbarians," had come into direct contact with routine Roman organization and dissemination, by the middle of the second century, the many barbarians external to the provinces could view Roman life just by going down to the riverbank and watching Roman barges struggling against the currents. In some areas Roman towns and camps stood within sight of barbarian villages, a development that was scarcely beginning in the second century. Marcus Aurelius deployed a true frontier army, which in peacetime manifested all the technology, organization, and prosperity of his civilization. In the long run, as far as barbarian life was concerned, the Roman army was more decisive in peace than in war.

In Roman military camps everywhere soldiers went about their appointed tasks, lived in barracks with four or more men to a room, and shared cooking and marching duties with these same bunkmates. On campaign they shared a leather tent. Large grain storage facilities dominated the edges of both camp and town. At first the camps were built of the most readily available material, usually wood. In some places this was replaced by stone construction within a generation as a sign of commitment, as well as for a somewhat improved defense. In both town and camp, sanitation was a visible concern and to keep it working there had to be running water, fed by gravity to the latrines and fountains usually supplied by pipes or aqueducts from higher ground, even when the town itself was on a river or stream. Life in a barbarian village and in a Roman town or fort were not comparable. In antiquity idyllic poets writing from their desks in splendid villas and libraries romanticized rural life, generally it seems without much firsthand exposure.

There was never any doubt that in the interwoven balance of urban and rural life, the former was the dominant partner. This was also the case along the frontiers from the second century onwards. The rural neighbors supplying Roman townsmen included barbarians living beyond the provincial boundaries as well as an increasingly dense network of market-oriented Roman farms (*villae rusticae*) scattered about the best lands nearby. There were many virtues in the rural life that the vast majority of the inhabitants of the ancient world lived. Indeed, many, perhaps most, basic Roman values derived from the countryside, but for anybody seeking to portray himself as superior to his fellows the products of the towns rapidly became indispensable. In a society that lived close to subsistence, towns offered splendid and abundant foods, home furnishings, construction materials, and objects especially crafted for religious practice. They also afforded their populations a wide variety of entertainment and festivals. Public festivals in particular exposed visitor and resident alike to the social and religious structures of the community. In this regard, the ancient town was a complete community linked to the great urban centers, such as Rome itself, by shared rituals and obligations. The barbarian hamlets and villages also encased their inhabitants in a cocoon of regularity, but one much more narrowly focused than those of the Roman towns.

Behind the physical layout of the camps, life in them represented an even clearer demonstration of the values of Roman society. As one would expect, the foremost virtues of any soldier were courage and discipline. The former was ubiquitous among the barbarians, but the latter was often in short supply. Barbarians had little experience with subordinating the individual to the welfare of any group other than family, and this revealed itself in the fact that at no time do we learn of barbarians intentionally holding back forces as a reserve in battle. This was true even when the barbarians were led by one of their own who had returned from Roman service. The barbarian onslaught was frightening to behold, but if seasoned troops could hold against the opening charge, the outcome was scarcely ever in doubt. Arminius, the victor at the Teutoburg Forest, was a Roman veteran, but his victory on the battlefield was the result of a well-placed ambush.

Auxiliaries fought as Romans and, after A.D. 69, always under Roman command. In an auxiliary fortress the commander was clearly set off for special privilege by the size of his house, basically the dwelling house of a villa within the fort, whereas at this time there was little material differentiation among the barbarians. Drill and fighting mock engagements were Roman routines, but not a single text mentions barbarians practicing for war. Weapons and military dress were standardized within Roman units and sometimes, perhaps regularly, passed down from soldier to soldier upon a retirement as is attested by the names found on a few examples of armor. Barbarians wore regular clothing and used handcrafted weapons and shields. There is no need to recount the Roman army on campaign, but a glance at the panels of Trajan's column in Rome reveals numerous examples of soldiers from the auxiliary units engaged in building projects, setting up marching camps, attending to wounded colleagues at field dressing stations, and so on. The more personal contact barbarians had with Roman towns and camps, the more they were likely to be influenced, but changing rural societies was a very slow process and barbarian societies were decidedly rural.

The development of military infrastructure in the provinces proceeded soon after an area was conquered, if, that is, the Roman authorities believed it in their best interest to create a province. This was not always the case. In those areas with long established governments that were not bitter opponents, Rome created and supported client kingdoms. The transition from client kingdom to province was not necessarily violent and often their internal workings were quite well suited for Roman uses, particularly in the East. The already long history of supporting friendly kings continued under Augustus and the emperors. Client kings took on the responsibility of governance and local defense; paid tribute to Rome, which was both a symbolic and economic act; and absorbed the inevitable criticism directed against all regimes by their subjects. Tribute—no matter how small—was a token of *obsequium*, a tangible gesture to acknowledge a client's dependence on his patron. Rome did not extend its monopoly of force into these kingdoms but expected the client to maintain order and to shoulder a major role in regional defense.

Clients were not allowed to ally themselves except with Rome. Inside the client kingdom Roman merchants and traders were protected and advantaged. Perhaps the most successful client state was that of Herod the Great of Judaea. Although he owed his throne to Mark Antony, Herod flourished under Augustus, until his quasi-independent foreign policy apparently ran counter to imperial wishes. Among other client kingdoms were Mauretania, Egypt, and Noricum. During the third century Palmyra was a late but peculiarly successful experiment in integrating client status into the internal operation of the empire. As Cleopatra, Herod, and Zenobia of Palmyra discovered to their ultimate harm, there were limits to what they could do in the way of foreign policy. Each joined with Rome for mutual defense and could not conclude alliances with other powers or conduct offensive warfare without prior approval from Rome. Despite Roman intentions, one by one the client kingdoms inherited from the days of the Roman Republic failed to satisfy Roman interests in both East and West and were converted into provinces, but the client kingdom as such survived as long as the empire itself. The client kingdom was the way Romans dealt with recently subdued barbarians. When kingdoms did not exist to be made clients, Roman policy was to create them

Some client kingdoms attempted to break out of their diplomatic straightjacket. Others became embroiled in rebellion when subjects rebelled against their own kings, often because of the demands for revenues needed to pay Rome its tribute or to fund its role in regional defense. In Palestine, the case of Herod's successor dragged on for two generations, during which Rome slowly dismantled the kingdom's special status and transformed it into a regular province. Concerning Roman-barbarian relations, it is important to note that the provincialization of client kingdoms was not the result of a general policy under the emperors to favor provincialization. Rather, each failed on its own and was absorbed in order to achieve specific Roman interests in that locality. The reason

Rome never gave up on the idea of client kingdoms was that for simplicity, accountability, and cost effectiveness they remained the best option available.

In this sense, the Roman world continued to the farthest boundary and its most remote client state. But even then the influence of its image and products radiated much farther than its diplomacy. This dualistic concept of imperium—an empire without ends but segmented into spheres of greater and lesser control—seems never to have confused either Romans or barbarians, but the latter clearly did not always like it. Resistance took various forms, but rarely direct military challenge. Some may have chosen to demonstrate their rejection of Roman norms in their dress and cult practice, but discovering motivations behind cultural artifacts is fraught with difficulty.[46]

In the cases noted here, as long as a client kingdom existed, it served as a buffer to areas where Rome hesitated to become directly involved. Mauretania was an exceedingly complex area with a mountainous core that took many decades to pacify even after the collapse of its client kingdom. The Bedouins always remained free to roam the Sahara. The rich mineral resources of Noricum were long-exploited through the support of client princes there before Augustus made it a province. The late republican clients in the East sheltered Rome from direct confrontation with the Parthian Empire and with the highly unpredictable inhabitants of the Arabian peninsula and the upper Nile valley. The wisdom of this client policy was brought home in 53 B.C., when the Parthians defeated a major Roman army and killed its commander, M. Licinius Crassus. Augustus avoided direct confrontation with the Parthians and reached a settlement through careful diplomacy. Armenia was beyond either party's control and remained either a Roman or Persian client throughout most of antiquity. One precondition was paramount before Rome could support a client kingdom—it had to have a tradition of local government that would and could guarantee compliance with the agreed-upon obligations of the client to the empire. Egypt would have been a perfect client state, except for the political ambitions of its rulers, particularly Cleopatra, to act upon a broader stage than was allowed to a client. Egypt otherwise met all conditions: an incredibly long tradition of stable rule, a highly efficient tax system, and clear geographic importance as a buffer.

Among Rome's less well organized neighbors to the north, most if not all of these essentials were lacking. Although ancients believed that even remote lands were peopled, there was no obvious need for a buffer against the scarcely organized and sparse populations still farther removed. Often Rome's client neighbors to the north had no tradition of dependable rule and few mechanisms to extract tribute for Rome. Nonetheless, as Rome interacted with the external barbarians, its goals were to create conditions that would satisfy as many of these conditions as possible. Caesar manipulated old clients and created new ones, as in Britain. The emperor Claudius (41–54) was still interested in exploring clientage in Britain until it became obvious that this would not work. Rome consistently sought predictable and subservient neighbors while avoiding the creation of a hostile military force or a political regime that aspired to an independent foreign policy. Actuality always fell short of perfection. All these considerations are apparent in Rome's long engagement in central Europe, particularly in the area of Pannonia (essentially modern western Hungary and much of former Yugoslavia), to which we now turn our attention.

Five

Perspectives from Pannonia

Roman Pannonia provides many opportunities to sharpen and expand upon some of the generalizations made in Chapter 4. It cannot be taken in complete isolation from other provinces and events, however, for with a limited number of forces available, Rome was forever "robbing Peter to pay Paul." Sometimes what is apparent for Pannonia is much better illustrated by reference to data from other provinces. Trade between Romans and barbarians, for example, was ubiquitous, and to reveal the wide range of possibilities it is necessary to draw examples from farther afield than merely Pannonia. Nor should we forget that Pannonia was itself a Roman creation formed to administer a large and exceedingly diverse area. Here the two major climatic zones of Europe—the Mediterranean and north European—collided and, with them, the underlying lifestyles of their populations. In antiquity the environment changed people. The topography of Roman Pannonia includes the oldest mountains in Europe, pockets of steppelands, broad expanses of alluvial soils, and vast forests. Pre-Roman populations had long ago adapted themselves to these environments. Pannonia was first conquered by Augustus and Tiberius and remained a single large but heterogeneous province until divided under Trajan into two provinces. The Danube formed its northern boundary westwards from the great bend in the river north of Budapest and the eastern boundary south of the bend until almost modern Belgrade when the flow gradually returns to an eastwardly course. The drainage systems of the Drava and Sava Rivers fell within the province (and after the division around A.D. 100, the Pannonian provinces), but the rivers entering the Danube from the opposite bank drained watersheds outside Roman administration. In the last decade of the third century these two Pannonian provinces were themselves split into halves.

The total area of the Augustan province today would include all of western Hungary, significant parts of Serbia and Croatia, and small pieces of Slovenia and Austria. Most of the examples used in this chapter are taken from sites along the amber road in Pannonia Superior (Upper Pannonia) and from Pannonia Inferior (often also called lower Pannonia, that is, the downstream or eastern part). Pannonia Inferior provides a better than normal setting for exploring barbarian-Roman interactions, in part because so much of Roman attention was focused on this stretch of frontier during the Principate, but also because for the Hungarian section excavations on both sides of the Danube have been conducted by the same academic establishment throughout the twentieth century and are therefore more complete and systematic. This reflects the fact that the stretch from roughly Budapest south to the confluence of the Drava is the last section of the Danube that does not now form an international border. An important aspect of the following case study drawn from Pannonia is the difference that governmental investments in infrastructure made in setting the direction and timing of barbarian-Roman interactions. As in other frontier areas the role of the army was crucial, especially in the early decades, for the technology and life-styles that it manifested. On the Danube, there was another reason: the Romans were not the only expansive peoples with ambitions in Pannonia.

Caesar had planned an expedition against the Parthian Persians and en route hoped to cut short the political development of the Dacians under their leader Burebista, but fate did not treat either leader kindly. Both fell to assassins. Perhaps Caesar planned to strike at the Parthians by marching around the northern coast of the Black Sea and attacking southwards through Armenia. Whatever his intentions, our speculations about Caesar's grand design for his war against the Parthians should not blind us from seeing just how strategically important the Balkan peninsula was to the Romans.[1] Rome's long involvement with the kingdom of Macedonia and the Greek federations culminated during the second century B.C. with the incorporation of Greece and Macedonia into the empire as provinces. Thereafter Roman armies were routinely required in the East for pacification and the series of wars with the remaining Hellenistic monarchies, a phase that ended only when Cleopatra took her own life in 30 B.C. The Danube River and overland routes through the Balkans were the surest way to move troops eastwards from Italy. Bulk transport of troops was rarely accomplished by ship, for the winds in the shallow Mediterranean Sea are decidedly seasonal and can whip waves up to lethal heights within a few hours and the heavy seas sometimes last for weeks. To move an entire legion or more could only be done safely by marching it overland, and for swift movement their baggage could not encumber them. Control of the Danube would make it possible to ship heavy supplies with relative ease, while the men advanced at their own pace. The centrality of Pannonia geographically meant that the government concentrated its efforts there earlier and sustained them longer than in many other places, and as a result, Pannonia developed at a faster pace than did other provinces.

The rise of an independent and hostile political power in Dacia seems to have taken place as various indigenous centers vied for power after the fall of the Macedonian kingdom to the Romans. By the time of Marius, regional power bases had developed among various Dacian peoples, probably including the Cotini living to the northwest of what would become the Dacian heartland south of the Carpathian Mountains. If the Cotini were culturally Dacian, as seems very likely from the archaeological materials, rather than Germano-Celtic as Tacitus suggests, then Dacian cultural influence was strong from the Danube bend north of Budapest to the middle Danube at the very time that Roman power was just beginning to be exerted beyond the coastal provinces of the Mediterranean.

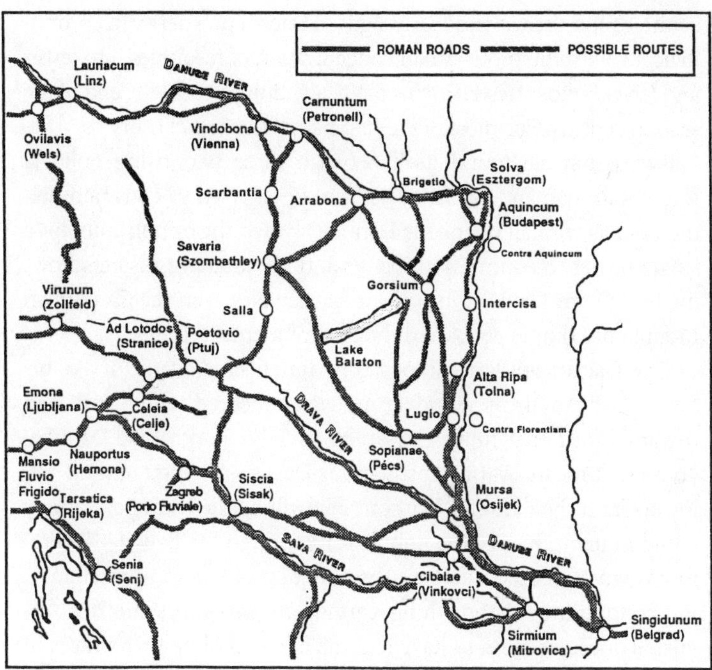

Roman frontier and hinterland: Lauriacum to Singidunum

Whatever the case for affinities with the Cotini, most of the population of northern Pannonia was Celtic. Ceramics and articles of dress suggest that in addition to some Dacian or Cotinian elements there were also pockets of population with craft production and decoration techniques similar to those of the Illyrians farther south. There is no point in pressing such possible ethnic affinities, however, for until and unless they were given a political purpose by somebody, the people were themselves almost certainly unaware of their distant cultural cousins living far afield. Nonetheless, no community can be truly endomorphic. Marriages and alliances always required reaching out beyond the neighborhood. These contacts were important to rural populations everywhere, and everywhere they went unrecorded in Roman texts.

Perhaps it is the tenacity of these extraterritorial but utilitarian bonds of community that can best account for extant similarities in ceramics and dress styles. Early signs of Dacian prosperity fit chronologically with the proto-urban concentration of resources into fewer and fewer hands attested archaeologically from around the end of the second century. For most of the first half of the first century B.C., the Balkan peninsula found itself between these two rising political forces—Roman and Dacian. The Danube satisfied to constrain neither, but as with all rivers, the Danube abetted the opportunity for a single power to control both banks and the drainage systems flowing into them. The Danube was no barrier. Not even the Carpathian Mountains completely barred the flow of men and trade.

The Dacian solidarity imposed by Burebista did not survive his death, and Augustus was determined to succeed where luck had thwarted his father Julius Caesar: he aimed to control the Danube. To do that meant war against various Dacian strongmen, their followers, and their clients. Without controlling the Danube, nobody could much influence the political situation in the Balkans. Therefore Augustus could not leave the conquest of Pannonia to chance. But conquering was one thing, carving out provinces another. Augustus does not seem to have had the creation of new provinces in mind when he began his Balkan campaigns in 35 B.C. Nor was a province created under his successor. Both Augustus and Tiberius preferred instead a loose clustering of client states each either dependent upon Roman favor or in fear of Roman armed intervention. Almost a century passed between the initial conquests and the establishment of a province.

In 35 B.C., Octavian (recall that he was not given the accolade Augustus until 27 B.C.) was a triumvir along with Marcus Lepidus and Mark Antony (Marcus Antonius). The triumvirs, like provincial governors, assumed their powers over territories, their *provincia*. Lepidus appeared content with his allotments, but Mark Antony was not. While Lepidus enjoyed the prerequisites of power, Antony was vigorously demonstrating his prowess by pacifying Judaea. Octavian could not sit idly by. Octavian's share of the empire as a triumvir included Illyricum, and, as with the case of Antony's Judaea, much of it was still beyond Roman control. So, like Antony, Octavian had to conquer parts of his assigned territory. There was, of course, a desire to continue his father's program of conquest, or at least to appear to do so. Our sources disagree as to which of these motives was primary. Appian writing in the first half of the second century and using Augustus's memoirs—unfortunately no longer extant—thought that Augustus's goal was to link Italy to the Danube in preparation for a war against the Dacians. Cassius Dio writing in the first quarter of the third century was skeptical of Augustus's self-declared strategic motives and discounted them in favor of a more personal explanation: Augustus's rivalry with Mark Antony. Cassius Dio was consistently against any expansion of the empire, and this may have colored his account. Modern scholars have lined up behind each view.[2] There can be no doubt that for Augustus history was what he could make of it, and that included Rome's struggles with barbarians. Whatever the motive, his route of invasion can be established with certainty.

With Augustus himself in the vanguard, his army marched along the Sava. He encountered major opposition at Siscia, where he mounted a thirty-day siege. After installing a garrison of twelve thousand in the former Pannonian stronghold, Octavian returned to Rome a bit battle-scarred but in glory nonetheless. Augustus himself made it clear near the end of his career that the spotlight of history should shine on only him and his successor Tiberius for bringing Roman power to Pannonia, the Danube, and beyond. In fact this was an understatement of Tiberius's role; he had saved the day for the Romans in Pannonia:

> The Pannonian peoples, whom before my Principate the army of the Roman people never approached, were conquered through Tiberius Nero, who was then my stepson and legate. I brought them into the empire of the Roman people and extended the frontier of Illyricum to the banks of the Danube River. When an army of Dacians crossed the Danube, it was defeated and overwhelmed under my auspices, and afterwards my army was led across the Danube and compelled the Dacian peoples to submit to the commands of the Roman people.[3]

This short statement glosses over the difficulty of the campaigns that had taken place and the complex relationships of the peoples whom he notes as having been conquered. Augustus also exaggerates the strength and unity of the Dacians and the level and scope of their pacification. So too does he ignore the contributions of Marcus Licinius Crassus, grandson of the triumvir by the same name. Crassus's campaigns in 29 and 28, while proconsul of Macedonia, made decisive progress against Dacian allies south of the Danube. In fact, his successes laid the groundwork for much of what Augustus says he and Tiberius accomplished alone. According to Cassius Dio, Crassus fell from grace because he sought the conqueror's share of the booty, disregarding the established practice that his conquests were those of his commander-in-chief, Octavian, under whose "auspices" he fought. Tiberius never made that mistake.[4]

The Pannonians had scarcely before entered the historical record, perhaps because they were eclipsed by their more politically powerful neighbors. As with the Celts and the Dacians, "the" Pannonians reflects an unfortunate grammatical usage in modern western European languages that did not encumber Latin, which had no such parts of speech. In American English "the" implies a singularity absent among most of the peoples living in central Europe. The region's dominant power, the Scordisci, was called Celtic by Pompeius Trogus (a contemporary of Augustus but probably basing himself upon Posidonius) but said to be of mixed Celto-Illyrian background by Cassius Dio. In the two decades prior to Augustus's campaigns the Scordisci had suffered greatly, especially after their defeat by Burebista. By Augustus's campaigns the Scordisci held sway over little of their former domain, being important only in the vicinity of modern Belgrade, but they still raided southeastwards as far as Macedonia. Raiding among the various barbarian groups present was a fact of life, one that could be transformed into trade, or some combination of the two, when a political force exerted itself in the region. The reverse followed upon the weakening of regional controls.

The decline of the Scordisci allowed for the emergence of new political forces, including such previously inept agriculturists as the Pannonians. In 35 B.C. unspecified Pannonians lay across Octavian's path, and they were to some degree in control of the strategically vital *oppidum* at Siscia on the Sava River. Appian's account depicts a situation in which the inhabitants of Siscia (Segestiké, therefore "the Segestani") appealed in vain for aid from fellow Pannonians in their vicinity, but these people were reluctant to get involved, preferring instead to flee into the forests. These same Pannonians, according to Appian, were unable to organize beyond the level of village and never lived in cities. But then, also according to Appian, some clearly lived in Siscia. Thus Appian made a very Roman distinction between *oppidum* and *urbs* (town and city), but when looked at functionally, the differences blur as the size of their populations converge.

Several strands of literary tradition lay behind Appian's narrative. As the works of Pompeius Trogus, Strabo, and others attest, the ethnographic opinions of Posidonius and Julius Caesar were influential throughout the early Principate. Appian also had available the Augustan memoirs. These imperial reflections surely took a very political approach, probably expanding upon the material still to be read in the greatest of all Roman inscriptions, the *Res gestae.* Ethnographic material such as Posidonius would have provided Appian's comment about the Pannonians being simple farmers living in villages, as well as describing diet and trade items. Augustus would have been concerned to explain taking hostages and the reasons why his attempts to capture Siscia took so long. So from the pen of Augustus would have come the story now found in Appian that the ruling families at Siscia were ready to accept Roman terms. They would surrender some of their children as hostages and provide supplies to winter over the Roman army there. In other words, they were ready to become clients. Augustus would have also noted that the ordinary farmers, whose crops would have gone to their conquerors, would have none of it. His handling of the campaigns was in keeping with the writing of his father on the conquest of Gaul.

At the opening of his campaign, Augustus defeated a group called the Iapydes, whom Appian, doubtless drawing again from Augustus, notes as having twice before repelled Roman armies and invaded Italy.[5] The stories of Augustus's repeated displays of manliness and martial vigor that pervade the historical record of his Pannonia adventures surely reflect his own official propaganda. An essential question, one that cannot be answered with certainty, is whether in 35 B.C. Augustus truly embarked on a campaign against the Dacians or, as his later conduct suggests, he was actually just moving troops along the northern flank of Illyricum in order to subdue it as a part of his triumviral domain.[6] If the latter, then later statements were retrospective and primarily comments made for propaganda. What is clear, however, is that by the time of his death almost fifty years after his siege of Siscia, Augustus had linked the control of the Balkans inextricably to Macedonia and to navigation on the Danube. He took credit for resolving the dilemma by driving the Dacians back to the northern side of the Danube. With the southern bank in Roman hands, passage by Roman warships was much safer but still not immune to Dacian efforts at disruption. Nor were the provinces to the south safe from attack. No Roman merchants regularly plied their trade on the Danube. If M. Licinius Crassus's only misstep was hubris, not disobedience to command, then Augustus deserves the lion's share of credit for planning the operations in Macedonia in 29, as he claims in the *Res gestae*. But in the final analysis, the struggle to control the lower Danube begun by his father had merely entered a new phase.

The surviving names of people and places suggest that the Pannonians were philologically most closely related to the Illyrians, who lived to their south, and so were an indigenous pre-Celtic people. But the Sava and Drava Rivers had long been meeting grounds for all sorts of cultural influences, merchants, and migrants, and a people as poorly organized as were the Pannonians would have absorbed much from others, just as had the Scordisci. This fluid situation is reflected in the still sparse archaeological data and in the distribution of Roman coins. North of the Drava the human topography changed. Having long been Celtic, Roman sources located their old nemeses, the Boii, there. Other than bearing the same name in Roman literature, the Celts of northern Pannonia shared nothing demonstrable with the Boii of third-century Italy. They were part of the general culture of the Danube basin of central Europe that included the northern Alpine foothills. Perhaps these Boii were somehow related to those Boii, whom Caesar noted as having left their homes somewhere beyond the Rhine to raid Noreia, the main stronghold of the Noricans in what would become the province of Noricum. Caesar settled some of these Boii as clients of the Aedui, but others seem to have remained in the area just west of Lake Constance. Caesar clearly reveals that people called Boii were spread across the transalpine zone with little or no cohesion.[7]

It is just possible that the Boian presence in our sources for the Augustan campaigns was but a literary convenience, a way of keeping the known historical cast together and of taking advantage of the rhetorical impact that their name provided. As with Julius Caesar, the authors of our extant literary sources for the Augustan conquest wrote works of literature, not works of history, as we understand that category today. Unlike Caesar, their craftsmanship was not tempered by direct personal observation, and so they are neither as historically valuable nor as interesting. These impersonal accounts tended to build upon the most memorable details offered by their predecessors with the result being that already flimsy historical material is made more dubious by further distortion and exaggeration as suited the later authors' needs. A brief examination of their twisted testimonies should reveal just how profoundly the Roman literary materials are tendentious. Indirectly it should reaffirm how tangential the barbarians were to those living in the imperial capital.

Strabo, writing under Augustus, records that after the Romans had pushed the Boii beyond the Alps, the Boii took up residence along the Danube with the Taurisci. There, he goes on to say, they fought against the Dacians until they ceased to exist, a detail developed by Pliny the Elder in his *Natural History,* where he notes that the Norici settled near lake Pelso (Balaton) in the deserted lands of the Boii. Strabo, not willing to let slip a chance for rhetorical effect, accepts a different suggestion, which he attributes to Posidonius: while the Boii were living in the Hercynian Forest, they had defeated the Cimbri and had deflected these great wanderers down the Danube to the lands of the Scordisci, Galatae, and Taurisci. Thus he provides the various people dwelling near the confluence of the Drava and of the Sava with the Danube a historical link to the Cimbri. Like the literary Boii, these three members of the "original," pre-Roman population are rhetorically linked to the inherent fear of invasion and disruption to Roman life so deeply associated with barbarian invasions since the Gallic sack of Rome. In fact, these Boii were even tougher than the Cimbri whom they are reported to have defeated in an otherwise unknown battle. Strabo even accepts Posidonius's flimsy attempt to connect the Cimbri with the Cimmerian Bosporus.[8] Surely these reconstructions are fanciful or at least overstated. In and of itself any mention of the Boii or Cimbri in Augustan literature is cause for suspicion, because their notice placed Augustus in a line running from Scipio Africanus to Marius and Caesar as a savior of Rome.

In addition to reflecting Augustus's imprint on their own sources, extant Roman literature provides evidence of how the Romans' sense of historical and personal evolution influenced their view of barbarian peoples. When discussing barbarians, Strabo, Appian, and almost all Roman authors credit them with very lengthy histories, often as in the case of the Cimbri linking them to remote and mythical ancestors. Their defining characteristics remained constant, as did the impact of their names. A name to a rhetorically trained author was like a primary color to an artist, something that one mixed to produce a desire shade. The barbarian peoples named in Roman literature did not need to have much in common with actual barbarians met by Roman armies in the field to achieve the desired literary effect. The Boii are a case in point. Their mention in connection with Augustus's Pannonian campaigns instantly established a grander imperial context for those campaigns. The name united both the Punic Wars and Caesar's campaigns in Gaul with the Roman struggle for dominion over the Danube. Like the stories of the Cimbri and Teutones, the name Boii lent power to those seeking credit for defending Rome from external aggression.

Such literary allusion to barbarians ultimately tells us much about the intellectual world of the Roman aristocracy, but precious little about barbarian societies. Attempts to put flesh on these sterile literary portraits from nonliterary materials are doomed to much failure and frustration. At best we can know something of Augustus, his general goals, and what type of barbarians he encountered. The fact is that Roman literature pursued the powerful, not the ordinary, and there was only one person whose power demanded attention, Augustus. Nonliterary data invariably speak of the humble, and of those Pannonia had plenty. Within a half century of Augustus's invasions, much had changed among the Celts of the

Carpathian Basin, but these changes went largely unnoticed in the literary traditions.

Rather than the demise of the Boii, inscriptions attest their survival under Roman rule. A Boian *civitas* was created along the Danube, and there are other indications that the group continued to be important in northern Pannonia for many generations after its conquest. Some Boii were later recruited into the auxiliary forces and served far from their homes, although it is impossible to be sure if these individuals were from the Pannonian Boii or those in Gaul, or how individuals of these later generations would have regarded their heritage.[9] Until the creation of a *civitas* with their name, "Boii" seems to have been another part of the nomenclature for local Celts in Pannonia and elsewhere that was in common usage among Roman authors. Although considerable archaeological work has been undertaken, many details of Celtic life in this area remain to be discovered. Many of their settlements are known only from surface finds or because they fell within the areas of later Roman settlements that archaeologists have explored.[10]

The siege of Siscia took thirty days because of its stout fortifications and location on an island in the Sava. According to recent archaeological analysis, *oppida* civilization was relatively new to Pannonia and the Carpathian Basin but had evolved rapidly within the last half century before Augustus. In general, what happened was a pooling of the diffuse agricultural societies living near small and traditional hilltop fortifications into larger communities. In his *Res gestae* Augustus does not say that Pannonia became a province, because he did not make it one, nor does he say that he created provinces further down to the Danube. He says that, by his efforts and those of Tiberius, he effectively extended Roman authority as far as the Danube, thus in some way fulfilling the task he had set for himself as the *triumvir* when he accepted the assignment of Illyicum in 40 B.C. In the absence of provinces, clients ruled for him. At least one central problem, however, goes unstated in the official narrative. Rome had entered an area that had no clearly dominant political power; no one was able to shoulder the responsibilities that went with being a Roman client, at least not for long, and so new clients had to be found or created. If these clients proved themselves unable to govern, then restructuring was predestined. Once involved Rome inevitably demanded more than the existing systems of local government could deliver. Frustrated by ineffective governments and outraged by unpredictable populations, Roman commanders turned to force. Villages and farms were burned; leaders were rounded up and executed, their followers enslaved. The Pannonian peoples rose up and rejected their client status. Their uprising was one of the most challenging that Rome ever faced from a conquered people.

The Pannonian revolt of A.D. 6–9 seriously challenged Roman control of the Balkans and the entire middle Danube, and threatened to undo much of Augustus's accomplishments to the northwest as well. Augustus immediately diverted Tiberius from his campaign to extend Roman authority to the Elbe-Harz Mountains and ordered him south to crush the rebels. It was the report of a fleet participating in Tiberius's expedition that apparently provided Tacitus with some of his material on the Cimbri remaining in Jutland. In support of his offensive, Tiberius had established support bases on both sides of the Danube where the amber road crossed the Danube—at Carnuntum on the right bank and at Devin on the left—and marching camps deep into barbarian territory. It seems unlikely that he and Augustus had sought to annex these territories. Rather than annexation, Rome sought to punish and install a new client system by which to control events beyond its borders. This policy of limited involvement remained in operation for the remainder of the first century.[11]

Serious attention now had to be paid farther south. Some veterans apparently stayed on at Carnuntum after the main force passed through. The deployment of troops and supplies needed to suppress the revolt cost the budget dearly. Velleius Paterculus, an officer of some note during the struggle, was an uncritical supporter of his commander, Tiberius Caesar. Paterculus makes it clear that one of the reasons for the severity of the revolt was the level of military training and the command structure that existed among the Pannonians and their allies because of their long exposure to Roman arms and culture.[12] The revolt essentially ended Roman efforts to conquer the peoples between the Rhine and Elbe Rivers and the area southwards from the Elbe to the Danube—that is, approximately the modern Czech Republic and Slovakia. The struggle expanded southwards from Pannonia to include parts of Dalmatia as well, thereby threatening to undo the entire client system created under Augustus.

Following soon after the Pannonian revolt, the Roman defeat in the battle of the Teutoburg Forest in A.D. 9 all but sealed the fate of central Europe as far as Roman government was concerned. If any desire to cross the Rhine in force still existed, it was dashed by a revolt in Gaul in A.D. 21. Roman emperors henceforth limited their efforts beyond the Rhine and upper Danube to maintaining bridgehead positions and keeping their barbarian clients in order. Rome never extended its direct administration beyond the Rhine and Danube except south of a line running between Mainz on the Rhine and Eining, near Regensburg, on the Danube. In this area—ultimately called the Agri Decumates, essentially modern Baden-Württemberg in southwest Germany—the rivers were too small and shallow to be of much consequence for defense or trade. This salient was eventually abandoned, but not for two and a half centuries.

Roman concerns to monitor the flow of men and materials beyond these borders continued. In the south along the middle and lower Danube, Rome had by no means given up on expansion. Even in the north a few strategic objectives were still in Roman hands including the Lippe River valley, the principal east-to-west transportation corridor leading into the middle Rhine. The valley of the Lippe was still home to Roman garrisons several decades after these revolts. In general, however, it was only after Roman authorities completed the repositioning of army units to the external borders of these provinces in the early second century that regular supervision of the rivers and particularly their fords became routine. After the disaster of A.D. 9, Augustus and the Julio-Claudian emperors settled for the security of patron-client relations. The difference between clients east of the Rhine and north of the Danube from those within Pannonia was, however, fundamental.

The barbarian clients beyond the *limes* were in a sense free; no

Roman veterans were settled there. Those former barbarians in Pannonia henceforth had Roman legionnaires, veterans, merchants, and various other civilians living in their midst as a protected and privileged minority. Like all "inner barbarians" those in Pannonia were also free, free to live as their customs demanded, but they did so in the shadow of Roman sovereignty—the rule of both people and land—with all the restrictions upon their political independence that this entailed. Beyond its frontier, Rome, of course, was never sovereign, but it nonetheless greatly influenced the indigenous people and the ways that they conceptualized the lands they occupied. Provincials could retain their traditions so long as these did not run counter to Roman law, to which they were all subject. A colony was established at Emona (Ljubljana) and legionary camps at Poetovio (Ptuj) and at Siscia. Naval detachments patrolled the Drava from Mursa (Osijek) and the Sava from Sirmium (Sremska Mitrovica) and Gomolava. Roads were built or improved along the southern bank of the Sava River, and the old amber road was upgraded to better link Poetovio, Emona and the garrisons along the Sava to Italy. A mix of civilians and veterans also settled at Scarbantia (Sopron), at Cileia (Celje) along the amber road south of Poetovio and at Novo Mesto near Emona. Rome thus assured its control of transportation and communication along the old amber road and the Drava and Sava Rivers, but the Danube still flowed on without visible Roman presence along its banks, despite the fact that it was the official border of the province.[13]

From Velleius's perspective, Tiberius had only to defeat Maroboduus and his Marcomanni to finalize his goal of extending Roman power to the Elbe. Then the Pannonians undermined everything by revolting. Velleius did not have the advantage of hindsight on these events, but Cassius Dio (ca. A.D. 230) would have been quick to point out that the Marcomanni were a time bomb waiting to detonate along the middle Danube for the next two centuries. When ordered to engage the rebellious Pannonians, Tiberius was at Carnuntum, which would become the capital of Pannonia Superior and is now essentially a suburb of Vienna. Tiberius was leading the southern arm of a giant Roman pincer movement within which he planned to entrap Maroboduus and his followers. The other arm, under his legate Sentius Saturninus, would strike due east from the Rhine. Together they would trap Maroboduus in Slovakia, called by Velleius "Boiohaemum," apparently "the homelands of the Boii," but no longer occupied by them it would seem.[14]

Had Maroboduus allied himself with Arminius to the north instead of fighting him as he did, the entire Roman client system behind the Alps might have dissolved at once in the wake of Arminius's victory over Varus in A.D. 9. Their combined forces then could have posed a mortal threat to Rome. This was not to be, for the two men could not get along. Tacitus recalled Maroboduus as the last sacral king of the Marcomanni, but Tacitus was wrong. The Marcomanni were relatively new on the scene, and Maroboduus was trying to position himself as a sacral king, not merely to those who had rallied to him in the face of Roman attack, but over all others in the area. The great war leader Arminius would brook no such pretensions. Maroboduus's attempt at sacral kingship failed. In A.D. 19 Roman meddling resulted in Maroboduus being rejected by his followers and seeking asylum inside the empire. He died of old age, dissipated after eighteen years as an imperial ward in Ravenna, his usefulness limited to the threat he posed to the peace of his old people. The Romans could have restored their royal hostage any time they felt that the Marcomanni were in violation of their clientage, but that need never arose. Maroboduus was replaced by Catualda, who held power for but a year before a certain Vibilius ousted him. Rome befriended each in turn.

Tacitus's account of these events provides a clear example of how Rome controlled and influenced the barbarians remaining beyond its direct administration: by welcoming exiles into the empire, and then by threatening the return and support of those exiles; by obtaining special trading privileges for Roman merchants, especially those licensed to procure supplies for the army; and by pitting one claimant to leadership against another for Roman favor.[15] In a peculiarly ironic twist of events, the exiles also provided Roman emperors with numerous occasions to proclaim their clemency, another of the primary virtues of a Roman leader and the reverse side of his manly prowess demonstrated by his victories. Ethnic identities played little role in actual Roman policy that was always first directed to individuals. Nor did their "barbarous cultures" enter into Roman calculations in the field despite the fact that barbarians were portrayed in official propaganda throughout the Principate and in contemporary literature as culturally inferior and potentially a threat to the urban world of the Mediterranean.[16] The emperors shaded their message to fit different audiences.

The presence of Boii and other groups well known in contemporary literature at the moment of the conquest of Pannonia had the effect of establishing a cognitive base line, against which any newcomers stood out. Not all these newcomers need to have been enemies bent on invasion, however. Some, perhaps most, were "peoples" of Roman creation, organized around old regional centers, some of them once Celtic, where they lived or to where they were brought. Roman authorities shifted newly conquered barbarians around inside the provinces with the same care that they allowed external ones to immigrate. By the reign of Claudius (41–54), Rome had created governmental districts (*civitates*) from the newly conquered populations for all of Pannonia, and these in turn formed the basis of the new province that Claudius created. In the case of Pannonia as elsewhere these *civitas* organizations remained basic local administrative units just beneath the provincial government throughout Roman history, although their names and boundaries might well be changed subsequently. Some *civitates* were named for peoples never before attested to in Roman sources, perhaps because they were too insignificant to have merited a place in the narratives of conquest, perhaps because they were entirely new creations. Others took their names from larger groups well known from Roman history such as the Boii. But, even then, there must have been many lesser group names current among the Boii, names that have escaped our sources, and these names thus had local meaning and were available to become the names of *civitates*. Caesar had done the same in Gaul.

At first the *civitas* units were administered, although it is hard to justify the use of that term, as if they were client kingdoms but under the supervision of a Roman military officer. This was in keeping with their primary role in local defense at this time, but with the slow establishment of effective provincial government and larger forces of auxiliaries, these *civitates* were disarmed. Instead of tribute, the inhabitants paid taxes depending on their status and that of their community. The real leaders of the *civitates* were men from the principal families who had supported Roman conquest. Naturally *civitates* had no foreign policies and no independent military forces. In northern Pannonia they collectively formed a buffer zone around the few Roman towns along the old amber road running southwards from Carnuntum (Petonell, Austria) on the Danube southwards through Scarbantia (Sopron, Hungary), Savaria (Szombathely), Salla (Zalalövo, Hungary), Emona (Ljubljana, Slovena), and on to Aquileia (Italy) at the head of the Adriatic Sea.[17] These cities still dominate their regions today.

Tiberius settled some veterans and auxiliary units at strategic places such as Carnuntum, Scarbantia, and Salla, and to these Claudius added only modestly at a few sites along the Danube. His reign, for example, witnessed the upgrading of the wood of earlier camps to stone. Claudius also continued the practice of establishing veteran colonies such as at Savaria. No significant Roman units were as yet assigned to Pannonia. The amber road itself was gradually straightened and paved to Roman standards, although when it passed through settlements the twists and turns remained. These first Roman towns along the amber road where founded upon the site of or near Celtic *oppida,* as was the case of Siscia on the Sava. As Roman military camps and urbanization slowly spread along the Danube, other Celtic *oppida* served similarly. This was so commonly the case because *oppida* already commanded the strategic sites, and because some of them had become the capital of their *civitas.* The Celtic *oppidum* of the Eravisci became Roman Aquincum (Budapest) in the second half of the first century.

Civitates everywhere, including Pannonia, had very little direct Roman influence throughout the first century A.D. unless they happened to be Roman commercial centers or lay along Roman highways connecting them to other commercial centers. In early Roman Pannonia this meant along one of two stretches: near the amber road or along the Sava River in the southernmost part of the province. The Pannonian *civitas* system, just as in Gaul and elsewhere in the West, was designed around preexisting Celtic regional communities. As implemented it was an artificial system erected to assure maximum control at minimum expense, as with Pompey's client state system in the East or Caesar's in Gaul. In effect, Rome took over governmental responsibility but left daily affairs to the indigenous leadership. Again, as elsewhere, until the "year of the four emperors" (A.D. 68–69) even local defense might be left in the hands of local recruits serving under native leaders. This despite the fact that they fought as Roman auxiliaries and were paid from the taxes levied in the province. Claudius's new province was at peace throughout his reign as it had been since Tiberius shattered the native rebellion.

Upon this structure ultimately rested the fate of barbarian-Roman interactions. It is no wonder then that preexisting trade relationships that took advantage of water transport, pre-Roman pathways, and personal contacts, continued for decades after the conquest. This is evidenced, for example, by the presence of ceramics in Pannonia characteristic of the inhabitants of non-Roman lands to the north and east. In addition to the amber trade, the survival of earlier trading patterns is quite apparent in the distribution of pottery usually associated with Dacians found in northern Pannonia. The most entrepreneurial individuals from among the new Romanophile—but still native—elites were even better positioned to take advantage of trade than their predecessors had been. Their political connections now placed them in closer contact with sources of Roman goods, while their traditional family and client networks went on operating beyond Roman provincial boundaries. Contacts in *barbaricum* gave them access to raw materials like amber, precious stones, minerals (particularly gold), hides, and preserved foods. Roman connections gave them coins and manufactured items produced locally or imported into the province.

The new indigenous elites were ideal middlemen. Trade with the barbarians never ceased to be important in Pannonia, and in the early decades there were still no mechanisms to tax or regulate it, no customs officers at markets along the river, and very few troops guarding against unregulated traffic using or crossing the Danube. As was true when the Romans expanded into southern Gaul, trade was a factor in their expansion into Pannonia, but neither in Gaul nor here was it the primary cause. Nonetheless, basic market forces were always at work.

The amber road was virtually the only important route for long-distance trade in Pannonia prior to the establishment of Roman control of the entire Danube. By the opening of the third century that great river had eclipsed all other arteries of trade including the amber road. The first Roman settlements occurred in veteran colonies along the road, and, as a result, it was there that villa agriculture developed. Amber was uniquely northern, for the only source of high-quality material was the southern shores of the Baltic Sea, where it washed up in exportable quantities. Amber satisfied all the basic criteria for long-distance trade; it was light in weight, in high demand for jewelry among all those living around the Mediterranean, and thus it was profitable for trading over such great distances. No other commodity could rival it in all these categories, not even slaves. Slaves could walk to market, like other livestock, but they were costly to obtain and had to be guarded at all times. The high demand for slaves inside the empire meant, nonetheless, that slaves from the North were marketed to the Romans from early times. Ultimately Germanic languages adapted the Latin to create a word, *mango,* for a slave trader.[18] There are a few other north European trade items known from Roman literary sources, but most of these references date to after the first century.

Salt was important where it was available in large quantities and could be transported profitably to distant markets. The continental coasts of the English Channel and the North Sea, in particular, were centers of production, but salt continued to be mined in the Alps, as it had been for centuries before Roman occupation. The Alpine areas became provinces under Augustus, thereby securing those sources of salt as well as many other minerals available there and almost nowhere else in Europe. The rivers that provided administrative boundaries also gave merchants an ideal platform for trade, both regional and long-distance. Along these transportation corridors towns and villas could specialize in highly refined products, because they could get them cheaply and safely to markets even at great distances. There must have been a considerable demand for specialty items, especially in areas where the imperial military and civil aristocracies competed for prestige. This specialization was not simply a function of manufacturing techniques, for sometimes it was a matter of taking maximum advantage of what nature provided. For example, certain geological pockets along the great rivers produced better strains and sometimes completely different types of cereals. Salted products were always much sought after among all ranks and ethnic backgrounds. Like nearly everything else, diets were becoming regionalized as inhabitants on both sides of the Rhine or Danube in specific market regions shared products unique to their local cultures.

Metallurgy as practiced in *barbaricum* was not competitive with Roman products. This was true across the entire range of metals. For iron this was because the Roman water-forced air forging techniques were able to produce and control much higher heats than barbarian hand-bellows commonly used. Jewelry was much in demand in *barbaricum*, and the best gold and silver pieces often reflect Roman craftsmanship. Barbarian cattle and sheep were traded along the Rhine and Danube to Roman butchers. Special sausages were in demand among the Roman troops, and dyestuffs made from grasses in central Europe were used in hair coloring popular among Roman women. There even may have been a special officer in the Roman fleet on the Rhine charged with acquiring beer, doubtless from the barbarians. Northern barbarians were gifted wood-carvers and produced many outstanding pieces of personal jewelry, but in the first two centuries their tastes were being influenced by Romans rather than the reverse.[19]

Furs and hides of all types were valuable among the barbarians and were also traded to the Romans, but what the barbarians had most to offer was not their clothes but their bodies as soldiers and later on as laborers. In the early Principate barbarians serving in the imperial guard earned a reputation for loyalty and severity, but the full impact of barbarian eagerness to serve Rome did not become apparent until after the empire had shifted its emphasis to the frontiers. The technical problems of distinguishing the pathways of influence from the available archaeological data are compounded by "Celtic survivals" long after an area had been politically and militarily taken over by Romans. Celtic survivals and adaptation were quite apparent in Pannonia.

On the Roman side, exports included ceramic vessels ranging from simple pottery to the finest red tableware, or terra sigillata, the latter especially after the middle of the second century. Glassware was in high demand among all northern barbarians. Certain types of cereals were easily sold, as was metalware of all types. Burials in peat bogs in northern Germany have revealed some of the same items, often quite perishable, that made their way into *barbaricum*. These included bronze statuettes of Roman gods, fine textiles and dyed fabric, silver spoons, bronze mirrors, finger rings and other items of personal attire, and even gaming stones. Similar materials made from metal have been found all along the frontiers, but only an oxygen-depleted environment such as peat preserves organic matter. Wine was to the Germans what beer seems to have been to the Roman boatmen on the Rhine: something they just had to have in regular supply. So important was this trade that Germanic languages borrow the Latin *caupo* for wine handler. The degree to which the Marcomanni and their neighbors used Roman coins among themselves remains unclear, but it seems highly likely that those living directly adjacent to the frontier did so. Many coins have been discovered in these areas, but one type is telling. The key indicator is the presence of significant bronze coinage, the small change without which a daily market economy based on coinage could not function. Second and early third century Roman bronze pieces are frequently found in *barbaricum* neighboring Pannonia, but they are especially common finds along the barbarian bank of the middle Rhine.[20]

Tiberius and Claudius settled veterans at or near the key *oppida* along the amber road: at Carnuntum (the chief city of the *civitas* of the Boii), Scarbantia (*oppidum Scarbantia Iulia*), Savaria, Salla, and so on southwards. Many of these locations had long been recognized for their strategic importance to road traffic and so already had resident Celtic populations or at least Celts living nearby. The new settlements were sited to guard local road junctions or to command promontories; all had good water sources. Water supplies and transportation were always vital considerations in site selection for any settlement, be it Roman or Celtic. Like veteran colonies elsewhere the first veterans in the new settlements surveyed the lands near the town, carved out a checkerboard system of square plots (centuriation), and divided them up for distribution among themselves. Beyond their immediate neighborhood, they had few interests. Those natives unfortunately living on any land desired by Romans veterans lost it, but they were not necessarily simply evicted, for their labor was sorely needed. Some doubtless found ways to lease back parts of the lands that they had lost to confiscation. Towns along the amber road and the Sava River grew steadily during the first century, despite the early repositioning of troops to the Danube that began under Vespasian and his son Domitian. Their hegemony ended when, after the end of Trajan's Dacian campaigns, the emperor systematically shifted troops to the Danube defenses, leaving very few in the interior.[21]

When Vespasian came out the victor in the military struggle for supremacy in A.D. 69, he had little cause to fear a barbarian invasion across the Danube, especially because some of the Iazyges had provided him with support during the civil war. Indeed, his main concern was the army itself and the various dissident officers that might have hidden themselves within it. For him the enemy was not so much the barbarians as other potential Roman claimants to the throne. Thus he had many reasons to disperse his troops and to station them as far from Italy as he could while still keeping them in the provinces.[22] Domitian accelerated the deployment of units to the Danubian forts in the course of his poorly recorded wars against the Quadi, Marcomanni, and Dacians. Although Salla lost its military importance when its garrison left for the Danube, the town survived. Salla went on to become a *municipium* only under Hadrian, whereas Scarbantia reached this status under the Flavians. Along the Sava the civilian status of various communities was elevated, with colonies technically being established at Siscia and Sirmium and new *municipia* at Neviodunum and Andautonia.

For Cassius Dio the cause of conflict along the Danube and its widening scope was Domitian's various moral failings as a leader, exemplified by his total disregard of treaty obligations towards Roman clients. He is reported to have simply ordered troops to cross the Rhine without provocation, despite the fact that Rome had treaties with these people. Dio offers no explanation for Domitian's forays into Dacia other than the rise of Decebalus there. For Dio, Domitian was out for glory to match his father's and thereby to secure his place in Rome. Whether such victories actually took place or were merely propaganda distributed to the masses through coinage was irrelevant, at least to the Domitian portrayed in our consistently hostile sources. When no opportunity for booty existed, he is said to have demanded outrageous tribute from his foreign clients. At least Cassius Dio understood Rome's obligations to its clients and so, of course, did most Roman emperors.

Upon his death, the Senate damned Domitian's memory. Every record, every public monument was to have his name excised, and with this act the senators made it virtually impossible for subsequent generations to rediscover his accomplishments. Dio's account is quite successful in stripping the long-dead emperor of whatever glory he still had in the early third century, but surely there was little worthy of praise left to find. Today it is hard to accept such uncritical transference of his obvious difficulties with the Senate to a damnation of his conduct in the provinces and on the frontiers, where archaeological data suggest that many significant actions were successfully undertaken during his reign. Whatever the cause of his war with Decebalus, the Marcomanni and Quadi refused to provide Domitian with troops, as they had for his father. He retaliated.

Perhaps the most interesting passage in Dio's troubled text rhetorically is Domitian's treaty with Decebalus in which the emperor is alleged to have provided him with an annual tribute and artisans skilled "in all crafts both for peace and war."[23] In other words, Dio is saying that the Roman army had won a victory over the barbarians, which their grossly incompetent emperor had then given back to the defeated. For Dio, Domitian had dishonored Rome by, in essence, becoming the defeated king's client. Worse than that, he gave away the secrets of Roman power, its military technology. Could Dio have read Shakespeare, he would have marveled at Antony's speech at Julius Caesar's funeral pyre, but he would have misunderstood the irony when Antony said, "I come to bury Caesar, not to praise him." Dio buried Domitian one last time. The Romans had to wait for Trajan before they could celebrate victory over the Dacians.

With the troops freed up after his destruction of the Dacian kingdom, Trajan began building and manning watch posts with Roman garrisons beyond the Danube in order to monitor the Marcomanni and Quadi more carefully. These outposts were maintained at least into the reign of Hadrian.[24] By his commitment of a permanent armed force north of the middle Danube, Trajan probably sought to regain the respect of those clients who had been remiss in living up to their treaties with Rome. In manning outposts there, Trajan took the first steps towards ending the rule of client states. By analogy to Britain and Judea, the next step was provincialization. These were not actions that would have gone unnoticed by the barbarians living there. Despite the redirection of Roman investment to the Danubian forts, most towns along the amber road continued to prosper, although growing perhaps a bit more slowly than before. All had attained the requisite features of Roman urban centers by the ascension of Marcus Aurelius (161–80): temples dedicated to the Capitoline Triad and the other principal Roman gods, stone architecture, major public water and sewage projects including baths, and an amphitheater large enough to accommodate most of the town's adult population. Trajan was particularly philanthropic in Pannonia.

In the countryside the indigenous population remained most numerous. The more remote from the amber road their villages and hamlets happened to be, the less their lives were affected by the Roman presence. Trade items and Roman ceramics were rare. The area south and west of Savaria, for example, had almost no detectable contact with Romans. There people continued to live in small villages practicing subsistence agriculture, their elites frequently burying their loved-ones in mound graves.[25] In general this lifestyle went unchallenged throughout the first century. There was some intermarriage, as can be seen on a few inscriptions that record the deaths of people with Celtic names. The fact that this was done with Latin inscriptions itself attests to a certain level of Romanization, but even near Roman settlements the natives were reluctant to give up their traditions.

Only after Trajan's redeployments did these towns become major economic centers with populations that required more foods than could be produced locally. Merchants responded to the new demand by importing new items from Gaul and Italy as is attested by the many examples of ceramic vessels, which carried much of the trade, and by the fine terra sigilatta that graced the tables of the wealthier elements of Roman society. Given the ready markets for foodstuffs, Roman villa agriculture spread to Pannonia in the course of the second century. Literally thousands of such commercial farms have now been identified through various surveying techniques. This process began in earnest after the Second World War, when scholars began to gain access to military aerial photographs. Current methods use a variety of magnetic, low-level nuclear radiation, and wave technologies, along with increasingly high-resolution satellite imagery. Altogether they have taken surveying into a new dimension. The villa life-style that was once thought to have been the life-style of the Italian rich now turns out to have been widely distributed across the western parts of the empire, even making an occasional appearance in the East. Little by little the best land outside the immediate areas of the towns was developed by individuals into agribusinesses (to use modern terminology, *villae rusticae* in Latin). To make a profit these new rural farms had to be situated upon the best soils, well drained and watered with easy access to markets. In Pannonia, most faced south to take advantage of the sun in winter.

The rural inhabitants of eastern Pannonia (which became Pannonia Inferior, ca. 120) were influenced by Roman practices much later. Although some camps had been established along the Danube before the opening of the second century, the completion and integration of the defenses had to await the return of Trajan's army from the Dacian wars. There were no first-century veteran colonies in eastern as contrasted to western Pannonia. Here too there were elements of the native population that were not Celtic, but they were also in the minority. Except for the area near camps, rural life in eastern Pannonia remained essentially pre-Roman until the end of the second century and, in some cases, even into the fourth. Villa agriculture had to await the development of urban markets, and where no markets emerged, no villas did either.

The site of an *oppidum* of the Celtic Eravisci, the area of Budapest (Aquincum), attracted early Roman attention. By the middle of the first century, two auxiliary units were in garrison along the Danube, fordable here as at the site of Brigetio (Komárom-Szöny). Both sites went on to become legionary camps. Brigetio is poorly explored, but Aquincum is one of the best understood of all legionary centers. In 89 the II Adiutrix legion was transferred to Aquincum from Britain. In 106 its commander became the governor of Trajan's new province of Pannonia Inferior, with Aquincum as its capital. At Aquincum the *canabae,* a town originally of huts that sprang up right next to all legionary camps, housed the families of the soldiers, merchants, shopkeepers, and various other occupations essential to soldiers but not provided by the army. In addition to the *canabae* was the civilian town, exactly one Roman mile from the camp, as Roman military law required. The division of Pannonia into two provinces left Pannonia Superior with two legions (at Carnuntum and Brigetio) and Inferior with one (Aquincum). This division remained in place until 214, when Caracalla, who was quite active upstream in Raetia, transferred the legion I Adiutrix and its camp at Brigetio to Pannonia Inferior and shifted provincial boundaries accordingly.[26]

A governor with two legions under his command not only outranked his colleague in the other Pannonia province but, more important to the empire, he could concentrate twice the heavy striking power of a legion upon the empire's most dangerous opponents. Trajan saw this threat as coming from the recalcitrant Marcomanni and Quadi; Caracalla focused his imperial military might on the Carpi and Sarmatians (Iazyges) in the Hungarian Plain. Hadrian was the first governor of Pannonia Inferior, *legatus Augusti,* and his palace built in the area of the *canabae* at Aquincum was one of the largest and most lavishly appointed constructions ever undertaken in the Pannonian provinces. As Emperor Hadrian made the civilian town at Aquincum a *municipium* (probably in 124). Aquincum had entered its golden age.

Legionary baths were built at Aquincum early in the second century and by midcentury the town and *canabae* had lost their original wood and mudbrick buildings. They had been rebuilt in stone and were usually carefully decorated. Two amphitheaters were also built at this time, one for the civilian town and one associated with the camp. A large barracks for gladiators was built outside the civilian amphitheater, and the military amphitheater outside the camp was primarily used for training and as a place where the commander could address his men. An aqueduct linked fourteen "sacred springs" to the camp with diversions to the town and *canabae* along the way. A *collegia* of citizens was active in support of the II Adiutrix legion. At the end of the century, Septimus Severus (193–211) raised both town and *canabae* to *colonia,* the highest possible urban status.

As in western Pannonia (after 106 Pannonia Superior) so too in eastern Pannonia, the development of villa agriculture in the countryside had to await the evolution of markets. These first arose around the camps. As Aquincum hit its stride under Trajan and especially under Hadrian, villas developed nearby. Near Aquincum domestic living space flowed outwards from the civilian town in all directions. Around 150, the so-called Villa of Hercules was built, perhaps by a former legionary commander or other very high-ranking officer. This villa and other purely residential estates are usually called *villae suburbanae* in order to distinguish them from the rural villa farms (*villae rusticae*). Although the former was splendid, the latter would have had a much greater effect upon the native populations. This pattern was repeated to a lesser degree all along the Danube, where the smaller size of auxiliary camps supported a smaller number of villas. The best understood of these communities is Intercisa (Dunaújváros) downstream from Aquincum.[27]

Intercisa, seventy kilometers downstream from Aquincum, was also built in the early second century to command a ford of the Danube. Nearby Celtic settlements provided the inhabitants of its early *vicus militaris,* the name for a civilian settlement that grew up around auxiliary camps. The camp itself held five hundred cavalrymen (an *ala*) and their mounts. The main road of the camp was also the principal artery of east-west transportation for the area, and along it passed merchandise on its way from central Pannonia to the heart of the Hungarian Plain. By the end of the century the civil town had out grown its bath, and a new one was built outside the town walls. As in all Roman settlements, the cemetery stretched along the main road just outside the town boundaries.

The same community cemetery provides confirmation of the forces at work throughout Pannonia that were creating a new society. Many of the graves are quite simple, pit types in which the cremated remains were scattered into the soil and reburied. There must also have been wooden markers over these graves indicating where these places were, because later burials avoided disturbing them. Inhumation and cremation graves were evenly distributed about the site. Slowly stone markers came into use, first among the soldiers and then among the civilian graves. Because this was a cavalry regiment, the headstone often showed the soldiers mounted, along with another figure or two, perhaps representing their stewards. The gravestones of the native population sometimes included a scene of a wagon with team being urged on by a driver. The women were always shown in native dress, characteristic hairstyles, and dress ornament. This was a largely self-sufficient farming community, which supplemented grains and vegetables with wild game and fish. Until the end of the third century it was illegal for natives in Pannonia Inferior to grow vines, thus restricting this most lucrative industry to Roman enterprises. In locations where good arable land coincided with strategic military interests Roman and Celtic farmers lived side by side.[28]

There were relatively few Roman towns of importance between the amber road and the Danubian forts, but one deserves our special attention as it did that of the emperors—Herculia (Gorsium). Herculia lay astride an important road junction where three major highways crossed, and so here Claudius established an auxiliary camp, which attracted the local Celtic population. Soon the fort had spawned a civilian community (a *vicus*) of simple clay huts with floors dug into the soil. Although the early fort disappeared ca. A.D. 100, the subsequent town followed the same street plan as the original fortress. The town became the center for the imperial cult for the entire province, and Trajan and Hadrian built a lavish temple complex to honor themselves and their predecessors there. From the beginning the town had the usual temple to the Capitoline Triad, but to this was added Trajan's precinct, and then sanctuaries and dedications to the most important gods of this and subsequent periods. Finally during the late empire, Christianity found a home here too. By the second half of the second century, these religious centers included temples and altars dedicated to many of the major mystery religions of the East that had become popular among the soldiers and merchants: for example, Jupiter Dolichenus (after Dolichis, a site in Syria). The presence of eastern merchants is even attested by the bones of a camel, doubtless used by some merchants trading with Gorsium.

As the center for the imperial cult, Herculia was the meeting place for the provincial council, through which representatives of all the various communities in Pannonia Inferior annually made sacrifice and pledged their loyalty to the emperor. Private residences stretched far into the suburbs. To support such a large and prestigious community, Herculia had to maintain large storage facilities (*horrea*), the remains of which have been excavated. The extraordinary flowering of religious life at Herculia is but one indication of the rapid expansion of official investment in the province during the second century. To some degree this was true everywhere in the empire, but in those areas not previously urbanized such as Pannonia Inferior, this effervescence of imperial patronage took place in an environment that had little private philanthropy to start with. In the cities in Pannonia Superior that developed earlier and from nongovernmental sources, private donations to public works can be seen to decline as government moves in. By the middle of the second century, those living in the Pannonian provinces were much more dependent on their government than were the original veteran colonies, but this may be said for many parts of the empire. Doubtless the many architectural and cultural refinements at Herculia had a powerful influence upon those natives living in what had been the *vicus* of the original camp, but their story is best told, as usual, from their burials.[29]

The cemeteries tell a story of very gradual assimilation. Simple

Celtic burial practices long survived alongside their Roman counterparts, the latter distinguished by the use of tile vaults composed of the standard Roman building tiles manufactured for roofs and heating systems. First-century Roman tombstones depict the interred male in military dress, whereas women are seen in traditional indigenous garb. This arrangement is hardly unique to Gorsium—in fact, it is typical of funerary monuments wherever Roman soldiers were stationed in the frontier provinces. At Herculia (Gorsium) the tombstone erected by Q. Flavius Titucus for his mother, Flavia Tattunis filia Usaiu, during the second half of the second century is particularly instructive. Clearly a Romanized lady of considerable means, Flavia lived to her eightieth year. From her name it seems that she was herself the daughter of a Romanized Celt. She wears her hair symmetrically wrapped in a turbanlike headdress; her native dress is embroidered around the cuffs; and around her neck hangs a thick collar ornament (torques) of twisted filigree. In life such gold torques would have broadcast her high position in any Celtic community she happened to visit. Below her bust in relief, two yoked oxen pull a four-wheeled covered wagon with a man holding the reigns. A funerary altar (an *aedicula*) brackets Flavia with a Corinthian column on either side. Two porpoises swim in the top corners. A Latin inscription introduces her to the passersby. The classical altar as temple (*aedicula*) denotes the assurance of the Roman gods at death, but the wagon directly beneath her announced that her journey would be in Celtic conveyance.[30]

The Roman character of the tombstone is clear, but so are its Celtic aspects. Flavia speaks to both worlds at once. Native women who "married" Roman soldiers thereby intertwined their family with that of a respected man with a secure income. Upon his retirement and enrollment among the ranks of citizens, he could easily move laterally into the governing elite of the community, especially if he had made the rank of centurion. Then too his spouse and their children were also legitimized and became Roman citizens. Thus the marriage of a daughter to a Roman auxiliary soldier might be a major step in the advancement and assimilation of an entire barbarian family (in this case one of indigenous provincials) to the dominant culture. Because so many of the auxiliaries came

Grave monument to Flavia Tattunis filia Usaiu, Herculia (Gorsium), ca. A.D. 150–200. Courtesy of Szent István Király Múzeum, Szekesfehérvár.

to Pannonia originally from places far distant, these unions of soldier and civilian created a new Roman, one not Italian and not really local. These were men and women of complex heritages.

Here as elsewhere as the second century wore on, more and more auxiliaries were locally recruited, often serving in the same units as had their fathers and grandfathers. Thus, at Gorsium and at every other town that had a strong military presence, the century and a half after Augustus produced a progressively multicultural society that was held together by its acceptance of Roman forms and ideals. This new society was a combination of Roman urban values, military personnel, and native custom. The gravestones with scenes of wagon burials are an extraordinarily evocative testament to the creation of such a subculture among the native elites in Pannonia. Second- and third-generation Pannonian aristocrats discovered that many of their traditional Celtic aspirations were best expressed though the media of their conquerors.

Flavia's son must have lived in a complex cultural community in Gorsium that would have readily understood the visual vocabulary presiding over his mother's grave, for why else would he have borne the expense of so impressive a monument, one of the best cut and preserved in all of Pannonia. Examples of Celtic wagon burials of elites are common across much of Europe. As the Greeks and Romans believed that after death one journeyed across the river Styx, paying the boatman Charon his fare, so too the Celts across Europe thought of an afterlife obtained through travel. But unlike the peoples of the Mediterranean littoral, or the much later Vikings with their ship burials, the Celts foresaw an overland trip. As in *Beowulf* and the great seventh-century ship burial at Sutton Hoo, where the kings are cremated in a ship full of everything that they might wish to see in the afterlife, Celtic elites could afford to bring their own equipment and transport, a wagon with team. In the Rhineland, mounds dating to the second half of the first century served to protect and announce the location of the remains of the diseased. More often than not their conspicuous appearance attracted early grave robbers.

The mound burials in Pannonia were virtually identical to those along the Rhine—for example, the burial of the wealthy father and son (ca. A.D. 100) at Inota northeast of Lake Balaton. These mounds are complete with cremated remains and horse trappings, which were also typical of such burials in the Rhineland. Also included are examples of Roman terra sigillata pottery and glass, as well as ceramics of local manufacture and weapons. The horses themselves are buried separately nearby.[31] Real wagon burials were not only obviously Celtic; they were very expensive. The ritual evolved soon after the opening of the second century into purely symbolic forms for matters both of taste and cost: first, the driver was seated in an open wagon with the ossuary (a wooden coffin) visible; then later, he was joined by the deceased and/or family members, seen sitting in an armchair on the bed of the wagon. Sometimes a slave sits at the rear (ca. A.D. 110–50). The depiction of an altar with a covered wagon, as seen on Flavia's tombstone, follows in the second half of the century with or without the family depicted sitting inside. The wagon burial symbolism was still being used in the early third century. These developments of a hybrid Celtic-Roman burial style among the indigenous nobility occurred only in the neighborhood of Roman military camps and related settlements. Here too Roman influence among the lower orders of the natives is apparent in their increasing use of Roman tiles to create a burial chamber. Areas farther away from Roman camps were unaffected, and there simple Celtic burial practices continued for many decades without modification.[32]

Although Rome continued to recruit external barbarians and to allow carefully selected and tested groups admission into the empire itself, the main Roman agents affecting barbarians beyond the *limes* were trade and diplomacy.[33] By the middle of the second century, after the development of the frontier camps and supporting settlements along the river south of the great Danube bend, those living in the Hungarian Plain experienced an increased Roman influence. Roman trade was carried on in ways that reflect a very good understanding of barbarian tastes and financial resources. For example, the pottery in which items were shipped to them tended to be smaller and less dominated by luxuries from Gaul and Italy. This trade entered the plain along well-established routes both overland, especially from Aquincum and Intercisa in Pannonia and from Roman Dacia to the east, and along the rivers, notably the Tizta. Some Roman objects found in sites on the plain may have been the result of booty, but trade can account for most. Companies based along the Rhine dominated trade among the barbarians on the plain more than they did trade in the interior of the province, to the extent that Italian and southern Gallic wares were being crowded out by the opening of the second century.[34] Apparently the firms from the Rhineland had perfected the size, type, and price that worked best among the barbarians. Transportation costs were also lower for products coming down the Danube than for those crossing the Julian Alpine passes. Despite the considerable profits accruing to the state from taxing trade, the primary concern of the Roman government concerning its barbarian clients remained the assurance of their peaceful compliance to treaties. Trade was sometimes used as a weapon in that endeavor.

A half century of peace followed the creation of the two Pannonian provinces in 106. Romans supported its favorites as kings, bestowed subsidies and occasionally gave armed assistance to their clients against their neighbors.[35] Perhaps new treaties that went unrecorded had sanctioned even Trajan's establishment of monitoring stations. During these peaceful decades Roman governors lavished their attention on public projects, the result being that Pannonian towns soon had all the amenities of the finest cities of the Mediterranean world. They needed only to keep them repaired. Rome's principal neighbors along the Danube responded well. They kept to their treaties, traded peacefully along the river, welcomed Roman merchants and itinerant craftsmen, and generally avoided war among themselves. The barbarians had fully accepted the limits of their client status and did not raid Roman towns across the Danube. Because there was still rather limited contact between them, changes among the barbarians and in techniques that Romans used to handle their neighbors were very modest.

The development of the Pannonian provinces indicates that, without sustained face-to-face contact, trade alone was not much of a force for change among ordinary people. Naturally the amber route continued to run northwards from Carnuntum through *barbaricum* all the way to the Baltic coast, and there was an organized trade through and with those in the Hungarian Plain, but only on a few routes. Unfortunately peace was not something that Roman historians found very interesting. Their genre had, in fact, little room for it. So while the philosopher Aelius Aristides spoke rhapsodically of a golden age, of a time beyond warfare, the peace also meant that those on the peripheries had nothing to say to the Roman literary elites and so are unmentioned. Peace almost cost the barbarians their role as the eternal enemy in Roman literature. The minor wars of Domitian and even the great ones of Trajan and Marcus are not very well reported and would be much less so were it not for the survival of the columns of victory set up to honor the latter two emperors. Real wars did take place, but the Roman aristocracy seems to have lost its enthusiasm for the subject. The long peace in Pannonia was, however, about to end.

War can disrupt a militarized frontier in two ways. The first manner is obvious: invasion across the frontier by one party or the other. The second way is less striking but can be just as stressful to existing relationships: war elsewhere. Shortly after they became emperors Marcus Aurelius (161–80) and his brother Lucius Verus began to prosecute a war in the East against the Parthians. Major engagements required Rome to shift units from other frontiers so as to concentrate and maintain a sufficient strike force. Because of the long peace along the Danube, Pannonia lost the II Adiutrix legion at Aquincum and numerous vexallations (temporary detachments) from its other legions. Auxiliary units in this campaign as always played a major role, fighting alongside the legions.[36] The loss of the II Adiutrix was partially made good by the temporary assignment of a different frontier legion to Aquincum, but the withdrawal of such entrenched troops put civil life into turmoil on both sides of the river. Of thirteen legions committed to defending the northern provinces, three were pulled out and sent east. Auxiliaries and vexillations were not so essential as whole legions. Jobs were lost and trade floundered. With the war over, the men returned to their units, or the units returned to their primary billets. Some of these men, however, brought back more than their share of booty and battle-won glory.

On 12 October 166, Lucius and Marcus celebrated their victory over the Parthians with the entire splendor that an imperial triumph could provide. By then a smallpox epidemic had broken out in the capital, having been contracted by Roman troops in Syria in late 165 or early 166 during a siege and brought home.[37] As the historical experience of Native Americans lamentably reveals, smallpox is frightfully destructive, especially in populations that have had no prior exposure. Estimates of the mortality rate range widely, but 7 percent to 10 percent seems reasonable with perhaps rates up to 15 percent common among army units and in Rome itself. In the worst instances the local rates of death could have soared to as high as 80 percent. Probably somewhere between 3.5 and 5 million Romans died during the quarter century that this plague lingered.[38] The more isolated the location, the less likely is the outbreak of the infection, but the barbarians along the frontiers were not isolated. Although not a single Roman source mentions the disease afflicting them, the merchant activity on the Danube attests that the river was a highway, not a barrier. Highways carry people, and people carry disease. The Roman command was quite aware of the importance of trade to the barbarians. Marcus sought to limit the trade to certain locations during his wars in order to punish the Marcomanni, the Quadi, and their allies. Nonetheless, he depended to some degree upon them provisioning his troops. In 171 Quadi requested, but were refused, renewed access to Roman markets.[39] During these wars various barbarians pleaded for admission (*receptio,* literally to be received), despite the blood that they shed fighting the Romans. The emperors, notwithstanding what must have been genuine hatred after thousands of men had fallen, usually accepted them.

The epidemic must figure into any explanation of these actions, but scholarly literature has yet to reach consensus. The standard explanation for expanding barbarian immigration is that the empire needed as many settlers as it could recruit to occupy vacant lands,[40] but perhaps we should consider more seriously the plight of the barbarians. The Roman army had the best medical support that the ancient world could provide, except naturally to those elites able to pay for a doctor like Galen, Marcus's private physician. Medical and pharmaceutical instruments are commonly found on the sites of camps and during the excavation of towns along the frontiers. Perhaps despite the high loss of life in both the army and Roman towns, barbarians still believed that the empire offered a better refuge. We cannot know. The long struggle between Romans and barbarian invaders and settlers left its imprint on every site that we have discussed thus far, but particularly among the towns along the amber road. It also changed the ways in which Romans and barbarians interacted.

Tiberius had fought Maroboduus near the headwaters of the Elbe (Albis), where the Marcomanni first came together and where they remained during the early decades of the first century. While Claudius, Domitian, and Trajan committed more and more resources to the fortifications along the Danube, the Marcomanni and others such as the Quadi gradually shifted their dwellings southwards, particularly along the March River (Marus), which flows into the Danube a short distance downstream from Carnuntum. Other barbarians settled along the Waag, which empties into the Danube, opposite Brigetio, and the Gran Rivers, while in the meantime the intensity of distribution for sites in the Elbe watershed decreases. This pattern is surprising for a people supposed to be locked in an interminable war against Rome. Basically they were setting up house on the doorsteps of their supposed enemy. These were not military adventurers either. The archaeological data reveal a clear shift in concentration and general distribution of sites throughout these river valleys as would have been necessary to sustain a society of subsistence farmers. Beginning under Trajan, in some places slightly later, Roman soldiers manned perhaps a dozen outposts in this territory. These were relatively simple structures with little defensive capability other than stone walls (fifty to eighty centimeters thick) and a ditch. One had at least two small baths. These sites were abandoned at the end of the Marcomannic Wars, but some were reoccupied in the fourth century.[41] Such outposts could have served an offensive function, but their distribution and construction suggest rather that they were there to monitor these clients whose former loyalty had been found less than complete but whose present circumstances seemed promising.

The state of the evidence and its dating cannot establish a primary cause and effect relationship for this southwards shift. Roman authors of course saw all changes in habitation as being generated by external pressure, thus migration and eventually invasion, but these barbarian settlements do not appear to have been overtly aggressive. The growing mutual interdependence clearly emerging from the archaeological record stands in sharp contrast with the literary accounts of violent raids and relations under Marcus and others, but these accounts are meant to relate the circumstances and causes of war rather than the mundane interactions of peace. Roman authors portray what seems to be an almost unbroken series of wars and battles, each presenting an opportunity to test the character of the emperor. Because Roman traditions going back to the origins of the city disdained unjust or uninstigated offensive war, these authors found a universal explanation for war in the barbarian's lust to loot Roman provinces. According to such principles, barbarians were pressing against the barriers at all times, either in search of booty or because somebody else was pushing them from behind.

Instead of stemming from pressure—that is, rather than accepting the standard Roman principle of causation—this gradual shift of barbarian settlements southwards seems related to Roman decisions to deploy troops on the river. As we have seen this was a decision made only in part because of concern with barbarians. It was at least equally important to disperse the army and thereby make military usurpation less viable. Regardless of which of these two factors was more important in deciding to reposition the army forward to the empire's administrative borders, the shift precipitated an economic boom along the middle Danube. New opportunities lured formerly isolated rural populations to sell their surpluses in Roman markets and then to move closer to those markets. The administrative structures and transportation systems that Rome perfected assured that the process would begin within the provinces, but once begun there was no way to either reverse it or to limit it to the Roman side of the frontier. Roman efforts to manipulate it were episodic and ineffectual. Such diplomatic use of trade overlooked the essential nature of all trade: there are buyers and sellers on both sides. Trade barriers hurt Romans and barbarians and therefore could not be sustained. More Roman presence meant more trade and employment for more barbarians. More barbarians in an area served to focus Roman attention.

The government set about reworking systems of clientage to take the new circumstances into account, but along the middle Danube clientage failed to produce the level of predictability that changing Roman conditions required. By the death of Antonius Pius, clientage was largely replaced in this area by an even more dependent barbarian relationship in which a few Roman troops were billeted in their midst to monitor their compliance. But compliance to the new standard required barbarian leaders to impose even greater control, yet any increase in their political strength ran counter to Roman desires for weak neighbors. Thus this area, which seemed outwardly stable, was inherently unstable long before Lucius and Marcus withdrew much of the garrison for service in the East. The highly visible Roman presence had made tranquillity possible.

The war in the East did not go well, and in 165 Marcus had to raise two new legions, the Second and Third Italian Legions (II and III Italica). This was the first time in the century that the number of legions was increased, and, as their name suggests, they were as usual raised in Italy, but unlike in former times these were also destined for its defense. The new legions took up positions vacated as existing units were withdrawn for the Parthian campaigns. As if things were not bad enough, rebellions broke out in Spain and elsewhere. Recruitment requirements were abandoned, and even slaves were accepted.[42] Some increase in the number of legions was overdue. By shifting the main strike forces to the frontiers, the Roman army had not only relocated its extraordinary capacity for economic and social development. This came at the cost of seriously impairing Rome's ability to compose large armies for offensive action. Pannonia is a case in point, but the same factors were at work everywhere. The trend had barely begun when a little over a half century earlier Trajan assembled the largest force in Roman history to invade Dacia. The wars with the Marcomanni, Quadi, and Iazyges along the middle Danube bring the interdependency of the frontier society into focus. They were needed as allies, at least as silent neighbors, but they were happy with neither. Invasion and counterinvasion were the order of the day. All along the Rhine and upper Danube the entire client system sooner or later imploded and then exploded.

According to Cassius Dio the barbarian invasions along the middle Danube began in 166 with the unauthorized crossing of some six thousand Langobardi and Obii. The Langobardi among others were new to the frontiers. Tacitus had noted that they were famous far beyond their numbers, rejecting *obsequium* although surrounded by "numerous and powerful nations." The Roman commanders Vindex and Candidus (of cavalry and infantry, respectively) easily repelled the invaders.[43] An anonymous late Roman imperial biographer writing near the end of the fourth century reports that a vast barbarian conspiracy lay behind it.

> Not only were the Victuali and Marcomanni throwing everything into confusion, but other tribes, who had been driven on by the more distant barbarians and had retreated before them, were ready to attack Italy *if not peacefully received.*[44]

> Then from the borders of Illyricum even into Gaul, all the nations banded together against us—the Marcomanni, Varistae, Hermunduri and Quadi, the Suebians, Sarmatians, Lacringes and Buri, these and certain others together with the Victuali, namely Osi, Bessi, Cobotes, Roxolani, Bastarnae, Alani, Peucini, and finally, the Costoboci.[45]

Dio goes on to report that in battles along the Rhine the bodies of barbarian women were found in armor, and that on the lower Danube, the Astingi (another group that had its day only centuries later) were on the move with their entire families.[46] On the face of it, something is already surreal about these accounts. The anonymous biographer does not mention Dio's Langobardi (Lombards) and Obii, which may actually be to his credit because these people were then believed to live far to the north of the Marcomanni near the Baltic Sea. Whatever the case they did not become prominent in Roman history for another half millennium; they were admitted into Illyricum in 540 and then invaded Italy. Scholars who have sought to find them a home at so early a date as the second century have assigned them to modern Poland. They usually place the Obii slightly closer to the Roman world. Such geographic assignments are very problematic.

For most of the twentieth century scholars routinely connected the second-century invasions with the beginnings of the long Gothic migrations that were thought to have originated in Scandinavia: the Goths crossed the Baltic pushing out the Langobardi, who in turn shoved the Obii southwards, and so on. Simply put, these scholars combined ethnographic traditions that were created during the fifth and sixth centuries, when developing monarchies such as the Longobardi in Italy sought to strengthen their dynastic claims by creating genealogies of distant ancestors, and the ancient view of migration and historic change. The child of this academic marriage was the theory of the *Völkerwanderungzeit* (the era of the migration of peoples). Accordingly, the Marcomannic Wars were but the first act in this drama, which took two and a half centuries before it had run to its inevitable conclusion, the fall of the Roman Empire. For the proponents of this theory, it was not hard to agree with the fourth-century biographer and envision an immense hoard with Lombards (Langobardi) in the vanguard smashing their way across the Rhine frontier into Gaul. History is rarely so simple.

In the second century Roman authors knew no Langobard leader by name. None had yet tried to create a dynasty. The Langobards had no kingdom and no political force capable of achieving the armed might taken for granted by Dio. By stressing first-time invaders such as the Langobards, Dio reinforced his theory of causation. New peoples were pushing the old allies across a weakened frontier into a vulnerable empire. The Langobards' reported allies included virtually every barbarian then known and several who were not. Of women and families much has also been made by modern interpreters, but because this was so clearly a standard way for Roman authors to underscore the seriousness of specific barbarian threats, it too cannot be accepted at face value. On the other hand, these were dark days for Roman armies along the frontiers—that much is indisputable. There may even be something in the tradition that, before invading, these barbarians had sought permission to immigrate peacefully and that this was not forthcoming. The arrival of new immigrants, not the entry of new groups into the historical record, required careful planning and supervision. With war raging in the East, no troops could have been spared to process any new arrivals. The admission, perhaps long deserved in many cases, had to be postponed. Archaeology has not been able to confirm these migrations and never will, because such large-scale movements of people did not take place.

If Vindex, the Roman cavalry commander set against the Langobards in 166 according to Dio was in fact the same man as Marcus Macrinius Vindex, the praetorian prefect and commander of the northern armies directly under the emperor, then that alone would indicate a major invasion by somebody. Vindex was a rather common name. A Vindex died four or five years later fighting the Marcomanni, at which time he was a praetorian. But even identifying the men in these two incidents as one and the same does not prove a major invasion in 166. Vindex may have won his victories in 166 as a local commander and only later became Praetorian, or he could have taken credit as supreme commander for the actions of any of his subordinates. A unit of auxiliary cavalry, an *ala* of five hundred men or less may have repulsed "the Langobardi" and other small groups. Candidus's infantry force may have been of similar size. There is no indication in the sources of Roman troop strength, not even an attempt for rhetorical effect. A thousand Roman soldiers could have made quick work of a few thousand barbarians. The main point for Dio may have been the novelty of the Langobardi rather than their numbers and that their presence confirmed his view of a mass migration from the German heartland.

Whatever the size of the first barbarian invasion of the middle Danube, Dio and the fourth-century biographer give us a clear example of how ancient authors used migration to explain invasion. By conceptualizing people moving from the farthest north to the middle Danube, Romans provided what was for them a rational causative framework for the complete collapse of their frontier system from the northern Rhine southwards to the middle Danube. The anonymous biographer adds a conspiracy theory and thereby greatly magnifies the pressure upon the Roman frontiers. While very few scholars have ever accepted the idea that a conspiracy could have been concocted among barbarians so far distant from one another as the coasts of the Black and Baltic Seas, until quite recently few seriously doubted the migration and pressure theory itself. In this scenario pressure always existed because barbarians always wanted to invade.

Reduced to its basic premise, the pressure theory runs as follows. To hold back barbarian pressure, Roman forces had to thrust outwards or hold the line everywhere. A major break in Roman ranks sent a tidal wave of savages flooding into the provinces just as we find by combining the two accounts just noted. Whenever Roman forces were removed to another theater, the barbarian pressure won out, with the result being a universal Roman collapse. If Roman forces were only weakened, then it took longer. The entire frontier defense system could break down without any Roman troop displacements at all if a third party entered the picture and increased the normal barbarian pressure by pushing from behind, again just as in the preceding account. Genuine catastrophe came about when pushing from the rear or the withdrawal of the countervailing Roman forces augmented normal pressure or left it to be more effective respectively. Because the origins of these explanations are embedded in the psychology of the ancient sources themselves, the pressure theory has proved itself very hard to resist.

Marcus Aurelius's biographer also captures Marcus's palpable lament as recorded in his *Mediationes* (Meditations or Reflections), which was largely composed over the course of a decade spent mostly on campaign near Carnuntum. In these pages Marcus writing as a Stoic philosopher accepts his duty, but he also appears increasingly weary of his burden. And well he should, for with but one exception the wars boiled down to a series of bitter skirmishes between small units slugging it out in the forests. The scenes on the column set up to commemorate Marcus's victories are at least as severe as are his memoirs. There is a visible tenseness, anguish in the muscles and facial expressions as Marcus inspects the captured or when a barbarian chief pleads for admission. Barbarian villages are

Marcus Aurelius crowns a new client king (for Armenia) before his troops. Part of the spolia placed on the Arch of Constantine. Heads of emperor and king reworked for the arch.

destroyed; new client kings are crowned; Roman camps arise. This war was serious, bloody, and brutal. Unrecorded on the column but quite apparent in the literary accounts, disease continued to reap a bountiful harvest year after year.

The coins of Marcus, and until his death in 169, those of Lucius Verus unintentionally open another window on the nature of these struggles—a host of victories, some of them apparently quite modest. The first coin issue with Victoria Germanica was not until 171, probably commemorating a victory over the Marcomanni in the neighborhood of Carnuntum. No triumph was staged in Rome until 172, when another coin reverse depicts the emperor accompanied by his troops crossing the Danube by bridge. Three boats are

Barbarian king submits to Marcus Aurelius. Part of the spolia placed on the Arch of Constantine. Head of emperor reworked for the arch.

seen on the river as well. The generic portrayals of Germans seated before trophies in defeat gives way to scenes celebrating the defeat of Sarmatians on the Hungarian Plain in the course of 175–76. Of the Sarmatian images one seems especially poignant, that of a Sarmatian woman and man seated before a trophy. His hands are bound behind his back.[47] All issues are for generic victories over barbarians. The Marcomanni, Quadi, and others are assumed under the title German; the Iazyges, Cotini and others in the area of the Hungarian Plain are included under Sarmatian.

From the barbarian perspective matters were different. When it became clear that Marcus and Lucius would launch an offensive in 168, the barbarians sued for peace at once. Their entreaties were ignored, and the campaign surely would have begun had the epidemic not racked the army. Lucius died of a stroke as he and Marcus took their doctor's advice and headed back to Rome for the winter of 168–69. It was not until 170 that Marcus could reopen his offensive. The Romans were soundly defeated with a reported loss of twenty thousand men.[48] The barbarians followed the Roman retreat with a major counteroffensive that rolled over the remnants of the Roman garrisons all the way to Athens and Italy. The newly raised legions were unable to prevent northern Italy from being pillaged. Until now, such levels of cohesion and coordination on the battlefield had been extremely rare among barbarians. The Marcomanni and Quadi were able to take advantage of the Roman road system in Pannonia to attack virtually every town along their route. Roman towns along the amber road sustained particularly heavy damage, only repaired under Septimius Severus (193–211).

By the end of 171, Marcus was able to push the barbarians back across the Danube, probably by accelerating their booty-laden departures with small harassing actions. The next year witnessed a Roman invasion in force into the lands opposite Carnuntum where Roman outposts had until recently observed Marcomannic villages. The Marcomanni were defeated and genuine fortresses were constructed in their territory. The Quadi, who may have played little part in the invasions to date, had nonetheless sheltered Marcomannic refugees from the Roman invasion. Their turn to face Roman steel came in short order, and they mounted a vigorous resistance. So determined were they that on two occasions Marcus's forces were reportedly saved only by divine intervention—the miracles of the Lightening and the Rain. Each was commemorated iconographically as well as in the written histories. In both cases barbarian forces were supposedly on the verge of victory, when natural phenomena struck fear in their ranks. Roman sources including the Marcus column and coins attributed these battlefield reversals in the face of the barbarians to divine intervention. The barbarians in the legends are portrayed as cowing before the superior power of the Roman gods, which may well have been true.

After their defeat the Marcomanni were forced to withdraw their settlements to beyond ten miles from the Danube and prohibited

Denarius of Marcus Aurelius struck at Rome, A.D. 175/76. Obverse legend reads, M[arcus] Antoninus Aug[ustus] Germ[anicus] Sarm[aticus]. Reverse shows two barbarian prisoners sitting on shields under a trophy. Courtesy of the British Museum.

from trading with the Romans. By the opening of 175, Marcus had rewarded them for good behavior by reducing the cordon sanitaire to five miles and by designating days and legitimate market points along the river. Five miles seems to have been a standard distance, but an exception was also made for the Iazyges. They had to live twice as far from the Danube as had been stipulated for other peoples, including by then the Marcomanni and Quadi; that is, they too had to withdraw up to ten miles. This was perhaps in exchange for their being allowed much freer travel privileges than was customary.[49] Clearly the Romans understood the level of dependency among the barbarians, if not their Roman trading partners, and used trade restrictions as a weapon of coercion. But even the relative freedom granted to these barbarians seems to have been too much for the emperor.

Shortly before Marcus's death in 180, Dio reports that some twenty thousand troops had been garrisoned in fortresses complete with baths among both the Marcomanni and Quadi, positioned to keep watch of their every move.[50] The Quadi found such supervision intolerable and sought to depart, fleeing entirely from Roman influence, but that Marcus would not allow and ordered that all roads be blocked. Again and again during the last year of Marcus's life he took steps to reorder the middle Danubian area. It is all but certain that the troops deployed among the Marcomanni and Quadi were intended to become the garrison of a new province called Marcomannia. So too his troop depositions along the principal roadways crossing the plain were but the forerunners of a garrison for the new province of Sarmatia.[51] The largest population group in Sarmatia was the Iazyges, who had served Rome against the Quadi well enough to win a very interesting exception when Marcus renegotiated their clientage treaty. Unlike all others, the Iazyges were granted permission to cross a Roman province (Dacia) in order to maintain their traditional contacts with other barbarians living in what would today be Moldavia. The frequency and extent of their visits were left to the discretion of Dacia's provincial governor. Marcus was careful not to allow them free passage on the Danube in their own boats or access to islands in the river along the way.[52] The sense of this passage is that they were to use Roman shipping and not disembark except at towns with Roman garrisons.

In this way, these favored barbarians were encouraged to continue their contacts and familial relationships with people external to the Roman frontier system. Such contacts could hardly have been commodity-oriented because of the distances and travel restrictions, but rather they must have been very important to the Iazyges and Roxolani socially, even religiously. Perhaps there were numerous and long-standing marriage networks involved or cult rituals needing attention. Whatever was so important to the barbarians, their special concern for retaining contact is strong testament to the importance of pre-Roman networks among the barbarians even when living at considerable distances from one another. The Romans were the newcomers to these relationships and appreciated that they could destroy them only at great risk.

Marcus concluded numerous new agreements with barbarian clients. In general these were reaffirmations of older treaties, but now it seems he pressed for more specific commitments and signed with several new parties such as "the Naristi." These agreements when taken together reveal an intent to use one group to monitor and stabilize another; for example, by exploiting the animosity between the Quadi and the Iazyges, Marcus tied each to Rome for their own self-interest.[53] These new treaties formed the core of Roman dealings with barbarians and so were noted in imperial records no longer extant but used by our sources. Marcus's choices of kings were accepted.[54] For new and, as it turned out, transitory groups such as Naristi, their status as Roman clients elevated their leaders to a new level. Barbarians knew that the emperors would sign treaties with only kings. So now for the first time the Naristi and others like them had a vested interest in their own kingship, and their kings had a vested interest in treaties with Rome. Without passing through some sort of screening as clients, the odds were very small that you or your friends would ever be granted permission to enter the empire as immigrants. So if that was your goal, you had better create a kingship recognizable to the Romans. Thus Romans molded barbarians into acceptable neighbors. Rome placed restrictions on all clients. Not even the Iazyges were allowed to assemble freely or to trade with other barbarians (except in the peculiar context of the visitation privileges that the Iazyges had with the Roxolani). Thus each barbarian group negotiating with Marcus Aurelius was free to be a client of a single patron, Rome.

Many Roman soldiers and civilians either had been captured or had deserted to the barbarians during the early years of the struggle, but by its end the tables had been turned and barbarians fled to Roman encampments. Roman captives had to be returned prior to any renegotiation of client status.[55] Barbarians who were captured were sold into slavery. Deserters were not returned against their will. Many barbarian groups sought immediate admission inside the empire, but not all were received. There was a clear ranking of peoples. The level of tribute exacted varied, as did the duration of the agreements. Every source indicates that despite some selectivity, the emperor admitted, that is, "received," a great many barbarians into the empire during these years, but not until they had been defeated and had given their formal submission before imperial officers. At least this formality is what we see on the column and read in Dio and the biographer, but field conditions must have dictated that many of these were small unit or even individual defections rather than important chiefs dedicating themselves and their people to the emperors in person. Even when a king made the pledge for his people, the Romans did not necessarily accept his entire group and no large group was allowed to remain together inside the empire. During his wars Marcus "recruited new auxiliaries from among some Germans to fight against other Germans"[56]—that is, he recruited along the Rhine and upper Danube to fight against the Marcomanni and those along the middle Danube and vice versa.

When Marcus died in 180, Rome was poised to complete the program of conquest that had seemed within reach when Tiberius was recalled from the headwaters of the Elbe to meet the uprisings in Pannonia. Once again this was not to be. Commodus, who had been personally involved in much of the fighting and who was on his way back to Rome when news of his father's death reached him, saw things differently. Rather than for some sinister motive or from some lingering jealousy of his father's fame, it seems that wiser heads saw how terribly overextended Roman armies were and how much more important it was for the new emperor to be seen moving about the empire and its capital rather than being tied up leading campaigns beyond the Danube. Whatever the case, the time had now long past when a major campaign could be conducted in the absence of the emperor. Once Commodus decided to leave for Rome, peace had to follow and soon. The Second and Third Italian legions were assigned to Lauriacum (Linz, Austria) and to Castra Regina (Regensburg, Germany) on the upper Danube. They stabilized these areas and invigorated their economies for the next three centuries. The ravaged towns of Pannonia were refurbished, their public works expanded, their monuments reset, and new ones dedicated with the return of imperial stability under Septimius Severus and his dynasty (193–235).

Commodus left relations with the barbarians along the Pannonian frontiers in good order. Invasions ceased to be important, but henceforth emperors were expected to frequent their troops, inspecting men and fortifications or personally leading their armies, particularly against the Persians. Rural areas in Pannonia that had become interdependent with the towns continued to witness an expansion of *villae rusticae* and market agriculture. But few lingering indications remained of the traditions of the peoples conquered two centuries before, except for those living in truly remote areas who clung to local customs. Septimius was particularly active at Budapest and at Gorsium. The civilian town at Aquincum (Budapest) was elevated to a *colonia,* while in 202 the emperor personally dedicated a new temple for the imperial cult at Herculia (Gorsium). The return of the old prosperity is also reflected in the growth of residential areas, where some of the new dwellings were truly lavish. A temple was also erected for the god Jupiter Dolichenus at this time.

In A.D. 212, Septimius's son, the emperor Marcus Aurelius Severus Antoninus Augustus, better known by his nickname Caracalla, issued the following edict:

> [So that] I may show my gratitude to the immortal gods for preserving me in such [. . . perilous times (?)]. Therefore I believe that in this way I can render proper service to their majesty . . . by bringing with me to the worship of the gods all who enter into the number of my people. Accordingly, I grant Roman citizenship to all aliens throughout the [Roman] world except the *dediticii,* local citizenship remaining intact. For it is proper that the multitude should not only help carry all the burdens but should also now be included in my victory. The edict shall [increase] the majesty of the Roman people."[57]

Whatever its exact cause, or even its effective radius among the Roman population, the edict all but eliminated internal barbarians. All free men and women were now citizens. Within a short time the many gradients of urban status such as *municipia* and *colonia* too disappeared, because the relationship between residence and citizenship was also dissolved by Caracalla's action. There were still some people whose backgrounds or criminal records would have excluded them from the citizenship, so too the *dediticii,* but the document reverses the traditional questions. Slaves were excluded. An individual was now regarded as a citizen, and the exceptions were noncitizens. This inversion of tradition had been long in evolving, and in that sense the edict merely acknowledged the shift. Nonetheless, as Septimius's raising the status of the civilian community at Aquincum from a *municipium* to a *colonia* attests, distinctions of rank and citizenship still had meaning prior to 212. Townsmen had been proud of the enhanced honor that their municipal elevation carried, and they broadcast it throughout the empire.

Perhaps Caracalla considered how Rome's very complex legal

and bureaucratic procedures would be simplified by his act, as they indeed were, but his motives given in the text are vague. The name Marcus Aurelius had long ago become a very common name as auxiliaries receiving their citizenship upon retirement had taken the name of the reigning emperor, Marcus Aurelius Antonius, especially in Pannonia, where the second century emperor Marcus had spent so much of his reign. Many of Caracalla's new citizens now took up his official name, also Marcus Aurelius, as their epitaphs attest. Frequently these men can be distinguished from one another by reference to their traditional names present on the inscription as well. Henceforth, however, the use of the old Roman trinominal names wanes rapidly, because being a citizen soon lost much of its distinctiveness.[58] The name Marcus Aurelius still had a future, however, for the reigning emperors towards the end of the third century revived it.

Among the most controversial aspects of the edict is the exclusion from citizenship of the *dediticii*, which can be most simply translated as "those having recently submitted [or dedicated] themselves to the empire." Within this category would have fallen any new barbarians "received" into Roman service. Many of these barbarians, however, had not been technically defeated and had therefore not "submitted," but rather they had petitioned for admission. In republican times slaves who had been convicted of a crime were called *dediticii* and could never become citizens, but third-century barbarian recruits were not slaves. Indeed *dediticii* were fully free and could own slaves. One of the few legal restrictions placed upon *dediticii* that had carried over from the republican era and was destined to continue far beyond the third century was the prohibition upon them making legal testaments—that is, they could neither inherit nor dispose of property through wills. The edict makes no provision for the barbarian recruits themselves to ever become citizens, and we know from much later legal sources that units kept records indicating those with the status of *dediticii*. Their children would probably not have carried these restrictions, because the edict seems clear enough that anybody born free inside the empire was now a citizen. Outside of the army, no one probably much cared to ask whether you were a *dediticius*.

The edict, in effect, announced that relations between Romans and barbarians had become routine. A special category existed within Roman law for the newest arrivals, which by virtue of its formality attests that the frontiers had created a zone of sustained interaction in which new immigrants were to be expected on a regular basis. Brief outbreaks of warfare, to be sure, were expected, thus the implicit requirement that barbarians be defeated before being received, but warfare was to be an exception to peaceful coexistence. The frontier operated as a gateway to the empire, the army as the gatekeeper. Many new recruits were needed to stock the armies; a majority of barbarian immigrants found new homes in the camps, others held a variety of jobs in and around the nearby towns, a few needed asylum. Admission was regulated and monitored and required a declaration of allegiance to the emperor, but it was worth bearing the legal impairment of being a *dediticii*. All frontier areas were not the same. Some areas remained sparsely populated, but most frontier provinces had the populations with all the requisite skills and talents to allow them to become virtually independent from the old Mediterranean core and some even from each other.

In Pannonia as elsewhere the once useful distinction between external and internal barbarians can no longer serve much purpose in our discussion because legally the internal had merged completely into the Roman population. Men with privilege still mattered more than those men without it, be they citizens or not. In the late empire the quality of one's education and cultural habits alone distinguished the best Romans from the lesser. The barbarians living on the opposite side of the Danube were not granted citizenship. To the extent that the empire still defined itself in terms of universal membership as certified by citizenship, the barbarians were now even more distinct. But legal definition was progressively unimportant, and the old cultural distinction between barbarian and Roman was beginning to disappear as well. Nurtured by peace, a new society was slowly taking shape. The peace and prosperity of Pannonia lasted, however, only about another half century before war and invasion resumed once again.

Six

The Barbarians and the "Crisis" of the Empire

The trend towards centralization during the Principate could be symbolized by the emperor's presence at the head of his armies in battle but was also apparent in the more mundane aspects of daily life in the empire. Little by little Romans had placed greater confidence in the central government rather than in local elites. The central government had responded effectively, enforcing its monopoly on the use of force to assure domestic tranquillity and foreign peace, and had provided the models and the funding for all sorts of urban infrastructures. The collection of taxes became similarly centralized, although the emperors never declared it as policy. One by-product of this prosperity was that cities were largely undefended, in part because they were then less able to spawn usurpations but primarily because to surround them with walls would have undermined the psychology of invisibility, which every emperor did his utmost to nourish. None of the great metropoleis had circuit walls able to withstand a siege.

The upkeep of civic buildings lay in the hands of local authorities, but major building initiatives required the attention of the emperor or his staff and, through them, a diversion of tax revenues. The imperial cult had taken on vast importance in the local communities. Local grandees no longer built temples; only the emperor or a member of his family did so. Pliny's famous correspondence with Trajan reveals just how beset with decision making the emperor was by the opening of the second century, and matters coming to the court grew steadily in number and complexity throughout the century. By the opening of the third century, the task of being emperor all but overwhelmed the officeholder. The provisionment of the throngs living in the city of Rome itself was perhaps second only to the army as the largest expenses in the imperial budget. Citizens of the capital were known to riot if the grain fleet were delayed. When multiple military crises struck simultaneously, the system collapsed, but it did not die. Centralization was too deeply engrained at the top for that. But by the restoration of the central government under Diocletian (284–305) those nearer the bottom had turned their backs to the old and had begun in earnest to seek different solutions to their problems.

The emperors were soon engaged in a similar quest. The three decades following the death of Decius in 251 witnessed emperor after emperor proclaim the restoration of former times or that society had entered a new era of peace and tranquillity, only to have reality contradict them within a matter of days or months. Emperors assured the people that they and their families were capable heirs of the Antonine monarchs, but their resources were incapable of retrieving that past. Rather they had to find new solutions with fewer resources while not appearing to threaten the existence of the sacred traditions upon which the empire long rested. Fundamentally the turmoil was a crisis in government, one between what was expected and what was possible. Romans themselves knew that these times were extraordinarily grave, and, despite imperial claims that a restoration was in progress, many doubted that the good times would ever return. They rallied in their neighborhoods and searched within themselves.[1] Self-help replaced a commitment to central direction so profoundly that no future emperor was able to reverse this shift. Ultimately nothing, not even time itself, was left unchanged. Slowly these sweeping alterations in ancient life left their mark on Roman-barbarian relations, but these transformations were not apparent to contemporaries, neither Roman nor

A sarcophagus portraying the battle between the emperor Decius (A.D. 249–51) or his son Herennius Etruscus Decius (made Caesar in 250, then coemperor with his father in 251), fighting the barbarians. Middle of the third century. Each emperor died fighting the Goths in separate battles in 251. The scene here is highly typical of Roman propaganda in general. It is impossible to believe that the apparently triumphal emperor, seen here on horseback urging on his troops, actually lost his own life and those of his entire army at the hands of the very barbarians seen here groveling for mercy. Courtesy of Museo Nazionale Romano, Palazzo Altemps, Ministero per I Beni e le Attività Culturali—Soprintendenza Archeologica di Roma—noriché la collacazione del repoerto riprodotto.

barbarian, who must have been hard-pressed to keep track of who their rulers were.

The Roman emperor Decius died in battle against barbarian invaders in the Balkans in June 251. As the sun rose that day he must have believed that he would soon reestablish the integrity of the empire's frontiers, secure himself as the founder of a new dynasty, and return Roman government and society to normal—that is, to the conditions prevailing under the Severan emperors. The barbarians—especially the Goths, who after defeating Decius went on to cause great suffering in Dacia and Thrace—have long shouldered much of the blame for the fact that this restoration of normalcy did not take place. What since the eighteenth century has been described as a century-long crisis has regularly been laid at their door. This "external menace" interpretation has recently undergone considerable rethinking.[2] There is no denying that northern barbarians eventually invaded many of the frontier provinces, some even making their way into Spain and Italy. Where they passed, they inflicted profound suffering. Families huddled in their farmhouses and cities with poorly maintained defenses were easy prey. By the end of the third century two large areas of the empire had ceased to be administered by Roman authorities.

On the other hand, there is also no doubt that the barbarians in turn suffered and were transformed by the breakdown of authority inside the empire and the resulting insecurity there as competing Roman armies sought their aid, recruited their youth, or plundered their homes. The death of Decius in battle against a foreign invader should not obscure the fact of his own rise to power in bloody civil war against Philip the Arab (244–49) and the progressive disintegration of orderly imperial succession that already manifested the most profound dilemma within the empire. The collapse of dynastic continuity dated back at least to the assassination of Alexander Severus (222–35) and in many respects had begun with the murder of Caracalla, the last son of Septimius in 217, and the internal conflicts during reign of the child-emperor Elagabalus (218–22).

Concurrent with the chaos in imperial politics, a new Persian dynasty, the Sassanid, sought to assert itself at Roman expense. As Roman troops departed the Balkan and western provinces to fight Sassanid armies, those remaining behind—barbarian and Roman alike—lost markets, jobs, and revenue. The best one could hope for was to be recruited into one of the departing units, but families surely knew that many of their loved ones would never return. Discontented troops raised numerous claimants to the imperial throne, usually their own commander. These men lived with their armies, and died at their hands, all the while staying near the frontiers. It was there that they conducted their business, including their intrigues. The warrior-emperor, rare until the reign of Marcus Aurelius, now became the norm and would remain so for a century and a half. Barbarians, rural Roman peasants, and civilian townsmen were all caught up in this turmoil of Roman civil war and the collapse of the regular patterns of government, but the disparities from region to region were stark. Civil war looms ever larger in our evaluations of the problems of this era, for these struggles pitted highly trained Roman armies against one another. No city or camp was safe, for walls could not long withstand their siegecraft. Their armies gave no quarter. Predictability was the first casualty. Profits were made at the expense of the suffering of others. Justice seemed to have vanished from the empire.

Any emperor delegating major military command faced great risk, for then his legate might claim a share of the throne; but if he did not delegate, he could face only one challenge at a time. This problem was hardly new but it reached new depths during the third century. Just when multiple theaters required a division of troops, the armies fought only for the emperor in front of them. This evolution was probably inevitable, given the nature of the emperorship and the scarcity of military assets. Although emperors did move some troops great distances for campaigns, the heart of Roman armies had to be rallied from among those units available within the region. Detachments from elsewhere supplemented these. If that core army were ever seriously depleted, then raising a similar force purely from troops transferred to the area was impossible in the short term. The rise of a new dynasty in Persia, combined first with Roman civil wars and usurpations and later with various invasions by northern barbarians, exposed the inherent fragility of the Roman military situation.

As did the new Roman dynasties, contemporary Sassanids had a need to demonstrate military prowess and thereby prove the favor of their gods and their right to rule. Within months of Decius's death the greatest of the Sassanid kings, Shapur, took Armenia back from Roman control. This new Persian belligerency greatly escalated the struggle with Rome that had gone on more or less continuously since the first Sassanids had thrown out the last of the Parthian dynasty and invaded Roman Mesopotamia (226–30), but even under Shapur there was no clear goal of territorial acquisition other than the reconquest of lands once Persian but lost in the course of Roman expansion. Retaking and securing the upper Tigris and Euphrates River valleys held by Rome for over a century was particularly important, but certainly no Sassanid king thought of replacing the Roman Empire with his own. Shapur pressed his advantage into Mesopotamia and Syria, and soon Antioch fell to his supporters. By 257 the emperor Valerian was relying on Odenathus of Palmyra to hold back Persian raids in the Syrian area, while he concentrated his forces against raids further north, particularly those of some Goths striking the Black Sea ports of Asia Minor. These Goths are usually referred to as the Black Sea Goths to distinguish them from the other Gothic speakers who had recently defeated Decius south of the Danube. These two Gothic assemblages remained distinct, but neither was able to create a coherent political system. There were just not enough men to fight both fronts in the East, and Odenathus had probably already proved his loyalty and usefulness by then. Valerian could stay on in the East and campaign because he had an able and trustworthy colleague back in Rome, his son, Gallienus, whom he had appointed immediately upon ascending the throne in 253.

Invasions by northern barbarians were tertiary to usurpation and the Sassanids in changing the nature of Roman society, its army, and government. When the emperor was off fighting Persians, armies in the other theaters of command often seemed incapable of action. Occasionally towns were left to stand alone with their skeletal garrisons and hastily assembled militias. This is in marked contrast to the case of Plautius Silvanus, governor of Moesia under Nero (54–68), who had boasted of his independence in fighting barbarians. Had Persia not rejuvenated itself under Shapur, it seems likely that conditions along the frontiers with the northern barbarians would have continued their peaceful evolution. At some point a future emperor would have had to subdivide the empire simply because the system was so complex that it was beyond one man's capacity to govern. In fact, by the opening of the third century most barbarians were themselves so familiar with peace and prosperity along the frontiers that they rarely initiated hostilities, especially not before conditions in the East required shifting large numbers of troops eastwards. Despite Roman withdrawals they were sometimes very reluctant to invade. For example, in 258 Gallienus (253–59 with his father Valerian, 260–68 alone) took troops from the Rhineland province of Germania Inferior and sent major detachments eastwards, but there were no raids there for at least a year, probably two, or even three. Small raids may have continued as usual but nothing needing the emperor's attention.[3]

A detailed imperial chronology for the third century has only recently emerged, so dismal are the records and so slender the hold on power of even the successful emperors. Even today many details concerning imperial ascensions, deaths, and campaigns remain obscure. One fact stands out: even in the midst of the most profound tragedies, nobody could imagine a situation without the empire—one society under one law and under one ruler. Although from the death of Decius onwards it became increasingly common for the empire to operate on the basis of three geographic divisions, centered respectively upon Gaul, Italy, and Syria, not a single ruler sought to change the increasingly theoretical unity of the empire. Not even Shapur could imagine a world without the Roman Empire. The three Roman political regions competed for domination over adjacent but not coterminus economic and cultural zones, because none of the three held sufficient fiscal resources and manpower to overpower the others. Looked at from a nonpolitical perspective, there were at least five major economic and cultural spheres in existence by the opening of the third century: (1) Italy with the neighboring Alpine areas and North Africa; (2) the Balkan peninsula including Dacia; (3) the western Mediterranean provinces including southern Gaul and much of Spain; (4) the northern transalpine provinces including Britain; and (5) the East, but not normally including Egypt, which since Augustus usually remained linked to Italy. During most of the third century no one regional political authority could muster sufficient strength to long hold more than two of these five regional clusters; thus there was an ongoing competition for power.

Frustrated by their imperial claimant's apparent weakness, troops and supporters abandoned one candidate after another. What political stability existed was provided by adherence to dynastic principles, but these were most effective at the regional level: Postumus and his line in the empire of the Gauls, Odenathus and Zenobia in Palmyra, and various generals from the central provinces, especially

Valerian and Gallienus. The aura of Italy and Rome sooner or later drew claimants from the periphery to the center, including ultimately Zenobia. Control of Rome and the acknowledgment of the Senate still conveyed legitimacy, but rivals to the center were always unable to deploy adequate resources there to replace the central government. Conceptually little had changed, but the realities of power had shifted dramatically. The periphery now provided the human resources and the ethos for a new empire, one progressively run as if it were an army in the field. The evolution of a mobile reserve force of cavalry began under Gallienus and helped stabilize the political situation. Future claimants from among its cavalry commanders had great success in competing for the emperorship, largely because by then the addition of a relatively small reserve force tipped the regional balance of power in favor of its commander and allowed him to mount a credible threat to other regions. Furthermore, it had the long-term effect of changing the recruiting priorities of the army towards lighter forces capable of operating more independently. In the haste to fill the ranks left vacant by moving men eastwards or battle casualties, barbarian recruits fit nicely into this new force. It needs to be pointed out, however, that as in so many other developments among barbarians, it was the Roman economy that produced the horses, it was the Roman command structure that held these cavalry formations together, and it was the Roman desire to expand their employment that gave them status. Maintaining large herds of horses trained to fight alongside infantry was beyond any barbarian people's ability. The horse was a powerful status symbol among barbarians, but it was an uncommon sight in battle.

These underlying economic and cultural zones reflected the difficulties and expense of long-distance transportation as well as the perpetuation of pre-Roman cultures. Just as Caesar had proclaimed, Gaul was divided into essentially three spheres, based upon levels of pre-Roman urbanization rather than the tribal alliances that he had emphasized. The most developed Gallic urban centers all lay in the south; at the other extreme were hamlet-based farmers. Every administrative region of the empire had a long history and had made its own peculiar contribution to Roman civilization. In general the native elites living in or near Roman provincial towns were the first to adopt Roman forms to express their concerns and values. Some needs were universal, such as that of protection from physical harm, but most called upon the gods for assistance in meeting the demands of daily life, and these latter requirements were not susceptible to political redefinition. That is to say, the environmental and topographic conditions existed whether or not Roman engineers and soldiers were present in a few towns.[4] Unless and until Roman towns and villa-based agriculture were deeply entrenched, the native communities and their traditions changed very little. These same principles can be applied to the barbarians living beyond Rome's borders and to the "reemergence" of native traditions within many of the western provinces.

By the third century the upper and middle Danubian provinces had become ever more interconnected economically with the Rhineland provinces. The Danube provided a cheap and safe way to transport goods, and it provided ready transport for troops. The northernmost provinces had similarly profited from the security that the Roman fleet on the Rhine guaranteed. These regional markets now provided most of the commodities that had in the first century come from manufacturing centers in the Mediterranean provinces. Because these new markets were themselves essentially self-contained, they also provided markets for rural populations that were often scarcely Romanized in their tastes. The regional centers thereby encouraged rural producers to expand their horizons. The major buyer of local products was usually the army, whose soldiers were themselves locals. Soldiers who had been recruited in the area used part of their pay to obtain those local specialties such as foodstuffs and handicrafts with which they had grown up. In some areas this complex evolution produced a renaissance of indigenous culture previously preserved primarily in the rural communities. This so-called Celtic Revival was a function of the success of Roman economic development and social integration at the regional level, not a sign of imperial failure. Individuals felt comfortable and secure in their local Roman settings and saw no reason to reject their ancestral customs that now might give them a valuable market niche. Great profits were to be made within the region, and highly successful administrative careers in the provincial and imperial governments did not always require relocation across the empire. This was especially the case in the Gallic Empire.[5] There was no more colonization, no more foreign conquest. New combinations emerged from the regional mixtures of local Roman cultures with their native touches and high culture of the imperial elites, but these new creations all took place within the peaceful evolution of Roman society. They were not revolutionary or anti-Roman.

After 212, not bothering to make the standard presentation of one's Romanness included not necessarily Latinizing your name or, as auxiliaries especially had done earlier, having two names, one in order to pursue a career in the military or other Roman trade and another for hearth and home. Now the Latin name could be omitted. Increasingly we find officials who recalled that their ancestors had been from such and such a barbarian group, long after they could have adopted the Roman practice of declaring in which city they held their citizenship. This freedom to be Roman and proud of your non-Roman background was demonstrated in many ways, such displays becoming common during the third century. The lure of Rome remained strong but culturally it was increasingly not Italian or Mediterranean in origins. The periphery was coming into its own, but those living there correctly thought of themselves as Roman. Even in the late fourth century, first-generation barbarian recruits more often than not abandoned their ancestral customs, hesitating to wear anything that might be regarded as appearing openly un-Roman around the camps, probably because it would have signaled that the recruit was "a country bumpkin." Great variety was possible in Roman military dress, particularly from the late third century onwards, but it was Roman nonetheless. One might say the newly admitted barbarians were more determined to be Roman than Romans were. This was in keeping with what was actually a long tradition of using one's ancestral dress styles to enhance one's overall Roman appearance. In Pannonia we have seen how women in particular retained peculiar ways of arranging their hair. Army officers exercised much latitude in their personal ornament. This can be seen still in the decoration of their dress armor, which they personally ordered and paid for but that was locally produced from a stock of figural representations. Aspects of Roman military dress had religious connotations that had evolved from Celtic decorative motifs during the early empire—for example, wearing the torques. Evolution continued to reflect a healthy and vigorous frontier society.

There is no indication that the consumers of local craft production and specialty items or Roman centurions were making political statements. None of the various "rebellions" of the third century can be shown to have been fostered or in any way related to the resurgence of "pre-Roman" tastes. The fact is that in remote communities there had always been a substratum of local products catering to local needs and still visible in peculiar pottery styles that were designed to prepare or serve local specialty foods. In those provinces with rugged topographies and few arterial roads, families continued to live peacefully with few if any signs of Roman influence throughout the third century. Despite much recent interest, relatively little is known about rural life within the Roman provinces let alone beyond them. Our knowledge of Roman villa estates is a partial exception, but very few have been fully excavated and published yet. Nonetheless, the distributions of datable Roman wares and related local products found beyond the frontiers suggest that the same geographic and climatic factors prevailed there as within the empire.

Among some barbarians Roman wares had already become so commonplace that by the third century they seem to have no longer played a role in status definition. Elsewhere the reverse was true, especially as one moved farther away from the frontier. As we have seen through the example of Pannonia, by the end of the second century the fortresses and towns along the frontiers dominated the interior of their provinces and the areas beyond them. Rome now dominated the two principal transportation corridors north of the Mediterranean, and from these rivers zones of commercial exchange continued to radiate outwards in all directions. Beyond the frontiers interior trade routes continued as they had in pre-Roman times, for without Roman roads and state subsidies making overland transportation competitive there was no alternative. Trade remained largely restricted to luxury goods, although a few rivers flowing into the Rhine and Danube did allow for some heavier traffic, such as in the area north of the Danube between modern Vienna and Budapest. Those barbarians living along the great rivers, on the other hand, had almost full access to Roman products, even though this exchange was subject to sporadic manipulation. Anybody using these rivers for heavy transport had to have Roman permission and pay appropriate taxes.

Less significant routes into *barbaricum* had taken longer to develop and are more difficult to trace, but there can be no doubt that they existed in many areas. Second-century wall construction in Britain and on the continent created "man-made rivers." The walls that demarcated the limits of direct Roman administration also stimulated the development of barbarian societies beyond them, but they did so without the benefit of navigable rivers acting as carriers and magnets for commerce. New zones of local commercial relationships emerged on both sides of these "rivers" that had no pre-Roman basis, for Roman conquerors had not paid much attention to such matters, and others later had cause to regret their lack of foresight. Where pre-Roman cultural interactions had well-established patterns of regional exchange, these were inevitably realigned, often with incomplete success. Military engineers laid out roads and defensive systems to take advantage of the topography, to provide for line-of-sight contact between small fortifications, and to keep track of populations. At first these walls divided people, but they did not affect many because they ran through sparsely populated areas. Gradually, however, as did the rivers, walls too united people. While Roman legions directed much of their attention to internal politics, during the third century their sporadic and predatory conduct towards barbarians pushed some into greater involvement in their own political structures.

The Persian wars monopolized most Roman effort after the death of Caracalla, and little attention was paid to the West or the Balkans except as sources of men and material. Nothing speaks more forcefully of the generally peaceful state that existed with barbarians in the West than the fact that emperor after emperor could stay in the East, where more often than not emperors fell at the hands of their own troops in civil wars. In fact, only Decius fell fighting barbarians. Around midcentury local problems involving barbarians along the frontiers began to coalesce, particularly in Dacia and along the middle Danube neighboring the Pannonian provinces, but secondary Roman efforts led by provincial governors, their aides, junior imperial colleagues, and even unauthorized local militias were successful at containment and restoration. This was true at least as late as 257. In 253 Valerian was hailed as emperor, first by his own men and then by those of the reigning emperor Aemilianus, whose rule had not yet lasted a year. Valerian immediately named his adult son, Gallienus, his coemperor. Politically things looked good with a strong general in the East and his able son in charge in the West. Then in 259 the Roman governor of Lower Germany, Postumus, revolted. Among the casualties was Gallienus's son, the young heir apparent, the coemperor Salonius. The rebellion was the result of an internal power struggle having nothing to do with the barbarians.

Rather than marching on Rome, Postumus set about shoring up the Rhine frontier, which needed recruits to fill the gaps left after Valerian had ordered more and more troops eastwards. Restoring manpower and confidence to the army on the Rhine and manning the long section of wall and ditch that ran from Mainz to the Danube upstream from Regensburg left Postumus with no realistic chance to settle affairs with his rival in Rome, the bereaved father, Gallienus. For manpower, Postumus had to turn to barbarians. Disaster struck in the East. Within a year, Valerian had been captured in battle against the Sassanid king, Shapur, but still Postumus (259–68) showed no intent to invade Italy. Instead he established his own imperial government, named his own officers to traditional imperial posts, and transformed the old Celtic, but by then long since Roman town of Trier into his capital. His breakaway regime, the "Empire of the Gauls" (259–73), outlasted him by five years as his three short-lived successors struggled to survive. Their capital Trier was later taken by Constantine I as his official residence north of the Alps and so foreshadowed the shift of the working capitals of the late empire to towns closer to the frontiers. Most towns in the interior of the provinces still had only the thin, largely symbolic walls that had marked them as urban centers during the second century.

While Postumus held forth at Trier, Gallienus relied upon the Kingdom of Palmyra under Zenobia and Odenathus, (Zenobia's supreme general, later paramour, and finally husband), to contain the Persians. The Persian rulers were to prove that they were quite content to nibble at the empire rather than trying to overthrow it. Gallienus thus was able to concentrate his personal efforts at the restoration of Roman control in Dacia and the Balkan peninsula. He made substantial progress there, sometimes with force, at other times through negotiations that transformed invaders into allies at the cost of Roman tribute. Probably through necessity, Gallienus had begun to experiment with mobile units and to consolidate them into a major support force of cavalry under his personal command when he himself fell in a plot led by his generals in 268. The worst years had, however, passed. Claudius (268–70), as his honorary title Gothicus suggests, was able to complete the suppression and pacification of the Goths who had invaded Thrace. Aurelian (270–75) defeated barbarian invaders in Italy and began the construction of a circuit wall for Rome, which further inspired cities elsewhere to look to their own defenses.

Aurelian also ended the independence of Palmyra, capturing its queen Zenobia and leading her in triumph through Rome before pensioning her off to a life of leisure. Shortly before his death he brought what was left of the empire of the Gauls back under the central government. Probus (276–82) began to restore the frontier provinces throughout the empire, but most of his efforts were incomplete when he too fell at the hands of his troops. Most of these emperors and their rivals were generals from the Danubian legions, but this was merely a reflection of the circumstances that made this area the principal theater of imperial operations and recruitment rather than some special characteristic of the Balkans. Restoration took decades and, despite the tremendous efforts of Diocletian (284–305), many projects were not completed until Constantine I brought an end to civil war. Indeed the theme of "the restoration of the good times" became a banner slogan under Constantine and his dynasty.[6] Even then, however, the "restored empire" was a different one from that which Septimus Severus had ruled.

By 300, after a half century of civil war in which rival armies besieged each other's towns and looted the countryside, the political, economic, and, in some ways, even the cultural center of the empire had moved to the frontiers. This shift brought the barbarians as well as the Roman armies and their dependents into the center. From their perspective they lived in the middle, and the Mediterranean cities were ever more remote and peripheral to their daily lives. Unlike in previous eras of civil war, the half-century-long competition for power (ca. 235–85) relied heavily upon barbarians recruited directly into Roman units or serving various claimants as armed allies. With so much manpower committed in the East, there was little choice but to accelerate the recruitment of barbarians and to encourage their leaders to act on Rome's behalf. While one rival Roman camp recruited and made alliances, another Roman commander moved to neutralize these efforts by supporting rival barbarian leaders. When there were no disgruntled neighbors to set against a rival's barbarian allies, then one could undermine the existing leadership by supporting a rival family within the barbarian community. If this did not work, recourse could be had to raiding barbarian villages. In this endless game of personal diplomacy, raid and counterraid, barbarian groups and the Roman armies each could claim that others had been the aggressors. The escalating cycle of violence and betrayal seemed to have neither a beginning nor an end. Offended honor could always justify attack and subterfuge. Some barbarians living near the frontiers must have felt as if they had grasped a whipsaw. By the end of the century as law and political order returned to the empire, an ethos that rewarded violence had established itself more firmly than ever before among the barbarians. The nature of the empire had also changed.

Until the middle of the third century most of the population of the frontier provinces lived in the countryside in open settlements and in *villae rusticae,* but as insecurity grew this life-style gave way. During the Principate thousands of such open sites existed in the German provinces from Belgica through Noricum. Some had prospered for many decades, while others failed and were abandoned.

Most were able to take advantage of the quickening economic life, and their owners lavished their gains on the further development of their estates. When this rural landscape began to change, all *villae rusticae* did not suddenly disappear, nor did those that did so vanish simultaneously. Nonetheless, the trend towards defended nucleated settlement had begun in many places by the third century's end. Towns reflected similar concerns. In the early years of the century few Roman towns had any defensive capability. Even urban centers in the frontier provinces were defended only by relatively weak fortifications, mostly built during the second century. Because the army was expected to take the offensive and confront invaders in the open, urban walls were primarily observation platforms, able to detour hit-and-run raids but hardly capable of withstanding a siege. Second-century towns revealed their status by their walls, but those walls were not their primary defense. When the century ended, most cities had encased their urban centers with stout up-to-date walls complete with protruding towers with preset and overlapping fields of fire for artillery.[7] For men living in the frontier provinces, as in the more central provinces, civilian careers had competed successfully alongside those related to the army. As civilian life retreated behind walls, one obvious career path remained, the army.

Barbarian villages were more stable. Life there continued as always but with ever greater signs of involvement with Roman markets, despite a sharp disruption in their economies during the later half of the century. Although they were at least as vulnerable to raids as Roman townsmen near the frontier, no barbarian villagers built defensive walls. Presumably some modest fortification was within their technological competence, but it was probably prohibited for these Roman clients. Some youths sought and gained admission into the empire through military service or joined a band under a particularly strong warrior allied to a Roman general or about to launch a raid against some other village or the empire, but most barbarians remained tied to their villages.

Yet there too something had changed. Now, almost as a self-fulfillment of Roman ethnographic stereotypes, some members of these traditional communities wished neither to be farmers nor to be under orders as regular Roman soldiers. For these, war had become a way of life with the Roman army serving as both part-time employer and adversary. Their way of fighting was excitingly independent of discipline. Leaders raised the battle cry for or against Rome, led the charge, and typically died a violent death. Very few long survived. This new warrior elite attained a sense of shared purpose with others in their regions such as had scarcely been witnessed before the opening of the third century. Only the Marcomanni were so capable before and for very similar reasons. On the one hand, Rome played a major role in this barbarian achievement, for its recruitment was greatly facilitated by the existence of indigenous political authorities capable of signing on as effective units with little or no training. There was no time to train armies during civil wars. On the other hand, successfully invading the empire also required a new level of cohesion among the barbarians. In either case, without Rome far more would have remained simple village farmers. Previously when such native political power had arisen, it had been crushed by vigorous and sustained Roman intervention; now it was a fact of life, nurtured by Roman commanders whose demand for soldiers reached deep into *barbaricum*.

We are left largely in the dark as to most details concerning internal development among the barbarians. As for everything else concerning the third century, the reason lies in our sources. Their style and vacuity have seemed to many scholars to offer proof of great drama and of imperial decline. Grand theories provoke discussion but rarely hold up to scrutiny. No matter how many times we stir the images, our historical kaleidoscope simply lacks sufficient elements to create a clear picture. Until quite recently modern historians were in accord that the third century was a period of continuous and universal crisis, primarily because they could not recapture the political narrative and little else mattered to them. Since the eighteenth century, especially since the publication of Edward Gibbon's *Decline and Fall of the Roman Empire* at the end of the century, barbarian invasions (including the Persian) were singled out for primary responsibility for the collapse of the Principate with its supposed openness and freedom. The fact is that most of ancient history has been written from the literary sources, through which historians have deduced causation by setting events in chronological order, but for the third century even the barest chronology is difficult, sometimes impossible to obtain. The few extant contemporary accounts offer widely conflicting analyses and are for the most part unhistorical as judged by the standards of Roman historians themselves. Against this background modern historians trying to understand the northern barbarians have tended to fill the voids in the literary evidence with theories supported in a most tenuous fashion by connecting the barbarians as depicted in Tacitus's *Germania* (ca. A.D. 100) to those of the late fourth and fifth centuries, for whom supposedly better records exist. This approach is fraught with problems, for neither anchor will hold against the tide.

Just as the *Germania* blends contemporary reality and inherited myth to connect with readers at the opening of the second century, authors in late antiquity recast the barbarian in new roles for their own audiences. Neither portrait can serve as a secure guidepost. Ancient ethnologies as most thoroughly represented by the *Germania* make it seem all too obvious that northern barbarians were simply violent and that this natural state of barbarians contrasted with men in civilized societies. Accordingly, all that was necessary for barbarians was the opportunity to be violent, to invade the civilized world, and to plunder its riches. Roman authors did not see barbarian violence as something that had developed among barbarians or was evolving towards greater destructiveness. Barbarians were by nature violent. Caesar and Tacitus both noted a curious fact; civilization theoretically worked against the perpetuation of their warrior ethos by undermining their martial spirit. The danger of running a straight line from the barbarians of Caesar, through those of Tacitus, to those of the late empire is to overlook the acceleration of Roman-generated violence that occurred during the third century. It was this violence and the violent means necessary to end it that produced a new and characteristically late Roman frontier environment. Often rival Roman armies cultivated this new military ethos among the barbarians and, in so doing, destabilized existing barbarian societies, enhancing the position of war leaders at the expense of traditional family and village structures. Without Roman initiatives, the violence that sometimes erupted along the frontiers would probably have been much less and certainly would have not lasted for over half a century. Nor would it have infected areas far removed from the frontiers in all directions. These new ideas have resulted from historians turning to nontraditional sources and, having done that, reexamining the literary material.

Archaeology has helped fill in some of the gaps in our understanding, and so too has the increased understanding of Roman coinage, the effects of its usage, and its distribution in *barbaricum,* but the light of inquiry has seldom penetrated far in the study of daily life among ordinary barbarians. Most important, archaeology has provided us with a different temporal framework, one based not on regnal years but on the stratographic analysis of single sites. Numismatics has played a major role in establishing a better chronology of imperial succession and has contributed mightily in underscoring the importance of Roman recruitment among the barbarians. The study of inscriptions has also contributed some striking insights, along with new interpretive problems. Setting up public inscriptions was always expensive and already by the third century relatively rare, but given our paucity of data, a single inscription can be decisive. The many pieces of the puzzle have yet to come together; they may never be brought to do so. After a century of excavation, particularly intense since World War II, it is clear that there was an increasing familiarity between barbarians and Romans along the frontiers almost everywhere. Trade and employment during the later half of the second century and the first half of the third were bringing this about. The domestic vitality around the frontier camps that supported Roman urban and rural development spanned the rivers. This can be shown in the distribution of Roman coinage and in the types of items one finds in excavations in *barbaricum,* but it did not yet extend much into the manner of domestic construction or the outline of barbarian villages. Until midcentury both sides of the river were adjusting to an increasing population, and more and more barbarian villages were being built along the frontiers where access to markets was much easier.

In the archaeological record most major crises virtually disappear. Almost invariably life goes on regardless of human calamities.

Clear evidence of identifiable dramatic incidents is extremely rare. Even when evidence of the latter is striking—for example, arrowheads still imbedded in the walls of a fortification, bodies left unburied or ceremonially sacrificed—it is by no means obvious who the actors were. Were they Roman soldiers bent on revenge against a rival army, or barbarians fresh from crossing the frontiers turned to plunder? In the western provinces, although many towns and open settlements suffered greatly, virtually no fortification can be proved to have been successfully assaulted by barbarians, although many can be shown to have been attacked by somebody. For example, when Maximinus Thrax (235–38) came to power over the last of the Severans, he ordered his troops everywhere to strike at the cult centers of Jupiter Dolichenus, the favored god of the Severan family and divine protector of their dynasty.

One such place of destruction offers a striking testimony of the brutality of civil war and a powerful reminder of just how dedicated to the gods of their emperor soldiers could be. At Pfünz, Germany, the garrison was massacred inside the fort with its standard-bearer found still lying in the midst of the most sacred objects of the camp, the armorial insignia and the statue of the god Jupiter Dolichenus. The bodies of the soldiers were not even stripped of their arms and armor. Had barbarians been responsible for the destruction at Pfünz, they would have certainly taken the insignia and the statue as well as the arms and armor.[8] The arms and armor would have been used or traded, the insignia and statue would have been held aloft amid dancing and celebration time after time. So precious was armor that it was sometimes stored in bog deposits, and there it awaited the next war, one typically against other barbarians. These soldiering tools need not have been acquired as booty, particularly not during the third century, for their Roman employers armed a great many barbarians. Native leaders received especially fine weaponry in recognition of their superior rank among their followers, and they retained their higher status under Roman paymasters. Thus, while in Roman service the native leader had two things usually denied barbarians: a position of honor not entirely dependent upon the result of the last battle, and a dependable flow of prestige symbols—Roman coins—with which to reward his followers. So even what seems to be obvious is rarely so during the third century.

New men like Maximinus Thrax claiming the emperorship had to decide whether to seek legitimacy as successors to previous regimes by associating themselves symbolically with them in their coinage, titles, religion, and other public statements. Alternatively they could reject such association and strike out on their own. Although many tried both approaches, no one had much success until Diocletian established himself on the imperial throne (284). He and the other tetrarchs established their own favored deities at the expense of former gods, while launching a major persecution of Christians. Diocletian took the surname Jupiter, his colleague Maximianus that of Jupiter's son and favorite mortal, Heracles. Their new identities thus simultaneously announced a new regime, a new source of divine protection, and clarified the patronal role of Diocletian as the foremost among equals and as the connecting link between the greatest of the gods and the empire. Each of their subordinates as heirs apparent took the title Caesar and announced their own divine connections. Armies followed the choices of their commanders.

If there is a positive side to the numerous disputes over the imperial throne it is the great number and often surprisingly broad distribution of the coins issued by the claimants. Because many emperors and usurpers ruled for months or at most a year or two, their coinage has a peculiarly finite set of dating parameters, which is sometimes of assistance to archaeologists in establishing a terminus post quem (a date after which the deposition occurred) for a stratographic level. Even approximating a terminus ante quem (the time before which) can be facilitated by the frequent issuance of coins. The violence of the era normally meant that people in the stricken areas were unable to return to their homes. Their personal savings were left hidden forever in their carefully concealed jars and boxes. There interred were their most precious possessions, including coins that they had carefully selected and deposited on a regular basis over the years. These hoards offer far and away the best mechanism for dating the abandonment of a site or the death of its inhabitants. Silver coinage was markedly debased after the death of

Alexander Severus and so presents several peculiar problems and opportunities. Much was spent immediately rather than being carefully saved for a rainy day. Conversely the monetary reforms legislated under Aurelian (270–75) made much of what post-Severan coinage had been hoarded nearly worthless, and so there was no point in bothering about digging up your savings. In these cases hoards may well have been left behind, but they may not attest to the death or dislocation of their owners so much as to their apathy. The coinage of Gallienus presents still other numismatic problems. Because his reign was by third-century standards quite long, from 253 to 260 with his father and then from 260 until 268 alone, establishing an internal chronology or sequence of issuance for his coinage is highly desirable, but this has proved to be largely beyond reach.

Gold coins were used to make the highest prestige payments such as to top officers, and it remained much more stable throughout the century. Tribute had to be rendered in gold. Because barbarians—those living peacefully near the frontiers, raiders or recruits serving in the Roman army—were also in need of small valuable items, they too surely pondered the worthlessness of contemporary coinage. Frequent coin issues, a few inscriptions attesting to imperial victories, the bare mention of barbarians distilled from works written long after the events, religious writings that saw invasions as validations of their gods' plans and powers, and the growing body of archaeological data cannot make up for the loss of the historical narrative and other literature integral to the period. Given the sorry state of our evidence the best that we can hope to discover are trends. Despite much recent progress, no discipline is very well served by the third century, traditional history least of all. At best our picture of barbarians, Romans, and their interaction remains poorly focused. Current investigators agree that, if there was a crisis at all, it must be carefully defined and limited chronologically and geographically, and that it should take into account the disparate nature of the evidence.

The first two decades of the third century are deceptively well documented, but then matters change. Largely devoid of literary sources such as traditional histories and imperial biographies, the five decades from the death of Alexander Severus (222–35) to the ascension of Diocletian (284–305) present profound difficulties for anybody exploring questions having to do with political and social history. Written records do, of course, survive, but typically they are sparse on details and late, merely summations of materials now otherwise lost. Some contemporary narratives concern spiritual matters, and others tell only of events in a single town and of its need for protection against a host of local evils. In Egypt relatively excellent material has survived, and there the tax collector was most feared, not barbarians, and not Roman soldiers. Although no extant contemporary account provides us with a continuous narrative of events for the empire as a whole, this sad fact does not necessarily mean that there was an imperial crisis, let alone that the northern barbarians were its principal cause. Nor can we overlook the fact that late third- and fourth-century sources, particularly panegyrics, fulsome in their praise of existing emperors, extolled the present at the expense of the recent past. Claiming restoration explicitly builds upon decline no matter when used. In contrast to pagan images of decline, later Christian writers chose to view these hard times as necessary trials leading to the triumph of their faith. Increased suffering was a sign of god's imminent coming, and for these Christian authors the barbarians (notably the Goths recast as the biblical Gog and Magog) were the agents of God's correction in preparation for his judgment. In both traditions barbarians mattered much more as vehicles for intellectual criticism than as real threats to the Roman world.

Thus, although such literary sources as exist may provide a context for discussion, more often than not they are simply irrelevant to investigations of the relationship between barbarians and Romans. There is one partial exception: the writings of Dexippus, an eyewitness and probably the leader of a successful Athenian initiative to bolster the city's urban defenses following the barbarian sack of Athens in 267. Unfortunately his work on the events of his lifetime is known only through fragments cited and thus preserved by others, notably the pagan Zosimus writing in the fifth century and the twelfth-century Byzantine chronicler Zonaras. Making telling the story of Rome and the barbarians even more challenging is the fact that the few relevant narrative sources that we still possess all used the same now lost chronicle cataloging emperors and their deeds. This highly influential source was probably not written before the opening of the fourth century.[9] It apparently recounted imperial campaigns against the barbarians but in a manner reminiscent of their coinage, that is, officially acknowledging "victories" with only the most merger elucidation. Even during the Principate emperors had been unable to resist the temptation to inflate their modest victories. During the middle decades of the third century, when more than fifty men claimed the throne or the right to succeed to it, such celebrations became commonplace. Their self-laudatory declarations were little more than propaganda contrived to encourage supporters and challenge rivals, who responded in kind. The psychological competitions for honor among would-be emperors were disseminated to their armies on the coins that they struck to pay them.

By far the ablest historian of the third century was Cassius Dio, but he was hardly a Tacitus. Dio's account breaks off in 229, but even so those portions of his work recounting the empire of the Severans, under whom he lived, are preserved only in fragments, which are mostly to be found in an eleventh-century Byzantine epitome that probably reflects a much later understanding of events. Because Dio is the best of the lot, appearing quite erudite by comparison to those who recounted events after him, his account of rapid moral, political, and military decline has contributed far more than it should have to theories of a general crisis. Dio provides a trajectory of events from which detour has proved to be very difficult: chaos following the assassination of Commodus and the raffling off of the empire by the Senate; a troubled restoration under Septimius that overextended imperial resources; this then followed by a period of rapid decline in the health of the empire beginning with Septimius's death and accelerating afterwards as his dynasty withered under the impact of murder and betrayal. With no sources comparable with Dio until the fourth century, historians more or less have let the ship sail onwards along the course that they believed Dio had set in 229. Thus set in motion, the empire spiraled into a prolonged crisis from which it could not recover until the strong hand of a true Roman, one with the old Roman character of sacrifice and perseverance, imposed order. The author of this deliverance was Diocletian, but the price he exacted was despotism. Although few now would accept such a simplistic reconstruction, its outlines still reverberate, especially with regard to barbarians. But what if Dio did not wish to tell the story as modern scholars have read his text? Then should not Rome's relationship to the northern barbarians also be subject to reconsideration?

In his way, Dio was a deeply conservative political and moral philosopher. He took a stand against territorial expansion as too costly and therefore unwise, and even the successes of Septimius in Britain and the East were seen as needless extravagances that strained imperial resources and removed the emperor for too long from Rome. Dio was equally adamant on the emperor's need to consult the Senate, something that was hardly possible from the frontiers where he was so often seen among his troops. Even had the emperors some how managed to consult the Senate, it is difficult to see how men so far removed from frontier life both spatially and psychologically could have offered much practical advice. During most of the third century emperors lived with their troops and turned to their families and other hard-bitten generals for support. The upper levels of the civil aristocracy, detached from military concerns and command by law, focused their attention on careers in the burgeoning imperial bureaucracy and on making money, although their code of honor did not allow them to say so. Although the traditional leading element of Roman society had never been deeply involved in the frontiers, their departure was nevertheless significant. It points to an empire that increasingly emphasized the provinces at the expense of the capital. The most fundamental of many changes during the third century was that the provinces that mattered were now those in the frontier zones.

In the time-honored manner of Roman historical criticism, Dio constructed his critique around character analyses; specifically, morally bad emperors led the empire into external crises. This approach inevitably draws the reader down a path chosen to illustrate the ruling emperor's moral qualities, and alongside it the barbarians stand as sentinels. Good emperors are victorious over them, whereas bad emperors rarely succeed. Most men fall in between, neither always good nor bad, with similar results for emperors over barbarians. While critical of Septimius, Dio was excruciatingly so of Caracalla (officially Marcus Aurelius Antoninus, 211–17), and of the "false Antoninus" Elagabalus (also officially Marcus Aurelius Antoninus, 218–22).

According to Dio, Elagabalus was completely dominated by his mother, Julia Soaemias Bassiana, and spent his brief reign in the East, having nothing to do with barbarians on the northern frontiers and little to do with the army. For Dio he was a pathetic child, the victim of consistently bad advice. Whatever the truth of the matter, the young emperor did not live to see his fifteenth birthday. Those around Elagabalus, however, were in fact well aware of their youthful charge's need to secure military backing, and to shore up his claims they created a false lineage for him as the son of Caracalla. These men survived several conspiracies and even the defection of the Syrian legions before falling from power. Dynastic claims clearly mattered both to the troops and to the Senate, whose authority, though much circumscribed, claimants still deemed essential in order to cloak their usurpations in legitimacy.

In comparison with his treatment of Elagabalus the fragments of Dio relating to his successor Alexander (222–35) are rather upbeat. Alexander was a true Severan, the grandson of Julia Maesa, sister of Julia Domna, wife of Septimius and mother of Caracalla, and he proclaimed it by adding Severus to his name, Marcus Aurelius Severus Alexander. Dio's account is hopeful of a restoration of the "good-ole days" of the Severans, but the extant narrative is very fragmentary. It ends about midway into Alexander's reign, when the emperor, still quite young, was hotly engaged against the Persians. Because both Elagabalus and, in the extant portion of Dio, Severus Alexander spent their entire reigns in the East, his treatment of their reigns adds little to our knowledge of the barbarians. Dio's account of Caracalla has been seized upon to fill this void. He reports Caracalla as having been personally and vigorously engaged against the barbarians along the northern frontiers. In his narrative of warfare against the barbarians, at first glance Dio seems to have lost sight of what he had said about the barbarians at the time of Augustus:

they "were adapting themselves to Roman ways, were becoming accustomed to hold markets, and were meeting in peaceful assemblages."[10] What happened to these peaceful barbarians? It seems that all was going along nicely until Caracalla projected his brand of brutality beyond the frontiers.

For Dio, Caracalla embodied the worst vices of his ancestors without any of their virtues. Whereas his Gallic ancestors were brave, he was a coward. Of his fine African inheritance, nothing remained but brutality, and his maternal, Syrian side survived in him only in spasms of villainy. Again for Dio, Caracalla spent all his time away from Rome and lavished too much money on his troops, raising their pay and staging various tours of inspection. During his so-called campaign against barbarians in 213, Caracalla supposedly ordered "a fort built here, a city there." But, Dio goes on to say, almost in a moment of comic relief, that he was actually just renaming towns after himself much to the bewilderment of the local inhabitants. He followed his lavish preparations for campaigns against the barbarians by recruiting them into the army, then betraying them. Assembling the new recruits before him in what they would have presumed to be for the standard recitation of the soldiers' oath of loyalty to the emperor, Caracalla signaled the Roman cavalry to slaughter the hapless volunteers, completely without provocation.[11]

This was not imperial revenge for their having invaded in the empire, for they had not. It was murder. Rather than restoring Roman honor, the emperor had dishonored the Roman name. Dio's entire narrative on Caracalla is filled with such invective, and few details other than construction projects undertaken during his reign in and around many of the army camps can be substantiated. Indeed, there is reason to wonder while reading Dio whether the emperor actually fought barbarians at all or even if he recruited many into the army. Other sources, such as they are, are more charitable to Caracalla, leaving no doubt that he did undertake an excursion of some type into *barbaricum,* probably departing from Mainz and traveling up the Main River and then southwards into Raetia. Warfare was hardly necessary, however, since this was a peaceful frontier, just as Dio's own comment about the barbarians under Augustus had forecast, and which his passages damning Caracalla actually take for granted. It was an area where the presence of the emperor would assure tranquillity without the need of violence. The point in all this for Dio was to underscore the fact that Caracalla's moral failings had greatly eroded Augustan peace and thereby had placed the empire at grave risk. Dio succeeded splendidly, but he tells us very little about the realities of life on the frontier.

Dio's account of Caracalla's campaign of 213, if in fact his is still there to be read beneath the epitome, contains a questionable first mention of the Alamanni. The next time that the Alamanni appear in our sources is in an anonymous panegyric dedicated to Maximianus in 289, after which they are increasingly prominent. The formation of the Alamannic confederacy is a problem for which many have offered an opinion. By the mid-fourth century and probably from its beginnings, the principle component of this confederacy was the Iuthungi. The Iuthungi are first mentioned when, along with bands of other barbarians, some passed near Augsburg on their way back from a raid into Italy late in the summer of 260. About a decade later (ca. 270) they were back in Italy but hard pressed by Aurelian, to whom they sent an embassy seeking peace. They are again mentioned towards the end of the century in an anonymous panegyric to Constantius I while Caesar (the title of a "vice-emperor" within the Tetrarchy of Diocletian), which proclaims them as living in their own lands, having recently been driven out of the empire. Ammianus Marcellinus, writing around 395 of events of 357, recognized the Iuthungi as a part of the Alamanni, but on this occasion they were still acting independently in violation of their treaty by invading Raetia.[12] Thus, if we ignore Dio, the trajectory of confederation seems rather clear: the Alamannic confederacy was built by loosely uniting Iuthungi and others sometime prior to 289.[13]

Much the same pattern presents itself for the Franks whose confederation also first appears in the record in 289. It included, among others, people called Chamavi in the panegyrics. The Frankish confederacy added new members from around 280 to 310, and it was still accruing small groups in the middle of the next century.

At the same time that new men were joining, others were allying themselves with Rome and still others were gaining permission to immigrate. The most likely inspiration for the rise of both the Alamannic and Frankish confederacies—actually acts of desperation rather than statements of belligerency—would have been in response to Roman offensives meant to reoccupy abandoned frontier fortifications and punish the barbarians and anybody who had given them succor. The Roman drive culminated in the brutal campaigns of Maximianus and Constantius. The western emperor and his Caesar starved them, pitted one against the other, never let the barbarians rally their combined strength, and defeated them piecemeal.

Aurelian (270–75) thought that the invasion of Italy by the Iuthungi was in clear violation of existing treaties and that they had to pay for their transgression. He saw to it that they did. Their embassy to him returned without success. The inhabitants of Italy seem to have taken them for Marcomanni, or at least the author of the late fourth century *Historia Augusta* did. Denying barbarian invaders food was often Rome's most effective weapon, one used over and over again in late antiquity. This strategy was more and more successful as rather soon towns were properly encased in defensive walls and adequately garrisoned. Facing such obstacles, barbarians had no chance of capturing major stores. Isolated farms were easy prey but could only feed a band or two and then not for long. After feeling their hunger pains a bit longer, the Iuthungi surrendered themselves to Aurelian. These were in fact small bands. Our source in this case is a fragment of Dexippus, as noted earlier an unusually reliable contemporary.[14] No leader was worthy of parading in triumph alongside Zenobia, and no triumph over them was celebrated. Thus not later than the Tetrarchy the rhetorical use of the name Alamanni carried weight. Although the meaning of the name Alamanni, like that of the Marcomanni, is not securely known, both suggest an assemblage of warriors rather than a distinct ethnic group. The reference to Alamanni in Cassius Dio is most insecure, for the text we have seems likely to have been subjected to emendation by the Byzantine chronicler and excerpter, as was fairly common. The Alamannic confederation was new, but already by 289 it had earned Roman respect. By the end of the sixth century, the Alamanni were well known. Agathias (ca. 530–80), continuing the histories of Procopius, tells his readers that the name derived from "the coming together of many peoples."[15]

Roman usage of the names of these confederacies was often indiscriminate. In times of war, Roman authors treated each as a specific group of people, whereas during peace their names frequently became convenient terms used to describe peoples living along vast sections of the frontier who, in reality, had no regular intercourse. Thus "Frank" and "Alaman" might describe every barbarian living along both the lower (Franks) and upper Rhine and upper Danube frontiers (Alamanni), and "Goth" served equally well for the rest of the Danube. The generalized use of these names is also notable in Roman coinage and epigraphy. Claudius Gothicus (268–70), for example, was the first to celebrate victory over the Goths on his coinage, and inscriptions might summarily celebrate the universal pacification of "barbarians" by an emperor by employing these as generic labels. This uncritical treatment of barbarian confederations in the sources tended to make them seem more than they were and gave them a permanency that they did not possess. Nonetheless, these confederacies could rather quickly become more than just convenient literary categories and greatly complicate Roman military operations. Like the Alamanni, all barbarian confederacies were multiethnic assemblages, notable opponents in war, but even then they had little central direction.[16]

"Carrot and stick" diplomacy worked for Rome almost everywhere. If you back the winning side in our domestic disputes, you will be rewarded. If you choose the losing side, you will suffer deprivation and loss of income. But if you invade without our permission, then we will hold you to have violated your agreement as our client. Offenders must be punished, no matter whether this retribution takes years and no matter if it be done at the hands of an emperor or usurper, for otherwise word may get out that Rome no longer enforces its treaties. The extant Dio cannot be trusted for its mention of the Alamanni or in most other details. For example, while Caracalla probably did recruit some barbarians into Roman service—all emperors did—his efforts were rather small-scale, involving probably only those directly along the frontiers. The type of evidence that supports the existence of major recruitment campaigns among the barbarians—especially concentrations of the current emperor's coinage deep in *barbaricum*—is entirely lacking for the reign of Caracalla, although it exists in abundance for his father's and later reigns.[17]

Although some of Dio's criticisms of imperial character were surely justified, it is now impossible to untangle the truth from his jaundiced, moralistic, and highly rhetorical portraits. He mentions northern barbarians only within the context of these highly contrived characterizations. For Dio the barbarians were just additional paints to be applied to the canvas.[18] Unless one accepts the epitomized version of his account of Caracalla's campaigns, there is no hint of disaster brewing in the North. Moreover, given the great confusion as to the Alamanni, Iuthungi, Marcomanni, and others in our sources from the fourth century onwards, it is quite likely that these later sources read history backwards.

The case will be made later that, contrary to the chronology seemingly provided by Dio in which the Alamanni existed as early as 213, the Alamanni came together as a confederacy around the Iuthungi and others first in the 270s and 280s. Thus towards the end of the third century the Alamanni and other new confederations provided common identities to the various people from whom they had emerged as a military elite and over whom they claimed to govern. The Goths and Franks, about each of whom even less is known for this early date than for the Alamanni, seem to have followed similar paths of military consolidation. At least in Roman eyes these barbarian confederacies ruled distinct territories comprised of numerous village communities, but such governments cannot be proved to have existed until the next century. There was clearly a limit to each side's trust in and knowledge of the other.

Another contemporary, Herodian writing ca. 240, also saw Caracalla in terms of his character, specifically his hatred of big cities, especially Rome. He reportedly much preferred life in the provinces, touring camps and traveling about. According to Herodian, he was extraordinarily popular among his troops and his barbarian allies.

> Setting out from Italy he arrived on the banks of the Danube where he saw to the business of the northern section of the empire. He took his physical exercise by chariot racing and fought all kinds of wild animals at close quarters. He spent little time over legal cases but he was straightforward in his perception of an issue and quick to make a suitable judgement on the opinions expressed. He also won the loyalty and friendship of all the Germans north of the frontier; so much so, that he drew auxiliary forces from them and created his bodyguard from specially selected men of strength and fine physical appearance. On many occasions he took off his Roman cloak and appeared wearing German clothes, including the surcoat they usually put on, embroidered with silver. He also used to wear a wig of blonde hair elaborately fashioned in the German style. The barbarians were delighted and absolutely adored him.[19]

Under these circumstances it is possible that his so-called campaign of 213 comprised little more than his taking a few vexillations from the nearby legions on a diplomatic mission. Thus Caracalla seems to have been content with "showing the flag" and thereby shoring up Rome's network of treaties among its client kingdoms. Peaceful coexistence was the norm, and this agreeable state of affairs evidently continued until at least midway through the reign of Alexander, when the text of Dio breaks off. Herodian's account ends with events in 238. Northern barbarians were not sitting around their campfires eagerly waiting for the first sign of Roman weakness. The emperor did not need masses of new troops, because he was not at war.

One of the few things about barbarians other than a few names that emerges consistently from the literary sources is that from not later than the 250s there was a gradual increase in the level of political and military cohesion among several groups of barbarians. When the empire split into rival camps with the usurpation of Postumus, the 180-mile-long *limes* running from Mainz on the Rhine to near Eining on the Danube collapsed. This exposed the hinterlands to any armed band that happened along for whatever reason.

The years 259 and 260 must have been especially difficult, for barbarian raiders made their way into Italy and Spain. No power was prepared to counter them, especially after they had passed through the frontier provinces. These new groups were but the forerunners of the barbarian confederacies that came into being during the last decades of the century. Ultimately rather large barbarian groups were able to conduct extensive raids, some lasting as long as a year. On a few occasions, when they could count on Romans for technical assistance, they even attacked fortified centers. Only a few cases in the literature mention third-century barbarians trying to conduct sieges. In most of these examples they attempted to build and deploy Roman-type siege craft, with at times ludicrous results.[20] Indeed, it is hard to suppose that these confederations had any purpose other than to invade their neighbors or to defend themselves against invasion. Normally multiethnic combinations of barbarians would have had great difficulty just assembling without Roman knowledge, for Rome controlled all transportation on the Rhine and Danube and had friends among almost every group of barbarians.

It is hard to see how life in barbarian villages could have been much aided by these military federations except as they provided some sort of defense against Roman raids. Prior to the third century such organization was peculiar to the Marcomanni, who had come together in earnest during the first half of the second century. As the Marcomanni had demonstrated, a barbarian confederacy could offer even an emperor as capable as Marcus Aurelius many trying moments. Foremost among these new third-century confederations were those of the Goths and, by the end of the century, the Alamanni and certain Franks.[21] As also under Marcus, however, what initially appears to have been united barbarian forces dissolves upon close study into a picture of various small bands ranging widely and only coming together spasmodically when confronting an imperial army. They possessed only a limited ability to coordinate the launching of an attack. Wise barbarians stayed clear of Roman camps and pitched battles. The Goths surprised Decius in a swamp, as later some Iuthungi sought to strike the emperor Aurelian. Other Goths were able to seize ships and eventually raided coastal towns along the Black Sea and even islands in the Aegean.

With the revolt of Postumus, Roman supervision broke down and the peace along the *limes* between Mainz and Eining quickly unraveled. Raetia and Germania Superior were particularly hard pressed because they stood between the two centers of power, Postumus at Trier and Gallienus in Italy. Serious barbarian invasions struck southwards involving many small groups, some appearing for the first time but only briefly before dissolving, as their members either died or sought new leadership. Violent alternation of composite groups coming into being and then vanishing was taking place along many sections of the frontiers.[22] Others disappeared after long histories, usually just trading one identity for a new one that they found more becoming or more useful, or that our sources did.[23] These barbarian groups included many that were later absorbed into the Alamannic confederation. Among the foremost invaders in 269 were some Semnones, who are associated with the Iuthungi in an inscription on an altar recently discovered in Augsburg. The inscription gives us further insight into mid-third-century barbarians and the nature of their invasions.

As the inscription states, the altar was set up to honor the actions of one Marcus Simplicinius Generalis. Augsburg (Augusta Vindelicum), the capital of Raetia and located on the main north-south road between the *limes* and Italy via the Brenner Pass, had found itself defenseless in face of attack by some "Semnones or Iuthungi" as they returned from Italy with numerous captive Romans in tow. Simplicinius, the acting governor, raised a ragtag army by rallying soldiers from Raetia and the nearby German provinces, who happened to be in the vicinity, supplementing this force with volunteers from among the civilian population. Together this militia defeated the barbarians and liberated their prisoners. The inscription ends with the date for the setting up of the monument, "September of the consulship of Postumus and Honoratianus," thus establishing that at this moment Raetia was a part of Postumus's so-called Gallic Empire.[24] Postumus and Gallienus competed for years over this central province, and it may have served both masters according to the prevailing winds of fortune, but details are lacking except for this inscription. It seems clear enough that although organized Roman military forces had ceased to exist in this area, nothing in the way of large coordinated groups had crossed the frontiers. The lack of organized defense in Raetia in 260 does not mean, however, that the Gallic Empire was too weak everywhere to defend its territories; in fact, just the reverse is true. Postumus proved himself quite able to defend Gaul from attack by both barbarians and armies of the central government; moreover, the prosperity that Gaul had achieved continued during his reign. Raetia was a border area between his empire and the central government, and the Augsburg inscription comes within a few months of his usurpation as he was desperately trying to rally support from all available quarters, so it should not be used to characterize his reign. This incident is a fine example of locals taking matters into their own hands. On the other hand, nothing much stood behind the undefended frontier provinces all the way to Italy and Spain.

The Athenian Dexippus might have been honored for courage like Simplicinius the Augsburger, although he never quite says that he took charge of fortifying Athens after the Herulian invaders decided to leave. Other incidents of local self-help against barbarians and usurping generals can be found around the empire, but the Augsburg inscription is one of the clearest examples yet discovered. Regardless of their origins, the marauding bands were too small and weak to assault defended centers, so they fell upon civilians. Augsburg and Athens were vulnerable because they were as yet without true defensive walls. Augsburg did have a second-century wall, but its main value was in conferring urban status rather than security. Because regular army troops were not to be found when needed, the locals had to fend for themselves. Roman captives were walking booty, this time freed before being ransomed or sold into slavery. Those caught out in the open, perhaps trying to defend their villas or deal themselves with passing marauders (not necessarily barbarians), might be butchered. In one famous case two skulls, apparently a man's and a woman's, both with their foreheads ritually smashed, were discovered by an archaeologist in the well of their *villa rustica* near Regensburg.[25] They too had had to face armed conflict without the aid of those to whom the state had given a monopoly on the use of force, the Roman army. The Augsburg inscription does not mention Alamanni, which is another indication that the confederacy had not yet come into existence.

Later sources, in a manner characteristic of so much history written under the emperors, told moralizing stories about Gallienus and illustrated them with quips about barbarians. For example, during the reign of Gallienus, in a story perhaps too reminiscent of Hannibal to be believed, groups of Iuthungi chose to bypass Rome, then still unfortified and virtually defenseless.[26] Both the Senate, apparently taking rare military initiative in another act of self-help, and the emperor, who was then in Pannonia, rushed forces into the fray. The Senate's hastily assembled force, despite its being reported as inferior in size to that of the barbarians, apparently succeeded in deflecting them away from Rome but thereby inflicted them upon the rest of the peninsula. The imperial army eventually caught up with and defeated some of them near Milan.[27] Writing in 361, Sextus Aurelius Victor explained the civil wars between Gallienus and Postumus as the inevitable result of Gallienus's moral depravity. Instead of tending to barbarian invasions, he "frequented taverns and eating houses, kept friendships with pimps and drunkards and abandoned himself to his wife, Salonina, and to his shameful love-affair with the daughter of Attalus, a king of the Germans, whose name was Pipa."[28] What kind of a patron, what kind of man, would run off with a client's daughter and avoid his responsibilities to the Roman people? Can it be any wonder that plague and invasion sought out his reign? The client system nurtured by the Severans was indeed disintegrating, leaving even Italy open to invasion, but only a moralist would choose this manner of saying so.

A decade later Aurelian moved swiftly when others also called Iuthungi (or Alamanni—the sources vary, but the former predominates) invaded Italy. In a rush to keep them from Rome, where senatorial opposition might rally against his recent elevation, Aurelian pressed them a bit too closely. The Roman army blundered into an ambush. The barbarian incursion had been against treaties concluded earlier, probably under Claudius if not Gallienus. Would any barbarian in 270 have remembered treaties signed by men he perhaps did not know, so long ago as a quarter of a life-span, that is, ten years before? The point is that the emperor and the Roman intellectual elite providing this story expected the northern intruders to know and live up to their predecessor's commitments just as the Romans would have done. Aurelian had learned a lesson, however, and bowed to the advice Fabius the Delayer had given Romans too eager to confront Hannibal five centuries before. Rather than continue attacking, Aurelian shadowed the barbarians until they were tired, hungry, and lost in the labyrinth of the Po River estuary before striking them a fatal blow. So in the moralizing schema of Roman history, one might read into these fragmentary accounts of emperors and barbarians in the third century the echo of a lesson: where the immoral Gallienus had failed against the new Carthaginians, the wise Aurelian succeeded and had thereby restored Roman honor just as Scipio had once done in the days of lost Roman glory.[29]

These stories lose sight of an important fact. Unlike the Carthaginians under Hannibal, the third-century invaders were just small bands with no paramount leaders. No source mentions any leaders among these particular barbarians, and in fact the names of very few barbarian leaders of any kind are recorded for the entire third century. This might seem odd until we recall that emperors only celebrated triumphs over kings, lesser men being unworthy of their august attention. There are two exceptions: the shadowy "king of the Goths," Cniva, whose name is recorded only in the sixth-century by Jordanes as part of a highly fictionalized Gothic ancestral tree; and a Frank, Gennobaudes, who gave himself up in 288 to the Tetrarch Maximianus Herculius to become a client king on the barbarian side of the Rhine. Cniva's Goths seem to have crossed the Danube and moved about to forage and raid in small groups in perhaps as many as four major clusters. They came together only to face the imperial armies and then dispersed again into raiding bands in order to continue their plundering a bit longer before returning home. Such raiders did not have much else in common, but nonetheless the Gothic challenge in the Balkans required concerted Roman effort for much of the rest of the century. Only under Claudius (268–70) were the last bands bottled up and destroyed.

The story of Gennobaudes is even more instructive. Here was a barbarian who seems to have sought out surrender and submission in order to cement his position among his own people still living on the barbarian side of the Rhine. There he indoctrinated his people in the art of Roman clientage. Like many other barbarian leaders since the late republic, Gennobaudes owed his elevation above his rivals to Rome, whose favor could just as easily pass to another. There is no clearer statement of contemporary clientage.

> So many kings, O Emperor, are your clients [*clientes*], when Gennobaudes recovered his kingdom, thanks to you, indeed received it from you as a gift [*munus*]. For what else did he seek by coming into your presence with all his people other than that he should reign at last with unimpaired authority [*integra auctoritate*], now that he had appeased you? He displayed you [that is presumably, a statue of the emperor] repeatedly, I hear, to his people, and ordered them to rest their gaze upon you for a long time, and to learn submissiveness, since he himself was subject to you. . . . Content to request the name of friend [*amicitiae*], he earns it by his submission [*obsequio*].[30]

Other new peoples did not produce leaders significant enough to leave even their name in Roman sources. The known and anonymous barbarian leaders during the third century owed their positions to the needs of the moment, but none of them mattered in the long run. Pushing Tacitus's ethnographic depiction of Germanic society forward in time by a century and a half—an admittedly dangerous gambit—barbarians followed these anonymous men for booty and honor until one or the other was denied them. Then they chose to follow another. All record of any third-century leaders of the Alamanni had disappeared before the mid-fourth century. An Alamannic confederation then deployed a rather complex system of subgroup leadership with petty kings under confederate leaders but made no apparent use of an ancestral mythology going back to the third century.[31] The tetrarchs humbled "many Alamannic kings"—that is, to say their forces defeated various anonymous barbarian leaders whose status had to be elevated in order to praise the emperor for having defeated them.[32] So too, except for the Roman client Gennobaudes, third-century leaders of the Franks remain unknown. The fact is that these barbarian confederations began as short-lived enterprises set up to facilitate raids into the empire, or perhaps in the case of the Alamanni to fend off a Roman attack. Some may have followed their best warrior into Roman service and then terrorized the countryside when their Roman general fell from power. Most barbarian leaders who survived the civil wars disappeared after returning home, but some ended up making a career in the Roman army. An Alamanni was one of the latter. Having risen high in Constantius's palace guard, he attracted the spotlight briefly when he became the first to hail Constantius's son Constantine, as emperor.[33]

The amorphous and ephemeral leadership of the barbarians in the third century also helps account for some of the numerous "victories" celebrated by Roman emperors and would-be emperors on their respective coinage. Numerous minor engagements were usually necessary, and each could be pressed into a separate victory. On the other hand, the keen competition for loyal armies among rival claimants to the purple led some to claim victory where none at all had taken place. Usurpers and emperors alike also sought to retain the support of their armies by striking coins, often with slogans of victory imprinted on the reverse. Coins were needed almost immediately after any candidate accepted the throne, for he had to pay the troops who had placed him there, and who could just as easily topple him. By midcentury many barbarians were serving in the armies of the various emperors and usurpers, some as special units and others as new recruits in existing units. Postumus (259–68) is recorded as having been especially successful at recruiting barbarians into his forces. His realm, the so-called Empire of the Gauls (although at one point it included Spain, Britain, and the German provinces) was ideally located for this purpose. Moreover, the withdrawal of so many troops from these areas to fight against the Persians made new recruitment imperative. With these renewed forces Postumus succeeded in defending most of his territory from Gallienus's forces and those of the barbarians, if not one and the same. Some of the coins used to pay these barbarians ended up far to the east of the Roman frontier. Even there Postumus and the central government in Rome can be seen vying to win over or at least destabilize their opponent's barbarians.[34]

Coin finds in central Europe attest that these recruitment and diplomatic efforts were very important, selective, and periodic, as distinguished from the normal flow of Roman precious metal through trade. The normal importation of Roman coinage brought about by regular economic, diplomatic, and ceremonial exchange apparently ceased around A.D. 250 and did not resume until the reign of Constantine I (306–37), although this varied slightly from area to area. Clearly some barbarian bands were lured into Rome's civil wars of the mid-third century despite the great distance that separated them from the nearest Roman camp. Here, far from the Roman frontier, the coins and other prestige items so far discovered, such as medallions awarded by the emperors to their favorite supporters, barbarian or Roman, probably circulated within a gift-exchange system. Barbarian leaders received coins from Roman generals and then redistributed them among their own supporters. The political importance of having a steady supply of prestige items should not be underestimated, as the Roman well knew. Receiving tribute payment was a matter of competition among Rome's barbarian allies, and its reduction or cessation was a cause of war.[35]

The peculiar distribution patterns and chronologies of Roman coins studied by numismatists suggest that at least some barbarian leaders turned their attention to raiding and warfare after the onslaught of Roman civil war in order to maintain their own positions, but that most were employed by Rome and paid upon discharging their commitments. The hoards found in central Europe, primarily in Poland, are unusually tight chronologically, suggesting a single payment of large sums rather than the result of raiding. Raiding would have yielded a distribution pattern within the hoards reminiscent of the typical bell-shaped curves statistically associated with normal circulation and personal savings.[36] Interestingly enough, the influx of coinage from sources such as payments for service as allies and tribute seems to have followed by a few years the breakdown of regular exchange, suggesting that a factor in the eagerness of these most distant allies to serve Rome was their need to renew their supplies of prestige goods.[37] This dependence upon Roman largess and the crises that its severance inflicted increased throughout the fourth century.

Under Aurelian (270–75), Roman troops were officially withdrawn from the province of Dacia, and by the end of the century the Agri Decumates (roughly a diamond-shaped area that had previously been administered by the provinces of Germania Superior and Raetia) had ceased to be ruled by Roman authorities. These former Roman lands were ultimately controlled by various peoples called the Goths and Alamanni respectively, but these alliances emerged only gradually and in some sense in accordance with Roman interests, at least in that they were both quickly if rather loosely tied into the client network. In both cases indigenous populations seem to have constituted a significant percentage of the population for many decades, but this and much else remains very difficult to gauge.[38] The rise of neither confederacy necessarily entailed a migration of people from far distant places. That is most clearly the case for the Alamanni, but the precursors to the Gothic confederacy are not as clear.

A relatively few new peoples gradually taking over military and political leadership with the departure of Roman authority can account for almost everything that we know about the Goths. Some of these families and their alliance networks must have previously arisen near Dacia, primarily to the east and northeast. There were plenty of pre-third-century local and regional military organizations in these areas, most notably but not uniquely the Carpi, so that new dominant families need not have "reinvented the wheel." In any case the majority of the populations was agrarian and as such had little reason and less capability to leave when a new tribute system replaced the old. In neither Dacia nor the Agri Decumates did barbarian hordes rush in to rekindle the still warm fireplaces left by the departing Romans. In both of the Agri Decumates and former Dacia there are suggestions that the new barbarians took over with the tacit approval of the empire. Under Constantine, Gothic leaders (*duces*) such as Ariaricus and Aoricus concluded client treaties, which were later honored.[39] In the West, finds associated with former Roman fortresses in the Agri Decumates may have belonged to allies settled there in accordance with a Roman desire to create a buffer to the new *limes* being constructed, which ended at Lake Constance.[40] Thus in both of these areas there was much restructuring of relationships, and in every case Rome found a place in the old system for the new barbarian leaders.

Along the middle and lower Rhine and middle Danube, where the presence and use of Roman coinage was commonplace, the economic effect of the collapse of regular exchange brought about by the civil wars and various invasions must have been most severe. The abundant evidence of coinage circulation, pottery, and glassware on the east bank of the Rhine and north of the middle Danube up to the mid-third century and then again afterwards reflects the increasing interdependence of barbarians and Romans through employment and trade. In these areas common regional economies were evolving, drawing labor and products together locally from all sources without much regard for formal administrative boundaries. This high level of interaction between barbarians and Romans along the frontiers had begun in earnest during the second century as Roman units and their accompanying civilian centers took root. In general diplomatic gifts, tribute, and booty played minor roles in this economic relationship.

By the opening of the third century the barbarians living along the Rhine were deeply engaged in the Roman trimetallic exchange system, using coins for purchase and as means to calculate and compare values. As one moved back from the frontiers, however, coinage lost its broader utility and became a prestige item used primarily in status rituals. The prestige trade in coinage in these areas had shifted from silver to gold even before the collapse of silver coinage, which began after the reign of Alexander Severus as the various regimes debased their silver issues. The contrast between areas alongside the frontier and those in the hinterlands can also be seen in the presence and virtual absence respectively of bronze coinage found in village burials. Through the reign of Alexander Severus trade across the frontiers was clearly robust with a wide variety of items being exchanged. This trade, including various types of ceramic and glassware, continued through all but the bleakest decades of the third century. Roman soldiers were active economically in *barbaricum* and conversely barbarians participated in Roman regional markets, where they recycled some of their Roman coins. Even Roman weapons turn up occasionally in *barbaricum,* despite much prohibitive legislation. In the worst hit areas all of this economic interdependence ended for a matter of about four decades, approximately the normal male life expectancy.[41] This fact bears underscoring. For the first time since the creation of Roman provinces in the non-Mediterranean West, in some areas an entire generation grew up that had little or no firsthand knowledge of the normal Roman-barbarian relationship.

The empire was a very large operation, and while some areas were ravaged, others profited by supplying the less fortunate provinces. Whereas hell broke lose from around 260 in the German provinces including Raetia, in Britain, for example, no invasions occurred, although some military forces there were shifted elsewhere. In fact, Britain prospered by supplying Gaul and the Rhineland provinces. Anatolia experienced little disruption despite a few widely reported raids. Some areas of Gaul took advantage of the distress elsewhere within the province to sell supplies. Barbarian invasions were usually localized, their duration brief, and their impact superficial, although some undefended towns and many open settlements suffered dramatically. This was often in contrast to the civil wars that pitted two highly trained armies against each other, both capable of besieging their rival's cities for months on end and living off the land while doing so. Major damage, although horrendous at places like Autun (Augustodunum), was limited to a few areas.[42] Nor should we forget that the relationship of barbarians with Rome was far from simple. Some barbarians were recruited and paid handsomely to fight other barbarians or rival armies; others were embittered by the unannounced and perhaps totally unwarranted destruction of their villages. Violence increased, and the state gradually lost its credibility as the guarantor of peace and prosperity, but even the upsurge in violence must be placed in context.

Low-level lawlessness having nothing to do with barbarians was endemic in the empire, as marginally employed people moved in and out of legitimate full-time employment. During the third century hard-core brigands, *bagaudae*—organized bandits and desperate citizens—appeared in several areas. These bands were intransigent opponents of the government or at least of its fiscal officers. By the end of the century domestic brigandage required sustained imperial attention, but the *bagaudae* had no direct connection to barbarians. Indirectly both groups may have profited from the same circumstances in that the increasing demands made by local generals for taxes and supplies may have pushed some men into their ranks. The barbarians cannot be blamed for a general breakdown in the rule of law, if indeed that occurred, for their activities were just one of many factors involved. Of course, for Roman aristocrats, barbarians were synonymous with incivility and Roman writing reflects that prejudice. Towards the end of the century, when emperors were able to cobble together enough loyal troops to hunt down raiding parties of barbarians in the West, they simultaneously employed these small units to suppress brigands. The era also witnessed a disruption in traditional patronage brought about by rival armies, *bagaudae,* and, in some areas, especially towards the end of the century, barbarian incursions.[43]

The imperial authority was now fragmented and unable to move fast enough to confront multiple military crises, let alone widespread lawlessness. After the death of Decius, when things deteriorated rapidly, local authorities often had to confront outlaws, ill-disciplined garrisons and deserters, and rumors of pending doom and barbarian attacks simultaneously and on their own. Examples are not hard to find in both the western and eastern provinces. The system had evolved in such a way that most types of local initiative, now so desperately needed, were technically illegal. It was thus extremely difficult for the central authorities to condone openly, much less praise, what they had to recognize as essential. Without much more evidence than is likely to be forthcoming, appraising the balance of these factors will remain highly subjective, but the primary factor in the West during the central portion of the third century was civil war. For the empire as a whole, the gravest concern was renewed Persian vigor.

Towards the end of the century, as a few emperors and other claimants managed to hold onto power long enough to do more than just announce hollow victories, new building efforts were undertaken almost everywhere. These projects visibly enhanced the defensive capabilities of towns and fortresses across the empire, especially in the frontier provinces, and began to address the psychological effects resulting from the loss of domestic tranquillity and government failure. The total amount of construction from ca. 270 to 320 must have rivaled similar periods in the glory days of the Principate, although the earlier era saw much more civilian building and often construction had generally been in a more lavish style.[44] Clearly once political stability returned, economic resources could once again be found. The military had priority in new construction, but it is also clear that building programs in most towns had already begun to taper off towards the end of the second century. By then many had achieved full municipal status and long had had all the accoutrements of Roman urbanity, such as roads, water systems, baths, temples, and public spaces. Built in stone, some of these still cause the tourists to wonder in amazement. Damage to these structures was difficult to inflict and relatively easy to repair. Repairs were completed, and functionality preserved. When necessary, some civil construction was undertaken during the third century. For example, Trier was elevated to the status of a capital under the Gallic emperors, and remained so under Constantine. Aurelian (270–75) began the construction of a circuit wall around Rome itself, which had long ago lost virtually all trace of the so-called Servian Wall built shortly after the Gallic sack of Rome in 390 B.C.[45] The building of urban defenses was among the last major economic stimuli from the Roman government in many towns.

The later half of the third century also witnessed repeated appeals to reassuring themes and iconographies common in the early Principate. In retrospect these attempts seem pathetically weak and surely failed to convince Romans that their past glory had been restored. Nonetheless the psychology of victory remained largely untarnished, and so emperor after emperor celebrated new victories over Rome's traditional barbarian foes. These efforts at reassuring the populace by claiming the revival of past grandeur foreshadowed the late empire's penchant for reusing architectural elements, *spolia* from earlier periods. *Spolia* manifested a deliberate attempt to achieve a sense of stability by invoking past glory. Their use was not primarily a way to save money, nor were they meant to deceive the population as is so often concluded in modern textbooks. Among such revived images, humbled barbarians held a prominent place.

The high percentage of late third-century building activity concentrated on military projects is not necessarily an indication of economic decline or of a new political imbalance in favor of the army. There had already been a shift towards military expenditure under the Severans. Despite their philanthropy to many provincial towns, the Severan emperors concentrated their resources on infrastructure having to do with the army. For example, highways important for troop transport were well maintained, others were not. Throughout the third century the military was the area most in need of innovation, whereas, except for defensive structures, towns were already well served. The need to defend cities against real barbarians was hardly so great as to account solely for such a vast commitment of resources as took place. Once again we must suspect other motives, particularly after stability returned. Local garrison commanders needed to attract support, and the central government needed to assuage the collective psyche by showing the army and the emperor doing something, literally in "concrete," in order to regain some of their lost eminence. The resulting system had so much built-in redundancy that it is hard not to suspect that local commanders also sought projects just to keep their soldiers busy. Such makeshift work, however, was not popular among the men, who would rather risk more to win more. Military unrest continued long after external menace had disappeared. The tasks of rebuilding public confidence and reshaping the military were hardly begun by century's end. Both processes continued throughout the next century, especially under Constantine the Great. A quest for stability also characterized barbarian internal development, and, up to a point, Rome encouraged this as well.

Despite the strides made towards greater political stability among a few barbarians, we are not suddenly exploring a new relationship between equals. This was far from the case. Unlike the pre-Roman Celts and Dacians, no subsequent barbarian communities ever reached urban size and complexity. Whereas Celtic monetary systems had evolved concurrently with Rome's until, in the final stages, some of it took on Roman standards, there was no reason for Rome's subsequent barbarian neighbors to do so. They had no economic need for an independent coinage because Roman coins were ubiquitous. Moreover, it never occurred to any barbarian people to challenge the Roman political and cultural dominance represented on coins. Roman coinage drew together all elements of frontier society.[46]

Unless one counts runes, which were restricted in use to religious offerings and may have originated in the course of the second century, no northern barbarian people ever developed a written language.[47] Given the very long interaction with Rome, this is somewhat surprising. Rome managed barbarian political evolution rather carefully and from the late third century, in particular, moved to destabilize and undercut its development by co-optation. The Romans selectively admitted barbarians into the empire and recruited them in small groups for military service while launching surprise raids across the frontiers. If northern barbarians learned to read and write, they did so only after being recruited into the Roman army. There they learned to navigate in the language of the army, Latin.

The sources are in complete accord that no barbarian group ever developed impersonal institutions or divisions of labor beyond that of a few specialized workshops and most of those only in the fourth century. Barbarian government, if that is not an oxymoron, still rested upon networks of family patronage tied together through marriage and gift exchange and was still subject to manipulation by Roman governors, who in the eyes of barbarians were Rome. In the fourth century a few barbarian groups managed to combine and extend local family networks into regional confederations, but these were associations with only one known purpose, warfare. Until the late fourth century barbarian religious practice remained entirely a local undertaking, and until a few warlords were successful in claiming divine favor, they were almost completely dependent upon Roman support in their efforts to found dynasties.

Major warfare alone combined all members of the community for short periods, but raiding on either side of the frontier was probably the business of war bands, whose members, in essence, temporarily adopted another family. Their leader was elevated by his stature as a warrior, but his actions were those of a traditional patron. All men had family ties, but just how extensive and invasive war bands were upon family bonds remains much in dispute.[48] Few if any third-century barbarian leaders managed to hang on for long without Roman support. Roman conduct along the frontiers effectively channeled barbarian social and political development, but when civil wars and the Persian threat diverted Roman attention, these highly segmented barbarian communities were able to come together as rarely before. The challenge posed by the northern barbarians, nonetheless, remained weak and poorly focused.

Whenever a Roman emperor or usurper was politically stable enough to muster an army and raise the fiscal resources necessary to deploy it, he was able to overcome the barbarians in his area. The plan was invariably to draw them into a set-piece battle and kill off their leaders, who could always be found in the front ranks where leadership literally was made and unmade. Following such a victory, the Roman general would recruit as many able-bodied survivors as possible. Occasionally a general actually seems to have picked a fight in order to lead his restless men to an easy victory and much sought-after booty. When neither emperor nor usurper was available, a purely local initiative could be successful against small groups of barbarians. Alas, a town or army so saved from destruction might well hail the local hero as emperor, either as a reward from his fellows citizens or in hope that he could find gold to pay the troops upon whose shoulders he now sat. Fortunately for all concerned, not all of those proclaimed decided to press their luck. Rather than leading their small army into the fray, some reached an acceptable accommodation with a more powerful and active player in this very high-stakes game. Real imperial claimants could choose to ignore the local savior and allow him to pursue an early retirement. The barbarians played at best a tertiary role in all this. In most theaters of operation, barbarians were more important in imperial propaganda than in the field. Nor were they responsible for the more general and profound transformations occurring within the empire during this turbulent century. Their concerns remained Roman military recruitment, aggression, and mutual retaliation.

One of the most ominous developments of the century was the willingness of frontier legions to take political power into their own hands against the traditional civilian elite of the core provinces. Given the circumstances, it is hard to fault these soldiers for not following the lead of those who seemed to know so little and to care even less about the realities of their lives. The decision (ca. 264) by Gallienus to forbid senators from army commands may have still further removed the political and literary elites from understanding the troops, but most of their class had opted out of military careers before the second century had passed. Roman armies never refused to fight barbarians, but the same cannot be said about their readiness to fight other Roman forces. Frequently two claimants would attempt to bring their armies onto the field, but before the first arms clashed, one would be killed by his own men in favor of the other. Only one emperor was actually killed in battle against a rival (Philip in 249 against Decius).

The large number of claimants to the imperial purple may reflect the isolation of army units on the frontiers, rather than their conscious challenge to the system. The soldiers' great reluctance to fight each other was not a sign of cowardice, for sometimes emperors were deposed by their own men because of their temerity in pursuing offensive operations against barbarians. What appears to be fecklessness among the troops might just as easily have been a tacit expression of their loyalty to the imperial system over and above individual claimants, as well as a declaration of their personal dependence on an imperial sponsor. Without the soldiers' ultimate allegiance to the system, the empire would not have survived. These same Roman troops apparently also regarded the barbarians in a traditional way, as needing to be taught a lesson, or more likely as an easy source of booty. Like many other third parties in history, a supposed threat of "barbarians" could be counted on to heal a schism within the political fabric.

After Aurelian (270–75) brought both the empire of the Gauls and the Kingdom of Palmyra to heel, things began to return to normal. One sign of this is the increased settlement of barbarians inside the empire, begun under Probus (276–82) and intensively pursued by Diocletian and Maximianus, in the East and West respectively. Probus is also said to have reestablished tributary relationships with barbarians and to have resumed the Roman practice of launching raids into *barbaricum*. Much of his effort at restoration seems to have been concentrated on the civilian communities, both towns and in the countryside, which had been so exposed to attack during the previous four decades. He was especially remembered for having introduced, or reintroduced, viticulture in many stricken western provinces. He may have done this because the demand for wine throughout the Roman world was no longer being met by traditional sources, many vineyards having gone to weeds during the troubles. Profits were to be made if provincial suppliers could be put back on their feet and their yields expanded. A systematic campaign of military building was begun under Diocletian and his colleagues in the Tetrarchy as they faced the task of realigning frontiers where the Agri Decumates had ceased to be. Dacia had been abandoned in all but name, leaving those Romans living along the Danube exposed and river transport at risk. Construction of forts and town walls continued for decades in an effort to fortify the Danube and demonstrate that the central government was once again exerting itself.[49]

Everywhere the emperors had to assure that supplies were concentrated and stored for troops on the move, for during the wars of the third century too often Roman troops found themselves competing for supplies with brigands, barbarians, and the local inhabitants. To guarantee supplies locally was not enough, for the army of the tetrarchs needed to be more mobile, first to chase down the various rabbles afflicting the provinces and then to compel them to relocate far away. Thus local supply depots had to be located along the principal transportation routes over which troops had to pass. Depots had to be maintained, bridges secured, and so on, and all this required taxes and careful coordination with civilian governments. It is no wonder that Diocletian's goal of containing the growth of the imperial bureaucracy failed so miserably. In most cases the work of the tetrarchs could not be sustained as originally begun by them, but in almost every category their work foreshadowed that of Constantine the Great. This was true in administrative reform, in the renewal of monetary stability through the creation of a new gold coinage, and in reasserting military and political control along the frontiers. Roman withdrawal from Dacia meant that the lower Danube no longer flowed through Roman provinces, for it now marked the northern administrative boundary of the empire. The emperor moved quickly and steadfastly, fortifying the entire length of the Danube that had been opposite the former province of Dacia, often with fortresses on both sides of the river. Small forts on the northern bank served as fortified landings points, bridge guards, and observation and customs posts as elsewhere along the frontiers. Rather than a largely overlooked backwater, the cities on the southern bank prospered greatly under the impact of imperial building and the need to meet troop requirements. Immense amounts of coinage were suddenly in circulation as taxes from across the empire were spent on construction and salaries.

The fortification work on the south bank was much more like that in the East than in the West in that whole towns were fortified rather than merely army camps. A significant civilian presence thus was maintained on the lower Danube, whereas upstream it was fading fast. Without the benefit of Roman investment in infrastructure and the presence of the military payroll, the old Dacian province north of the river rather quickly reverted to its pre-Roman ways. An exception to the diminishing financial involvement of the central government in the frontier provinces, the lower Danubian provinces prove the rule. Without the concentration of Roman capital expenditure nearby, life beyond the frontiers would have remained at pre-Roman levels for a very long time; with it, cities were built which attracted labor and supplies, lives were changed and profits made.

The provinces along the southern bank of the river were restructured so that a new province, Dacia Ripensis, came into being, in which some of the refugees from former Dacia may have settled. Troops no longer stationed in trans-Danubian Dacia manned the new fortifications, but more men were needed. It was not long before barbarians were attracted to the new prosperity of the region along this stretch of the Danube, just as they had been to the middle Danube and along the Rhine. The recovery of the rest of the western frontier provinces fell somewhere between the poles of former Dacia and Dacia Ripensis. The central government not only did not have enough resources to build and restore everywhere, but it saw no reason to try because in most areas the restoration brought with it a return to traditional borders. In other places in the West the civilian presence had already begun to wane. The government saw no need to artificially reverse that process, for there were more cost-effective ways to meet imperial needs.

In Gaul, parts of which were severely damaged, some barbarians were settled with the newly created status as *laeti.* Such groups are known to have served as military units under Roman commanders, "prefects of the *laeti,*" throughout the fourth century and perhaps even longer. *Laeti* were not drawn from one barbarian group but from the defeated remnants of various peoples, although Franks were probably initially especially prominent among them. Not all Frankish immigrants were *laeti.* Other Franks were also received into the empire, formally accepting its laws by swearing an oath of loyalty to the emperor and acknowledging their military obligations. Barbarians are minor characters in an anonymous panegyric presented in 297 before the tetrarch Constantius I, father of Constantine I. This oration praises Constantius in florid terms for his supposed courage in restoring the empire. More revealing, it implies that once barbarians had been defeated and humbled themselves before Roman authority, the recruitment process and the rights and obligations that went with it were again matters of routine:

> In all the porticoes of our cities sit captive bands of barbarians, the men quaking, their savagery utterly confounded, old women and wives contemplating the listlessness of their sons and husbands, youths and girls fettered together whispering soothing endearments, and all these parceled out to the inhabitants of your provinces for service, until they might be led out to the desolate lands assigned to be cultivated by them . . . now that the Chamavian and Frisian plows, and that vagabond, that pillager, toils at the cultivation of the neglected countryside and frequents my [provincial] markets with beasts for sale, and the barbarian farmer lowers the price of [our] food. Furthermore, if he is summoned to the levy, he comes running and is crushed by discipline; he submits to the lash and congratulates himself upon his servitude by calling it soldiering.[50]

The panegyric concludes by invoking Constantius directly:

> [I]nvincible Caesar [Constantius], whatever land remained abandoned in the territory of the Ambiani, Bellovaci, Tricasses, and Lingones turns green again under cultivation by the barbarians.
>
> Indeed in addition, that city of Aedui, which is most devoted to you, and in the name of which I must render special thanks to you, has received by virtue of the victory in Britain very many artisans, which those provinces have in abundance, and now rises up with reconstruction of old houses and the repair of public buildings, and the restoration of temples.[51]

Some of these recruits soon found themselves in Upper Egypt.[52] Images of barbarians taking up their plows as tillers of Roman soil become one of many standard depictions of barbarians in virtually all later Roman panegyrics. Normally these images cannot be pressed for details, but this early panegyric presents an unusual degree of geographic specificity, which thereby adds considerably to its general credibility. By the end of the third century the once vaunted Frankish confederacy, the very people whose bands had reportedly terrorized the empire as far as Barcelona in 259–60, was no longer an adversary. Some had been combined with others as *laeti;* others had been settled under traditional mechanisms of *receptio* (that is, legal immigration); others were being taught the virtues of clientage to the emperor by their Roman-sanctioned king, Gennobaudes; still others remained on the barbarian side of the Rhine and so did not fall into any of these categories, and therefore remained unnoted by the panegyrist. The lower Rhine was rapidly denuded of regular Roman troops, leaving the *laeti* and the various Franks as the defenders of the empire they had once pillaged. These areas remained secure for over a century, when Frankish loyalty proved itself anew. By then a highly complex multicultural society had come into being in this region. In the area of the Agri Decumates, Roman allies were either already there or were soon to move in. A new system of fortifications was fashioned that followed the Rhine to Lake Constance and the Danube to Ulm and then turned sharply southwards along the Iller and finally overland with a system of man-made defenses, also to Lake Constance. For a while barbarian settlement in these areas remained sparse. Other areas required other measures.

Tetrarchic medallion from Lyon. Drawing courtesy of Dr. Pierre Bastien. Photograph courtesy of the Staatliche Münzsammlung München.

The panegyrics contemporary to the Tetrarchy hail the four governors' victories across the empire: the defeat of usurpers in Britain, the cleansing of the Germanic provinces and Raetia of barbarians, the carrying of the battle to the enemy, their bold victories on the Danube, their concluding peace with the Persians. The bitter struggle against the Alamanni in which Diocletian, Maximianus Herculius, and Constantius had all played personal roles comes up for repeated praise. Under their aegis barbarians found the door open to peaceful settlement and became farmer-soldiers in Gaul and Thrace. Along the middle Danube, Sarmatians and Quadi were defeated. The barbarian alliance of Goths and Carpi that had smashed through Dacia and crossed into Thrace was driven out, or allowed to leave. A core element of this alliance had been the Carpi, who were split and weakened by selective admission onto Roman soil. Their recruitment was probably orchestrated by the tetrarch Galerius. Some Carpi were settled in the Pannonian provinces, while others found new homes in the Drobrudja at the mouth of the Danube, a bleak posting by any standard. Although Rome claimed repeatedly that they were annihilated or subjugated, like the Franks not all Carpi sought safety through admission into the empire. Some remained outside and independent despite all Roman attempts to transform them into good clients.[53] In all this, there was scarcely a note concerning the legacy of the civil wars. After all there was little glory in recounting fratricide; better to praise our rulers with stories of barbarians, humbled and downcast before their majesty.

A medallion struck by the tetrarch and imperial colleague of Diocletian, Maximianus Herculius, with his junior colleague, his Caesar, Constantius I, captures the process of welcoming barbarians with a slightly less punishing air. On the coin obverse barbarians petition the two seated rulers for admission (*receptio* or reception) and receive their permission. On the coin reverse, these same barbarian families merrily cross over the Rhine on the bridge linking Mainz (Mogontiacum) and Castel(lum).[54] The medallion is an official commemoration probably given out to the commanders responsible for the event. According to Roman law and custom an official reception such as that depicted on the medallion and celebrated in panegyric followed the defeat and submission of a barbarian people. Their petitioning was part of the formal act of *obsequium,* the ceremony by which a subject acknowledged a more or less permanent state of submission. In reality, however, the emperors were not present, only their representative, the local governor or commander, nor were all recruits defeated foes. In fact, much recruitment was of individual chiefs or small groups not worthy of the emperor's time or concern.

Panegyrics complement the images on medallions and coins. When barbarians encountered Roman troops and were forced to fight, the results were predictable, and so were the Roman reactions. "For you, Emperor [Maximianus Heraclius], thinking that the war should be waged with the stratagems of your divine foresight rather than by force, let the rest of the enemy, whose great numbers were ruinous to them, fall prey to the extremes of famine, and to plague after famine, intending then to employ bands of troops to capture them to adorn your triumphs."[55] When they stood their ground, this passage continues, they were slaughtered, as Maximianus is reported to have done to some Eruli, naturally by his own brilliant leadership on the field of battle.

Similarly, recalling several victories garnered between 302 and

305, an anonymous panegyric addressed to Constantius's son Constantine extols one particular Roman victory over barbarians near Vindonissa (Windisch, Switzerland), a recently refortified and garrisoned outpost guarding the main north-south road between the new tetrarchic frontiers to the north and Italy. There Constantius is said to have left barbarian bodies to rot as a warning to others.

> Why should I recall the victory in the territory of the Lingones, made notable by the wounding of even the Emperor [Constantius] himself? Why the fields of Vindonissa, strewn with the corpses of the enemy and still covered with bones? Why the huge multitude of Germans from every nation, which, enticed by the freezing Rhine, had dared to cross over on foot to an island which the same river encircles with its divided course? There they were cut off by a sudden thawing of the river, and, besieged by boats immediately sent out against them, were compelled to surrender in such a way that they had to choose by a common lot who among themselves were to be given up to captivity (a very difficult thing), and [who] to carry home with the remnant of their number the obloquy for the betrayal of their fellows.[56]

We may dismiss the claim of multitudes crossing the frozen Rhine as just another example of rhetorical exaggeration, but the scene is interesting nonetheless. The story is told only here and so cannot be verified, but what may lie behind it is the demise of a modest winter raiding party, a band of starving barbarians seeking plunder and supplies. The ice suddenly broke trapping them on an island, where units of the Rhine fleet forced them into submission. Some decided to accept Roman terms, but others were ferried back across the river, whipped pups, so to speak, and had to face the scorn of their colleagues.

The panegyric as a literary genre takes the standard portrayal of barbarians to a new level, one that corresponds with a new kind of emperorship. The emperors of the late empire were wrapped in ceremony, draped in purple and seated aloft from their subjects, symbolically dwelling nearer the gods than mere mortals. Their high level of literary exaggeration was so notorious that Ammianus Marcellinus writing ca. 395 mocks it; naturally he did not think himself guilty of the same.[57] During the third century warfare among barbarians themselves became common once again and was encouraged, whereas in the days of the Principate Rome had often sought to stabilize relationships among its barbarian clients. By the end of the century Burgundians and Alamanni, formerly co-conspirators in invasion, were exchanging blows, the latter coming out short. Likewise, various Goths were killing Vandals and Gepids. Exciting one barbarian against another was a hallmark of Roman diplomacy when there was no chance of fomenting changes among the barbarians towards leaders more respectful of Roman treaties. And so, as another panegyricist declared, "the speech of all men eagerly proclaims: 'the barbarians are armed, but to fight each other! The barbarians have conquered, but conquered their own kin!'"[58]

Such were the goals, and, except for the fact that most new recruits were soon transferred far from their homeland, the realities. Once peace had been restored to the frontiers, emperors resumed the traditional balancing act of seeking stability while not allowing barbarian political organization to mount dangerous military challenges. Regular admissions of barbarians continued throughout the rest of imperial history as a reward for good behavior and in fulfillment of recruitment needs, but the great rush to accept immigrants, such as we see in the tetrarchic panegyrics, subsided and was not renewed for a century. Once again, Romans and barbarians were held together by common bonds of daily necessity. In most cases, the return to peaceful clientage succeeded, but it took many decades before the confederacies that had come into existence during the third century were tamed.

The medallion and the panegyrics noted here naturally make the most out of Roman victories, but in every case what was actually taking place was the controlled admission of barbarians into the empire. After being at least formally defeated, some but not all barbarian petitioners were accepted as immigrants under the provisions of Roman law. As always the lure was Rome. Once inside the empire the barbarians served how and where Roman authorities wished. The notoriously fictionalized *Historia Augustae* (composed ca. 395) says of the emperor Probus that he accepted barbarians and then transferred and settled them in groups of about fifty to sixty. Some he ordered transferred throughout the provinces in small detachments; others he scattered among the frontier garrisons. Despite the questionable source, this particular picture of the reception of barbarians inside the empire is in accord with all other available data—small groups of barbarian immigrants serving far from their homelands. This pattern was still common practice when the *Historia Augustae* was composed. The small detachments can be traced by their names, for typically they were named for the original men recruited into their ranks. Earlier, new units of the auxiliary during the Principate had been named in the same way. Many new units were similarly raised from barbarians at the end of the century. Indeed, several different units with the same ethnic name might be created simultaneously and given numbers so as to distinguish them from one another. The *Historia Augustae,* like the panegyrics that in part inspired it, notes that most groups of barbarians had to be defeated many times. This all but universal theme gives an author an opportunity to reflect upon the emperor's perseverance and other glorious qualities. More important, it points to the very fragmented nature of barbarian societies and their inability to transfer personal relationships to group conduct. Some barbarians went directly into the army, but others were better suited to be farmers. Roman authorities processed them all.[59]

Because those admitted were routinely sent elsewhere, and soon, new treaties signed even a few years later in the same area and with the "same people" were not really agreed to by the same people, at least not from the barbarian point of view. A barbarian, who might have been quite willing to commit his family for generations, just as any client would to a patron, would scarcely have done so for a group identity that had so little demonstrable effect on his life. A warlord could vow the support of his band so long as he lived. A king could commit his dynasty and thereby hope to direct the future conduct of his people, but such kings were virtually nonexistent. The few hoping to become such leaders were betting on Roman support. From the Roman perspective the fact that barbarians had such great difficulty appreciating that commitments made by one generation of individuals bound the next was a source of constant frustration. By allowing barbarians to immigrate, Roman authorities solved several problems simultaneously. In the case of Gaul there was a need for labor to till the soil and to defend it, the latter not being a matter for slaves. Selecting only those barbarians worthy of trust meant that Rome also dissolved whatever barbarian political consolidation had occurred since the breakdown of normal relationships along the frontiers. Those young recruits posted to the farthest corners of the empire became Romans there long before they were ever to see home again. In short, *receptio* gave the processes of acculturation time to work.

Thus, as the fourth century opened, barbarian-Roman relations were regaining their accustomed equipoise, but both sides of the equation had changed. The new assemblages of barbarians were tough, warrior societies, sufficiently strong to outlast the very empire that gave them rise, but their leaders still needed Roman backing, if not employment. The confederations were volatile organizations, but they could be managed. In fact, if Rome could truly harness their leadership to the old task of guaranteeing stability and predictability, the existence of the new barbarian confederacies might work to Roman advantage. Fewer and more powerful clients could bring greater security rather than less.

Roman cultural, social, and economic influence among the barbarians also reasserted itself as late third-century emperors restored order to the frontiers. It was then that some one set up shop among the barbarians in Thuringia to produce high-quality Roman-type ceramics. This transfer of Roman kiln-firing technology to the barbarians remains without parallel in other areas, but Roman diplomatic gift exchanges, payments to chiefs, veterans returning from their service in the Roman army, and the lure of frontier markets were ubiquitous. The Romans were apparently especially concerned with nonmilitary influence in the Thuringian area after Roman military defenses between the Rhine and Danube fell into complete disarray.[60] Trends apparent before the collapse of organized Roman political process continued after a hiatus of half a century.

The Roman Empire too had changed. Now there existed an unveiled despotism, which, although it had been evolving for a very long time, had been steadfastly resisted all the while. New lines of fortifications ran along the length of the Rhine and Danube. Their elements were more closely spaced and easier to maintain than those of the Principate were, and their men were increasingly drawn from both sides of the frontier. The Roman countryside behind them was being fortified in great depth in order to provide for the needs of the soldiers. Provincials living in areas exposed to attack or outbreaks of lawlessness were searching for ways to defend themselves, and that usually meant investing in walls and towers and moving to be nearer to them. Similarly the inhabitants of the frontier provinces were discovering ways to profit in peace without much recourse to the central government. The imperial court was both physically and symbolically farther and farther removed. Paradoxically, just as provincials along the frontiers were taking greater precautions to ward off barbarian attacks, they were becoming ever more dependent upon barbarians for labor, both in civilian marketplaces and especially in the military.

The century and a half that followed would witness the evolution of both of these trends. Rome's efforts to monitor and manage the barbarians along its frontiers inevitably had to take into account greater interdependence between Romans and barbarians while still pursuing policies designed to control frontier violence. The need for peace was never more obvious, since now a few barbarian leaders could inflict great harm when pushed too far. Symbiosis punctuated by eruptions of war seemed to be foretold. Periodic outbreaks of major violence occurred, and petty offenses to honor and property once again became routine irritations.

During the Principate, most internal barbarians had become Romans, while those beyond direct Roman administration were marginal to Roman civilization, literally and figuratively existing on the fringe of Roman civilization with its great cultural and political centers nestled along the Mediterranean Sea. By 300 the periphery had become the center. It was not merely the place were emperors were made and unmade, for it was the focal point of a uniquely military culture with its own values and largely self-sufficient economies. It had its own career paths requiring service only in the frontier provinces. When Gallienus made it illegal for senators to hold military commands, he set them on an independent course and liberated the new military elite from competing with them for power and influence. Henceforth soldiers never had to depend on the old cultural elite for personal advancement. They used this new cultural freedom to generate a unique subculture that evolved separately but within the parameters of general Roman society. When the peripheries became central, the external barbarians became insiders in a new society. They still lived beyond the direct Roman administration, but they lived in the heart of the frontier zone that nourished an emerging composite society in which the old borders were slowly dissolving. The fruits of this coexistence within the militarized zones dominate the remainder of the Roman history and the rest of this book.

Seven

Barbarians and the Late Roman Empire

The main features of the late Roman Empire were already apparent by the death of Diocletian in 305, but they continued to evolve throughout the following century and beyond. Except for Christianity, the contours of the late empire were most apparent along the frontiers. These trademarks included a new civil administrative system that channeled imperial government through dioceses under vicars to a proliferation of provinces each under the supervision of a governor. Between the dioceses and the emperor stood four regional prefectures plus the urban prefectures of Rome and Constantinople. In the immediate frontier zones, both civil and military governments were merged under the district military commander, the *dux,* whose authority very often included troops stationed in several adjacent provinces. His forces were spread thinly along the frontier in small but highly fortified encampments, between which ran the all important *limes* road and in many places a line of watchtowers within sight of each other.[1]

Other than the *dux,* the only point of convergence of civil and military governments in the late empire was the person of the emperor himself. The emperor stood at the apex, far above the fray, and progressively out of touch. For much of late antiquity there

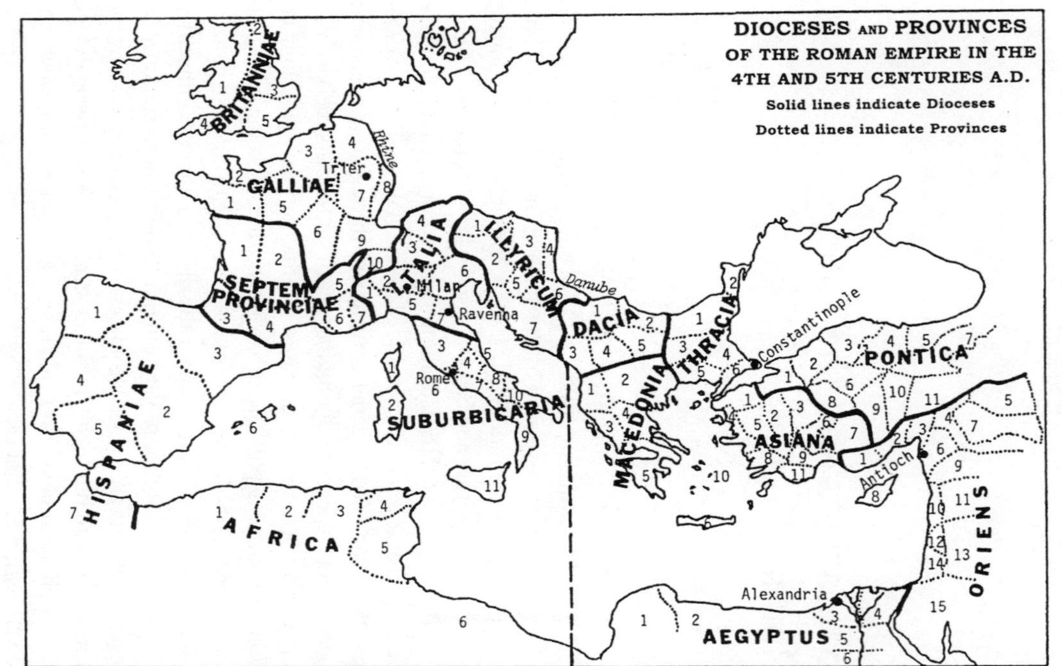

The Late Roman Empire showing dioceses and provinces. Courtesy of Indiana University Press.

Key to Map

Western Division

Britanniae
1. Valentia
2. Britannia II
3. Flavia Caesariensis
4. Britannia
5. Maxima Caesariensis

Galliae
1. Lugdunensis III
2. Lugdunensis II
3. Belgica II
4. Germania II
5. Lugdunensis Senonia
6. Lugdunensis I
7. Belgica I
8. Germania I
9. Maxima Sequanorum

Septem Provinciae
1. Aquitanica II
2. Aquitanica I
3. Novem Populi
4. Narbonensis I
5. Viennensis
6. Narbonensis II
7. Alpes Maritimae

Hispaniae
1. Gallaecia
2. Carthaginiensis
3. Tarraconensis
4. Lusitania
5. Baetica
6. Insulae Balearum
7. Tingitania

Africa
1. Mauretania Caesariensis
2. Mauretania Sitifensis
3. Numidia
4. Africa
5. Byzacena
6. Tripolitania

Italia
1. Alpes Cottiae
2. Aemilia
3. Raetia I
4. Raetia II
5. Liguria
6. Venetia et Histria
7. Flaminia et Picenum

Suburbicaria
1. Corsica
2. Sardinia
3. Tuscia et Umbria
4. Valeria
5. Picenum Suburbicarium
6. Roma
7. Campania
8. Samnium
9. Bruttii et Lucania
10. Apulia et Calabria
11. Sicilia

Pannonia (to ca. 400);
Illyricum (after ca. 400)
1. Noricum Ripense
2. Noricum Mediterraneum
3. Pannonia I
4. Valeria
5. Savia
6. Pannonia II
7. Dalmatia

Eastern Division

Dacia
1. Moesia I
2. Dacia Ripensis
3. Praevalitana
4. Dardania
5. Dacia Mediterranea

Macedonia
1. Epirus Nova
2. Macedonia
3. Epirus Vetus
4. Thessalia
5. Achaea
6. Creta

Thraciae (? Thracia)
1. Moesia II
2. Scythia
3. Thracia
4. Haemimontus
5. Rhodope
6. Europa

Asiana
1. Hellespontus
2. Phrygia Pacatiana
3. Phrygia Salutaris
4. Asia
5. Lydia
6. Pisidia
7. Lycaonia
8. Caria
9. Pamphylia
10. Insulae
11. Lycia

Pontica
1. Bithynia
2. Honorias
3. Paphlagonia
4. Helenopontus
5. Pontus Polemoniacus
6. Galatia
7. Armenia I
8. Galatia Salutaris
9. Cappadocia II
10. Cappadocia I
11. Armenia II

Oriens
1. Isauria
2. Cilicia I
3. Cilicia II
4. Euphratensis
5. Mesopotamia
6. Syria
7. Osrhoene
8. Cyprus
9. Syria Salutaris
10. Phoenice
11. Phoenice Libanensis
12. Palestina II
13. Arabia
14. Palestina I
15. Palestina Salutaris

Aegyptus
1. Libya Superior
2. Libya Inferior
3. Aegyptus
4. Augustamnica
5. Arcadia
6. Thebais

were two emperors, usually relatives: one in the West, the other in the East. In moments of great crisis, they did their best to assist each other. The bureaucracy that surrounded them virtually guaranteed their isolation. This bureaucracy evolved as a parallel institution to the army, the support of which was its primary task. Every emperor from Diocletian to Theodosius I (379–95) spent much of his time with his troops, touring garrisons, authorizing modifications to defenses, and personally directing campaigns. Emperors knew their army well; they had to.

Civil war loomed in the background but might erupt at any time. Constantine defeated his last rival, Licinius, at Byzantium in 324, renaming after himself the expanded and, as he himself had just witnessed, almost impregnable city. Constantinople not only stood guard over the Hellespont but also provided the emperors with a residence not far from the new frontier on the Danube. Elsewhere, Constantine spent much of his reign at Sirmium (Mitrovica) in Pannonia Secunda, one of seven provinces now making up the diocese of Pannonia, and at Trier, which he greatly embellished over what it had been when it was the capital of the empire of the Gauls. Henceforth Trier was the center of the imperial government beyond the Alps and received its own special defensive system, as did Constantinople. Like Constantinople and Trier, the working capitals of Milan and Sirmium were close to the frontiers and the troops who guarded them. Constantine paid Rome little attention after allowing his men to sack the city following his victory over Maxentius at the Milvian Bridge in 312. Much more important than even his new capitals was the interpretation of a vision that he had before his battle with Maxentius. By 315 the Christian XP appeared on his triumphal medallion, and other depictions following soon thereafter. By his death in 337, the Christian god alone stood with and for the Constantinian dynasty, but conversion to the new god had barely begun. Progress was especially slow in rural areas, where religion was deeply rooted in both belief and the politics of patronage.

Constantine's medallion is peculiar for another reason: for the first time an emperor is depicted as a general of the cavalry. On the obverse, the emperor himself is pictured in a three-quarter frontal pose with the helmet and the full battle dress of the commanding

Silver medallion of Constantine the Great, ca. A.D. 315. Note the Christogram as a special plume at the extreme left side of Constantine's helmet. Obverse above. Reverse below. Courtesy of the Staatliche Münzsammlung München.

general of the cavalry; on the reverse, he appears addressing his men, who are standing around him with their mounts.[2] The increasing prominence of cavalry was already clear under the Tetrarchy, and by the end of the century the command of the imperial cavalry was the highest honor in the Roman army, and cavalry units were ubiquitous in the frontier provinces. These developments reflect changed threat. Major confrontations in the field were rare, but small raids by barbarians and brigands were not. Cavalry could move quickly to chase down the culprits before they could get away. Infantry units were expected to hold key installations and to take the field in force in the rare case of a major invasion. Constantine is seen here with his cavalry, because it had been crucial in his victory at the Milvian Bridge over his rival Maxentius, not because of a battle against barbarians. Barbarians entering into the Roman army were welcomed into these cavalry units. Some units raised during the fourth century were largely recruited from one specific people and bore their name just as during the Principate. And also as in the Principate, these units received replacements through normal recruitment and were commanded by regular career army officers. Once again the initiative in innovation lay in Roman hands, but henceforth barbarians knew that horsemen had the best chance of being recruited into the Roman army and that, once in, they would have greater prestige and pay. Nevertheless, when a major battle between barbarians and Romans did take place, both sides fielded large infantry forces. Horses, although prestigious, were very expensive and, except in war, nearly worthless. No special training was required to stand with the mass of barbarians and charge, just courage.

Within Roman society there was a progressive division of the population into the haves and the have-nots, characteristically referred to in Roman law, even that edited under later barbarian kings, as the *honestiores* (those with honors, that is, the office-holding families) and the *humiliores,* those without, the humble. At the top of the *honestiores* stood the imperial administrative elite, who controlled the highest echelons of the civil government. They came from all over the empire to serve in the capitals of the new provinces, in diocesan government, and at the imperial courts.

a

b

The insignias of the *Comites sacrarum largitionum* from the *Notitia dignitatum,* denoting some of the products that they manufactured for the emperors including coins, fibulae, belt buckles, ingots, and treasure chests. (a) Western; (b) Eastern.

Their numbers and wealth were sufficient to support an empire-wide luxury trade as they sought to portray their privileged status in art, food, language, and religion. For them the imperial courts set the standard, which they tried to emulate. This small but extremely affluent minority commissioned some of the finest works of art produced in this period. Much of this was produced in a few centers near the capitals and exported to the imperial elites in the provinces. Another group, the barbarian elites both in Roman service and beyond the frontiers, was also interested in the finest available. Some of the extraordinary jewelry and highly ornate weaponry were produced in government workshops under the direction of the Counts of the Sacred Largess—one served in the West and the other in the East—because these items were routinely needed as gifts from the emperor to his closest officials and foreign visitors.[3] Beneath this upper administrative crust were the more numerous and, in many ways, more interesting local governing classes, just as in the days of Principate. Their culture was a scaled-down version of that of the imperial elites—with locally produced items replacing the exotic imports of the imperial elite, and standardized works of art rather than originals decorating their homes and standing watch over their graves. Prefabricated and poorly finished or locally designed sarcophagi held their mortal remains. Mass-produced ceramics graced their tables. Nonetheless, they must have been envied by most of their fellow citizens.

Symptomatic of the bureaucratic state that the empire had become, was the large body of law that a complex system of courts administered. Such bureaucratic micromanagement had long been a part of life in Egypt, where Roman administration inherited the elaborate system of administrative districts (*nomes*) from Ptolemaic times. The first systematic collection of the laws applicable to the empire was completed under Theodosius II (408–50), after much effort at recovering the texts of the laws, many of which had been promulgated while the emperor was outside the capitals.[4] The resulting codex, the Theodosian Code, reflects the bureaucratic desire to categorize and systematize the entire population, making it appear that the empire had become little more than a vast labor camp in which the poor freemen toiled endlessly to pay their taxes under the ever watchful eyes of bureaucrats. But this dismal picture seems to have been merely a lawyer's dream, far from real life. Ample evidence exists, for example, to reveal continued geographic and economic mobility despite repeated legal regulations enacted to restrict it for the sake of accountability. The upper and business classes traveled widely, and all manners of people were making the decision to enter monastic communities or to follow other pathways to their gods. Trade and commerce remained strong with a wide variety of goods circulating locally and regionally, including into *barbaricum*.

Everywhere we see signs of tension, experiment, and creativity: new styles of dress, intense philosophical and religious debate, experimentation in the visual arts, the turning on their heads of certain basic family values such as the goal of childbearing, the replacement of superficial unity by a restless and open search for new forms of identity, and the reliance on nongovernmental means of problem solving. This diverse world of tastes and values lay just beneath the surface of a monolithic and domineering imperial court. Furthermore, it is important to recognize that the barbarians were very much a part of the Roman world and so participated in much of this excitement and bewilderment. Perhaps the most important late Roman bureaucratic achievement was the maintenance of the Diocletianic system of tax assessment and collection that, while still acknowledging the primacy of the family as the taxable unit (*caput*), tempered its assessment with systematic review of property holdings and resources (*iugum*). The survey of property (the indiction) normally took place every fifteen years and became a common means of dating local documents.[5] The barbarians living beyond the administrative borders were ultimately affected by all these developments, but most immediate was the impact of the military reforms begun by Diocletian and completed under Constantine I. These reforms aimed at maximizing the efficiency of individual units by more carefully matching function and size, and of the army as a whole by building an extensive supply and support system behind the frontier garrisons. This system required a major financial outlay to erect and maintain it, and at some point budgetary constraints entered into imperial calculations.

As the Tetrarchy withdrew regular Roman units from the area of the Agri Decumates and completed the withdrawal from trans-Danubian Dacia, the emperors had no choice but to rethink the deployments in at least those areas. In fact, their efforts went far beyond them to include the entire empire. In the most threatened areas some new fortifications had already been built along key roadways by a few of their predecessors, but these early efforts merely reflected an immediate need to oppose invasion. During the third century rival Roman armies and barbarian bands had seriously impaired rural production far into the interior of many provinces. If this situation was to be reversed, a way had to be found to move troops from one area to another with minimal disturbance to the local producers. That meant perfecting a system of roadhouses and supply depots and of finding ways to protect important transportation hubs, such as bridges and naval stations. Each had to have enough defensive capability to slow the progress of invaders moving along the same routes and sufficient storage capacity to meet the needs of armies on the march. As the system evolved, it had a high level of built-in redundancy that would have permitted a sizable force to march with limited baggage even after some of the support centers had fallen to the enemy. The result was a system of heavily fortified strong points along the trunk roads connecting the frontier defenses to the interior provinces and command centers. The task was further complicated by the need to provide fodder for the increasing number of cavalry units that made up the western armies. Army-owned-and-operated production centers supplied raw materials for weapons and other crucial military and diplomatic items. The latter were usually luxury goods, including fine apparel to be given as gifts to barbarian leaders and ambassadors. When these payments were not forthcoming or were reduced, it was considered an affront worthy of war.[6] Already in the early third century the emperors had demanded special payments in kind to assist them in supplying the army. In the course of the fourth century this grew into a special grain tax (*annona*) levied for the soldiers. The annual *annona* was a regular feature of military pay, and the newly created supply depots were ideal storage and collection centers.

For the barbarians living alongside the frontiers one other aspect of the Diocletian-Constantine military program may have mattered more than all others; contraforts were built on the barbarian side of the river frontiers and sometimes deep inside barbarian territory.[7] Like other aspects of the military, the development of contraforts began in the late third century and went on throughout the fourth, but even then it was not something unique to the late empire. A few bridges had spanned the Rhine and Danube much earlier, for example, at Mainz and Budapest, but in general ferries plied back and forth. These ferry points were often sited where formerly inhabitants had forded the rivers in order to trade on the opposite bank. Fords shift as the course of rivers change, but by the time that the contraforts were built centuries of trade had created easily discernible routes for wagons and men across Roman territory and on into *barbaricum.* In some places the ruts can still be seen, just as they can be along sections of America's Oregon Trail. Contraforts were built to secure these points as fortified landing areas for troops in case of war, and the barbarians in whose territories they were built initially hated them. War sometimes followed.[8] Because war was infrequent, however, their normal function must have been monitoring trade, just as the fortlets at the gates in Hadrian's Wall had done already for centuries. That is, the troops there acted as customs officers, searching for contraband, such as weapons going into *barbaricum,* and assisting in collecting taxes and fees on products coming into the empire.

The tetrarchic medallion from Lyon that presented us with a stylized portrayal of the admission of barbarians (depicted in the previous chapter) can also give us a sense of the normal coming and going along the frontiers during peacetime. It is not hard to visualize other families striding enthusiastically across the bridge at Mainz to attend to the regional market, hoping to sell their agricultural products stacked high on carts and wagons, perhaps with a few children bouncing along in wide-eyed wonderment. At the normal river crossings, wagons would have had to pay a ferrying fee and obtained permission to ford. In any case, there was money to be made and spent. The contraforts did not discourage barbarian settlement along the Rhine and Danube, but instead they probably assisted it. If war broke out, their defenses provided bridgeheads to land troops and supplies. One may wonder, however, whether the local barbarians would have run in fear or set up kiosks to welcome Roman soldiers passing through to rebels deeper in the interior. In the late fourth century as the Roman command reduced troop levels in many areas, it abandoned most of the watchtowers and smallest fortlets. It had little choice; there were just not enough men at the forts to stand watch in the towers. The fate of the contraforts remains unclear. Some may have continued their monitoring even during the first few decades of the fifth century. There is no evidence that this system collapsed in a holocaust of invasion.

By the middle of the fourth century this intensive system of defense and supply was largely in place, but subsequent emperors, notably Valentinian I (364–75), tinkered with and strengthened the infrastructure still further. In some cases building activity continued into the early fifth century. The Roman general Arbogastes, a Frank by ancestry, led a punitive expedition across the Rhine from Cologne shortly before he joined Eugenius's attempted usurpation in 394.[9] In the late Roman army the units under the various regional *duces* constituted the first-line frontier defense and were known as the *limitanei.* These units were less valued, and so were paid less than those serving under the command of a *comes,* from which officer these units collectively took their name, the *comitatenses.* The various *comites* set up their headquarters where they had access to the best communications and logistical supports, often in the principal town of the diocese, while their troops were billeted elsewhere. Large troop concentrations were reserved for field operations, and most training took place in the individual units. Armies were built by assembling these units, but they rarely had occasion to practice combined operations. Tactics were quite limited, and so discipline was crucial. The main strategy remained to force the barbarians to fight a pitched battle in which Roman troops would be able to withstand the initial charge and outlast their opponents. The major tactical innovation came from Roman attempts to use heavily armored cavalry, the *cataphractari,* which had evolved in competition with the Sassanids and was now combined with the traditional heavily armored Roman infantry. But concurrent with the development of heavily clad cavalry and infantry was the use of small units of lightly armed troops. Barbarians were especially well prepared to enter the latter category of service, if, that is, the Romans provided them with horses.[10]

During the reign of Constantius II (337–61) and later fourth-century emperors, special concentration points for the large mobile field armies were built in a few areas. These centers were characterized by vast storage capacities where surplus production from imperial and private estates in the area as well as the proceeds from the *annona* could be kept safe. Such a place was Fenékpuszta lying west of Lake Balaton in Pannonia Prima, where in the late fourth century a very large encampment was built with but minimum internal buildings. The realignment of unit priorities that occurred during the fourth century in favor of the comital armies was combined in many places with the further dislocation of the civil administration to the new provincial capitals necessarily created by Diocletian's administrative reforms. The result was an ongoing shift in the patterns of state investment in infrastructure and personnel towards these new centers.

Those areas favored by this redirection of capital flourished, whereas other areas withered. Concentration upon the mobile forces of the *comitatenses,* meant that units of the *limitanei* often shrank. Some became second-class members of the *comitatenses* and were listed as *pseudo-comitatenses,* at least for purposes of accounting. The original purpose of the reassignment of former *limitanei* as *pseudo-comitatenses* was probably to provide temporary replacements for the core units of the infantry, but their paper designation stayed with them for the remainder of their existence. The distinction between them and the genuine units of the *comitatenses* blurred with time. By the opening of the fifth century, most personnel in the remaining *limitanei* were of recent barbarian ancestry, and in some cases entire sections of the frontier had been delegated to barbarian allies for defense. But this withering away of the old military frontier was but a part of a general trend for traditional boundaries to lose their meaning and new ones to gain prominence. Experimentation and change on a local level replaced central planning.

Elite units of the *comitatenses* were directly attached to the emperors and fought under their personal commands while they were on campaign. By the end of the century these troops were distinguished as palatine. They were not billeted together, but were instead scattered about towns near Constantinople or one of the other imperial residences. Barbarian recruits might find themselves in any unit of the *limitanei* or *comitatenses,* but rarely did they serve close to home. Most were already volunteers rather than defeated opponents when Julian debated whether to send them to Constantius, as he had been ordered. When each side raised the war cry before the charge, it was the same from both ranks, the barbarian *barritus.* By the third quarter of the fourth century men of barbarian ancestry were filling a high percentage (the exact figure is out of reach) of all new recruits and were well represented in the officer corps.[11] The last quarter of the century found men of "barbarian" ancestry at all levels of command, including the very highest. They, like the other senior members of the military establishment, had advanced to the top through fierce competition, but one purely within the army. The senior civilian staff and the lofty members of the old senatorial elite competed among themselves. Ultimately, however, everybody sought the ear of the emperor at court, which followed wherever the emperor went. Once men of barbarian origin were holding top military posts, they associated at court with the civil elites, with whom they contracted alliances secured by the marriage of their children or even of themselves. Among the lesser soldiers intermarriage was common, and legislation prohibiting it was either ineffectual or intended to punish specific units for disloyalty and so were temporary measures.[12]

By the middle of the fourth century, the eastern and western armies were further divided under two overall commanders, one for the infantry (the *magister peditum*) and another for the cavalry (the *magister equitum*), the latter having priority in honor. This cumbersome system gave way to combined operational commands under Theodosius I (379–95), but he lived long enough to complete this transformation only for the eastern army, where the five top generals held palatine or regional commands over both horse and foot soldiers. In the West the earlier system continued on paper, although there too the need for combined field command superseded tradition. From Stilicho's time (395–408 as commanding general in the West for the emperor Honorius) the supreme general held the position of commander-in-chief of both branches, *magister utriusque militiae* and, as such, was the power behind the western throne. These various unified field commands more accurately reflected the joint operations necessary for successful warfare everywhere. Cavalry in specialized units of heavily armored horse and rider could hold its own even against disciplined infantry, but the latter still formed the backbone of the Roman army at Strasbourg in 357 and in 378 at Adrianople. Some units of cataphracts took part at Strasbourg, but none is mentioned at Adrianople. The total strength of the army at the death of Constantine I is a matter of debate, but surely it was not less than 400,000 men spread across the entire empire. Estimates of the size of the late Roman army at various stages of its deployment, unit names, and their relative worth are based on the list of command and support structures from a peculiar document known as the *Notitia dignitatum* and from the excavation of some actual fortifications.

The *Notitia*, a semiofficial table of organization of the late-fourth and early fifth-century Roman army, accounts for much of our information about the army's operational structure, but it is notoriously untrustworthy because it seems to have been partially updated at various times. The eastern portions are less complete and do not reflect changes after about 392, whereas some western sections may have received revisions as late as 420. The last systematic revision of the western section was most probably carried out under Stilicho in preparation for the renewal of his campaigns against the eastern empire, thus around 406. Archaeology has been able to determine the size of some late frontier fortifications with certitude, but many more lie beneath modern towns and so are out of reach. Neither offers much security for numerical calculation. More often than not, the legionary camps of the Principate have become major modern cities, and revealing what portion of them remained fortified in late Roman times has proved to be very difficult. The only double legionary fortress on the Danube, Viminacium in Serbia, was a major late Roman meeting place for the emperors Theodosius and Gratian. Yet it remains largely unexplored and is daily threatened by a hydroelectric project.

The same juxtaposition of violence and peaceful coexistence that we have explored in previous chapters culminated in late antiquity. The relatively long periods of peace and stability are rather surprising given the origins and nature of the new barbarian confederacies, which after all owed their existence to war. But as we have seen in the previous chapter, booty was rarely their principal source of income; rather, they served as allies or as special units recruited into the Roman armies. As allies they had received annual payments and were urged to plunder the allies of rival Roman generals. These tribute payments were more than symbolic, for the chiefs who received the payments had themselves a carefully established hierarchy of subordinates awaiting their shares. Such exchange demonstrated to all the hierarchy of dependence: the emperor at the top, next the barbarian chief, and finally chief's supporters. Barbarian dependence was not always adequately appreciated by Rome, but the abuse of obligation by the imperial patron was deemed sufficient cause for war. When a barbarian chief failed to dispense largess to his followers, barbarians thought it was time for new leadership. With the reestablishment of frontier defenses, war against the empire became decidedly more dangerous. Petty raids were different. They were commonplace events and uncontrolled by the confederate leaders.[13] So how did Rome manage to stabilize the inherently unstable situation as well as it did? By using the time-honored means at hand. It supported cooperative barbarian leaders against internal rivals, it acknowledged the role of these leaders in regular Roman recruitment efforts, and it recognized their need for prestige through cash subsidies and gifts. The cast of characters had changed but not the script, although new plots and counterplots were added.

When Rome lured the war leaders themselves into service in the Roman army, they gave them special recognition, making them junior officers. By the end of the century, the rank awarded them was that of military tribune. Normal economic intercourse was even more important. The trend towards nucleated rural settlements in many of the frontier provinces sooner or later left many areas needing settlers. Throughout the fourth and early fifth centuries, as the frontier provinces gradually lost and redistributed population, the need for farmers (who might be pressed into militia service in an emergency) increased accordingly. As more barbarians were admitted, the sense, if not the reality, of insecurity grew, leading to more retreat from areas exposed to lawlessness, which then left more land untilled and therefore untaxed. The face of the frontier provinces changed. To men of letters in the Mediterranean provinces, lawless and barbarian were synonyms were for uncivilized. The rule of law, Roman law, still defined civilization. By this definition the frontiers were slipping into barbarism or, more precisely, falling under the rule of soldiers. Labor was also in short supply around the camps and fortified centers on the frontiers. Although finances were tight and becoming tighter, military commanders completed priority projects as ordered.

The army was professional despite being a frontier force charged with supplying itself with some of its own provisions. There were many jobs that soldiers and Roman civilians would not do or that could be accomplished more cheaply using barbarian laborers. Inscriptions and the philological evidence from the Germanic languages reveal barbarians living in an agrarian world dominated by kindred and the village. By far the most important source here is the Gothic Bible composed by Bishop Ulfilas, after he and his followers had immigrated to Moesia around 360. Many barbarians also had regular contact with Romans, and some lived in Roman towns. The reverse was also true. Romans living in the frontier zone saw barbarians all about them conducting daily business; Roman merchants had long frequented barbarian villages, and Roman deserters served important chiefs. Goths served as day laborers, soldiers, female companions, and wives, and also bought and used Roman olive oil, wine, and other refined products.[14] Archaeological investigations have confirmed the wide distribution of Roman wares, the intensive use of Roman coins in areas directly adjacent to the frontiers. Despite intensive surveys not a single urban development has come to light among the barbarians. The vast majority continued to live in villages. All evidence underscores the fact that daily commercial intercourse between Romans and barbarians increased in importance throughout the fourth century. Ammianus Marcellinus's opinion that virtually all barbarians lived within a few miles of the frontier was not far off the mark.[15]

This is not the pattern that we would expect if we just read the literary sources, according to which violence was sometimes extreme. Some of Julian's soldiers managed to sneak across the Rhine and "butchered everyone they found, men and women of all ages, like so many sheep." In an act of utter desperation, Valentinian declared a bounty on barbarian heads, only to have to rescind his offer when cartloads of heads indiscriminately arrived for collection. With such graphic stories available it is easy to lose sight of the long peaceful periods that characterized every frontier.[16] Nonetheless, brigands and barbarian bands occasionally did plunder Roman villas, killing entire families. Fear grew. Understandably the trend towards defended nucleated settlements, already visible in the later half of the third century, picked up pace. Despite the desire by some to get out of harm's way and move to safer abodes, peace was still the norm. Our ability to recognize peace is rendered much more difficult by the fact that ancient historical narrative as a genre focused on war, and so did imperial propaganda.

Just as in the days of Augustus, most Romans still believed that war and the emperor's role in it reflected the moral health of the empire, its people, and the favor of the gods. Valentinian and his brother Valens continued the tradition of extolling victory over barbarians in an effort to assure the populace that all was well. They routinely proclaimed the universal pacification of the barbarians on inscriptions and coinage region by region. They were conquerors of the Germans, Alamanni, Franks, and Goths—thus in these generalized terms, over all the barbarians on the Rhine and Danube Rivers from the North to the Black Sea. Such assurances were routine, matters for propaganda that were repeated even on quite inconsequential building inscriptions throughout the empire.[17] Even the most unwarlike emperor Honorius (395–423) struck coins and medallions showing himself in full armor celebrating victory over barbarians. In fact, he spent his reign as a pawn in the civil wars and plots hatched by his generals, some of them men of barbarian ancestry. All was not well, however.

By the end of the fourth century, traditional imperial virtues and the emperors themselves were ever more remote. In many areas of the frontier there was a marked decline in the level of construction and maintenance. This trend had begun in most frontier provinces much earlier, but from the time of Valentinian it was increasingly obvious as he himself discovered in Pannonia. By the end of the fourth century the fortifications along the lower Danube, begun under Constantine the Great and his dynasty, were no longer attracting a disportionate share of imperial revenues. The stimulative effect of imperial investment had leveled off even before the wars following the battle of Adrianople. Whereas once emperors had traveled extensively on inspections and public appearances, now they were aloof. The iconography of Theodosius, the last great warrior-emperor, often depicts the emperor as closer to God than man, closer to an abstract perfection of ruler than flesh and blood. The same symbolic quality had long been present in the use of the cross and Christogram to represent the support of the Christian god. Compare, for example, Theodosius's portraits on coinage to those of earlier emperors. His is less naturalistic, more rigid and ethereal. His coinage frequently abandons the use of profile in favor of the frontal image. He looks at you and through you. His image is that of "Emperor," less that of an individual emperor or even of a dynasty than was common heretofore. In making Christianity the official Roman religion shortly before his death in 395, Theodosius moved it from the religion of his dynasty to that of the empire. At some point Romans and barbarians would relate to one another as Christians, but that still had sometime to come. As the imperial government expended less interest and resources along its frontiers, these areas became more self-sufficient and independent culturally and economically. There barbarians and Romans were slowly becoming one and same.

The political necessity of victory, and victory over barbarians rather than other Romans, far outlasted the need for triumph on the battlefield. Just as barbarian leaders needed Roman titles and subsidies to remain in power, so too the Roman emperors needed victories or at least the celebration of them to retain the psychological reins of power. For the leaders of both, there was much political posturing, but we see it only from Roman sources. There is considerable evidence that during the fourth century various barbarian confederacies created more durable political structures with hierarchies of power carefully delineated and rewarded to reflect status within the confederacies and their constituent parts. There is also strong evidence that Roman authority intervened in these developments.

Civil war was never again combined with war on the eastern frontiers, but there were several close calls. Indeed, it seems that it was only luck that kept civil war and armed conflict with the Sassanids separate for so long. Trouble was brewing on the eastern frontiers, for example, when Magnentius rebelled in Gaul against Constans and thus the Constantinian dynasty in 350. An even greater disaster loomed a few years later when Julian (360–63) challenged Constantius II (337–61) for the throne. Fortunately for civil peace, Constantius took sick and died before the two Roman armies clashed. Julian lost little time before beginning his ill-fated invasion of the Sassanid Empire in which he and much of his army perished. His successor Jovian (363–64) had little choice but to extricate the survivors by ceding Roman territory to Persia. His act saved his army but damned his memory forever. It made brandishing one's spear in the direction of the Persian Empire a necessary part of a new emperor's first gestures. Jovian's public acknowledgment of Roman weakness was widely seen as an unprecedented dishonor to the Roman name, but perhaps more important, despite all the bellicose posturing, except for a brief period under the emperor Valens the treaty held throughout the remainder of the century.[18]

The exception, however, proves the rule, for in 376 while Valens was engaged against the Sassanid Persians, thousands of Goths took flight from their own civil wars and foreign invasion. These refugees sought legal immigration (*receptio*) into the Roman Empire en masse, and Valens, busy gearing up for an eastern campaign, regarded their appeal as a great opportunity for recruitment. So he agreed. Unfortunately the flow of refugees severely overtaxed Roman preparations for receiving and dispersing the new immigrants, and what should have been just one more peaceful transition to Roman service deteriorated amid starvation, assassination, and finally open warfare. Valens rushed troops to the threatened areas on the Danube from the East. After this army barely escaped annihilation, he took the field himself, only to perish. Although the rebellion of those Goths admitted for resettlement under Valens occurred towards the end of a period of difficult war and negotiations with barbarians on the Rhine and upper Danube, Valens's nephew and imperial colleague, Gratian, was able to conclude treaties there and rush to aid his uncle. In fact, between now and his death in 383, Gratian and his field commanders presided over routine settlements of various Goths, Taifali, Alamanni, and Sarmatians, from Gaul and Italy to the Balkans.[19] The personal relationship between uncle and nephew was strained, but nothing suggests that it would have led to open warfare. Valens chose not to wait for reinforcements, attacked, and died as a result.[20] Even then neither the eastern nor northern frontiers erupted in widespread violence. The new emperor Theodosius, working with his younger but senior colleague Gratian, was able to contain the seemingly victorious Goths and their hangers-on in the northeastern Balkan provinces. He went on to isolate them in small groups and defeat them.

The most important stabilizing factor during the fourth century was that at no time did Rome face military campaigns on multiple fronts either from invasion or civil war, nor did Rome ever lose the initiative despite fearsome losses in 377 and 378. This general equilibrium meant that throughout most of the fourth century Roman-barbarian relations could resume their normal course of general peace, punctuated by petty displays for internal consumption on both sides, and by moments of open and violent hostilities. The last quarter of the fourth century and first quarter of the fifth witnessed an intensification of military confrontation between barbarians and Romans, but by then it was already becoming difficult to distinguish one from the other in the frontier areas. More often than not even the violent episodes coming near the end of the century were not the result of inherent hostility but rather the dysfunction of political structures either within the empire or among the barbarians.

Warfare between the great barbarian confederacies and Rome was rare during the fourth century and even more so in the fifth. Really big battles were fewer still. In terms of tactical details, Julian's victory at Strasbourg (Argentoratum) in 357 over Alamanni is by far the best reported late Roman battle against barbarians, despite the fact that the battle of Adrianople in 378 was more important. The battle of Strasbourg will serve to illustrate one set of special circumstances, one compared favorably by Julian's admiring historian to Marius's victories over the Cimbri and Teutones.[21] Otherwise there were varying levels of local skirmishing, occasional raiding in both directions, and much daily commercial and personal exchange. Julian boasted that he had made the defeated barbarians rebuild the fortifications on the Rhine that they had set out to destroy. If true, their labor surely increased their knowledge of Roman construction practices. All fourth- and fifth-century barbarian confederacies were diverse ethnic amalgamations and were very difficult to assemble and maintain. Roman diplomacy was complex and effective in stabilizing relationships with them nonetheless. Even before the conclusion of the Roman civil wars that destroyed the Tetrarchy, Constantine I had begun a successful policy of negotiation and diplomacy along the Danube with Sarmatians and the various Gothic-speaking groups then dominant there. He did similarly well along the Rhine, where barbarian embassies appeared before Constantine and his sons at their court at Trier to work out the details of their relationships. Constantine's sons Constantine II, Constans, and Constantius II, and their cousin Julian continued these policies. Keeping the peace meant keeping the alliance system of client states not only intact but responsive to Roman interests. Each ally had to keep to its place. Rome, as patron, had to live up to its obligations as well. Such a balancing act was not easily established and harder still to maintain, but it allowed peaceful intercourse to take place.

Ammianus is by far our best narrative source for Rome and the barbarians in late antiquity, but his work is far from the model of reliability it was once thought. Like every other ancient Roman historian, Ammianus filtered his personal bias through the rules governing the genre in which he wrote. He had his favorite themes and actors. As Julius Caesar and Tacitus did before him, Ammianus loved to engage in traditional ethnographic portrayal. Once he even returned to the Gauls of Julius Caesar, rather more for entertainment than for serious background material. When finding himself writing as an ethnographer, Ammianus's barbarians exhibit odd anatomical details. Alamanni are especially tall, for example. His most striking description is of the Huns and Alans, scarfaced, swarthy, bowlegged, warming their meat under their saddles, wearing the skins of field mice. Like all barbarians they are inherently free, not knowing the meaning of slavery, respectful of their gods, and loyal unto death to their leaders in battle. They lived in the unvisited climes of earth, and now they flowed over the land like the melting mountain snow.[22]

Ammianus's account of the barbarian invasion stands as another reminder of how steadfast was the Roman concept of historical change; change for Ammianus was not evolutionary but the result of new people imposing or trying to impose their inherent qualities upon others. Within the historical genre recounting barbarian invasions was still a primary vehicle used to heighten personal contrast between leaders, in Ammianus's case, between Constantius II and Julian. Ammianus drew biographical portraits of emperors as had Suetonius and to the same end. He unjustly and in self-contradiction attacked the overt "pacifism" of Constantius II towards the barbarians so as to give greater praise to his rival Julian, who is portrayed as the restorer of Roman vigor, dignity, and prosperity. Constantius is depicted as weak, shrinking from the task at hand; in contrast, Julian seized the moment and distinguished himself as the savior of Gaul. Whereas the former delegated command, the latter rallied a defeated and demoralized army around him. Although appearing reluctant, Julian accepted the purple toga of emperorship offered him by his troops, who ardently hoped to remain close to their homes rather than fight in Constantius's wars against the Persians. Instead, Julian marched them eastwards thousands of miles to engage Constantius in civil war.[23]

In his adherence to the canons of his chosen genre, Ammianus seems to have been just the most gifted of the late ancient moralizing historians. Zosimus writing sometime after the sack of Rome in 410, but following the same line, says of Constantius that "he was at a loss of what to do," whereas Julian took control of events. But then again both Ammianus and Zosimus were pagans, and Julian was their hero. He could do little wrong. Constantius was a Christian, though regarded as a heretic by the time that both Ammianus and Zosimus wrote, and could do little right. According to Zosimus forty cities had fallen before Julian managed to annihilate sixty thousand barbarians on the field and to drive countless others headlong into the Rhine near Strasbourg.[24] Ammianus, who was with Julian, gives a detailed casualty report: six thousand Alamanni dead (one-tenth of Zosimus's total) and countless others washed downstream. He says the Romans lost 243 dead, including 4 military tribunes—Bainobaudes, tribune of the Cornuti; Laipso, the commander of the cataphracts; Innonentius; and one other whose name he could not discover. Inadvertently Ammianus provides us a nice example of a loyal officer of Frankish ancestry, Bainobaudes, commanding a unit of barbarians recruited elsewhere.[25]

The barbarian confederacies now were better able to take defended cities but still usually failed. Cologne fell briefly under Frankish control in 356, but in the same year the Alamanni besieging Julian in Sens left after a month of frustration.[26] An example of barbarians taking a city by assault was still exceptional, at least in the eyes of Ammianus the eyewitness. Perhaps the Franks got lucky. Did Zosimus inflate the number of cities sacked by the same factor of ten? Regardless of the numbers of dead and levels of destruction, Julian was able to confront the barbarians in the field. The battle of Strasbourg culminated a series of punishing offensive operations. What were the circumstances leading up to this epic slaughter? Was it, as conventionally depicted, a traditional victory over uncivilized barbarians bent on plunder?

Prior to the battle, Julian had led a highly destructive series of raids across the Rhine, burning crops and undefended villages. Now that the barbarians had taken the field, Julian planned to smash them in a great pincer movement between himself and general Barbatio, who had moved to Augst on the upper Rhine at the order of Constantius. Ammianus variously calls them Alamanni and Germani, again betraying his indifference to the details of barbarian societies. In the weeks prior to the battle, however, some "barbarian *laeti*," noted by Ammianus as "particularly ferocious raiders," had independently attacked Lyon.[27] Something is not being told or is being intentionally obscured. All sorts of "barbarians" were obviously moving about, raiding and being raided, some of them *laeti*, who had otherwise proved themselves highly dependable as guards along the lower Rhine. The start of this general disintegration of law and order along the Rhine and upper Danube was not caused by barbarian invasion. It was the revolt of Magnentius (350–53), the commander of the palatine legions. Just as in the previous civil wars, once it became clear to Magnentius that the emperor Constans would not recognize him as his colleague, the usurper had sought to raise an army. This had meant recruiting heavily from among barbarians and rallying all Roman troops that might come over. The latter included *laeti*, among whom he had himself lived. Perhaps he was a barbarian who had changed his name, although that practice had become rare since the edict of Caracalla. The reverse was now just as likely among those destined for a military career in the late army. More than likely Magnentius had once served as a prefect in charge of a unit of *laeti*.[28]

Recruiting barbarians may not have been an easy task, even for a man with his experience and connections, for Magnentius was not the only recruiter. Competition was intense. Constans too, like his father Constantine, had been active in crafting alliances with Rome's barbarian neighbors and in welcoming them into the empire.[29] Barbarians concluded agreements with men and families, not with abstractions. Promises were kept or, if broken, avenged. Some of Constantine's treaties with Gothic leaders were still honored by them after the death of Julian, more than a half century after they had been signed, but only because they believed that they were obliged to his family.[30] Once Magnentius had rebelled and killed Constans, the personal ties of patron and client that had been concluded between barbarian chiefs and imperial representatives of Constans were nullified or at least placed in doubt. New ones had to be formed, and formed quickly, but no sooner had some old barbarian allies of the Constantinian house gone over to him than Magnentius led them to their own destruction in Pannonia.

After Magnentius's death in 353, Constans's sole surviving brother, Constantius II, took pains to root out every last supporter of the usurper, but in the process he provoked still further rebellion. Meanwhile Constantius did restore some of the Constantinian alliance system along the Rhine and his diplomatic efforts continued. In 355 Silvanus, a very well educated and high-ranking infantry commander north of the Alps, rose in revolt with a broad base of support. Like many top commanders then at the imperial court, he was a Frank by ancestry. Surely Silvanus was from the same circle of top military advisers as Magnentius had been.[31] And as he had done to those who had rallied around Magnentius, Constantius moved to hunt down and execute all Silvanus's followers. In other words, the background to the battle of Strasbourg was one of a long series of Roman civil wars and their suppression. During these troubles various diplomatic initiatives to potential barbarian allies were attempted, often with apparent success. Just as in the third century, Roman civil wars pitted barbarians against each other, confused their diplomatic relationships with Rome and among themselves, and inevitably led some of them to fight for the losing side.

Julian, both as Constantius's relative and as Caesar, at once set about punishing all those who had bet on the wrong side. His central objective was to redirect wayward barbarians back to the alliance system of the Constantinian dynasty, that is, to himself as Caesar and to Constantius II as emperor. Julian augmented his army by recruiting every able-bodied volunteer, and with these he chased down armed bands raiding the countryside. Around Autun, where the walls had been neglected and the garrison was completely moribund, veterans settled nearby rallied and lent a hand. Surely Zosimus exaggerates when describing Julian's early efforts to raise an army in Gaul around the pitiful core of 360 men given him by Constantius by taking "any recruit available," veterans, and other volunteers. In what is surely rhetorical license run wild, Zosimus tells us that Gaul's regular soldiers reportedly froze in fear at the mere mention of the word "barbarian." As Ammianus reveals, however, normal recruitment had long meant accepting numerous barbarians, and many of Julian's recruits came from among those barbarians who had remained loyal to his dynasty. Any towns destroyed during these years most likely fell victim to rival armies rather than barbarian invasions, as when a unit of *laeti* attacked Lyon. Ammianus also notes, however, that there was no glory in defeating rebels and so no reason for him or Julian to celebrate it.[32]

During the rest of the century whenever civil war broke out among the Romans, both sides immediately intensified their normal recruitment efforts among the barbarians. As had been the case throughout Roman imperial history, the foundation of a new dynasty favored rebellion. Shortly after Valentinian and his brother Valens came to power, Procopius rose to challenge them and brought his barbarian allies into the fray. When the emperor Theodosius was tied down in one of his Balkan campaigns, usurpation tempted some. Civil wars broke out between him and the usurpers Magnus Maximus (383–88) and later Eugenius and his general Arbogastes (394). In the latter rebellion, Arbogastes, a highly educated member of Symmachus's literary circle, whose family background was Frankish, helped lead a rebellion of the leading senators in Rome. In these civil wars most new barbarian recruits joined the existing units with their heavy complements of "former barbarians," that is, those already serving as Roman soldiers. A few others fought as special detachments. The final battle between Theodosius and the usurper Eugenius and his general Arbogastes pitted two closely matched Roman armies in a desperate struggle. The most striking similarity of the two armies was that both were led by Roman generals whose fathers or grandfathers had immigrated into the empire: the Gothic Gainas and half-Vandal Stilicho with Theodosius, Arbogastes at the head of the rebels. Their armies fought for two days with terrible losses on both sides, especially among the newly raised barbarian units.

Fate gave Theodosius little time to celebrate his victory. On 17 January 379, he died of illness, leaving behind his two young sons, Arcadius and Honorius, under the guardianship of Stilicho. Court intrigue and civil war shaped the brothers' reigns, and as always, so-called barbarians took sides. Foremost among them was Alaric, literally a man of legend, adept at both courtly politics and leading men in battle. Most but not all troops in Alaric's various commands were northern barbarians. Most spoke Gothic and a little Latin. All hoped to make the most of their careers in the Roman army, although Alaric's dreams were of a higher order, of becoming a Roman general; for this he fought both for and against both eastern and western emperors.[33] Neither Alaric nor Arbogastes had been the leaders of their native confederacies, but they knew how to use the old networks to raise armies. Roman civil war gave barbarian leaders a chance for honor and a means to reward the loyalty of their followers, but if they bet on the losing side, they lost everything.

By the middle of the fourth century every barbarian confederacy for which we have adequate records had developed a complex system of internal ranking. These systems were often very complex because they had to provide each member chieftain appropriate recognition when it came time to field the composite army. Sometimes we can even watch as these leaders build and maintain their own regional hegemony. The Alamanni confronting Julian in 357 had two supreme kings, five subkings (*proximi reges*), ten princes (*regali*), and numerous lesser nobles, who commanded, according to Ammianus, some thirty-five thousand men in battle. When the call to arms went forth, many of these had to come from far off rural districts (*pagi* in Latin). Romans recognized, for example, the Lentienses living near Lake Constance as members of the Alamanni, despite their remoteness from those along the middle Rhine. One of the high kings of the Alamanni now went by the Greek name Serapio, though his original German name was Agenarich. His father had changed the name out of his fondness for Greek, a bit of which he had picked up as a diplomatic hostage in Gaul.[34]

Another clearly ranked barbarian confederacy was that of the Quadi, with one king at the top, and beneath him his son, a *regulus* or prince, followed by a *subregulus,* then various other nobles. The Quadi's neighbors, the Sarmatians, had evolved a similar hierarchy, with subkings, princes, subprinces, and various nobles spread over many widely dispersed groups. The Goths living in former Dacia and those along the Dnieper had equally complex ranking systems. The former was headed by a *thiudans,* or in Ammianus, a *iudex* or supreme judge, which was slowly becoming hereditary; the latter culminated in a king ruling through multiethnic and graded ranks of princelings.[35] Regardless of his rank within a confederacy, each barbarian chief was free to raid at will, take hostages and hold them for ransom, negotiate alliances, and take and sell slaves. The territory of each was recognized by the other chiefs of the confederacy, so at least in that regard the barbarian elites supported each other. Some leaders were able to extract regular payments from their subjects, using the force of their attendants, sometimes numbering a few hundred, to coerce payments.[36] No chief had authority over the followers of another or had anything to do with the villages under another's control. A chief's status was recognized by his personal display, by his wealth and generosity, and most especially by his leadership in battle.

The chief was expected to lead the charge when the war cry rang out; his followers were dishonored if they survived his death. The power of the supreme king(s) was hardly supreme. Such a leader could not always stop the wars that he had begun and had trouble limiting the scope of the violence of his followers. As far as the Roman authors were concerned, these confederations were constantly rising up and being defeated. After a while, like the Phoenix, they would be back challenging Roman arms again and again.[37] In every case, the confederate structures were primarily, perhaps exclusively used to unite the barbarians in a region for war against Rome, offensive or defensive, and to then negotiate treaties with the emperor at the conclusion of hostilities. Wars between confederacies were rare, primarily because of the distances involved in confronting each other. Furthermore, Rome discouraged such warfare among its clients because it inevitably led to instability along the frontiers. The Burgundians with whom the Alamanni often found themselves at odds deposed any of their kings who led them to defeat. Councils of elders can be seen from time to time, and we a catch a glimpse of village life among some of the Goths through the life of the Christian martyr, Saint Saba.[38]

The account of Saint Saba reveals that the ordinary villagers feared but otherwise had little to do with the local or regional war chiefs, who passed through their communities from time to time, but they would have probably responded quite differently had war been on the horizon. Had war come, they would have fought on foot, as did other northern barbarians. Leaders and their closest followers alone rode into battle. The village remained the center of daily life, the place where families, pets, and livestock all lived together as they had time out of mind. Kindred still grieved for their lost loved ones and defined membership in the normal community.[39] But whereas the village remained the bedrock of society, warrior confederations were inherently unstable. The tension between the two was ultimately resolved by dynastic succession among the leadership of the bands and the grafting of principles of familial leadership onto the warrior ethos, but these developments were a very long time in coming.

One successful Roman approach was to split the confederacies by offering treaties to selected chiefs or engaging them in series rather than giving them time to assemble their full might. The case of Vadomarius of the Alamanni provides a clear and detailed example of this practice. Vadomarius was one of the top kings of the Alamanni and a very worthy opponent indeed for Constantius II early in his reign. Nonetheless he ultimately accepted peace and became a trusted ally of Constantius, who regarded him and his Alamanni as sufficiently trustworthy to send them against Julian at the outbreak of his rebellion. After Julian discovered the secret pact, he invited Vadomarius to a banquet, where he ordered him seized and placed under guard. Next Julian ordered Vadomarius to dismiss his attendants and send them back to their homes. Having thus isolated Vadomarius from the source of his power, Julian sent him to Spain. This was hardly the end of Vadomarius's career, for next we find him as a Roman general in Phoenica, then commanding Roman forces in the Balkans against the usurper Procopius for Valens, and finally on the eastern frontier on Valens's campaign against Shapur II and the Persians. Vadomarius's son, Vithicabius, by 375 also king of the Alamanni, was murdered by his own men at the order of Emperor Gratian, who suspected his loyalty.[40] Thus the attempt by Vadomarius to found a dynasty did not last a single generation.

Upon occasion Rome was able to send one confederation against another and so to save its own troops.[41] The story of Vadomarius and his son reveals both sides of Roman handling of barbarian leaders, recruitment and treachery. Often they were two sides of the same coin, its scenes repeated many times over the next half century.

As if the lives of Romans and barbarians were not sufficiently entangled, some barbarians were able to move back and forth between Roman service and high rank among the barbarians. Mallobaudes is a case in point. Such individuals enjoyed elite status in both societies. A Frank by birth, he worked his way up the ranks of the Roman army from junior officer before retiring back to *barbaricum* where he became a Frankish king. Later we find him back in the Roman army as *comes domesticorum*, at that time commander of the emperor's household guard, a very important position indeed.[42] There was nothing inherently disloyal in Mallobaudes's actions, in fact just the reverse. Imperial armies had all sorts of barbarians in their ranks. Enterprising barbarians were clearly able to negotiate their own way through frontier society by playing both sides alternately as occasion demanded; they made the most of their multiple identities. Some decided to return to their homes beyond the frontiers permanently, and some carried Roman customs with them into the grave.[43]

The most successful (but in the long run disastrous) meddling in the internal affairs of a barbarian confederacy occurred when Valens supported the Gothic prince Fritigern against his confederate superior, the *thiudans* Athanaric. Athanaric was an old opponent who had perhaps insulted Valens by refusing to set foot on Roman soil even long enough to sign a treaty. As a result the treaty signed between Romans and Goths in 369 was concluded on a ship moored in the Danube. Fritigern rebelled against his overlord just as the entire confederacy was forced to deal with the arrival of the Huns and Alans on its doorstep. When Athanaric proved too much for Fritigern, the latter appealed for armed Roman intervention. As a token of his submission as a client, Fritigern accepted the emperor's religion, Christianity. This was what had long been expected from a client or a new recruit, swearing his oath of loyalty to the emperor. Although the emperor was originally supposed to be a god, the Christian emperors had to abandon that claim. The oath recorded by Vegetius as of ca. 400 is a Christianized version, noting the new role of the emperor not as God but as God's interlocutor on earth:

> So when recruits have been carefully selected who excel in mind and body, and after daily training for four or more months, a legion is formed by order and auspices of the invincible emperor. The soldiers are marked with tattoos in the skin which will last and swear an oath, when they are enlisted on the rolls. That is why (the oaths) are called the "Sacraments" [*sacramenta*] of military service. They swear by God, Christ and the Holy Spirit, and by the Majesty of the emperor which second to God is to be loved and worshipped by the human race. For since the emperor has received the name of the "august," faithful devotion should be given, unceasing homage paid him as if to a present and corporeal deity. For it is God whom a private citizen or a soldier serves, when he faithfully loves him who reigns by God's authority. The soldiers swear that they will strenuously do all that the emperor may command, will never desert the service, nor refuse to die for the Roman State.[44]

Fritigern appealed to Valens as a client to his patron, pointing out that, if granted, his request would further both his own and Roman goals. Could a patron deny a client protection? Fritigern failed to obtain the aid requested, but, anticipating that his challenge to Athanaric would fail, Valens granted him and his followers admission. What Valens, who was then preparing to engage his army against the Persians, did not know was that by then much of the barbarian population north of the lower Danube was fleeing southwards towards the Danube and the presumed safety of the Roman frontier.[45]

Four centuries after Roman armies first encountered barbarians in southern Gaul, much had changed, but not the most basic ways in which men understood their relationships to others. Foremost among these was, still, the relationship of patron and client. Julius Caesar's clients were tied to him personally. By the time of Augustus, however, Roman imperial institutions, particularly the army, acted as patron, and the office of emperor guaranteed Rome's observance of its commitments. How barbarians actually understood the institutionalization of Roman patronage was another matter. Fritigern had a strong claim to protection within the empire. The barbarian confederacies, in part because of their endurance and emerging political structures, had the potential to be ideal client states. As the Frankish "king" Gennobaudes had dramatically demonstrated to his followers towards the end of the third century, being supported by Rome as a client carried with it heavy obligations. The heaviest were observance of your patron's gods and a willingness to fight your patron's enemies.

Romans too felt the weight of treaty obligations. Constantine the Great had to intervene on the side of his clients the Sarmatians when they could not withstand Gothic raids. After he defeated those Goths, who had violated the area accorded to Sarmatians, the emperor began a series of contraforts and bridged the Danube at Sucidava. Under his son Constantius his armies also took the field against the Sarmatians themselves and various others along the northern bank of the Danube.[46] Constantine's new building programs and clarifications of the client status of the barbarians north of the Danube continued tetrarchic policies and applied them in the area of the former Roman province of Dacia. Rome could manipulate access to its own regional markets whenever it wished. But as was already the case under Marcus Aurelius, monitoring trade was one thing, its long-term restriction quite something else. The latter hurt everybody because so many people were to some degree involved in the regional economy.

Naturally imperial propaganda recalled its attempts to control barbarian access and Roman invasions of *barbaricum* as appropriate humiliations for barbarian misconduct. There were many victories celebrated on coins and treaties signed, but the scale of "punishment" and the tone of humiliation were so much a part of Roman political and cultural rhetoric that it is difficult to place much credence in them. These actions and this type of rhetoric were the standard responses of a Roman patron creating or disciplining a client. As in all such relationships the obvious inequality was acceptable within limits. Punishment was acceptable, and barbarians surely knew the risks, but once the offense had been redressed, normal conditions were expected to resume. Sometimes punishments were deemed inappropriate or were seen as having no basis. Thus the Alamanni protested Valentinian's reduction of Roman tribute payments. So too the building of permanent structures in barbarian lands meant that the fundamental relationship was being altered with little likelihood of a return to the status quo ante. The client felt justified in stating his concerns.[47]

Constantine's client system on the lower Danube lasted until the events leading up to the battle of Adrianople (378). Ammianus tells us that after three years of war (364–67) in which access to Roman markets had been denied and their crops destroyed by Roman raids, the Goths under Athanaric "begged for peace."[48] This should not, however, be interpreted as a sign that these Goths, let alone other barbarians, were deficient in agriculture. They were dependent upon commerce in which they sold agricultural products and anything else they had in excess, in return for finished products of all types, most especially refined bulk metal and metal objects, wine, ceramics, and olive oil. Perhaps they offered a slave or two on the local market, although to sell a slave they may have been able to deal with Roman slavers operating within or close to their own realms. These men then sold their human cargo throughout the empire.[49]

The war had begun in the context of the usurper Procopius's request that the Gothic chiefs provide him with recruits, as, he reminded them, they had agreed to do under his ancestor Constantine. Unfortunately for the Goths this was only the beginning of their woes. In some of his most moving passages Ammianus relates the story of whole families roving the banks in search of food while awaiting permission to cross over to Roman territory (in 376) and of their life in the concentration areas under unscrupulous Roman officers. They did not revolt even when offered dogs to eat in trade for their children.[50] For the next several decades food was a critical issue among barbarians caught up in war or when moving about the empire without the written authorizations that would open Roman storage facilities to them. In fact, supplying the dietary needs of their followers became as important for barbarian leaders as rewarding them with tokens of prestige. One of the main conditions governing the settlement of the barbarians inside the late empire was guaranteeing them adequate food supplies until they could harvest their first crops. Land was routinely offered as a part of any frontier settlement and continued to be a central issue when in the fifth century large numbers of barbarians were settled in the interior provinces—for example, when Honorius's general Constantius settled Goths in southern Gaul in 418.[51]

The Quadi accepted their client status along the middle Danube, a status they had negotiated with Constantius. There they lived quite peacefully until Valentinian decided to build a military outpost deep within their territory. They could accept contraforts: Valentinian and Constantius had built nine of them just between Budapest and Belgrade. But what Valentinian had now in mind was not a contrafort but a remote listening station and monitoring point. Constantius had apparently built one in Sarmatian territory earlier, doubtless over the Sarmatians' opposition. The Quadic confederation was called together, and war ensued. The murder of their confederate king at the order of the commander of the Roman frontier forces (the *dux*) only made matters worse. Barbarians crossed into the Pannonian provinces in 374, cutting a swath through undefended farmlands, carrying off some property owners and their slaves, killing others, and driving Roman livestock back with them across the Danube. Walled cities were avoided. Despite all this destruction and Valentinian's misguided announcement of a bounty upon barbarian heads, a peace was concluded.[52]

The reasons that Julian so often encountered urban defenses and even fortresses in a poor state of repair was not that they had yet to recover from some recent attack, but rather that the client system had worked so well that cities like Autun had thought funding their maintenance programs unnecessary. Constantius II trusted his barbarian allies and had confidently relied on them, first to fight Magnentius and then to support him against a member of his own family, Julian. Burgundian clients attacked the Alamanni as ordered when the latter threatened Roman territory, and so on. The system still worked. Whenever it broke down, wars ensued, lasted longer, and were bloodier. Escalating violence inevitably eroded the trust that was at the heart of any successful patron-client relationship, and the longer it lasted the more difficult it was to heal the wounds. When peace finally came, however, the emperors moved quickly to restore and improve the system so that it would better defend their interests. But in the case of the Alamanni, after a decade of turmoil, the relationship could not be just returned to its pre-Magnentius state. Fortifications had to be rebuilt and strengthened, thereby reasserting in a highly visible fashion the coercive power of the patron, the Roman state as embodied in the emperor. Although dressed in very stout walls with the capacity to rain artillery fire from its towers, these fortifications also served as markets with the barbarians.[53] The later function was reserved for peace, and the former for war. The Romans really had no alternative but the tried-and-true client system, because none of the barbarian groups with whom they dealt had institutionalized diplomatic responsibility.

Sometimes the restoration of the client system was relatively simple, favoring one chieftain over another. At other times it was much more difficult and required selective admission (*receptio*) or even the relocation of thousands of people to other areas beyond the frontier with all the resistance such actions caused among both the emigrant and the indigenous populations. Rebellious clients wishing to retain their position in Roman eyes and therefore, among their own followers, had to make recompense. Julian forced many such leaders to supply him with building materials, recruits, and even slaves to be used to rebuild the forts guarding against these same barbarians along the Rhine. Valentinian compelled Quadic chiefs to provide him with recruits. It is hard to imagine a more humiliating test of their restored loyalty. Romans such as Ammianus knew that, as the patron, Rome had no right to invade and destroy its client's lands and villages without provocation, but they also knew that an excuse was rarely hard to find. Emperors were remarkably successful in their endeavors to maintain and rebuild client systems, for as in all such relationships the patron held all the trump cards. Rome continued to dictate terms well into the fifth century, and by then the goals of both patron and clients were changing. Not all Roman efforts went smoothly. Constantius's attempt to admit some Sarmatian clients called Limigantes ended in chaos, and when the reception of the Goths under the client prince

Fritigern fell apart, it led directly to the battle of Adrianople in 378 and the death of an emperor.[54] The outlines of Rome's relationship to its barbarian clients were familiar; Julius Caesar would have understood the objectives of Julian the Caesar perfectly.

By the fourth century, although no northern barbarians lived in cities, they had made some significant strides in local, district, and regional political structures. Corresponding to these structures were signs of a heightened awareness of geopolitical boundaries. Rome encouraged such developments among its clients as another way to stabilize its neighbors. Little information reached the Romans about warfare among its clients unless and until one or the other appealed for aid. More often the issue was settled quickly, perhaps as a matter of honor rather than of territory, and in that case the Romans would have had nothing to say. The Burgundians and Alamanni had a long conflict over salt pits and had erected a system of boundary stones to mark their territories. The Sarmatian Limigantes rejected the areas Rome had assigned them and crossed the Roman-imposed boundaries to raid their neighbors against Roman wishes. Rome had earlier intervened to separate the Limigantes, who claimed to have been the "former slaves of the Sarmatians," from their former masters. Romans thereafter referred to the Sarmatians, whom they had rescued from their former slaves, as the Free Sarmatians, probably to remind them that they owed their freedom to Roman intervention. Despite the clarity of the Latin, it is not clear how one should understand "slaves" in this context. It is obvious that the Limigantes were at least former dependents of the Sarmatian ruling elite, if not literally their personal slaves. The term Limigantes is reminiscent of the Greek *perioikoi,* "those living around." Although as a group they were enslaved by the Spartans, they were recruited into the front ranks during the final stages of the Peloponnesian War. The *perioikoi* farmed their own lands, but had none of the rights of Spartan citizens. This is far different than being a chattel slave serving in the house and fields of the master.[55] Perhaps some of the peculiar earthen walls running through Slovakia and eastern Hungary had territorial as well as defensive functions connected to Roman relations with various Quadi and Sarmatians respectively. If so, they would have been in accordance with Roman efforts to clarify responsibilities among their clients by tying them to particular territories. The best-attested wall-building effort in *barbaricum,* that of Athanaric in his effort to ward off Hunnic invaders in 376, was stated to run along a border with another barbarian people, the Taifali.[56]

Had there been an alternative way to conduct relations between Romans and barbarians, it might have been tried, but there were no options. Over and over, new treaties had to be negotiated, some because clients rebelled, others because emperors, old or new, knew that they needed to renew the personal qualities of the Roman relationship with barbarian leaders, old or new, in order for the terms to be effective. In some areas the process was especially trying. Petty wars with various members of the Alamanni were frequent during the 360s and a major invasion took place in the mid-370s—even northern Italy was not spared. The rapid escalation of violence that had served Julian so well was renewed under Valentinian, who by his death in 375 had personally taken the war to the enemy and had made frontier fortifications much more formidable. Despite building stouter walls and more watchtowers, the Romans never found an alternative to renegotiating treaties with barbarian chiefs. Eventually treaties alone were sufficiently respected to provide peace, submission to Roman authority, and the fulfillment of the promises.

Thus the barbarian confederacies constituted a permanent conundrum for the Roman government. In order to assure that barbarian leaders could enforce the peace they had to be strong enough to impress their followers. This in turn required Roman support and cooperation, for unless the chiefs could reward their followers with gifts and occasions to gain honor, they were replaced. Furthermore, because stability in the Roman client system required that internal warfare among the barbarians had to be limited, Rome placed substantial resources at the disposal of the chiefs. The Roman government, operating through the local and regional army commands, funneled its recruitment efforts and most commerce—including, it seems, the slave trade—through these chiefs. In addition, the great chiefs received regular tribute payments in the form of coins and other gift items in carefully negotiated quantities and types appropriate for redistribution among the followers. But even this was not enough. Rome also had to accept its barbarian clients' need for occasional warfare, preferably low-level violence, as each chief demonstrated his merit in battle. Thus Rome discouraged war among its clients but turned a blind eye towards their petty struggles. As Ammianus noted, the latter were usually over before Rome even knew that they had occurred. So, on the one hand, the more power a barbarian chief had, the more stable was his hold over his followers, and the more he could deliver to Rome. On the other, the more power the confederacy had, the greater the threat it posed to the frontier and, ultimately, to Rome.

The Romans were subject to similar whims. New emperors and especially new dynasties had to manifest their martial vigor, and that could only be done by defeating barbarians. If the client system was functioning smoothly, then some sort of opportunity to publicize this welcome news needed to be manufactured. This might take the form of a tour of the frontier defenses with much ritualized diplomacy designed to confirm the emperor's status as patron, or perhaps a limited military exercise with maximum follow-up propaganda. Both sides inevitably crossed the line between acceptable demonstration and committing acts that broke the peace and thereby undermined the client system. Open violation of an agreement was an affront to both Roman and barbarian honor and had to be punished, but that need not have meant a major war, just carefully managed posturing. Under these circumstances Romans and barbarians learned to live in an artificial setting in which peace was temporarily set aside for war and then tranquillity returned. The ethos of the warrior was tempered by the needs of the politician. As in most other aspects of ancient life, war and peace were surrounded with rituals of dominance and submission. The gods had to be invited to lend a hand.

Sometimes it took a decade or more to end a war, but even then it was possible to rebuild the peace. The wars with the Alamanni in the 370s resulted in an alliance system that allowed for peaceful co-existence along much of the frontier. It lasted for over half a century, especially if we take into account that much of the unrest in the 380s may have been associated with the revolt of Magnus Maximus and hence a repercussion of Roman civil wars. The Gothic *receptio* did ultimately yield troops for the empire, although not in the time frame that Valens had imagined. Rather, it occurred over the course of two decades, and even then only after repeated efforts at containment and recruitment. Any barbarian with political and military power had to be brought into the network. As soon as a Hunnic chief had fought his way to the top of the heap north of the Danube, Rome entered into negotiations with him to guarantee peace and to provide the imperial government with military support.[57]

Foreign relations for barbarian leaders were extensions of family, friends, and dependents, a small circle expanded by diplomacy and united by ritual. Treaties, marriages, gift exchanges, taking and redeeming hostages—all were personal acts, not things undertaken for a state. Thus these were what anthropologists call "chiefdoms," not "client states." The Roman government understood this, took advantage of it, and to some extent was itself still governed by the same principles. The Roman code of honor had always been best conveyed through legends of individuals giving their lives for family and of families sacrificing themselves for Rome. In Roman myth and barbarian life anyone who found himself outside the circle of kindred and friendship was in grave danger. They were literally outside the law and could expect the worst. They were at the mercy of the strongest and meanest. Roman meddling and the numerous agreements signed with clearly understood and mutual obligations suggest that Romans continued to regard barbarians as in some sense clients and as such as "insiders," that is, as living within a greater Roman Empire. Certainly fourth-century barbarians knew but one EMPIRE, and they probably saw themselves as a part of it despite the annoying checkpoints that they encountered along the frontiers. One tends to forget that similar customs controls existed between provinces, not just with the external barbarians.

Philosophers had long wrestled with the issues raised by the postulation of universal values. Another version was set forth towards the end of the fourth century when the neo-Platonist Themistius offered a late pagan vision of the relationship between mankind and empire. For him, the emperor was the supreme patron—not just to his fellow Romans, as Augustus had thought, but to all mankind. The new imperial task was to educate all men in the arts of civilization, most especially the barbarians, and through education to lead them all to a life of peace.[58] There are echoes of Vergil here, for Themistius's culture too rests on "the rule of law," but no longer do we read Vergil's admonition to Aeneas that he must first "beat the haughty down." For Themistius the force of Roman culture and the lure of peace were more powerful than the sword, but his level of abstraction was too esoteric even for the imperial court. His barbarians were created merely for philosophic convenience, but nonetheless there is, even in Themistius, a strong paternalism and so clientage. His mythical barbarians are like all men, clients of a new cultural patron, his most enlightened imperial majesty, and so in late antiquity as in earlier ages as clients the barbarians belong to a Roman "empire without end," just as Jupiter had prophesied to Vergil's Aeneas so long ago.

For Julius Caesar, Celtic culture stood as a buffer between Roman and German, between civilization and barbarism. Culture defined and divided people. But Themistius's universal empire was something else, something new, for it offered a vision of a greater unity and of a greater empire. His pagan philosophic vision lost out, however, to another universalistic dream, that of a Christian world in which emperors were intercessors between man and God. Frontier society was far removed from the imperial courts where intellectuals of all types entertained. Themistius did not really know barbarians, and none knew of him. Nonetheless frontier society, not just those on one side of a river boundary, was changing, giving up worn-out formulas.

One of the hallmarks of the Principate had been the vitality of the urban enterprise in the provinces. Even in most frontier areas urban centers grew nearby legionary and auxiliary camps. Some pre-Roman proto-urban centers, *oppida,* were transformed into provincial towns; others were abandoned in favor of new towns built at important road junctures. Commerce flourished in all of these urban centers, first where Roman veterans helped assure the peace but ultimately throughout the provinces. When the army was moved to the frontiers, this economic stimulation moved with it. Rural areas were less affected, and those remote from Roman settlement and transportation corridors still less so. By the end of the second century villa agriculture, producing surpluses for local and regional markets, could be found wherever villa owners and operators had access to good soil and buyers for their products. The keys to villa success had always been markets and security. If either lapsed, villas were soon hard pressed. Such hard times were increasingly in evidence during the fourth century in the frontier provinces and became chronic early in the fifth.

By the late fourth century several goldsmithing traditions, including Roman and Persian, had come together to produce distinctive gold ornaments made by setting garnets in cloisonné. This style was extremely popular among the highest levels of the Roman army and among barbarian elites still resident in *barbaricum*. By the middle of the fifth century men wearing it could be found from the Balkans through Gaul. Some of the best-known examples come from the burial of Childeric (ca. 480), a king or prince, a Roman officer, and the father of Clovis, king of the Franks. Because those who could afford these great works of personal art were invariably elites, and because many of these elites occupied the highest ranks in the fifth-century Roman army, the style is not truly barbarian but, like so much else, both Roman and barbarian.[59]

An even better example of a decorative style that was peculiar to the frontier—and, hence, Romano-barbarian—is that of the so-called chip-carved style of personal ornament. Here again the manufacturing technique of using molds and the lost-wax method of production augmented by very precise incising and polishing meant that it was usually produced in Roman shops. The origin of the chip-carved style dates to the mid-fourth century. It then evolved for several centuries, culminating in the early medieval animal style. The latter is best known to Americans and British from the great golden belt buckle from the early seventh century in the ship burial found at Sutton Hoo, England, and in medieval wood carving such as that still to be seen on the prows of Viking ships.[60] This style was very popular among all ranks of the late Roman army, in which of course numerous Germanic recruits were to be found. For maximum visibility, they wore it on their broad military belts, from which hung all sorts of small paraphernalia.

Late Roman chip carving. Courtesy of Rheinisches Landesmuseum Trier

Chip-carved metalwork was surely diffused by soldiers retiring back to their ancestral homes, but more commonly it arrived there by trade. What we see as small cuts that glistened in the sunlight seems likely to have resulted from the merger of Roman metallurgy with decorative styles that the barbarians had developed earlier in wood, and for which no examples now exist. The distribution pattern of chip-carved jewelry is striking. Very few examples have been found more than 150 kilometers from the frontier in either direction, but many hundreds have been discovered within that zone. Obviously this was a style that appealed almost exclusively to the militarized society of the late Roman frontier.[61]

Ammianus Marcellinus, in the process of narrating a Roman raid across the Rhine in 357, describes what at first seems to be a highly atypical barbarian settlement: "Upon their departure our soldiers marched on undisturbed plundering barbarian farms rich in livestock [*opulentas pecore villas*] and crops. Sparing no one, they dragged the inhabitants away and took them captive. Then they set aflame their houses, which were carefully built in the Roman way [*ritu Romano constructa*]."[62] His assertion that some barbarians were living as Romans, perhaps some even on villa-type farms, is very gradually being confirmed along some sections of the frontier, and what better things to raise in abundance than fresh meats and vegetables. These were not transported great distances at state expense, and so did not have to compete with subsidized products. They were sold in the regional markets or directly to Roman procurement officers obtaining military supplies. Excavated examples of Roman-type building in *barbaricum* are very rare and the dates and identities of their occupants remain controversial.

The area beyond the middle Danube has recently produced substantial remains of Roman-style buildings, many dated to the fourth century, especially its second half. Several sites suggest that building using Roman technique began to penetrate into *barbaricum* here during the third century, which in this area was a relatively peaceful period, and continued to expand during the fourth and even into the fifth. In one case a rather simple Roman-style building from the later fourth century lay in close proximity to a barbarian settlement. In general the small finds from these sites are quite diverse, with local handmade ceramics found lying alongside Roman imports. The same can be said of small metal items for personal use. The broader context for these Roman-type constructions is unclear.[63] Although elsewhere complete examples of Roman building styles in *barbaricum* are as yet lacking, examples of Roman building materials, especially roofing tiles, making their way into *barbaricum* are rather common. In any case, the importation of Roman manufactured elements such as heavy Roman building materials required water transport, and so their use was limited to those areas relatively close to navigable rivers.

The area that Julian's soldiers brutally destroyed may have held several Roman-type farm buildings, not just an isolated great estate. The phrase "in the Roman style" may simply have meant "built" with Roman materials or even just "built in stone."[64] According to Ammianus, the soldiers themselves suggested that they could ford the river, and they did so pushing their shields ahead of them as sort of "kick-boards." One does not have to let one's mind wonder too long to imagine a group of soldiers sitting idly around camp watching the Rhine tumble past and seeing a way to get from one side to the other at night. So with the permission of their commander, they gave it a try. In order for this scenario to play out, the barbarians had to live virtually within sight, just across the river, and this is precisely what we would expect. Archaeology in the hinterlands of the uppermost Danube and Rhine reveals that already by the mid-fourth century, villa agriculture was retreating to the areas of the forts, perhaps spurred on by the wars in which Julian had engaged.[65] At the same time, however, there was a continuing symbiosis of Germanic and Roman cultures along and beyond the frontiers.

Simultaneous with the retreat of villa life to secure enclaves was the development of hilltop settlements on both sides of the frontiers. On the Roman side these were sometimes within sight of still functioning villas. Once again, topography and security joined hands to determine which types of settlements, if any, would prosper. Beyond the Rhine and the Danube, Rome's barbarian neighbors too were moving into more defensible locations, particularly along the rivers flowing into the Rhine and Danube at Mainz and Regensburg. Because these towns were home to Roman garrisons of some type at least into the early fifth century, the growth of highland settlements among the barbarians along the ridgelines of the streams feeding the Rhine and Danube could only have been with Roman support and encouragement. The broad chronology of their development, stretching it seems from around the middle of the fourth century well into the fifth, suggests, however, that there was no true policy at work here.

Roman authorities probably saw this move towards defensible communities as in keeping with their own concerns for defense and encouraged it beyond the frontier as likely to produce a buffer zone of friendly barbarians. The same pattern and basic chronology for hilltop settlements existed in the area of southwest Germany, along the Rhine in the area west of Lake Constance, and in Switzerland where the Rhine cuts its way deep into the Alps.[66] These sites are characterized by their elevation and defensibility but also by their highly composite material remains. For example, some items of personal dress exhibit styles common in sites near Roman camps, while others are much more traditional mixtures of colorful beads, combs, and decorative pins long traditional in the area. The first area along the frontiers to produce such a strong fusion of barbarian and Roman traditions was northern France, which by the middle of the fourth century had a material culture made up of Roman and barbarian influences that spanned the Rhine in both directions. This is the same area where the Tetrarchy and Constantine had successfully settled Franks and *laeti*.[67]

Some of the people living in the barbarian hilltop communities seem to have been relatively new arrivals in the area from farther east. One such group has been detected beginning around the middle of the fourth century and continuing into the fifth century. So far they are identified only by their peculiar grave artifacts, especially their very dark hand-turned ceramics that they used originally for cremation burial. Many examples of this peculiar pottery have come to light during the excavation of cemeteries near Roman camps and across the Danube from them. On the basis of the distribution pattern of these distinctive grave goods, it is clear that from the middle of the fourth century the Roman army along this stretch of the upper Danube was quite successful in recruiting barbarians into its ranks from the entire watershed. Once in the Roman army, however, they could end up serving elsewhere. Their distinctive artifacts have come to light in Gaul and a few much farther away. Most of these recruits stayed nearer to home. Some scholars have opted to refer to this archaeological group as "Elb-Alamanni," but that seems to beg the question of identity, since there is nothing to suggest that the Alamannic confederacy had anything to do with these local developments.[68] Nor would there have been many opportunities for youths growing up in barbarian villages near Roman camps or in the high plateau settlements other than service in the Roman army, for such small garrisons needed little in the way of supplies. The good economic times of the frontier economy had passed. Farming was now largely subsistence agriculture, producing only those surpluses marketable in the local economy. Much the same thing was taking place deeper inside the Roman frontier provinces extending into France and Switzerland. In the few places where good soil, stable markets, and security still prevailed, villas survived, sometimes even into the first decades of the fifth century.

As a result of Theodosius's successful recruitment strategies on the lower Danube, east-Germanic recruits entered the army and were assigned duty elsewhere. A range of items formerly peculiar to areas north of the lower Danube where the Goths had lived, before taking flight from civil war and the Huns, have turned up in datable contexts in Roman military cemeteries along the Rhine and upper Danube. This was a long way from the Balkan area where these artifacts originally appeared. Thus the hypothesis that, because these men found their final resting place on the upper Danube and the Rhine, they were recruited as a result of Theodosius's successful effort to restore order to the Balkan provinces following the Roman defeat at Adrianople. Ammianus cast Rome's struggle in epic terms. Just as Marius had eventually crushed the Cimbri and Teutones who had spread out over Italy, as Marcus Aurelius had rid the empire of barbarian plunderers, and as Claudius Gothicus and Aurelian had restored peace and Roman honor to the frontiers, so implicitly had Theodosius redeemed the current disaster.[69]

Archaeological finds of such Balkan goods are datable to the last quarter of the fourth century by stylistic analysis of the Roman goods interred with them, most of which relate to their owner's position in the Roman army, where official dress and armorial symbols changed very slowly and in a uniform manner. The same process that brought east-Germanic men also brought their families into the empire, including some women whose skulls had been forced into oblong shapes by tightly wrapping their heads as babies. Perhaps their parents were Huns or Alans or at least wanted their daughters to attract one, because such cranial deformation was favored among the Hunnic ruling elite. In the cemeteries at these sites lie the remains of a decidedly mixed garrison population. Some burials have little or no goods of Germanic provenance; others have less sign of Roman provincial culture; but many lie in between, with some artifacts falling into either stylistic category. The nature of the unit—*limitanei* or *comitatenses*—made no difference, for barbarians were recruited and integrated into all units of the army.

Although the people living in both Roman and barbarian highground settlements had their homes on the hilltops, they continued to farm the rich valley soils just as in previous centuries. These settlements were the result of ad hoc decisions made by locals. Roman officials and camp commandants had no specific military interest in agrarian communities, but they may nonetheless have regarded their presence as supportive of local defense. The government concentrated its resources at a few camps and towns, and the systematic and interlocking pattern of forts, towers, supply depots, and roadhouses faded into insignificance. There were not enough men in the small garrisons to spare for watchtower duty, but also the barbarians they were supposed to watch were extremely well known by this time and may not have needed watching on so regular a basis. Elements of the fourth-century army's building efforts remained, but by the early fifth century people had few occasions to use even the regional command system. When trouble appeared, the cultivators sought refuge in the forts. Agriculture and most other labor were carried on within sight of the walls. Without the watch system, nobody provided them advance warning. Each fort, or military complex, along with the farmers huddled nearby, had to fend for itself. As the integrated defensive system came apart, so did the relevant borders that it had long guarded. The new frontiers were local. Raiders could appear from any direction and under any banner. As the fifth century progressed, they might be led by men wearing Roman uniforms and boasting Roman titles of rank. The fifth century can be seen as a shakedown period for new military regimes established on the last configuration of the Roman frontiers.

By 425 some stretches of the frontier may have been entirely in the hands of Germanic auxiliaries, who, although under the command of their own officers, were attached to the Roman army. Thus these units were more independent than were the *laeti* with their Roman appointed prefects. But much remains unclear. Part of the general uncertainty about late Roman military deployment and command systems results from the problem of dating the various sections of the *Notitia dignitatum.* The *Notitia* does not mention any barbarian auxiliary units at all, although there is no doubt that many such units were then in existence and sometimes served alongside regular units in battle. If there is a general explanation as to why no barbarian auxiliaries are listed in the *Notitia,* it should lie in some clerical practice. One suggestion is that because barbarian auxiliary units by this time served under their own leaders, the clerks had no way to insert them into a table of organization based on the normal chain of command. This does not, however, mean that these forces were not regarded as parts of the Roman army, or that areas protected by them were "abandoned." Instead what seems to have been happening in various areas along the frontier is that the military system was catching up to the realities of life. Just as along the lower Rhine, sections of the upper Rhine and Danube had, in effect, ceased to function as meaningful boundaries and the best source of protection in the area was the barbarians living in their villages nearby. They were given the task.

Despite the litany of invasion and destruction recorded in the literary materials, as late as 350 many individuals in the western frontier provinces could have lived out their lives without fear of awakening to the sound of looters or soldiers ravaging their homes. After 350 and the collapse of the client system during Magnentius's revolt, this peaceful innocence was progressively less common. By the end of the fourth century much had changed. By then most frontier fortifications had been reduced very substantially, and as a result many watchtowers had ceased to function because the small garrisons of the nearby forts could no longer man them. Along the uppermost Danube and Rhine Rivers, villa agriculture had withdrawn to the immediate vicinity of the camps and in some places had begun to take on the appearance and functions of medieval walled villages. In some areas such as near Regensburg, even the best soils had been abandoned, leaving nobody in the undefended countryside. Nonetheless villa agriculture did not disappear completely even here, because the forts, although reduced in size, still needed supplies and still provided local protection. Areas around provincial capitals, such as Augusta Vindelicum (modern Augsburg), where civil and military officers congregated, also satisfied the requirements for nearby villa production into the fifth century in many cases. But even small road stations such as Fussen at the northern base of the Alps seem to have supported a small community as long as the road linking Augsburg to Italy through Salzburg and the Brenner Pass remained in use, perhaps in some cases well into the fifth century. About halfway between Fussen and Augsburg the road ran through a large area of gravel plain just west of Munich, where once stood a small late Roman outpost. Some villas survived on the plain into the early fifth century but only in a shrunken state. Elements of the *villa rustica* that had once existed there remained but now as a compound containing several small buildings within a defense enclosure.[70]

Trier with its own defensive system was also a center for villa agriculture, apparently even after much of the government moved south to Arles around the opening of the fifth century.[71] Archaeology reveals that during its very long afterlife the inner city proper became progressively rural. Areas once overbuilt with housing and government buildings were cleared and transformed into gardens. A famous comment about Trier's inhabitants being reduced to living in and defending the amphitheater may be simply a rhetorical exercise showing perhaps that the citizens of Trier were struggling to retain their Roman heritage and the traditions of an imperial capital. The same ruralization in an area clinging to urban status may have been the case at other urban centers. Most Roman cities survived into the Middle Ages and beyond as episcopal seats and pilgrimage centers, and today these old areas are densely settled. Archaeology follows in the wake of urban renewal, hardly the type of systematic exploration needed to determine the chronology of late Roman urbanism. But no matter how one looks at the settlement data from the Rhine and upper Danubian provinces, one comes to the conclusion that the independent urban vitality of the Principate had largely expired by 400. Thus these provinces were left with reduced military garrisons and considerably reduced urban markets. Villa agriculture, even if security was not an issue, would have had to adjust. As villas declined in number or were transformed into walled villages, whole areas were left without complex agriculture, without urban markets, and in some cases without human habitation. Barbarian village economies competed to provide a share of the agricultural needs of the nearby Roman camps. By the middle of the fifth century along the Danube upstream from Kunzing (that is, west of the Inn River and within the province of Raetia Secunda), villages with few if any Roman artifacts began to reoccupy lands that may have remained relatively clear of trees even without active agriculture. These people too might be called Alamanni, but the typically isolated settlements were hardly those of a coordinated confederacy. The men could have been summoned after the harvest for a raid or two at best.

If we had ventured east to Passau and crossed the Inn into Noricum or went still farther to the Pannonian provinces, we would have found a similar outline of development but one in which Roman urbanism and its accompanying defensive requirements were much more tenacious. Here the network of villas lasted longer than in the western and northern frontier provinces, but eventually the same patterns emerged. The military evolution was also similar to that in the northwestern provinces but not identical.

When Constantius II (337–61) pulled together forces in the Pannonian provinces in order to create the mobile field army he needed to fight civil wars and Sarmatian invaders, he initiated a process that forced the gradual transformation of all other aspects of frontier defense. His successors throughout the remainder of the century could not help but further engage these efforts, building and strengthening. Then, around the end of the century, the system was transformed one final time. This may have been one effect of Theodosius's civil wars against Eugenius and Arbogastes in which troops were scrounged from the entire region, even including the defenses in the Julian Alps to the south. The fortifications immediately on the frontier (those manned by the *limitanei*) were reduced. Some units were incorporated into the field army, while a few remained in place. Watchtowers were abandoned for lack of watchers. The soldiers serving in old frontier forts were primarily the new barbarian recruits. They typically retained much of their former tastes in food and dress, and so are identifiable in the archaeological data as related to those still living in *barbaricum*.[72]

The general trend of Roman strategy was to withdraw all or part of major military units into the interior of the provinces to produce a concentrated and mobile force. On the one hand, this resulted in a rapid decline of the towns on the frontiers and the increasingly common presence of people of recent barbarian ancestry in the army and as new settlers in the countryside. This was the case in much of Raetia and the Rhineland provinces, for example. On the other hand, the concentration of human and fiscal resources upon provincial capitals and a few other towns in the interior helped some of them prosper as never before. Thus Sopianae (Pécs, Hungary), which became the capital of the late Roman province of Valeria in the diocese of Pannonia, flourished. Simultaneously Aquincum (Budapest) in the same province went into decline, as emperors reduced its garrison and shifted the organs of provincial government to Sopianae.

Villa agriculture followed troops and the imperial bureaucracy into the interior, thriving, for example, around Sopianae. Areas of the countryside far removed from the pockets of prosperity continued as always, basically unchanged from pre-Roman times. In these isolated villages and hamlets families produced for local consumption and lived in huts with sunken floors as if nothing had happened during the last half millennium, and, of course, for them little had. But elsewhere, where provincial Roman traditions had established themselves in decorative and manufacturing techniques, these transplanted ways too continued through the first quarter of the fifth century. Often items thought to be peculiar to barbarians living on the other side of the Danube, as far away as former Dacia, appear alongside pottery and jewelry characteristic of the native provincial population. The ethnic identification of such complex burials is conjectural, if not counterproductive, for clearly much of Valeria and other Pannonian provinces were experiencing a profound realignment of cultural values that in each area produced a unique blend of traditional Roman, Roman provincial, native barbarian, and immigrant barbarian. After around 425 this aggregate culture received new components from much farther to the east, materials and traditions common among the peoples of the steppes of south Russia, such as cranial deformation, elaborate horse burials, peculiar mirrors, and ceramics.[73]

Wherever markets for the products of villa agriculture survived, villas did too and at the same level of prosperity. Most of the fourth century was a period of visible prosperity, and it remained so until almost the end of the century and in some cases awhile longer. The move to nucleated settlement occurred in this area but later than in the frontier provinces farther west. High-ground retreats played little role, in part because the areas near the frontier were on the plain of the Danube, and there were no suitable sites. There was a greater effort on behalf of the Roman government to sustain its military and economic commitments here but, in the end, without much success.

Less clear is what happened along the lower Danube. Here the imperial government became embroiled with various barbarian groups, beginning with the Goths in 376, and then turned upon itself. The murder of Gratian in 383 inaugurated a period of civil wars that raged more or less constantly and pitted various generals against one another and tested the willingness of the courts of East and West to help each other. Feeding all this strife was a virtually continuous recruitment drive in the Balkan provinces and across the Danube that lasted for more than a decade following the official end of the Gothic wars in 390. The Balkan provinces and the Danubian frontier had to be maintained for the same reasons that they had been conquered under Augustus. They linked West and East, but with the rise of Constantinople as the rival and in most ways the superior of Rome, the need for security in the eastern

Balkans rose to paramount importance. What is clear is that throughout this roughly quarter of a century, barbarians were recruited into the army from all quarters. Also clear is that the provincial cities, all having been rebuilt in the fourth century as fort-cities with imposing and formidable defenses, survived these trials. Villa agriculture in adjacent areas likewise survived.

Fewer and fewer fourth-century Roman soldiers with Germanic names changed them to Roman names; after 400, none can be found to have done so. Nonetheless, naming one's children and choosing what name to use yourself was a matter of personal choice, much as it had always been. During the Principate, when auxiliary soldiers retired as citizens they had had little choice but to use a convenient Roman trinomial name, but that reason largely ceased in the third century after the extension of citizenship under Caracalla. Those German men who did change their names, and whose families had the money to later set up grave inscriptions recording their changes, had all become officers before retirement. In every known case, they also gave Roman names to their sons. As Ammianus and all other sources make clear, outward signs of Germanic ethnicity in the fourth-century army had progressively less impact on one's military career. By the end of the century, Germanness had ceased to be a negative factor at all. Late Roman soldiers of Germanic extraction, for whom a few inscriptions preserve their names, predominated in some units. They were apparently quite happy to continue their heritage. For one thing, sons of veterans had an edge on the competition for early promotion. This was repeatedly decried in imperial legislation, doubtless to no avail. During the fifth and sixth centuries, when men of barbarian ancestry filled all military ranks in the West, parents who wished their sons to pursue a military career might even abandon the Latin names that their families had carried for several generations.[74]

The increasing presence of Germanic recruits during the third century predictably left its mark on the epigraphic record. Ethnographers agree that if you change your name, it is almost always because you think that the new name will benefit you in some way. Conversely, if you go by a name that identifies you as a minority and could change it but do not, presumably that benefits you in some different way. Identifying yourself or your child as a member of a group provides a "hook," a connection to something through association with the group. By the end of the fourth century, nothing was to be gained by changing your Germanic name to a Roman form. Some level of Latinization of names was always unavoidable—if, for example, you wished to use your name in written form, which was not possible in barbarian languages except in runes. From the late fourth and early fifth centuries outside the empire we find Roman-type signet rings, for example, inscribed with the Latinized Germanic names.[75]

The fourth century appears to have been a period of accelerating change with continuing examples of concern about retaining part or changing one's entire name, as well as of unrestrained use of Germanic names without modification.[76] The old soldier Ammianus Marcellinus thought that to have a meeting of a group of army officers without barbarians among them was "a rarity these days."[77] Among those making it to the top were men like Victor, known to be of Sarmatian stock, and the Frank Silvanus, who had borne their Latin names to lofty generalships. By the fifth century there were no longer compelling reasons to bother changing your name regardless what type of career you pursued.

The demise of the importance of being or not being of barbarian ancestry did not erode other needs to make personal identification, however. Through their names or those of their children men could identify themselves with their military units, for example.[78] Adding still further twists to an already complex situation, some barbarians married slaves who were remembered only by their Roman names.[79] In such circumstances ethnic and cultural boundaries were blurred, but they were still there to some extent. For those wishing to demonstrate their Roman identity matters were a bit different. In the camps and few urban centers, people doubtless still thought of themselves as Romans. But what else, we might ask, were they to have thought? What they thought being a Roman meant was probably very problematic. They may have connected it to their profession, or perhaps there was something special about their family or their circle of friends. Even the literary elite found being Roman a difficult concept to define. The tidy legal definition had blurred and all but disappeared after Caracalla extended the citizenship to virtually everybody inside the empire, and instead Ammianus speaks of *Romanitas,* the quality of being Roman, but never defines what he or his contemporaries meant by that. Literacy for the elite was the hallmark of a Roman but not all Romans could read. At some level all members of society would have professed loyalty to the emperor. Many identities functioned among Romans according to their owners, including the newest recruits and Rome's barbarian clients' occupations and social positions.

The army had many networks affecting promotions and social affiliations, including religion, be it pagan or Christian, and networks of patronage and friendship. Within the late Roman army, for example, such friendship circles existed as social groups, sometimes with special cult practices held in common. The unduly accelerated promotion of the sons of veterans attracted the attention of imperial legislation. Sons of officers received preferential treatment and early promotions.[80] Officers married their children to other officers in marriages that cemented alliances inside as well as outside the army. The great general Theodosius the Elder saw to the military training of his son the future emperor, and his old friends may have been instrumental in his son's elevation to the purple. Examples abound of sons getting a leg up the career ladder because of their father's standing in the army. In that regard, as the century waned, even a vague allusion to a Germanic affiliation may have helped; there is no longer any evidence that it could have hurt one's career. There may also have been groups of men with similar regional or ethnic backgrounds, men who shared special traditions, perhaps dialects or previous and current service together.

None of these personal and group relationships undermined the vague but ubiquitous sense of being Roman. The Roman cultural paradigm was much alive and well, still capable of absorbing barbarian newcomers but not into the old civilian world of the Mediterranean. For example, those barbarians whose families had practiced cremation with the use of the special ceramics gave them up within a generation after migrating to Roman camps. Other recent immigrants found occasions to wear clothing and jewelry traditional to their families, if only around the house or as small, inconspicuous items worn on their army uniforms. Native religions were still practiced with special instruments, but probably only in the privacy of their outwardly Roman homes.[81] Some things, however, remained as they had always been.

In speaking derisively of Caracalla, Herodian writing in the third century had commented that the emperor sometimes wore "a blonde wig elaborately fashioned in the German style" and that the barbarians loved him, apparently taking his false hair as a sign of his respect for their traditions.[82] The standard Roman view of barbarians was that they all wore their hair long, especially the nobility, but that was not always the case. The Alamanni did, but the Goths had cut their hair and adopted the short style traditionally favored among the Romans. Nevertheless, official monuments still depicted all barbarians, including Goths, with long flowing hair. Nor did all barbarians change their hairstyles when they lived among Romans. For example, as late as the sixth century, Vandals living in North Africa could still be distinguished by the way they wore their long hair knotted on the top of their heads and held there by distinctive hairpins.[83]

The barbarians were not all the same and never had been, but because in literature and imperial propaganda they still served the same singular purpose—to be humbled before the power of the emperor—they were still portrayed as one people, thirsting after Roman blood and booty just as in all the centuries past. A slight crack in the monolithic portrait of barbarians occurred when Christian authors emphasized Alaric's decision to grant Christians asylum in churches while his men sacked Rome in 410, but even this incident is actually just a transition from pagan stereotypes to Christian ones. Barbarian Christians were all seen as devoted Arian heretics, and as such they stood somewhere between pagan barbarism and full Christian piety. The same cultural dichotomy that had inspired Julius Caesar was being rewritten for a Christian empire. Arians were now supposed to occupy the middle position where the Celts of Gaul had once stood.

The extent to which the barbarian confederacies promoted a lasting sense of group identity among their members is a subject of intense current discussion. Americans are fond of thinking that all immigrants to the United States should become "real Americans" in three generations or explain why they failed. Despite its wide currency, this is merely an ideal and never has existed anywhere as a norm. Currently American ethnologists speak of cycloidal progress with much starting, stopping, and occasional retreat to older forms. The children of immigrants may dress and act like members of the majority, but the grandchildren may emulate the grandparents and so start the process anew almost from scratch.

There also appears to be a correlation between assertions of ethnicity and external factors such as wars with the "old country." German Americans, for example, essentially stopped proclaiming their German origins during and after World War I.[84] Italian Americans in the nineteenth century were fiercely proud of their cities of origin but could not have cared less about being Italians, a nation just coming into being. They did not think of themselves as Italians until it made sense for them to do so in the competition for economic and political power in the ghettos of America. They became "Italians" in the States.[85] The German-Roman experience exhibits some signs of undergoing a similar range of evolutionary processes within the empire. Exactly in reverse of what ancient ethnographers believed, identity is never fixed in space and time, not political and not ethnic. Old ones expire and new ones emerge. The barbarian confederacies of the fourth and fifth centuries were a start at what later became identities, but they were only a beginning and there were many fits and starts.

If Athanaric was the third in his family to be recognized as a *thiudans*—even if this position were not a continuous appointment but only one acknowledged by other nobles during extreme crises —a start towards shaping a group identity of the Tervingi Goths around this family had begun.[86] A start perhaps, but then came Fritigern, Huns, and Alans, leaving a splintered confederacy with part clinging to Athanaric, who still refused to enter the empire, and part seeking immediate entry into Roman service inside the safety of the Roman frontiers. Athanaric finally swallowed his pride and also accepted service in the empire, but he died two weeks later in Constantinople in January 381. His followers were dispersed through the normal processes of recruitment and reassignment to garrisons along the Danube without complaint.

Another Goth, Alaric, emerged from obscurity around 390, but not at the head of an independent nation of Goths. Alaric's foremost desire was a generalship in the Roman army. He got his wish, first from the government in Constantinople, but he lost it. Then he got his wish granted again, this time by the western government in Milan (later Ravenna), but he lost it for a second time. Then and only then did Alaric claim the title of *rex Gothorum* (king of the Goths) and begin his famous sieges of Rome. It was a last resort, taken only after all legal attempts to realize his cherished dream of Roman command had failed. Later a dynasty of Visigothic kings would base their claims to rule upon the legends of Athanaric and Alaric.

One factor in the withering of distinctions that has been alluded to only briefly is religion. Very little can be said about pre-Christian religion among the Germanic barbarians. This remains true even if we take into account archaeological information, much of it from bog deposits in northern Germany and the Low Countries. The picture does not change much when we carry back with us into Roman times Norse legends compiled during the Middle Ages, some as late as the thirteenth century. Although these approaches have yielded some interesting suggestions, generalizing to all northern barbarians creates a false picture of religious and cultural uniformity. What little direct evidence we have about barbarian religions demonstrates that regions far distant from one another shared little in detail. In each area unique local cult practices and traditions defined religion, just as was true among the Romanized populations of the provinces. Although the names of the gods of the late Roman barbarians cannot be guessed at without recourse to medieval recollections, contemporary archaeological data suggest that Germanic barbarians shared many of the same cult practices as the Celts: occasional human sacrifice, a love of divination, and a host of rituals connecting men to spirits associated with special natural features, especially springs. Although there is no evidence of a class of priests like the Druids among the various Germanic barbarians, as in most societies in which cult must be observed in rigorous detail, priests performed the sacrifices. The Burgundians not only had priests but ranked them. The foremost one had a spiritual rank equivalent to that of their king, but unlike him could not be deposed.[87]

One reason why Germanic and Celtic religious ideas are similar may be that much of Celtic religious practice was common in areas east of the Rhine before the Romans took over Gaul. Although Gallic influence across the Rhine had continued under early Roman rule, a similar willingness to borrow cults specifically Roman is not apparent. Nor is there evidence that barbarians outside the empire ever Romanized their native religious practices as was common within the provinces. Occasionally the statue of a Roman god comes to light in a bog deposit, but these instances are very rare, and the objects were probably booty items buried as treasure saved for a rainy day or as part of empowerment rituals. Some, perhaps all, clients kings acknowledged the emperor's special religious function as a part of their obligation.[88] Although we cannot know many of the details of barbarian paganism, we know enough to be certain that what we would call religion occupied a central position in their lives and in their communities.

In contrast to their pagan practices, Christianity was of little importance to the barbarians until they entered the empire. Christianity among the Goths in the second half of the fourth century was a religion of a handful. Only after their admission into the empire did the Goths living in Moesia under their bishop Ulfilas, whose ancestors were apparently taken as captives by Goths raiding Asia Minor, create the documents upon which all discussion is based.[89] Ulfilas was himself a contemporary of Athanaric. These documents include the Bible translated into Gothic by Ulfilas and a calendar of feasts in memory of Goths martyred during the persecution launched by Athanaric. The "Life of Saint Saba," one of those martyrs, is extant in Greek. Although by late Roman standards this documentation is impressive, it tells us much more about the search for self-identity among Gothic Christians inside the empire than about Christianity outside the empire. What these sources do tell us about the period before their admission into the empire is that Gothic Christians were very few in numbers and that they lived in almost complete isolation from others of their faith. Saba, for example, was sheltered by his fellow villagers, none of whom was a fellow Christian. Of the other celebrated Gothic martyrs, many were women. This reflects that fact that women were more likely than men to experiment with a new religion for their families both inside and outside the empire, for their actions had less impact upon their family's social and political fortunes than those of their husbands.

Despite efforts by Ulfilas, there was no organized Gothic Christian community north of the Danube. In the late empire Christianity was a Roman religion, and there were no organized missionary programs carrying the Word to the barbarians until the sixth century. Christianity remained for the barbarians the emperor's faith. There is no way of knowing how or even when the first barbarians became Christians. Because Roman soldiers would have sworn to the god of their emperor, who had been Christian since Constantine the Great, barbarians retiring to their ancestral homes would have carried Christianity with them. Strikingly, however, none are recorded as proselytizing their kinsmen. Other former Roman soldiers were notable missionaries for the faith, but only among Romans. Christians were sometimes taken back to *barbaricum* as captives, and ransoming them was an act worthy of special recognition, be it preformed by the imperial household or by private citizens and bishops. So captives may have first brought their religion to *barbaricum,* but Saba and the other Gothic martyrs were neither former soldiers nor Roman captives.

Athanaric launched a persecution of Christians that seems to have been a political act intended to counter the growing internal rebellion against his authority. It seems likely that what most provoked the dissidents was Athanaric's determination to further his dynastic claims to supreme leadership. In any case, he suspected Roman support lay behind his rivals, particularly Fritigern. He was probably correct, for Fritigern and his followers ended up petitioning the emperor for protection and, once inside the empire, offered their conversion as an act of loyalty. At some point Athanaric ordered cult statues to be carried about his domain and public sacrifice made. That he could do so is itself another testimony to the scope of his power and the advances that he had made towards territorializing the claims to leadership for his family. Suspected Christians were required to eat the meat offered in sacrifice to the cult. Saba, of course, refused. Such a ritual of purification survived in various Christian forms throughout the Middle Ages: in one version a priest carried a reliquary about the fields, following which there was community-wide celebration and feasting. We do not know what deity Athanaric meant to be carried through the countryside, but for this purpose any would do. That he was able to order and carry out such a persecution attests that with him the *thiudans* had real authority. Following his order, the great men (*megistanes*) fanned out across their territories and sought out Christians, but they had great difficulty locating them. The leaders demonstrated over and over that they had little knowledge of their villagers, who were quite wily in hiding Saba.[90]

As the facts of Athanaric's persecution reveal, barbarians saw religion in terms of patronage. So too did the most Romans, especially those in the countryside where their gods performed as was expected of spiritual patrons. Divine patrons bestowed favorable weather to those areas where their human clients had performed the appropriate sacrifice in the agreed-upon manner. Gods played an active role in the village life. If the ritual of sacrifice was omitted or incorrectly done, the gods did not hear or, hearing, were not obligated. In some of its Christian forms this favor was very specific. Rain might fall only on the fields of the true believers, while the pagans and weak Christians watched their crops perish from drought. A snowstorm might arise from nowhere to protect believers from harm. Signs and portents were deeply rooted in all pagan religions, both barbarian and Roman. Identifying and interpreting them were among the earliest issues to confront Christianity, which solved or at least defused these problems. Peasants were linked together as a community of worshipers. The borders of inclusion in that community were fixed in times long past by marriages, friendship, and as clientage to the greater families among them.[91] Together they honored their gods, and in private they honored those which had blessed their family with health and children. These were not matters subject to change. When a family or village added a new deity to its pantheon, this was generally to include in the spiritual dimension a new patron in the secular world. Thus Athanaric had reason to suspect Christians as being clients of the Roman emperor, and as clients their relationship was not purely religious. Thus the villagers protected Saba, one of their own, but did not take up his faith.

As long as the barbarians were outside the Roman provinces, they had little reason to risk upsetting the balance of cult practice linking them and their gods. Had the emperors required their barbarian clients to acknowledge Roman gods when treaties were renegotiated, some would surely have added an expression of respect in their cult rituals. Local commanders may have been delighted had that happened, but they did not ask it. The third-century Frank Gennobaudes brought the imperial cult into his domain of his own accord. Requiring religious conversion of its diplomatic clients was just not the way Romans dealt with international politics before the reign of the eastern emperor Justinian (527–65). On the other hand, clients had always shown respect for the gods of their patrons. When barbarian kings ruled in the West, they showed little interest in converting their pagan neighbors. This changed really only with the Carolingians. Inside the empire it was a different matter, but even there until the late fourth century Christianity was essentially an urban phenomenon. Many rural areas remained almost untouched until late in the fifth century. Some were slower still, but by 400 Christians were present in all-important urban centers even in the frontier provinces. Even then what conversion meant is hard to say, but the emphasis on converting kings and princes is telling. Patronage still mattered a great deal, correct belief less.

Conversion of belief and ritual was a painfully slow process. As the case of the Saba and the Goths demonstrates, it did not necessarily depend on bishops. The most effective agents of conversion were holy men and women whose life-styles convinced others that they stood closer to God. The archetypal late Roman Christian, Saint Anthony, tried to recluse himself in his peasant hut. His self-effacement helped spread his fame far beyond his Egyptian village, attracting crowds of pilgrims to his cell. Saint Martin of Tours is said to have cut his soldier's cloak in half to share with a fellow traveler that he thereby converted. The owners of a large villa might sponsor a local fellow known for his religiosity to be priest. He and his dependents, living in the villa or nearby, might use an area formerly set aside for cult worship as a Christian meeting place. Sometimes he lived partially at village expense in a house provided to him by the landlord. This too reaffirmed the intimate relationship between patrons and clients, both human and divine. Bishops in the nearby towns were not universally pleased by these challenges to their authority.[92] When the barbarians took up residence within the empire they too were subject to these forces as well as the theological currents within Christianity, but in general that was not until the second half of the fifth century.

Ulfilas and most of the Goths entered the empire when the emperors favored a limited form of Trinitarian Christianity known as Arianism, after the name of its most powerful champion, Arius a priest of Alexandria. Accordingly, the Goths generally took up Arianism and, presumably with it, the emphasis on the centrality of the Father within the trinity. Gothic-speaking Christians were instructed in Arianism by means of the Gothic Bible, the oldest copy of which was preserved in Italy. This was only to be expected because Christianity is a text-based faith and the Bible was available in Gothic, but there is actually extremely little Arianism or any other theology in the Bible itself. The marriage between Greek philosophy and Christian theology had not yet occurred when the last book of the Bible was written. Gothic Christian liturgical equipment such as censors and candelabras were indistinguishable from those of any other Christians. Just how much theological rigor was appreciated among barbarians or poor illiterate Romans in the countryside is uncertain. So too is how much their alleged adherence to heretical beliefs isolated them from the rest of the population. We have almost certainly overemphasized the divisive role of barbarian Arianism.[93]

In the frontier provinces barbarian recruits and barbarian settlers first came into contact with Roman gods through their contact with indigenous Romans, however one defines that. Because a high percentage of Roman soldiers were of barbarian ancestry, communication was no problem, and the military life-style integrated them socially and religiously. Settlement in the countryside brought new and old together in the extremely conservative environment of rural patronage—if, that is, the areas of settlement were not completely vacant. The powerful among barbarian newcomers were members of the warrior elites of the barbarian confederacies. As such they were accorded special status just as if they had been Roman officers, which of course many became upon entry into the empire. Farmers and farmers, soldiers and soldiers, elites and elites—no matter where one looks ethnographic distinctions were mattering less and less, but so were cultural variables. After the middle of the fifth century large armies are unknown. In much of Europe city residents were clustered around a few religious centers.

All towns with bishops in 400 survived the Middle Ages, although, except in Italy, all became very small. Towns and urban values remained, just as people calculated in Roman or derivative monetary units, although they had rarely seen a coin. In such a world, a world of villages and warlords, the final distinctions between barbarian and Roman lost meaning. In late Roman legal terms, the barbarian *honestiores* merged with their Roman counterparts, and sooner or later the *humiliores* followed suit—soldiers and farmers, sometimes one and the same, sometimes not. The distinctions that lay at the heart of this book were vanishing without anyone taking notice.

Epilogue

The civil war between the courts of Honorius and Arcadius following the death of their father Theodosius I in 395 not only inaugurated a new phase of military and political development but accelerated the convergence of barbarian and Roman. Once again each side pressed its barbarian allies for recruits, but the well was running dry. The West was especially wracked as various Roman armies contended for control of the western empire or major sections of it, rather than for the emperorship itself. The house of Constantine and then that of Theodosius had managed to instill an aura of divine protection around the throne, making usurpation by those outside their dynasties much more difficult. Theodosius's successors lacked the military and political ability to rule; they merely reigned. Generals fought for power, not the purple. The civil wars of the third century had brought barbarian recruits, allies, and enemies deep within the empire, but then armies had fought for the emperorship. Maximianus and Diocletian drove out the barbarians but then welcomed many of them back. During the fifth century Roman armies commanded by Roman generals—both typically of barbarian ancestry—fought each other for regional preeminence. These struggles for hegemony took an especially heavy toll in northern Gaul, where the last competitor left standing was Childeric. The old intellectual category "barbarian" was no longer worthy of much attention.

The forces that had created a unique frontier society did not come to an abrupt halt in the early fifth century any more than Alaric's sack of Rome in 410 destroyed the Eternal City. As we have seen, styles of personal attire continued to evolve from their fourth-century roots throughout the fifth century and beyond. There were nonetheless significant changes in the amalgam binding the elements of the synthesis together. The withering of the distinctions between Roman and barbarian continued even as new distinctions arose only to disappear in their turn as still others emerged. The pace of change quickened noticeably as the century passed its halfway point and more and more semi-independent groups of barbarians were settled in the old core provinces of the Mediterranean.

The settlement of barbarians in the western empire placed powerful frontier generals over Roman civilians as well as over their barbarian-Roman soldiers. The barbarian kingdoms that speckled the western landscape were patchworks of regional solutions to the problems that the settlements of barbarians caused. They had more similarities than differences because so many of the participants shared common backgrounds. First came the settlement of the Goths in Aquitaine in 418; then the Burgundians were established as a frontier force along the Rhine (413) and later were resettled amid Roman landowners in Savoy (443); and Zeno ordered the Ostrogoths to Italy in 489. The latter learned the game so well that they could play adeptly. Theodoric, the greatest of the Ostrogothic kings (489–526), settled various Gepids and other Germanic groups along his northern frontier in what is today southern Bavaria. What most distinguished Theodoric's actions from those of Theodosius the Great a century before was that a barbarian king rather than the emperor or a member of his court had implemented it.[1]

One way for the new regimes to earn respect was to associate themselves with supposed past glory that would justify their claims to lead in the present. They took shape as leading families of the new barbarian kingdoms sought to expand their power over the large territories that they had either inherited or conquered from the Roman emperors. One vehicle with which they sought to do this was family genealogy. More often than not these genealogies were invented or at least greatly embellished. Kings routinely laid claim to putative ancestors back to the fourth century or even earlier.[2] The family of Theodoric was thus traced to Ermanaric, a "hero of the resistance." But Ermanaric's decision to take his own life rather than live to see his people subjected to Hunnic bondage was deemed unworthy, and so it was transformed into a story of heroism and vengeance.[3] Such historical fabrication was only one aspect of the process of barbarian state formation. Theodoric's Ostrogoths, like their Greutingi forebears and all other late Roman barbarians, were a diverse group that was hard to rally around abstractions. They responded instead to the bonds of family and patronage. Whatever pre-immigration identity the ancestors of Theodoric's Goths had achieved while living above the Danube dissolved and was reformed during their time within the Hunnic empire and once again inside the Roman Empire. So too, those seeking a Visigothic political identity rekindled the flame of Alaric's line, the Balthi. Clovis may have had to fashion a Frankish identity from whole cloth despite a long association with the empire.[4]

As the barbarian kingdoms evolved into self-governing polities, their existence took the already widespread search for new personal and group identities in new directions.[5] New groups like individual leaders needed historical legitimacy. One tradition traced the Franks back to the Trojans, thereby achieving for the Franks in Gaul a myth of origin analogous to the relationship of Aeneas to the Romans. Similarly inspired Jordanes, a Goth himself, wrote the *Getica*, in which the Balthi and Amali shine forth as the rallying points for Visigoths and Ostrogoths respectively.

During the fifth century virtually every so-called barbarian kingdom could find among the titles of its founders that of *magister militum*. It was the core around which the new kingships arose: Alaric and Athaulf, founders of the Visigothic kingdom of southern France and Spain; Gundobad, king of the Burgundians; Theodoric the Great and his father Thiudimir, founders of the Ostrogothic royal family; Childeric, father of Clovis, and so on. All were at one time proud to hold the title of *magister*, general of the Roman army.

As these leaders struggled to go beyond the limits of their generalships they explored ways to build on the power implied by late Roman titles or commands. From their base as *magister,* barbarian kings modeled their governments on that of the empire, often having the regional government with which they were more familiar in mind rather than the distant imperial court which they had never seen. They became lawgivers, prominent Christian figures; by the sixth century some were even adopting elements of the monastic virtues just as the imperial household was doing in Constantinople, and some even issued coinage within the Roman standard. Nonetheless, despite their best efforts, the artificiality of it all is readily apparent.

Sooner or later the traditional Roman aristocracy found ways to negotiate a special niche in the barbarian kingdoms; often they did so through their control of the Christian churches, their rituals, and holy sites. Until they lost the initiative to their aristocracies, the kings called the tunes. The indigenous Roman aristocracy now had to respond to barbarian kings much as Celtic chiefs had done to the conquering Romans of the first century B.C.[6] Roman titles and alleged family glories were hardly sufficient to create strong governments, but then nobody seemed too much concerned about central authority after the middle of the fifth century. The trend towards self-help that emerged so frequently during the third century continued unabated.

Although inventing ancestors may seem rather bizarre today, in this way as in so many other things, the barbarians were part of a much broader social movement. People—whether Roman or barbarian or something else—were searching for new identities, because those inherited from the imperial and pagan past were no longer satisfying. So too in creating genealogies the barbarians were in good company. This type of endeavor was occupying their contemporaries all across the empire as they also sought to define membership and relationship within new communities, but among the barbarians the process lasted even longer.[7] There were lists of Christian martyrs, lists of bishops, lists of saints, lists of officeholders both civil and military, Christian and pagan; for the barbarians there were lists of ancestors who were suddenly royal long before there was either a king or a people. In an age when everybody was searching for identity, the search by barbarian kings to define a kingdom made them a part of the greater society rather than a cancer within it.

The presence of the Huns was not fully felt until after the opening of the fifth century. The massive destabilization of frontier relationships caused by the Huns culminated with the attempt by Attila and his brothers to create and maintain a supraconfederacy, which they held together from the 420s until shortly after the death of Attila in 453. Within months of Attila's death his empire fell apart as the clash among his brothers opened the way to civil war and the revolt of the various barbarian confederacies that had been subject members of the Hunnic empire. The centralization of the Hunnic empire under Attila virtually assured that any major conflict between him and the Roman Empire would confine itself to a single point of attack. The supreme Roman general in the West, Aetius, a man who knew Hunnic society intimately, was able to anticipate and defeat this straight-ahead assault. When Aetius did so on the Catalaunian Fields, he did so with the help of his own barbarian allies, who had by then begun the long process of fashioning a place for themselves within the empire into which they had been invited to live.[8] Once the Hunnic empire had disintegrated, gone was the need to defend against the old barbarians. Without these conditions the terms "Roman" and "barbarian" accelerated their search for new meanings.

In an odd but touching baptismal inscription from Lyon, grieving parents are comforted by whoever set up the inscription, sometime not before the second half of the fifth century. Although they had lost their two sons "of barbarian seed" (unnamed and so probably infants at death), they had had the boys baptized. Thus, the inscription goes on to say that the boys were no longer outsiders to the Christian faith. The parents, who had themselves put off their own baptism, could take heart. They had given their sons to God, who had now taken them into his care. In this case a barbarian was somebody outside the Christian or perhaps Catholic faith, as opposed to Arian heretics.[9]

Gregory Bishop of Tours (ca. 580) placed great store in the fact that his Franks were orthodox and that their principal rivals, the Goths in southern Gaul, Spain, and Italy were Arian heretics. Gregory's apparent vehemence must, however, be considered within the context of the continuing formation of the Frankish monarchy and the role that he wished the episcopacy to play in it. Not surprisingly Clovis was remembered by the Gallic bishops for his Constantine-like conversion to orthodox Christianity, whereas in Italy one author remembered Theodoric as dying of dysentery in a public latrine just as had Arius, the accursed founder of the Goths' heretical faith.[10] Christian charity did not extend to heretics. In at least one case, brigands outside the control of the so-called barbarian kings were called barbarians. By the end of the fifth century "soldier" and "barbarian" were virtually synonymous. Gothic barbarians were clearly regarded as being "soldiers of the state [the *res publica*]," for example, in Ostrogothic Italy.[11] The term "Roman" too was changing, beginning its gradual departure from the ancient world in the fifth century with the increasing prominence of the pope and papal ritual. By the eighth century, in western Europe Roman typically meant Catholic Christian.[12]

Ironically the great alliance that "The Scourge of God," as Attila came to be known in medieval Europe, built created the need for a momentary pause to the internecine warfare among the western generals. With Attila's death and the rapid collapse of the Hunnic coalition, Roman-barbarian generals continued business as usual. Roman institutions withered, died, or were transformed; the army was among the last to go. As institutions receded, patron-client relationships reemerged as the backbone of society. There were no great barbarian invasions. The so-called barbarians were now the frontline troops of the Roman army. They fought behind their Roman general against his rivals, region by region. They took advantage of whatever taxes he could collect to pay them and all the booty they could carry. In some areas the Roman garrison mentality survived far into the fifth century. But isolated garrison troops claiming to be Roman, still thinking themselves to be Roman soldiers, did not constitute a Roman army. Except along the Mediterranean, towns shrank almost to vanishing, but in most places their Roman names have survived in mutilated form.[13] This indicates that somebody living nearby, if not inside their ruins, kept fragments of the urban tradition alive. But progressively isolated towns are not an imperial government. Men and women whose ancestors had been Roman or barbarian believed they lived in the Roman Empire and they were right. There was no temporal end to the "Empire without End," but now it existed as Christian Europe. Whereas for Augustus it had been an infinite chain of human bonding, for Saint Augustine it was merely a pale reflection of the Heavenly City.

The task at hand for the barbarian leaders after the settlements was novel. Most tried hard to respond to the progressive collapse of imperial government without violating basic imperial principles to which they still adhered. Every region experienced a different set of problems and usually at very different times. The task of building a state within the empire that all these later barbarians faced was unprecedented. The best most kings could do was to dress themselves in Roman garb, both literally and figuratively, while they dealt with unrelenting recalcitrance from within their own military elite. They were often more successful among the native Roman ruling class than with their own soldiers.

In the case of Ostrogothic Italy, day-to-day Roman administration may have actually improved. Spain too fared well enough, particularly once the Visigoths took it over (ca. 500) and put a stop to the wars ravaging the peninsula. Rather mundane civil government continued in Gaul throughout the fifth century, at least in the south.[14] For all these "barbarians" there remained one empire and one ruling family. The *Orbis Romana* was not in doubt. This dilemma pushed them ever deeper into new political, social, and religious waters. The late fourth-and early fifth-century development of a new Roman army composed primarily of men of barbarian ancestry had prepared the way, but much of the landscape was unfamiliar. By 400 holding a regal or princely title as a sign of traditional prestige among one's fellows was rather unexceptional for senior officers in the Roman army, but to rule as king over a territory within the empire was another matter. Nor did it matter much whether this territory was officially assigned or taken by force. It continues to be a matter of scholarly dispute just how and when various newcomers arrived in Britain, but some were already there by the end of the fourth century, recruited as Roman soldiers, and more followed. Even the Vandals who fought their way across Gaul and Spain before taking ship to Africa in 429 ultimately had to confront the problems of permanent government over Romans and barbarians alike. So too did the Lombards, whose arrival in Italy in 568 was quite unpleasant and most unwelcome for the bishops and what was left of the imperial government.

During the fifth century almost everywhere in the West, the shift in favor of the military over the civilian, already apparent under Valentinian I (364–75), gained momentum. In rural areas soldiers were integrated into the general population, which felt a strong need for security. Most took up the plow; a few looked for adventure. In the urbanized provinces where the Roman-barbarian armies, their families, and supporters settled, soldiers had to accommodate themselves to the needs of the townsmen. The emperor Justinian (527–65) can be credited with dissolving the unity of the Roman world, not the barbarian kings. In order to justify its reconquest, Justinian had first to declare the western empire's loss. Forced to react, contemporary barbarian kings had no choice but to see themselves differently, especially those who came up against Justinian's armies. Even then what is most striking is how the unity of a Christian empire survived among them as the central vision of life on earth.

As Rome shifted ever more military manpower to duty stations deep inside the empire, the logistical support that had maintained the armies on the frontiers departed with the troops. As a result of the barbarian settlements, imperial economic initiatives, which had waned markedly anyway after the death of Valentinian, disappeared. Only the coastal cities of the Mediterranean remained interconnected, whereas those men and women living in the hinterlands addressed their economic problems locally or not at all. The tax cycle tying urban centers of the Mediterranean provinces to the camps and towns near the frontiers—a centuries-old windmill redistributing wealth—became progressively irrelevant. Nonetheless it is important to recall that there was a great deal of regional variation in all this: in the deployment and redeployment of troops, in the level of urban survival, and in the reallocation of economic resources. Not all frontiers lost their garrisons, and they certainly did not all do so simultaneously.

The only systematic withdrawal of Roman troops from garrison duty in the frontier provinces took place in Noricum at the order of Odovacar, "king of Italy," in ca. 480. Elsewhere feeble garrisons of *limitanei* sometimes stayed in place for generations, in a few cases up to the end of the fifth century, with little or no support from the central government. Many of the factors at play went back a hundred years or more, but what distinguishes them in the fifth century is the almost complete absence of the imperial government in decision making. Concurrent to the settlements, Roman governmental and military institutions fell into disrepair and disuse at both the regional and local levels without any clear order or single rationale. The barbarian kingdoms took over whatever remained of Roman military personnel and integrated them into their armies. The newly settled barbarians were quite capable of waging war. Without the Visigoths, who stood shoulder to shoulder with Aetius's "regular Roman army" against Attila and his barbarian allies, losing their king in battle, Attila, not Rome, would have carried the day in Gaul.

The fifth-century settlements of barbarians in the interior provinces can be seen as the final redeployment of Rome's military resources. Once in their new homes Goths, Franks, and others discovered that the empire held out great promise for their own personal development. Examples exist of Germanic academics, book dealers, and civil servants, as well as soldiers. Aetius's panegyrist Flavius Merobaudes, whose Frankish ancestry is clear from his name, was perhaps the most famous. Several such men did, however, claim an especially noble descent.[15] Many remained in the profession of their forefathers—Roman soldiers and farmers. Stripping the frontiers of the Roman army's barbarian auxiliaries removed the most effective fighting units, and it also had the effect of removing the remaining rationale for defending the frontiers themselves. The barbarians against whom generation upon generation of Romans had ostensibly stood watch were no longer on the horizon.

The first two centuries of the Christian era had witnessed a transfer of culture from the coastal cities of the Mediterranean to the frontiers. This exchange had depended on the economic vitality spawned by the presence of the army along the frontiers. During the third and fourth centuries the flow of men and ideas increasingly moved in the opposite direction. With the settlement of barbarians in the Mediterranean provinces, the old exchange almost completely lost meaning as first one region and then the next went its own way. An exchange based on Christianity arose and replaced the old economic dynamo that had evolved to nourish frontier society. Bishops and their councils, monks in their quest for both isolation from their fellow man and closeness to their God, pilgrims plodding to the holy sites of Christendom, each and all generated, redistributed, and maintained a new society in which the old distinctions of Roman and barbarian had no place. These men and women were the vanguard of the later missionary efforts beyond the old imperial frontiers, but for now all attention was concentrated on converting the provincial countryside. Little by little an exchange of sacred texts replaced the formal epistolary of the traditional Roman aristocracy. The new Christian culture flourished in and was nurtured by the superimposition of values that took hold ever more powerfully as a result of the settlements. In this crucible, unyielding spiritual passion and agrarian conservatism fused with the rough-and-ready virtues of the late Roman soldier. Despite extraordinary effort, Christianity took a very long time to muscle its way into rural life. The life-style of the soldier was even more resistant to change. At the opening of the fifth century, Christianizing the warriors and peasants had scarcely begun.

Not all barbarians were welcome. There still had to be a place to put them and good reason to trust their leaders. Most barbarian settlers took up their new homes at imperial invitation, but the fifth century also heralded the first hostile penetrations of the empire that were to prove irreversible. First came the Vandals, who stormed across the frozen Rhine River on the last day of the year 406, when Roman garrisons along the Rhine rejected their pleas for food and shelter. Next entered the Huns, who after years of harassing the lower Danube were ceded Pannonia (ca. 425–30), only to use it later as a launching pad for raids deep into the western empire. The Huns were also the only true nomads to enter the Roman world prior to the seventh century. The presence of the Huns as a military superpower based on the steppes of Russia altered the cultural equation along the old Danubian frontier. The Huns had lived too far from the Roman frontiers to bear its stamp. All other barbarians were products of Rome's frontier culture to some degree, and most were quite welcome in the empire. Roman influence even reached the Lombards, the Vandals, and the various barbarians who established themselves in Britain, although often only indirectly.

The factors that led to a withering of distinctions in the West took even longer to manifest themselves in the eastern Balkans. A major indication that insecurity could no longer be reversed was the building of the great land wall across the peninsula protecting Constantinople and its hinterland under Theodosius II (408–450). Completed in 447, the wall was actually a complex defensive system: an inner wall having ninety-six towers each over ninety feet high, a lower outer wall also with ninety-six towers, and a moat and wide terrace in between. Constantinople was safe behind this immense fortification for the next millennium. Thessalonica was the only other viable Roman city in the area by the sixth century, and like Constantinople it too depended on its landward defenses and supplies arriving by sea. By the middle of the sixth century villa agriculture was almost unknown beyond the area of Constantinople quite near the great walls. A few miles beyond them even villages became rare. Justinian deployed the army along the Danube in forts, some rebuilt, others completely new. Now, however, the troops in these outposts had to be supplied entirely by the government in Constantinople at great and ultimately unsustainable costs.[16]

New rural populations did not arrive in most of the Balkans until the Slavs settled there in the seventh century. As earlier in the West, now in the Balkans, gone was effective central government. Gone was most of the economic recycling that the old imperial system had fostered and sustained. Gone were the traditional distinctions between Roman and barbarian. The Roman Empire was very slowly giving way to medieval civilization.

Appendix

Most Important Roman Emperors and Usurpers

After the regnal dates, the ruler's name is given in full and, in a few cases, a shorter form which also appears on coins. The regnal dates here are the years of rule as emperor not as Caesar (the heir apparent).

Augustus, 31–14 B.C.: Caius Octavius; after his adoption by C. Julius Caesar, Caius Julius Caesar Octavianus; after 16 January 27 B.C., Augustus.

Tiberius, A.D. 14–37: Tiberius Claudius Nero; after his adoption by Augustus, Tiberius Julius Caesar

Caligula, 37–41: Caius Julius Caesar

Claudius I, 41–54: Tiberius Claudius Nero Drusus Germanicus

Nero, 54–68: L. Domitius Ahenobarbus; after his adoption by Claudius, Tiberius Claudius Drusus Germanicus Caesar; on coins and imperial inscriptions, Imperator Nero Claudius Caesar Augustus Germanicus

Galba, 9 June 68–15 January 69: Servius Sulpicius Galba

Otho, 15 January 69–25 April 69: Marcus Salvius Otho

Vitellius, 2 January 69–20 (?) December 70: Aulus Vitellius

Vespasianus, 69–70: Titus Flavius Vespasianus

Titus, 79–81: Titus Flavius Vespasianus

Domitianus, 81–96: Titus Flavius Domitianus

Nerva, 96–98: M. Cocceius Nerva

Traianus, 98–117: M. Ulpius Traianus

Hadrianus, 117–38: P. Aelius Hadrianus

Antoninus Pius, 138–61: Titus Aurelius Fulvus Boionius Arrius Antoninus; after his adoption by Hadrianus, Titus Aelius Hadrianus Antoninus Pius

Marcus Aurelius, 161–80: Marcus Annius Catilius Severus; after his adoption by Antoninus Pius, Marcus Aelius Verus Caesar; as emperor, Marcus Aurelius Antoninus

Lucius Verus (coruler with Marcus Aurelius), 161–69: Lucius Ceionius Commodus Verus; after his adoption in the reign of Antoninus Pius, Lucius Aelius Aurelius Commodus Verus

Commodus (coruler with his father Marcus Aurelius from 176), 180–92: Lucius Aelius or Lucius or Marcus Aurelius Commodus Antoninus (Lucius Aurelius Commodus from 191)

Pertinax, 193: Publius Helvius Pertinax

Didius Julianus, 193: Marcus Didius Severus Julianus

Pescennius Niger, 193–94: Caius Pescennius Niger Justus

Clodius Albinus, 193–97 (in the beginning acknowledged as Caesar by Septimius Severus): Decimus Clodius (Septimius) Albinus

Septimius Severus, 193–211: Lucius Septimius Severus Pertinax

Caracalla, (198) 211–17: Septimus Bassianus from 196; Marcus Aurelius Antoninus

Geta, (209) 211–12 (together with his brother Caracalla): Publius Septimius Geta

Macrinus, 217–18: Marcus Opellius Severus Macrinus

Elagabalus, 218–22: Varius Avitus, as Caesar; Marcus Aurelius Antoninus

Severus Alexander, 222–35: Alexianus Bassianus, as Caesar; Marcus Aurelius Severus Alexander

Maximinus I Thrax, 235–38: Caius Julius Verus Maximinus

Gordianus I, 238: Marcus Antonius Gordianus Sempronianus Romanus Africanus Senior

Gordianus II, 238 (as coruler with his father Gordianus I): Marcus Antonius Gordianus Sempronianus Romanus Africanus Junior

Balbinus, 238 (together with Pupienus): Decimus Caelius Calvinus Balbinus

Pupienus, 238 (together with Balbinus): Marcus Clodius Pupienus
Gordianus III, 238–44: Marcus Antonius Gordianus
Philippus I Arabus, 244–49: Marcus Julius Philippus
Philippus II, 246–49 (as coruler with his father Philippus I): Marcus Julius Philippus
Traianus Decius, 249–51: Caius Messius Quintus Traianus Decius
Herennius Etruscus (son of Decius; since 250 Caesar), 251: Quintus Herennius Etruscus Messius Decius
Hostilianus (son of Decius; since 250 Caesar), 251 (also still under Trebonianus Gallus): Caius Valens Hostilianus Messius Quintus
Trebonianus Gallus, 251–53: Caius Vibius Trebonianus Gallus
Volusianus, 251–53 (together with his father Trebonianus Gallus): Caius Vibius Afinius Gallus Veldumianus Volusianus
Aemilianus, 253: Marcus Aemilius Aemilianus
Valerianus, 253–59: Publius Licinius Valerianus
Gallienus, 253–68 (up to 260 with his father Valerianus): Publius Licinius Valerianus Egnatius Gallienus
Postumus, 259–68 (Gallic Empire): Marcus Cassianius Latinius Postumus
Laelianus, mid-268 (Gallic Empire): Ulpius Cornelius Laelianus
Marius, second half of 268 (Gallic Empire): Marcus Aurleius Marius
Victorinus, 268–70 (Gallic Empire): Marcus Piavonius Victorinus
Claudius II, 268–70: Marcus Aurelius Claudius
Quintillus (brother of Claudius II), 270: Marcus Aurelius Claudius Quintillus
Tetricus I, 270–74 (Gallic Empire): Caius Pius Esuvius Tetricus
Aurelianus, 270–75: Lucius Domitius Aurelianus
Tacitus, 275–76: Marcus Claudius Tacitus
Florianus, 276: Marcus Annius Florianus
Probus, 276–82: Marcus Aurelius Probus
Carus, 282–83: Marcus Aurelius Carus
Carinus (son of Carus), 283–85: Marcus Aurelius Carinus
Numerianus (son of Carus), 283–84: Marcus Aurelius Numerius Numerianus
Carausius, 286–93 (British section of the empire): Marcus Aurelius Mausaeus (?) Carausius

Allectus, 293–96 (British section of the empire)
Diocletianus, 284–305: Marcus Aurelius Valerius Diocletianus
Maximianus Herculius, 286–305 (306–7, together with his son Maxentius): Marcus Aurelius Valerius Maximianus
Constantius I Chlorus (Caesar from 293), 305–6: Caius Flavius Valerius Constantius
Galerius Maximianus (Caesar from 293), 305–311: Caius Galerius Valerius Maximianus
Severus (Caesar from 305), 306–7: Flavius Valerius Severus
Maximinus II Daia (Caesar from 305), 310–13: Galerius Valerius Maximinus
Maxentius (son of Maximianus Herculius; usurper in Italy), 306–12 (Augustus from 307): Marcus Aurelius Valerius Maxentius
Constantius I Chlorus (Caesar, 293–305), 305–6
Galerius (Caesar, 293–305), 305–10
Constantinus I (son of Constantius I Chlorus; Caesar, 306), 307–37: Flavius Valerius Constantinus
Licinius I, 308–24: Valerius Licinianus Licinius
Crispus (son of Constantinus I), only Caesar, 317–26: Flavius Julius Crispus
Constantinus II (son of Constantinus I; Caesar from 317), 337–40: Flavius Claudius Constantinus
Constans (son of Constantinus I; Caesar from 333), 337–50: Flavius Julius Constans
Constantius II (son of Constantinus I; Caesar from 324), 337–361: Flavius Julius Constantius
Magnentius (usurper in the West), 350–53: Flavius Magnus Magnentius
Vetranio (usurper in Illyricum), March–December 350
Julianus II (Caesar under Constantius II from 355), 360–63: Flavius Claudius Julianus
Jovianus, 363–64: Flavius Jovianus
Valentinianus I, 364–75: Flavius Valentinianus
Valens (brother of Valentinianus I), 364–78: Flavius Valens
Gratianus (son of Valentinianus I), 367–83: Flavius Gratianus
Valentinianus II (son of Valentinianus I), 375–92: Flavius Valentinianus Junior

Maximus (usurper in the West), 383–88: Magnus Maximus
Flavius Victor (son of Maximus; usurper in the West), 384–88
Eugenius (usurper in the West), 392–94: Flavius Eugenius
Theodosius I, 379–95: Flavius Theodosius
Honorius (son of Theodosius I; emperor of the West, 393), 395–423: Flavius Honorius
Constantinus III (usurper in Gaul,) 407–11: Flavius Claudius Constantinus
Arcadius (son of Theodosius I; emperor of the East, 383), 395–408: Flavius Arcadius
Theodosius II (son of Arcadius; emperor of the East, 402), 408–50
Constantius III (coemperor of the West), 421: Flavius Constantius
Valentinianus III (son of Constantius; emperor of the West), 425–55

Notes

Chapter 1. Sometimes Bitter Friends

1. F. Braudel 1967, a classic modern survey which others, including myself, can only aspire to emulate in clarity and insight.
2. Vergil, *Aeneid,* 6.847–53, trans. R. Fitzgerald, 190.
3. See also J. Drinkwater 1996.
4. V. Rosenberger 1992, 66.
5. J. Elliot 1994, 12–13.
6. E. Gibbon 1776, 1.211, 4.163.
7. M. Fried 1961 and 1975; and N. Whitehead 1992. Although foreign-language publications are also cited in the notes, the goal of this study is to introduce an English-speaking audience to the subject. In that regard, a special effort has been made to include English-language titles and to cite primary materials from English translations but with standard classical nomenclature.
8. In addition to the anthropological literature, including M. Fried, there are numerous historical studies, recently augmented by the decipherment and explication of the Mayan language. Still useful for comparative insights from Chinese experience is Y. Yü 1967, which explores the development and significance of both inner and outer barbarians to Han China, contemporary with the Roman Empire.
9. S. Mattern 1999, 30.
10. For references to this fifth-century evolution, see the Epilogue, note 11.
11. See further A. Demandt 1989. Given that even after great industry we

cannot be sure of much more than who married whom, it is only a supposition that the increasing intermarriage among Germanic (that is to say, military) elite and that of the civilian uppercrust was inspired by hedging a family's bets, but one that seems well justified by circumstance. The most famous of these cases is Stilicho, whose father was Vandalic and mother Roman, and who then succeeded in marrying his own two daughters sequentially to the emperor Honorius (395–423). Another example from the very top tier is that of *magister militum* Bauto, who was able to marry his daughter Eudoxia to Honorius's older brother Arcadius, emperor in Constantinople (395–408). These showcase marriages should not, however, obscure the fact that the interpenetration of these elites had begun at lower echelons at least two decades before.

12. To offer but one example for the continuing rhetorical image of the barbarian savage, note Synesius of Cyrene (ca. A.D. 400) writing of Alaric at the court of Honorius as if he were a rustic barbarian when even he had to allude to the fact that Alaric was in fact *magister militum* and was not dressed as "a barbarian" but in the cloak of a general. Synesius is hardly unique in this regard (A. Cameron and J. Long 1993, 121; T. Burns 1994, 162–65; and on Synesius and the complex trajectories which terms such as barbarian were taking, A. Demandt 1989).
13. For example, Cicero, *Epistulae ad Q. Fratrem* (Epistle to his brother Quintus), 1.1.15; Tacitus, *Agric.* 4.
14. For example, Caelius Aurelianus, 1.258.35; on the legal evolution and meaning of the term in the fourth century, E. Chrysos 1973.
15. F. Barth 1969, 9, 14–15.
16. On Murranus, G. Mancini 1933. For examples of such bypassed barbarians, see P. Amory 1997, 21. The term *gentes* could be used to describe such people, although typically *gentes* referred to neighboring peoples geographically outside the empire. Internal *gentes* lived in isolation from the main currents of Roman influence and were thus "outsiders" to Roman culture and political control, despite the fact that they lived within the empire's administrative boundaries.
17. The results of the Osnabrück excavations will be forthcoming for many years. On the early finds that fixed the site of the battle, see W. Schlüter 1991 and J. Dornberg 1992.

Chapter 2. Recognition, Confrontation, and Coexistence

1. *Roman Republican Coinage,* 286/1 Munich, silver denarius, struck by the moneyer M. Sergius Silus, who placed his name in the genitive to indicate that the coin was his workmanship. This is the earliest known depiction of a Gaul on a Roman coin.

2. S. Dyson 1984, 128, 148–50. The importance of this peculiar topography was well known to Romans from early times; Strabo, 4.1.14, and on the Arverni, 4.2.3, but with an eye towards providing geographic instruction for readers of Caesar's *Gallic Wars* and later provincial developments under Augustus. Strabo quotes from Polybius concerning the still earlier accounts of Pytheas. On the early routes, see C. Hawkes 1977, 17–32.
3. D. Braund 1984, 92–98; E. Badian 1958, 1–14, 250–57; as late as 63 B.C., Allobroges were still tied to the Fabii, Sallust, *Bellum Catilinae* 41.4–5.
4. A. Rivet 1988, 39–44.
5. J. Collis 1995, 163–68. *The Celtic World* (ed. M. Green), the volume in which this article by J. Collis appears, is a very important contribution to the field, providing the reader with splendid essays, intelligible to nonspecialists but with timely insights for other scholars as well. The notes and bibliographies there provide a ready bridge to the scholarly literature in considerable depth and on a diverse range of subjects.
6. Julius Caesar, *Bellum Gallicum* (*BG*)1.1, remarks that in one of three sections of Gaul live those who in their own language are called Celti, but in Latin, Galli.
7. Few Celtic roads have been discovered by excavation in large part because of the fact that Roman and modern highways so often follow the same routes. Julius Caesar's routes and speed of march during his Gallic campaigns clearly attest to some type of road network linking major centers, for example, *BG* 5.47, 53.
8. P. Wells 1990, 442, 450–60; see also *BG* 5.12, 55.
9. *BG* 5.12, notes that the Celts in Britain used a standard weight for bronze and gold coins and iron tally bars. He does not mention that among the southern Gauls these standards corresponded to Roman as they did. In some cases Celtic and Roman coins of the same or very similar weights and purity have been found together. On these numismatic issues, see H.-J. Hildebrandt 1994–99. Caesar provides numerous examples of Gauls using coinage among themselves and to pay German mercenaries (e.g., *BG* 7.63).
10. P. Wells 1990, 448–50.
11. C. Crumley 1974, and virtually all subsequent scholarship.
12. B. Burnham 1995, 124–32.
13. S. Dyson 1984, 139–41.
14. Livy, 21.20.8–9, at least among those near Marseilles, but attested by Caesar and others to include most of Gaul. This social stratification is confirmed by the pattern of concentrated wealth in graves.
15. Diodorus Siculus, 34.23, S. Dyson 1984, 150.

16. One hectare is equal to 10,000 square meters, or 2.471 acres.
17. F. Maier 1986, 1–43, exploring parts of two areas within the defensive wall that were characteristic of dispersed settlement and livestock raising. The excavations at Manching have been ongoing for over half a century; the results are being published in the multi-volume *Die Ausgrabungen in Manching,* ed. W. Krämer.
18. *BG* 7.23.
19. J. Collis 1984, 8–14, using an enclosed area of at least thirty hectares.
20. J. Collis 1984, 65–84; for interesting comparative insights into modern clientage, see also S. Eisenstadt and R. Lemarchand 1981, 27–29.
21. Diodorus Siculus, 5.32.
22. D. Evans 1967, 266–69 (note that the title of this book, *Gaulish Personal Names,* uses the British English Gaulish in contrast to the American usage Gallic): (*teuto*), 439 (*Cimberius,* n. 4), noting that teuto is a very common element in names, especially but not exclusively among the Gauls and that several Germanic leaders mentioned by Caesar seem to have Celtic names, perhaps reflecting linguistic hybridization. As with archaeology, distinguishing things Celtic from things German is never easy and frequently impossible. For a traditional philological identification of the Cimbri and Teutones as Germans and from specific areas along the coast of the North Sea, see E. Demougeot 1978, 920–21, who agrees with earlier German scholarship, which located the Ambrones's homeland as the island of Amrun off the coast of Holstein (n. 58). On pp. 910–20 Demougeot provides a complete survey of the literary sources.
23. This is quite clear in the content, arrangement, and origins of our extant fragments, as in the edition and commentary by L. Edelstein and I. Kidd. Strabo is the principal source of these fragments.
24. Plutarch, *Marius,* 11.4–7. Herodotus, 4.46–105, on the Scythians. This is still one of the best literary accounts for any ancient barbarian people as well as being a fine example of the Greek view of European geography and ethnology.
25. The ethnographer and philosopher Posidonius of Apamea in Greece was personally familiar with the career of Marius, whom he served as an ambassador. He wrote of the wars of Fabius in southern Gaul and their ethnographic background, but his entire corpus of writing is known to us only as it was influenced by later historians. His approach can most clearly be seen in the *Gallic War* of Julius Caesar and is discussed in the next chapter.
26. A. Gellius, *Noctes Atticae,* 16.10.10.
27. Plutarch, *Marius,* 27.5.
28. Livy, 6.18–20. The moral of the story was not lost on Augustus, who

was careful to veil his acquisition of power and to depersonalize his own victories over barbarians.

29. T. Carney 1970, 30–38, with copious discussion of battle sites and tactics, especially in the notes.
30. *BG* 2.29.4–5; Rivet 1988, 53, n. 65. On the later place-names, *Inscriptiones Latinae Selectae* 4595 and 4596.
31. Tacitus, *Germania,* 37. Tacitus's phrase "Germanorum libertas" has given rise to the common description of the lands east of the Rhine as "Free Germany." He must have felt that his purpose was sufficiently served by reference to the Cimbri alone, for no mention is made of the Teutones by Tacitus. Another reason for this omission might have been that the Roman fleet, which reached Jutland in A.D. 5 as a part of a diplomatic move during Augustus's planned expansion eastwards to the Elbe, had not gone farther east.
32. Plutarch, *Marius,* 11.2–3, trans. B. Perrin, p. 489. The same story was apparently told by Livy writing ca. 30 B.C., in his book 68, but now can only be read in its epitome. After Plutarch the chain is unbroken until nobody any longer cared. See Cassius Dio, writing ca. A.D. 200 but only preserved in the Byzantine epitome of Zonaras for these events, 71.3; Ammianus Marcellinus, writing ca. A.D. 395, 31.5.12–13; and finally Orosius, 7.15.6, writing ca. 417. The smallest figure in the ancient sources for the Teutones is Velleius Paterculus's 100,000, see A. Rivet 1988, 53, n. 71, for all the ancient demographic guesses.
33. Florus, 1.38.3.
34. These traits characterized Celts as well, but in lesser extremes according to the ancients. J. Tierney 1960, who has assembled and translated the fragments of Posidonius from all available sources.
35. Livy, epitomy of bk. 13; Appian, *Roman History,* bk. 4, the *Celtica* (only extant from later quotations) ch. 13; and Tacitus, *Germania,* 37.2.
36. Livy, epitomy bk. 65; Florus, 1.38.
37. Livy, epitomy bk. 65.
38. *BG* 1.14.7, reminding him that the Helvetii took hostages—they did not give them. The uses to which Julius Caesar put these barbarians continue those of Marius and occupy much of the next chapter.
39. Plutarch, *Sulla,* 4.1.
40. Plutarch, *Marius,* 25.4. Roman sources should have been better aware of their own troop strengths than those of the enemy, but statistical accuracy was never the point of ancient narratives. Leading out the equivalent of ten legions may just have seemed impressive to the authors.
41. Florus, 1.38.10; the Sequanni role in his capture is only known to us from still later sources epitomizing earlier materials; on Boiorix, Florus, 1.38.18, and also Plutarch, *Marius,* 25.2.

42. *BG* 1.5, 7.9; the Roman camp of the Principate Boiodurum (in Passau Innstadt at the confluence of the Inn and Danube) also had this name element (J. Whatmough 1970, 1210); however, why and if this is so remains much disputed. Other than those mentioned by Caesar as living in Gaul, some seem to have gone to what will become Bohemia, others perhaps to Bavaria.
43. Livy, 23.14.11–12; on various possibilities for the name element, *boduo,* see D. Evans, 1967, 151. "The Boii" make a reappearance in Chapter 5, in which we pick up the theme of both Boii and the Cimbri again, but then for central Europe.
44. Frontinus, *Strategemata,* 1.2.6.
45. A. Rivet 1988, 44–55, provides all source citations and various arguments concerning these events. Caesar took care to secure the province and direct its resources to support his conquests of the remainder of Gaul.
46. P. Wells 1995a, 179–82. This article is exceptionally clear and forthright in its careful survey of the relevant archaeology leading up to this conclusion. As his notes and bibliography indicate, as the dating of the abandonment of Manching in particular has been pushed progressively back towards the opening of the first century B.C. by recent finds there and elsewhere, this hypothesis has become inescapable. B. Overbeck 1987, with a careful chronology based on coin finds, particularly hoards, comes to the same conclusion. Few would now hold out for 15 B.C., the traditional date corresponding to the establishment of the province of Noricum, under Augustus. Overbeck does not relate his findings to the reports of Cimbri and Teutones. P. Wells 1993, 151, does, offering the earliest expansion of the Germanic peoples as the most probable cause for the fortification of the *oppidum* at Kelheim ca. 130–120 B.C. In his later works, however, Wells does not press this theory.
47. A relative chronology is created for each site by the archaeologists when phases of construction and habitation are related to one another stratigraphically: one is older (generally deeper) than another, but their relationship is not expressed in years. An absolute chronology seeks to place the phases of the relative chronologies in calendar years and thereby to relate what is happening at all sites at any given time. Obviously in a perfect world, everything would have an absolute date, but archaeology is not a perfect science. What must be avoided is forcing an absolute chronology upon unwilling data, because this invariably leads to false interrelationships to other sites. By assigning phases (here C and D with their subclassifications), archaeologists seek to emphasize the stage at which a specific community found itself within a general cultural pattern. In this way each site can be assessed in an

evolutionary manner without its being forced into a precise absolute chronology with dated parameters. Such a classification scheme provides a way for archaeological chronologies to preserve patterns peculiar to each site while providing for the fact that the same development may have occurred at different sites at different times. This method of dating nicely reflects the loose cohesion and numerous variations within Celtic society. It is reproduced in this book only this one time so as to introduce the system to the reader.

48. This is one explanation of the coin hoards in south Germany: for example, at Lauterach (120–100 B.C.), at Schönaich (120–100 B.C.), at Langenau (ca. 100 B.C.). For a dating of these hoards and others to ca. 100 B.C., but not the interpretation here being pursued, see B. Overbeck 1987, 3–5. Dendrochronology also offers a range of reconstruction between ca. 125 and 100 B.C.: wood from the gate at Manching was cut in 105 B.C.; wood tested from the defensive wall at Fellbach-Schmiden to 123 (P. Wells 1987, 406). Neither numismatics nor dendrochronology provides motives. Certainly in the case of wooden defenses, repairs and fires must have been common occurrences. Hoards offer a more limited range of explanation, anticipated violence, and are more useful than single coin finds but the abstract nature of the images on Celtic coinage seriously impedes precise dating.
49. B. Melin 1960, 70–71, points out that the Roman geographic placement of the Teutones is ambiguous and that this probably derived from the similarly vague sources available to them, specifically the works of the fourth-century explorer Pythias.
50. P. Wells, 1995a, 174–75.
51. L. Hedeager 1992, 242–46.
52. Contrary to J. Collis 1984, 11, who explains the demise of the *oppida* settlements as being much more closely related to the movement of peoples from the Jastorf zone.
53. This is a topic of great interest to those specializing in the sociological applications of linguistic theory, particularly as advanced by G. Dumézil 1977, and applied to the early Celtic and Germanic myths. The new dynasties of the so-called barbarian kingdoms in the fifth century A.D. were able to use this societal recollection, as preserved in pagan ritual, as a part of the underpinnings of their kingship. Its earlier forms are taken up by Caesar and Tacitus, but generally misunderstood.
54. F. Suppe 1993, 156.
55. For example, long-term continuity of settlement is apparent in the area around Kelheim; see M. Murray 1993, 102–110.
56. J. Untermann 1989, 219, who explores how earlier philologists created these artificial divisions.

57. European scholars have generally lagged behind in this retreat; see W. Adams et al. 1978.
58. In general, see L. Shaffer 1992. The disappearance was all but universal and spanned the period A.D. 1250 to 1450; a very few sites such as Natchez were still occupied when Europeans arrived. See also T. Pauketat and T. Emerson1997.
59. L. Schele and D. Freidel 1990, 377–403.

Chapter 3. Through Caesar's Eyes

1. The problem of composition was already apparent to Suetonius, writing ca. A.D. 120, in *Caesar,* 56.
2. Diodorus Siculus, 40.4.1, records an inscription set up, apparently by Pompey himself, recording his Asian triumphs. For the material profits and political stakes, see E. Badian 1958.
3. For an exceptional window upon this phenomenon in the case of the nineteenth-century American explorers Lewis and Clark, see J. Allen 1975, particularly 109–26. Their contemporary Sir John Ross, apparently succumbing to his strong desire to go home, saw an end to Lancaster Sound in the Canadian arctic, although none of his men did. He thereby missed the entrance to the only navigable Northwest Passage; B. Lopez 1986, 310.
4. *BG* 1.11, the example of the Allobroges.
5. *BG* 1.5.
6. For formal friendship, *amicitia,* see in general P. Brunt 1988, 351–81. On its use diplomatically, see E. Badian 1958, 12. There are a great many examples in the *Gallic War,* including men who had made the most of the fact that their fathers had been hailed as friend (e.g., Teutomatus, *BG* 7.31).
7. *BG* 1.3, totius Galliae; 1.13, Dumnorix.
8. *BG* 5.39, 7.4, 7.40.
9. On Bibracte, see C. Goudineau and C. Peyre 1993.
10. *BG* 1.3, 1.33, 1.43. According to Caesar, Ariovistus had sought out Roman friendship. The Aedui were at best sometime allies (*BG* 1.45).
11. *BG* 7.32.
12. *BG* 1.9, "gratia et largitione."
13. *BG* 7.77.
14. *BG* 1.4.
15. So the Ambarri among the Aedui, *BG* 1.11; so the Bituriges, *BG* 7.13.
16. *BG* 1.29 and repeated in the ethnographic section of book 6 with the comment that it was done for secrecy within Celtic communities, *BG* 6.14. Caesar corresponded with Q. Tullius Cicero using the same technique, Greek letters for Latin words, *BG* 5.48. Use of an interpreter, *BG* 5.36. Caesar also sometimes employed a replacement cypher in his

correspondence, using the letter three to the right of that intended in the alphabet, Suetonius, *Caesar,* 56.

17. For example, the 120,000 Germans who are said to have crossed into Gaul later on, *BG* 1.31.
18. *BG* 1.11.
19. Slavery in antiquity has long inspired much interest. The modern bibliography far outweighs the ancient evidence, but this is even more the case for slavery among barbarian peoples.
20. *BG* 5.44, is not definitive, since the owner and his slave, although both Gauls, were inside Caesar's besieged camp.
21. *BG* 1.39, 2.33, 7.55.
22. C. Haselgrove 1987, particularly 108–10; L. Hedeager 1987, 132–33.
23. *BG* 1.38. Seizing Vesontio (Besançon), which contained "omnium rerum quae ad bellum usui," before Ariovistus arrived there by a series of forced marches day and night. Other examples are too numerous to list, but *BG* 7.14 is especially clear.
24. *BG* 3.13. Romans continued to use this Celtic design for river transport long after the conquest.
25. *BG* 1.22.
26. *BG* 1.19.
27. *BG* 1.31. Caesar states that at first the Germans numbered 15,000 but by the end of the year numbered 120,000. These calculations are impossible to believe. Ariovistus then orders the Sequanni to withdraw (*decedere*) from another third (*altera parte tertia*).
28. *BG* 1.31–33; invoking Marius and the Cimbri and Teutones again at *BG* 1.40.
29. *BG* 2.4, 2.29, 7.77.
30. *BG* 3.19.
31. *BG* 1.35.
32. *BG* 1.53, the marriage took place while Ariovistus was on campaign in Gaul. She and his other wife were later killed when Caesar's troops crossed the Rhine and routed the Germans.
33. *BG* 1.33, 1.44–45.
34. *BG* 1.34–37.
35. For example, by Caesar *BG* 1.30, 1.6.3; by Vercingetorix, *BG* 1.63, 1.7.4.
36. *BG* 1.17.
37. *Roman Republican Coinage* 452/4, Munich, struck from a mobile mint in Gaul (ca. 48–47 B.C.). Unlike earlier coins depicting killed or captured Gauls, this one does not give the name of the moneyer (compare to the illustration on p. 45) but that of the general paying his troops with it. Thus it also announces a new type of Roman leader, one not content with tradition.
38. *BG* 1.28. A. Berger 1953, 427.

39. *BG* 1.50–53. German mothers are reported to have been responsible for declaring the lots before any action affecting the people. The lots, according to Tacitus writing with Caesar in hand, were wooden tallies marked with symbols (*Germania,* 10).
40. J. Tierney 1960, provides an extensive and controversial discussion of these problems and offers a rearrangement of the fragments that seem to be contained in Caesar and other ancient sources on the Celts. On Posidonius in general, see *Posidonius. The Fragments,* ed. L. Edelstein and I. Kidd (1989). The fragments on the Celts include such items as their eating and drinking habits (frag. 67.3, 41), military tactics (frags. 68 and 275), and severing heads (frag. 274). There is less concerning the Germans. The only such comments that can be securely attributed to him are those about their eating habits (frags. 73 and 277b).
41. In addition to the works cited on Posidonius, see M. Laffranque 1964, 78, 120, 140. Posidonius is the closest to being a contemporary source for the ethnography of the Celts of southern Gaul, but of course his works are lost except as they influenced later authors such as Caesar.
42. *BG* 3.21.
43. W. Buckland and A. McNair 1965, 25; this remained the case throughout Roman history as far as legal theory was concerned. Also, A. Berger 1953, 528–29.
44. *BG* 2.4.
45. *BG* 1.37, 2.24, 5.35.
46. *BG* 2.6–13. In the case of Iccius, he was "summa nobilitate et gratia inter suos" (the most noble and respected among them).
47. *BG* 5.27, 2.6.
48. *BG* 5.4 and 6.8 concern Indutiomarus, one of Caesar's most troublesome Gallic allies. Caesar (*BG* 5.4) orders him to provide two hundred hostages, a number calculated it seems to weaken significantly Indutiomarus's power among those of his *civitas,* the Treveri.
49. *BG* 5.25 among the Carnutes; *BG* 5.3 among the Treveri; *BG* 7.39 among the Aedui, raising a commoner to eminence and thereby outraging the established elites.
50. *BG* 2.6. These included mantlets (covered shelters on wheels) and various other devices (*BG* 7.84) but not siege towers and similarly complex Roman equipment. The lack of Roman-style machinery must be what Caesar had in mind when he declared that the Gauls had no experience in conducting sieges. Their fortifications and internecine wars also suggest that they were rather skilled at it. Roman origins among the Nervii, *BG* 5.42.
51. Supplies and Belgae, *BG* 2.10, 3.1. Legionaries wintered over in 57 B.C. near Octodurus, today Martigny in Switzerland, to assist.
52. *BG* 2.13.

53. *BG* 2.27–31.
54. *BG* 2.33.
55. *BG* 3.28.
56. *BG* 4.1–2.
57. *BG* 6.5; Caesar clearly thought that the Ubii *oppida* could be defended.
58. *BG* 6.10.
59. *BG* 5.27, 5.55, 6.32. Caesar himself occasionally recruited Germans as mercenaries, (e.g., *BG* 7.14, 7.65, 7.70), but such augmentation was routine among the Gauls and had been a major factor in expanding the wars from their normal levels.
60. *BG* 4.20, where they are twice reported, once giving data to the Romans, once to the Gauls about the Romans. The Romans in residence among the Carnutes were among the first casualties of the general revolt under Vercingetorix in 52 B.C., *BG* 7.3.
61. *BG* 4.10.
62. *BG* 4.16–17.
63. *BG* 4.19. Although using the term *oppida* to describe these settlements, it is clear that, as in the case of British settlements, also *oppida* (*BG* 5.21), he is not speaking of the Gallic-type fortified urban centers but unfortified rural settlements, which were completely indefensible.
64. *BG* 6.40.
65. *BG* 4.16. "Populi Romani imperium Rhenum finire," a declaration that later history made reality.
66. *BG* 4.27, 4.30, 4.33, 5.11 Cassivellaunus; *BG* 5.14, 5.57.
67. *BG* 5.12, 5.21.
68. *BG* 6.11–19 on the Celts, 20–28 on the Germans. The essay opens, "de Galliae Germaniaeque moribus et quo differant hae nationes inter sese propronere" (concerning the customs of the Gauls and Germans and how these nations differ from one another).
69. *BG* 6.13, "sese in servitutem," but a translation of this as "enslaved" seems to miss the point. This is an attempt to explain the clientage system, not chattel slavery.
70. The only other reference to horsemen, "knights," does not address the class but merely a cavalry force levied from among all members of Vercingetorix's alliance (*BG* 7.66). The class or group (*genus*) is only noted in book 6, and then without elucidation. All Druid references are to be found in *BG* 6.13–16. These facts of presentation have engendered much academic debate.
71. The same cultural mix of adaptation and survival was going on throughout most of the Roman world, especially in the West, as a result of Roman military and political expansion. The Iberian peninsula provides many interesting parallels to Gaul. Romanization began earlier in Spain than in Gaul because of the Punic Wars, but conquering,

pacifying, and transforming the Iberian peninsula was a task never completed. Pompey and then Julius Caesar cut their teeth in Spain but left most of it unconquered. The constant demand for military action on the peninsula was a major factor that greatly accelerated the political imbalances that were to transform and ultimately destroy the Roman Republic. As in Gaul, Rome moved from the coast inwards, but unlike Gaul, the peoples of Spain never rallied together to present Rome with an Alesia-like opportunity to defeat the bulk of the opposition in one climactic struggle. Exploring the gradual changes in indigenous religion, as for Gaul, is a useful gauge to the penetration of Roman culture. For a start, see J. M. Blázquez 1996, 13–143; and L. Curchin 1997.

72. *BG* 6.24.
73. *BG* 6.2–4, 7.9, 7.75.
74. *BG* 5.29. At *BG* 5.54 Caesar acknowledges their plight: "tantum se eius opinionis deperdidisse ut a populo Romano imperia perferrent gravissime dolebant"; *BG* 7.38, Audean law superseded by Roman. Better to die than to lose the *libertas* given them by their ancestors, *BG* 7.1: "belli gloriam libertatemque." Vercingetorix appeals to the loss of liberty for all, "communis libertatis," *BG* 7.4.
75. On the postconquest evolution of Gauls into Romans, see G. Woolf 1998.
76. In all Caesar seems to have created 31 colonies, principally in Gaul and Spain but even a few in Italy. Augustus added another 74 colonial foundations during his long administration, among them some in Gaul, many in Spain. Spain repeatedly proved itself to be a greater challenge to the Romans than Gaul. P. MacKendrick 1957, 8, basing his statistics on the major study of Roman colonization by F. Vittinghof 1952. Assigning foundations to Caesar rather than to others, particularly Augustus, is problematic; see E. Salmon 1970, 128–44. For recent work in general on this topic, see E. Fentress, 2000, especially the contribution by G. Woolf 2000.
77. In addition to C. Wells 1995, see the beautifully illustrated work by a pioneer German archaeologist, R. Hachmann 1971, and the still fundamental study of Caesar by G. Walser 1956, but noting the many reservations placed upon it by H. Montgomery 1972.
78. Among such surveys, see most recently P. Wells 1999, drawn primarily for the upper Rhine and Danube.

Chapter 4. The Early Empire and the Barbarians

1. Suetonius, *Augustus*, 48.
2. S. Mattern 1999, 191: revolts alone, rhetorically at least, required annihilation.

3. Vergil, *Aeneid,* 1.278–79, "His ego nec metas rerum nec tempora pono: imperium sine fine dedi."
4. The *Tabula Imperii Romani, L-34,* shows the western boundary as unclear, but recent research suggests that it ran to the Tisza River, although the area up to the Carpathians may have been largely undefended. Continuing efforts are revealing unexpected levels of Roman influence here as elsewhere beyond the administrative and military boundaries that long have been called the Roman frontiers. The eastern boundary seems better established as running along the north-south road connecting a series of fortifications, most of them constructed to monitor access up the valleys. This system does not seem to have been preclusive even for defense, for the topography is penetrable in too many other locations.
5. A. Mócsy 1974a, 157.
6. P. Wells 1999, for a focus on the Rhine and upper Danube.
7. *Res gestae* 3, 4, 16, 28. Written towards the very end his life, the *Res gestae,* or "My Accomplishments" is a singularly important window into the cultural and political considerations that Augustus regarded as having been pivotal to his success. He claims in *Res gestae* 3 to have settled 300,000 men after the civil war.
8. I. Haynes, 1993.
9. There is an unavoidable ambiguity in using the name Augustus, which became the Roman term for what we have long called the emperor. Octavian did not receive the title Augustus, implying deepest respect, until 16 January 27 B.C., before which he used his birth name Octavian or *divi filius,* son of the divine Julius Caesar. After his receipt of the title Augustus, he preferred to be recognized by it.
10. There is no way to ascertain the population of even the city of Rome, let alone of the empire, but if we use the rather traditional estimates of between 65 and 100 million people—the former seems most likely and the latter almost certainly is too high—this produces the 1:250 to 1:300 ratio at the time of Augustus. The army of Severus may have exceeded 400,000, but the general population surely had not increased proportionately. If the overall population were less or the size of the army greater, the ratios become ever more forceful indicators of the level of sacrifice that Roman society accepted to maintain this military force. Naturally a precise comparison to current American troop strengths cannot be pressed because of the vastly different technologies employed to wage war and the fiscal means to raise revenues in a highly industrialized society. Nonetheless there are presently approximately 1.5 million Americans under arms out of a population in excess of 260 million, a ratio of 1:175. On the budgetary issues, B. Shaw 1999, 141–43.

11. *Corpus inscriptionum latinarum* (*CIL*)3.3385.
12. M. Speidel 1975.
13. That legionary commanders had to be senatorials continued to be the rule until the reign of Septimus Severus (193–211). On pay, see M. Speidel 1992 and R. Alston 1994a.
14. Correspondence preserved in the bog environment at Vindolanda in Britain has provided a unique window into these contacts. There members of the 9th Batavian Cohort wrote letters covering a wide variety of subjects of military and personal interest; see A. Bowman 1994.
15. Y. Le Bohec 1994, ch. 3 on "Recruitment," especially p. 71, on the numbers needed by the various services.
16. So suggests A. Mócsy 1974a, 154, for Upper Moesia as compared with the early recruitment of natives in neighboring Pannonia. On this Mócsy finds support from P. Holder 1980, 112.
17. P. Holder 1980, 112, 117, 120.
18. *CIL* 6.6236 from Rome, Suebus from Germania or the house of Germanus; see further I. Kajanto 1982, 51, with more examples. His list of tribes and peoples is hardly exhaustive. Gaepidius Theodorus by his mother Marciana, a domestic slave (*verna*), *Museum Veronense,* 259.5, Rome, undated, perhaps as late as the fourth century. Some barbarians married slaves who are remembered only by their Roman names, *CIL* 6.10951. Many other examples exist, e.g., W. Schulze 1933, 56–58, and O. Fiebiger and L. Schmidt 1917.
19. *CIL* 3.4991; O. Fiebiger and L. Schmidt 1917, no. 14.
20. The example of a certain signifier in the *cohors* I. Belgarum buried near Humac in Herzegovina in the second half of the second century: "Dassius, Bastarni [f. do]mo Maezaeus, [mile]s coh. I Belgarum" (O. Fiebiger and L. Schmidt 1917, no. 13)—Dassius the son of Bastarnus, who it seems was somehow on the estate of the Maezaei. Or see *Corpus inscriptionum graecarum,* 1.428. where a certain Amphion noted that his father was an Illyrian from ca. 250 at Athens.
21. For example, "Secundinius Verus natione Suaebus" (*Ephemeris epigraphica* [supp. to *CIL]* 4:345 no. 935, cited in W. Schulze 1933, 58), or Candidinius Spectatus and Candidinius Verax natione Badavi (*CIL* 6.3240). An especially valuable case, because it gives four examples in one, is that of Laurentius, son of Tzita (*CIL* 12396, from Glava in Lower Moesia, undated). Valerius Tzita here is remembered by his son Laurentius "suo carissimo." Laurentius notes that his father had named his other two sons Vitalis and Florentius. All had followed their father into the army, each noted on the inscription as *miles.*
22. B. Shaw 1999, 135.

23. For an example of the prestige of a veteran from Roman literature, see Ammianus, 28.4.20.
24. A Roman mile corresponded very closely to an American mile.
25. On the increasing use of stone building among the Marcomanni, see H. Böhme 1975. Most recent data can be found in H. Friesinger et al. 1994.
26. The SC mark continued on imperial bronzes into the sixth century, when it appeared on coins struck under the barbarian kings. By then there was only the dimmest memory of a senate worthy of consultation, but no new consultation ever took place. The SC joined a host of other imperial iconographic statements used to announce that all was well even when it was not; see B. Overbeck 1996.
27. Tacitus, *Agricola,* 30, trans. M. Hadas, 695.
28. Tacitus, *Agricola,* 20–21.
29. For example, revolt followed Ostorius Scapula's attempt to disarm the Iceni and other recently conquered British in A.D. 48; Tacitus, *Annales,* 12.31–39.
30. Mattern 1999, in particular 171–76, stresses the continuing importance of honor and dishonor among the Roman aristocracy and their literary world in dealings with non-Romans, while other historians (e.g., C. Whittaker 1994 and H. Elton 1996a) give more importance to the role that practical concerns played. Probably no society has departed entirely from the dilemma of honor and practicality in international affairs.
31. G. de Ste. Croix 1981, 510 from appendix III, a very convenient list of all settlements of barbarians upon Roman soil as compiled from literary sources. The archaeological materials, some to be adduced in this chapter, make it clear that the extant literary evidence reveals but a mere fraction of the traffic. De Ste. Croix provides all pertinent references to the ancient authors.
32. P. Console and R. Milns 1983, 183–84; *Inscriptiones Latinae Selectae,* 986.
33. Tacitus, *Annales,* 2.41, also commemorated on a coin struck for Emperor Gaius (Caligula), son of Germanicus, during his first year on the throne, A.D. 37; *Roman Imperial Coinage* (*RIC*) (2d ed.), Gaius, no. 57. Tacitus, *Germania,* 37.6, was unwilling to credit Domitian with retaking Germania, which his coinage proclaimed was the result of his wars in the area between the Rhine and Danube. Later authors continued the official tradition of damnation; for example, Seutonius (*Domitian,* 6.1) and, writing much later, Cassius Dio (67.4.1) regarded his campaigns as of no consequence. So too Florus, 2.30.21. Archaeological data support a limited version of his claims; however he did not re-

store the lost province of Germania. Germanicus was adopted by Tiberius in 4 B.C. shortly before his own adoption by Augustus.

34. *Res gestae,* 35.1.
35. H.-P. Schönbeck 1998.
36. Made a mockery of by his biographer, Suetonius, *Gaius,* 43–45.
37. Compare, for example, coin reverses depicting various barbarians: *RIC* 16, of Vespasian, A.D. 70/71, a denarius with a Jewish captive; *RIC* 278(a), a sestertius, of Domitian, A.D. 85, with a captive German; *RIC* 1443, of Lucius Verus, a sestertius, A.D. 165/66, with a Parthian prisoner. These portrayals originated in the late republic. See the denarius of Julius Caesar, *Roman Republican Coinage,* 454, 48/47 B.C., of a similar Gallic captive, but this type in general reflects the reduction of iconographic alternatives to a basic vocabulary that occurred under Augustus.
38. Examples of such displays of weaponry, symmetrical on the coin reverse, are common: for example, *RIC* (2d ed.) 73, an aureus of Claudius I, A.D. 41–45; *RIC* 295, A.D. 85; a dupondius of Domitian celebrating, according to the coin legend, a victory over the Germans; and *RIC* 584, a dupondius of Trajan, celebrating on the coin legend victory over Germans and Dacians.
39. Domitian, *RIC* 278(a), a sestertius, A.D. 85; and Marcus Aurelius, *RIC* 1021, a sestertius, A.D. 171/72.
40. A. Lund 1988 and J. Rives 1999 provide extensive commentaries as well as ample discussions of the ethnographic and geographic issues surrounding Tacitus, *Germania.* Some details of his work are paralleled in the archaeological data, but many others are historical whimsy retold to entertain and inform within the limits of the genre. Like other Roman commentators on barbarians, Tacitus weaves together stereotypic literary depictions and historic observations into a fabric that is now extremely difficult to unravel.
41. Tacitus, *Germania,* 7.
42. Tacitus, *Germania,* 42, trans. M. Hutton.
43. Tacitus, *Germania,* 43.
44. The contrast here offered by Tacitus is the classic statement of the difference between what anthropologists traditionally distinguish as the "big man" and the "king." Some combination of both is widely held to have been a core element in the rise of all advanced societies.
45. L. Hedeager 1987, 127–33. This is a highly theoretical and provocative essay, but linking archaeological data to passages and concepts found in Tacitus, *Germania,* as done here, is tenuous at best. So too are the theories of class development adduced as explanations for distribution patterns. Much of the data used was collected earlier; see H. Eggers 1951.

46. Many of the more traditional aspects of this problem were outlined in Pippidi 1976, but more recently discussion has focused on the interpretation of archaeological materials. This in turn has fueled heated debate around the so-called Celtic Revival in the third and subsequent centuries but with roots earlier.

Chapter 5. The Early Empire and the Barbarians

1. S. Mattern 1999, 60–61; even after Trajan's conquests at the opening of the second century, the geographic position of Dacia was poorly understood in relationship to the Mediterranean Sea and the "northern Ocean." The Balkans were very well known by comparison. V. Lica 2000 has recently reviewed all the sources and interpretations for Caesar's and Augustus's involvement with the Dacians; see particularly pp. 123–44.
2. Appian, *Illyrici,* 14–28 (one of the fragments of his *Roman History*); Cassius Dio, 49.34–43. For a detailed narrative of these events and a discussion of the source problems, see J. Wilkes 1969, 46–77, and A. Mócsy 1974a, 22–52.
3. *Res gestae,* 30.1, trans. M. Reinhold and N. Lewis 1990, 1.571.
4. Cassius Dio, 51.23.
5. Appian, *Illyrici,* 22–24. Appian was quite aware of the limitations imposed by his use of Augustus, *Illyrici,* 15. On Iapydes, *Illyrici,* 18.
6. A. Móscy, 1974a, 22, discounts any plan to wage war against Dacians; J. Eadie 1977, favors a more strategic view as seen in the *Res gestae.*
7. Caesar, *BG* 1.5; 7.9, 7.75. Archaeologically the relationship of the Boii in northern Pannonia to those in Bavaria is increasingly probable; L Horváth 1987, 41. S. Rieckhoff-Pauli 1980, fig.1, reflects the distribution of Celtic materials in central Europe including the Carpathian Basin. On Celts in Hungary, particularly the *oppida* just prior to Roman conquest, see E. Petres 1976; in general on their handcrafts, weapons, and domestic items, see also M. Szabó 1971 and E. Jerem 1995.
8. Strabo, *Geography,* 7.2.2.
9. Strabo, *Geography,* 5.1.6; Plinius, *Naturalis Historia,* 3.24; *CIL* 9.5363; for textual references, see *Paulys-Wissova,* 3.1.631–32.
10. The most accessible compilation of Celtic materials in Hungary will be *The Corpus of Celtic Finds in Hungary,* by various authors; to date two volumes are in print (L. Horváth 1987, M. Hellebranct 1999).
11. On Tiberius's limited goals and the exaggeration of them in Augustan propaganda, see also D. Timpe 1971, and for subsequent first-century policy, K.-W. Welwei 1986.
12. Velleius Patercullus, *Historiae Romanae,* 2.90.5; on Velleius's career, 2.104.3–4. On the costs, Cassius Dio, 56.16.4. On the recent ar-

chaeological data and their interpretation, see J. Tejral 1994 and M. Bálek and O. Ŝedo 1994.

13. In addition to A. Mócsy 1974a, see Z. Visy and D. Planck 2000, for a succinct, beautifully illustrated, and clear historical and archaeological development of the province, particularly its Hungarian sections; here pp. 11–13.
14. Part of the uncertainty surrounding Celts in Hungary has to do with the level of Celtic occupation of this area at this time. Some Celtic settlements had ceased, but others continued. The suggested causes range from natural disasters to conflict with Dacians. In the absence of literary sources, a resolution of this issue will have to wait a long time.
15. Tacitus, *Annales,* 2.44; 2.62–63.
16. For a marvelously easy way to visualize how Roman elites and the state viewed barbarians at this time, see P. Hamberg 1945, especially the photographs of second-century sarcophagi at the end of the volume, with Romans dominating barbarians (outlined in red on the overlays in Hamberg).
17. For Hungarian Pannonia, see now G. Hajnóczi et al. 1998, which provides not only an up-to-date guide with maps, photographs, a historical introduction, and a glossary of Latin terms, but also gives reliable references to the recent scholarly literature. This book is now the indispensable place to begin for those lacking Hungarian. For several of the largest sites there is also an older series of guide books published in English and German: for example, K. Póczy 1977, on Scarbantia; J. Fitz 1973, on Gorsium; and Z. Visy 1977, on Intercisa. The standard historical narrative remains that of A. Mócsy 1974a. One can start an inquiry into almost every site discussed in this chapter by starting with G. Hajnóczi et al.
18. R. Wolters 1990–91; analyzing the archaeological data, pt. 1 (1990), and then in pt. 2 (1991) the literary references; here, pt. 2 (1991) 88.
19. Although there is as yet relatively little in print on trade with the northern barbarians, this is changing rapidly as more and more archaeologists address the topic. At present, see R. Wolters 1990–91, here 85–105; U. Lund-Hanson 1989, and also 1987, 233–34; as well as H. Elton 1996a, 97–111. Much of Elton's evidence concerns the more demonstrable Roman long-distance trade with India and eastern Africa. The study of the reverse flow of Roman goods to the barbarians is still largely dependent upon the evidence collected by H. Eggers 1951, but this is now being augmented almost daily by new archaeological discoveries and advances in numismatics. No one has yet pulled these new data together in the manner of Eggers.
20. R. Wolters 1990–91, pt. 1, 22–23; pt. 2, 85–88.

21. For the natives and Romanization in the area of the amber road, which will become the heart of the province of Pannonia Superior, see D. Gabler 1994. For Scarbantia as *oppidum,* see Plinius, *Naturalis Historia,* 3.146; for a review of Trajan's construction efforts between Carnuntum and Brigetio, see D. Gabler 1989, 636–43.
22. D. Gabler 1989, 636; on Iazyges, Tacitus, *Historiae,* 2.81–82.
23. Cassius Dio, 67.3–7. To properly set the stage for his narration of Domitian's wars, Dio notes his execution of those Vestal Virgins he suspected of fornication (Cassius Dio, 67.3). As a result of his damnation, no detailed account of Domitian's actions outside Rome could or can be done.
24. H. Böhme 1975, 189–211.
25. D. Gabler 1994, 401–3, the area around each city is surveyed in this study with appropriate references to the most recent excavations and interpretations.
26. The division of 214 only shifted a small area to the northeast of Lake Balaton. Prior to 214 the boundary ran from the eastern end of the lake to the Danube bend; afterwards it shifted westwards to Arrabona, A. Mócsy 1974a, 198. Cassius Dio, 78.13.4, on his penchant for building in Raetia, as in other areas through which he passed, but this account is largely a rhetorical exercise directed against Caracalla.
27. G. Hajnóczi et al. 1998, 41–71. On the collegium, A. Mócsy 1974a, 126.
28. Intercisa is the best understood of the frontier fortresses, particularly because of the work done to elucidate the importance of the *vicus militaris* and the native populations, see Z. Visy 1977, 8–14; G. Hajnóczi et al.1998, 73–76. On rural society in general in Pannonia Inferior, see Z. Visy 1994, on wine restrictions, p. 431. For Romans taking over or perhaps even sharing rural villages, see the example of Tokod-Szorosok in L. Horváth 1987, 199–200, in the area of the Danube bend.
29. J. Fitz 1973; G. Hainóczi et al. 1998, 78–87.
30. For the Flavia monument in Gorsium, Z. Visy 1997, 46–47, plate 59. This volume examines over seventy similar monuments from Pannonia and offers the evolutionary interpretation given here. The Flavia stone is among the highest quality in its cut and preservation.
31. G. Hajnóczi et al. 1998, 87–88; S. Palágyi 1981. Burying nobility in similar mound burials complete with elaborate gear and horses nearby survived in much of non-Roman Europe throughout the imperial centuries only to come back into the empire during the fifth century A.D.
32. Z. Visy 1997, 92–106, and A. Mócsy 1974a, 147–50. The size of the ossuary itself apparently changed from a full body size to a smaller type suitable for cremation (Visy, p. 101). Although the evolution of

types is consistent overall, regional variations and the tenacity of older forms preclude an absolutely linear chronological development.

33. For an example of routine selective admission of external barbarians into Pannonia, see *Inscriptiones Latinae Selectae,* 985, admitted by the governor Tampius Flavianus.
34. D. Gabler 1986, 70–72.
35. Tacitus, *Germania,* 42, notes their peaceful acceptance of their clientage ca. A.D. 100.
36. Both legionnaires and auxiliaries are depicted on the columns of Trajan and Marcus Aurelius, see P. Hamberg 1945, for example, plates 12 and 15, Marcus with legions and barbarian chief in submission; and with auxiliaries, for example, plate 27 (the emperor addressing his troops before battle).
37. The passages in Galen are but fragments, but a compelling account can be found in his fourth-century biographer, *Historia Augusta* (*HA*), *Marcus,* 13.3–6.
38. R. Littman and M. Littman 1973. Galen, the personal physician to Marcus Aurelius, makes scattered reference to the disease in his extant work, too randomly for us to be absolutely sure that the disease was smallpox, but enough to rule out many other possibilities. Except for the scars left upon the survivors, all the other smallpox symptoms are mentioned.
39. Cassius Dio, 72.11.1–5.
40. A. Birley 1987, 170. This is far and away the best and most balanced account of these wars.
41. H. Böhme 1975, 182–97.
42. *HA, Marcus,* 21.6, making a comparison to the Punic Wars and thereby throwing into question this reference.
43. Cassius Dio, 72.1a. This book of Dio's history was greatly compressed by the Byzantine epitomist, with the result being that the textual obscurity for the beginning of the wars is particularly impenetrable. Tacitus, *Germania,* 40.
44. *HA, Marcus,* 14.1; note especially the terminology in the phrase, "a superioribus barbaris fugerant, nisi reciperentur, bellum inferentibus." The *HA* is fairly well grounded through the Life of Marcus, but afterwards fantasy reigns rather than emperors. The emphasis on the last phrase of the translation is my own. On the reliability of the *HA* on Roman-barbarian relations, see T. Burns 1979.
45. *HA, Marcus,* 22.2.
46. Cassius Dio, 72.11–12.
47. *RIC,* v. 3., Crossing the Danube, p. 234, no. 270; Sarmatians, p. 239, no. 340.
48. A. Birley 1987, 164, but surely Lucian of Samosata, *Alexander,* 48, can-

not inspire much confidence. His storyline with barbarians being mistaken for dogs and beaten to death is a splendid reminder of what Roman authors did with barbarians.

49. Cassius Dio, 72.15–16.
50. Cassius Dio, 72.20, recalls that archaeology has revealed that Roman monitoring stations had been built there prior to the outbreak of hostilities.
51. *HA, Marcus,* 24.5, 27.10.
52. Cassius Dio, 72.19; this passage in general relates to events of 179–80, but the treaty with the Iazyges is used as a retrospective example.
53. Cassius Dio, 72.21.
54. *HA, Marcus,* 14.3, for example.
55. Cassius Dio, 72.16.
56. *HA, Marcus,* 21.7: "emit et Germanorum auxilia contra Germanos."
57. The edict (the *Constitutio Antoniniana*) is known only from fragments and references to it in classical authors. Some like Cassius Dio (76.9–10) were decidedly jaundiced in their views of its merits and purpose, claiming that it was just a mechanism to raise taxes since Romans alone paid the inheritance tax of 5% destined for the troops. It was still remembered in the *Digesta* (1.5.17) of Justinian (527–65) as marking the moment when everyone living in the empire became a citizen. The best preserved text is a fragmented papyrus, Giessen papyrus, no. 40, col. I., which like virtually all papyri has gaps caused by the deterioration of the papyrus itself. In some cases these lacunae can be filled in a general way from the classical references to the text. Modern scholarship is as imposing and varied as the text is fragmentary and controversial: see particularly C. Sacce 1958.
58. The fact that throughout the third century emperors and claimants often took the name of Marcus Aurelius as a part of their official nomenclature no longer would have left such a mark on the official names of the retiring auxiliaries because of the rapid decline in the use of Roman trinomial names after the edict of 212. For example, upon his ascension to the throne in 284 Diocletian supplemented his name Diocles by including the names of his most famous predecessors in his new imperial name, Marcus Aurelius Valerius Diocletianus. Moreover, there are a few examples of barbarian soldiers taking the name Marcus Aurelius well into the fourth century.

Chapter 6. The Barbarians and the "Crisis" of the Empire

1. See the fundamental articulation of the governmental situation by R. MacMullen 1976; on the intensification of non-Christian spirituality, see D. Potter 1990.
2. J. Drinkwater, in press, who graciously allowed me access to his man-

uscript; C. Witschel 1999, who in surveying all the western regions of the empire including Africa, stresses the need for regional study. Witschel concludes that in general the events of the third century merely accelerated changes already underway in response to inherent structural problems in the empire. Although each region proceeded along similar evolutionary paths, they did so at varying speeds, before, during, and after the third century. What is especially surprising is the rapidity with which life returned to normal even in some of the areas most affected by the military and political trauma of the last half of the century. The social and economic fabric was marvelously resilient.

3. J. Eadie 1980.
4. In addition to the works cited in preceding chapters, see on Roman influences in Gaul during the first and second centuries especially T. Derks 1998, who demonstrates important differences between the urbanized south and other areas by marshaling archaeological and epigraphic material.
5. J. Drinkwater 1987, 249.
6. The apparent continuity of succession from the death of Gallienus is only just that, apparent. At least one usurper or heir punctuated the transitions here noted. The reigns of these claimants were less than one year and so disappear in this sketch, but see J. Drinkwater, in press, for a full accounting. *Felicium temporum reparatio* is a common coin legend on issues struck during the Constantinian dynasty. The people are also instructed as to the reason for this return to the happy times—the loyalty of the army. The martial vigor of the emperors is affirmed by frequent commemorations of victory over barbarians.
7. H. Bender 2001a, 185–88, 191; C. Witschel 1999, 338–44. The trend towards various types of defended nucleated settlements picked up momentum in the following two centuries, and will be explored more fully as it relates to barbarians in the following chapter. Artillery had evolved little since the days of Julius Caesar—in fact, from those of Alexander the Great. Various types of machines still used the torsion derived from pulling hair or rope to hurl various ballistae such as metal darts, wicker balls soaked in olive oil and set afire, and prepared stones of different sizes.
8. L. Okamura 1984, 184–90, especially his vivid reconstruction of the final hours of the auxiliary fortress and the convincing connection of the destruction of Pfunz to Maximinus. Otherwise for the importance of the eastern mystery cult of Jupiter Dolichenus to the army and the Severans in this context, see M. Speidel 1978. On third-century bog deposits, see J. Coulston 1990, 150. For an example of celebrating around a captured insignia, Ammianus, 27.1.6.
9. T. Burns 1979, on Enmann's *Kaisergeschichte* as lying behind even the

notoriously fictionalized accounts in the *Historia Augusta,* composed towards the end of the fourth century. J. Drinkwater, in press, provides a convenient overview of the available literary evidence from antiquity.

10. Cassius Dio, 56.18.2, trans. E. Cary (Loeb edition).
11. Cassius Dio, 78.13.4–6.
12. For the names being synonyms by the mid-fourth century, see Ammianus Marcellinus, 16.7.1. Near Augsburg in 260, as recorded on a newly discovered inscription, dated 11 September 260 by L. Bakker 1993, 378, and discussed further below. For 297, see *Panegyrici Latini* (*Paneg. Lat.*), 8 [4].9.3–4, ed. and trans. C. Nixon, in C. Nixon and B. Saylor Rogers 1994. All references prior to Nixon and Saylor Rogers to the *Panegyrici* are as in E. Galletier, which I indicate here and below in brackets, so in this case in the traditional (Galletier) numbering it is 4.9.3–4 rather than 8.9.3–4.
13. *Paneg. Lat.,* 10 [2].5.1, as numbered by C. Nixon, in C. Nixon and B. Saylor Rogers 1994. In addition to the Alamanni were Burgundians, Chaibones, and Eruli. The Franks also occur in *Paneg. Lat.,* 7 [6].4.2 dated 307, addressed to Maximianus and Constantine, and again in a panegyric addressed to Constantine in 310 in a way that makes it clear that they were hardly one people even at that date; a "diversis Francorum gentibus," *Paneg. Lat.,* 6 [7].5.3.
14. Dexippus, in Jacoby, *Fragmente,* 2A, frag. 100. Maximianus took as his official name Marcus Aurelius Valerius Maximianus, and his son, continuing the complex pseudodynastic links, chose Marcus Aurelius Valerius Maxentius.
15. Agathias, *Historiae,* I (A). 6.3. The literary sources for the Alamanni are assembled in the multivolume, *Quellen zur Geschichte der Alamannen,* here v. 2, p. 80. Subsequent literary emendation that turned third-century barbarian groups that were highly fragmented into later, better-known, and more centralized ones is probably true of other of our sources as well. For example, *HA, Claudius,* 6.2, juxtaposing Greutungi and Austrogothi, the former a well-documented Gothic invader and one of several peoples ultimately gathered together as Ostrogoths (Austrogothi), is likely an emendation of the *HA*'s tenth-century copyist.
16. On the categorical usage of these terms by Roman authors, see R. Wenkus 1977, 502, but the terms themselves were Germanic barbarian in origin. There is also an abundance of examples of the uncritical use of victories over Alamanni, Goths, and Franks, commemorated in such titles as *Alamannicus maximus* and *Gothicus maximus,* as well as the truly generic *Germanicus maximus* on coins and inscriptions.
17. This can be seen clearly in the patterns of coin distribution and the nature of the hoards in central Europe that are absent from early in

Septimus's reign until after 236: A. Bursche 1996, 72–76, 95–97. A case can be made against the traditional and literal acceptance of Dio on Caracalla, the scope and duration of the campaign of 213, and of the first appearance of the Alamanni; see L. Okamura 1984, 8–150, with careful attention to both numismatic and archaeological finds, particularly coin hoards (given in detail in appendix I, v. 2, pp. 466–82), as well as the suggestion for a route beginning at Mainz (pp. 60–61). Okamura is among the first to challenge the validity of Dio's account for the origin of the Alamanni, and data behind many of his suggestions have increased. I believe that the Augsburg inscription and the recently analyzed coin data from eastern Europe confirm most of Okamura's reconstruction of the rise of the Alamannic confederacy. There is, of course, no way to have absolute confidence in any theory.

18. For example, Cassius Dio, 78.3 on Caracalla's madness for money and evil nature; and Cassius Dio, 78.6.1, lack of virtues, and 78.31.2–4, death of Elagabulus, and J. Eadie 1996, 141.
19. Herodianus, *Historia,* 4.7.2–3, trans. C. Whittaker, 409–11.
20. The identity of those raiding Italy is securely known, the Iuthungi; the Franks are identified as getting to Spain, but only in Sextus Aurelius Victor (written 361). Sextus Aurelius Victor in this passage also calls the invaders going into Italy Alamanni, but, as is developed later, this is anachronistic, contradicted by contemporary evidence. So probably his reference here is to the Franks. Precise dating of this passage is not possible, but it probably refers to events around 260. The best literary account of Roman army deserters assisting in siege warfare in the third century comes from Zosimus (1.70) and concerns not barbarians but the revolt of Lydius the Isaurian against the emperor Probus. Contemporary Goths used Roman captives knowledgeable in seafaring to raid the Aegean and Black Sea ports (Jordanes, *Getica,* 90); see further T. Burns 1980, 21–24.
21. See A. Brulet 1996, 55–120, on the Franks ca. A.D. 250–400, on both sides of the lower Rhine as seen primarily in archaeological perspective. These collected essays are part of a rich catalog for an exhibition. The articles reflect current struggles with issues of identity and are leery of forcing archaeology into the descriptive system of the literary material, rare as it is, although that temptation is not universally resisted. See further, A. Wieczorek, U. von Freeden, and U. Koch 1999.
22. For example, the Chaibones of *Paneg. Lat.,* 10 [2].5.1–2, associated in the text with Eruli, themselves probably one of many Gothic-speaking groups, were most famous for their sack of Athens in 267. The Chaibones are known only from this one passage.
23. The Quadi, the primary opponents of Marcus Aurelius on the middle Danube, are last reported as invading Italy in alliance with the Ala-

manni in 270, Dexippus, Jacoby, *Fragmente,* 2A, frag. 100. The late fourth-century *HA, Aurelian,* 18.4, confuses the Marcomanni and the Alamanni, having the former invade Italy under Aurelian. What P. Geary 1999, 107, said of the geographer Pliny could be said about almost every Roman author, certainly including that of the *HA,* that they "delighted in combining as many sources as possible, mixing people long disappeared with contemporary ethnic groups." Under such circumstances it is easy to see how the Alamanni, who it seems ultimately absorbed the various peoples once called Marcomanni and Quadi, were sometimes confused with them in the sources.

24. L. Bakker 1993; important passages for our discussion are lines 3–4, "ob barbaros gentis Semnonum sive Iouthungorum"; and, of the assembled Roman forces, lines 6–8, "fugatosque a militibus provinciae Raetiae sed et Germanicianis itemque popularibus." Dating is based upon the last line, "Postumo Augusto et Honaratiano consulibus." Because Postumus is known to have held a second consulship in 261 and subsequent ones, none of which are noted on the Augsburg inscription, this must be his first consulship after declaring his usurpation, thus 260. Simplicinius is clearly acting governor (linel 1, "agens vices praesides"), not the governor, but at this point in Roman history officeholders who did not have the proper rank at the time of appointment might be *vices,* although there would have been no higher authority in the province. The inscription makes it clear that the Roman soldiers involved were not units of the Roman army, but for a different reading see J. Mackensen 1999, 200. Barbarians with the name Semnones are earlier recorded in Tacitus, *Germania,* 39.
25. This *villa rustica* at Regensburg-Harting also reveals the dependence of such farms on major markets. Its construction went hand in hand with the establishment of the Third Italian Legion in Regensburg. See H. Bender 2001b, 1–4.
26. Later authors such as Sextus Aurelius Victor (361), the author of the *HA* (ca. 400), and Zosimus (writing after 410) typically used the names Alamanni or Scythians for these and later invaders. But it is clear from the fragments of Dexippus (ed. Jacoby) that these were some Iuthungi, and so that is what I have called them here.
27. Probably in 260, the second invasion of Italy in as many years. Zosimus, 1.37.2: the hastily assembled Senatorial force is still reported as being larger than that of the barbarians; for that of Gallienus, Zonaras, 12.24, perhaps from Dexippus, has Gallienus outnumbered by 30 to 1, but victorious nonetheless.
28. Sextus Aurelius Victor, *Liber de Caesaribus,* 33, trans. H. Bird.
29. Dexippus, in Jacoby, *Fragmente,* 2A, frag. 100, calling them Iuthungi; see further, L. Okamura, 1984, 286–90. *Paneg. Lat.* 8 [5].10.4. Writ-

ing in the late fourth century or early fifth century the anonymous biographer calls these invaders Marcomanni; *HA, Aurelian,* 18.4, destroying scattered bands; Zosimus, 1.49.1, calls them Alamanni. Surely Dexippus is to be preferred over the competition.

30. *Paneg. Lat.* 10 [2].10.3–4, trans. C. Nixon, in C. Nixon and B. Saylor Rogers 1994, 68–69. On Cniva, see T. Burns 1984, 26–27, and B. Gerov 1963, 138–39, and B. Gerov, 1977.
31. There was an early medieval tradition current around 600 in Avenches, Switzerland, that Alamanni under a certain Wibilus sacked their city (Fredegarius, *Chronicon* 4), but this seems to be but a late addendum made for local purposes. Their fourth-century political system is discussed in the next chapter.
32. For example, *Paneg. Lat.*, 10 [2].6.1.
33. Sextus Aurelius Victor, *Liber,* 41.3, calling him an Alamannic king, of course.
34. A. Bursche 1996, 67–95, 123–34. This work draws heavily upon the statistical analysis of the coins and their patterns of distribution and then places these findings alongside the third-century chronology as currently understood. The following discussion of third century coin hoards is largely based upon Bursche.
35. For example, Goths attacked (probably in 238) after Philip the Arab ceased paying their tribute (Jordanes, *Getica,* 89). Prior to this, their annual tribute had apparently set the standard for the lower Danube. The Carpi, who dominated a loose alliance that included Goths, demanded at least as much as the Goths from the governor of Moesia Inferior, Tullius Menophilus (Petrus Patricius, *Historiae,* frag.8, writing in the sixth century and probably using the now-lost Dexippus), see also T. Burns 1980, 12–19.
36. Most simply, the statistical analysis of a regular deposition of randomly available coins produces a bell curve in which the last coins so saved are poorly represented and chronologically fall close to the end of the "savings account." The oldest and newest coins in "the account" are rare statistically because their relative availability has been reduced: the first because their type has already been "saved" and so gradually withdrawn from circulation by others; the latter because the saving period has been short. This pattern is the result of the facts, first, that coins could be used as legal tender for generations during which some would remain in circulation and, second, that most people saved on a regular basis. Such a person today might regularly throw his loose change into a large jar and not take it to the bank for years. For numerous historical examples and a more rigorous explanation, see K. Harl 1996.
37. Similarly A. Bursche 1996, 136.

38. So as to remind us of the current relevance of these third-century decisions, note the debate as to the extent to which a Latin-speaking population remained in Dacia and so formed the linguistic basis of modern Romanian. Argument continues to be intense, particularly among Romanian and Hungarian scholars. The undeniable Latinity of the Romanian language has been asserted as proof that Romania always remained culturally a part of western Europe. Romanians have traditionally held that the survival of a substantial Romanized rural population provided the essential explanatory linguistic link, whereas non-Romanian scholars have pointed out the absence of romance language in the records there for centuries after the Roman abandonment and posit a medieval reintroduction. See A. Du Nay 1996. On the emergence of Gothic peoples as a major factor on the lower Rhine, see P. Heather 1996. On the Alamanni, see K. Fuchs 1997, particularly articles therein by K. Frank and D. Geuenich, which trace the consolidation of these people beyond the frontier and then their invasion and settlement. Although somewhat dated, see also R. Christlein 1978. On the survival of Romans and the continued use of Roman materials in the Agri Decumates, see K. Christ 1960, v. 1, pp. 143–47, and, more recently, K. Stribrny 1989, who tends to exaggerate their continuing importance.
39. *Anonymous Valesianus, pars* 1, 31; and Jordanes, *Getica,* 79.
40. L. Okamura 1984, 274, makes this attractive suggestion and summarizes the evidence; however, it seems to me more likely that these developments occurred after Maximianus's successful campaigns to clear the area, rather than earlier.
41. R. Wolters, 1990–91, pt. 1 (1990) 21–23; and pt. 2 (1991) 98.
42. B. Bridget 1981, 287–315. A short duration for warfare among barbarians remained the norm at least as late as the end of the fourth century, when Ammianus noted that typically they had fought a war and returned to peace before Romans ever knew there had been a disturbance, 31.4.3. The wide variety of western experience during the century is recently surveyed by C. Witschel 1999. Compare, for example, Britain with little disruption; North Africa with only some minor disturbances from bedouins, and the German provinces including Raetia, which experienced profound distress from invasion ca. 260 and again ca. 280.
43. On low-level banditry as a normal state of affairs in the empire, see R. Alston 1994b and B. Shaw 1984. On the third-century *Bagaudae,* J. Drinkwater 1984, who rejects the earlier view that these people were the lower classes in rebellion against oppression.
44. For comparison the inclusive dates should include the final years of Aurelian but stop at the death of Licinius in 324, after which the mas-

sive construction projects to create a second imperial capital at Byzantium-Constantinople would surely distort any results.

45. M. Todd 1978, 15–20, its name derived from the legendary Servius Tullius, whose true identity and dates were lost to later Romans. It was restored for the last time in the age of Marius. On the defensive works begun under Aurelius, see further Todd, 21–45.
46. Even as late as the sixth century, the coinage struck in the barbarian kingdoms still held to the Roman system. The Roman gold coin, the *solidus,* remained the standard unit and the linchpin of the monetary system. There was some experimentation on the depictions on silver coins, and bronze coins when struck at all revealed much more ingenuity. Nonetheless, all coinage remained within an essentially Roman system until the Carolingian reforms of the coinage system replaced gold at the center with silver. See B. Overbeck 1996, and the literature cited there.
47. A written Gothic was created by bishop Ulfilas in the late fourth century. It was, however, restricted in use to a translation of the Bible and other purely Christian documents and was employed only among those Goths living within the empire. This quite limited Gothic might be counted as a written barbarian language and thus as an exception to the statement here, but it occurred very late and for purely Roman-Christian purposes.
48. Given the extremely limited data at our disposal, even the outline offered here is tenuous. After the collapse of Roman urban and governmental systems in the fifth and sixth centuries, barbarian societies were able to combine segmented family lineage and military command to fashion lasting political systems; see, for example, T. M. Charles-Edwards 1972, for the early Anglo-Saxons. Britain provides good examples since by the sixth century Roman urban civilization had disappeared.
49. For the literary references to Probus's settlements, see G. de Ste. Croix 1981, 512; M. Mackensen 1999, 203–22, for archaeological data from Raetia revealing that Diocletian should get credit there for the rebuilding of the fortifications. The area called the Agri Decumates corresponds closely to the modern German state of Baden-Württemberg.
50. *Paneg. Lat.,* 8 [4].9.3–4, trans. C. Nixon, in C. Nixon and B. Saylor Rogers 1994, 121–22, with commentary. The Chamavi and Frisians may have backed the British usurper Carausius and so merited special humiliation.
51. *Paneg. Lat.,* 8 [4].21.1–2. The setting for this speech is northern Gaul. This is the earliest recorded notice of *laeti,* although it is indicated that the first settlement of these barbarians as such had taken place sometime before, probably shortly after the foundation of the Tetrarchy. It

recognizes the Gallic victories of Maximianus Heraculius. "Maximiane Auguste, nutu Aruiorum et Treuvirorum arua iacentia Laetus postliminio restitutus et receptus in leges Francus excoluit." As Caesar, Constantius ruled the northern provinces of the coemperor Maximinus's western section of the empire under Diocletian's Tetrarchy.

52. *Paneg. Lat.*, C. Nixon and B. Saylor Rogers 1994, 122, n. 29.
53. *Paneg. Lat.*, 8 [4].5.2 and 8 [4].10.4. C. Nixon and B. Saylor Rogers 1994, 116, n. 17, and 125, n. 35, with bibliographies, for the "afterlife" of the Carpi and Carpodacae, as those remaining outside the empire were called. G. Bichir 1976 gathers together all data on the Carpi.
54. P. Bastien 1989.
55. *Paneg. Lat.*, 10 [2].5.2, trans C. Nixon, in C. Nixon and B. Saylor Rogers 1994, 62.
56. *Paneg. Lat.*, 6 [7].6.3–4, trans C. Nixon, in C. Nixon and B. Saylor Rogers 1994, 226. Constantius was emperor, Augustus in 305–6, thus his new title.
57. Ammianus Marcellinus, 31.10.5.
58. *Paneg. Lat.*, 11 [3].17.3; earlier as allies, 10 [2].5.1, and for the quotation, 11 [3].18.3; trans. C. Nixon, in C. Nixon and B. Saylor Rogers 1994, 101.
59. *HA, Probus,* 14.7, otherwise the source is filled with elements of traditional panegyric, which by the end of the fourth century included as canonical the turning of warlike barbarians into farmers, 15.3–4; defeated many times, 18.2. On the *HA, Probus* and its many elements borrowed from late fourth-century panegyric, especially that of Symmachus to Valentinian I delivered in 370, see E. Norden 1962, pp. 31–37, whose skeptical reading of the *HA, Probus* has been recently vindicated archaeologically (see M. Mackensen, 1999). In this case, however, the depiction in the *HA* of the handling of barbarian recruits is useful, although technically anachronistic, because all other evidence confirms that the policy already existed prior to the third century and did not change until the reign of Theodosius I (379–95) and then only partially. The fifth-century *Notitia dignitatum, or.* 28.25, attests to the existence of the eighth unit of Vandalic cavalry ("ala octaua Vandilorum"); the other seven are absent from the list, presumably having been disbanded by the date of composition of the *Notitia dignitatum* (ca. 400). On this very challenging document, see T. Burns 1994, 98–99, 149. There is no way to determine when these Vandalic units were raised, and the 8th could have been incorporated as early as under Probus or the tetrarchs, who are known to have fought some Vandals in Raetia and elsewhere (e.g., Zosimus, 1.68; and *Paneg. Lat.*, 11 [3].17.1). On the settlement and dispersal system used on the middle Danube during the third and

fourth centuries, see L. Barkóczi 1959, but with caution as to the precise ethnic identifications of grave finds.

60. S. Dušek 1992, v. 1, pp. 137–51.

Chapter 7. Barbarians and the Late Roman Empire

1. A. Jones 1964, 366–410, remains fundamental for the bureaucratic structure. On the late Roman army in general, see H. Elton 1996b, an indispensable work, long needed. There is no really adequate modern survey in English of the West in late antiquity, as Av. Cameron 1993, provides for the East. The most detailed survey by a single author for the entire era in any language is A. Demandt 1990; Av. Cameron, B. Ward-Perkins, and M. Whitby 2001, offer the latest collective effort.
2. B. Overbeck 2000, on the medallion and influence in numismatic representation during the subsequent two centuries, and still valuable, A. Alföldi 1932. The study of Christian conversion has entered a new phase as interdisciplinary approaches bear fruit; see T. Burns and J. Eadie 2001, 265–379, for some new approaches. Constantinople did not get its major land walls until the middle of the fifth century; Trier's came about in the fourth.
3. On the functions of the *comites sacrarum largitionum,* see A. Jones 1964, 369–70, and the *Notitia dignitatum* (*oc.*11.1 and *or.*13.1).
4. J. Matthews 2000.
5. A tax survey could be initiated at other times by the emperor or his agents; for example, Julian did so to reassess taxes after civil war and invasions in Gaul, Ammianus, 17.3.1.
6. This had been the case in the third century as well, but for a fourth century example, see Ammianus, 26.5.7, in 365 and the Alamanni. Many of these great hoards have attracted scholarly debate, among the many discussants, T. Burns 1984, 41–49, 112–15, 139. Most emperors were very careful to provide the correct gifts for men of various ranks, and this can be seen in several hoards found in *barbaricum* with materials from their reigns. Theodosius's actions in this regard are frequently noted in the sources, T. Burns 1994, 65–67.
7. In addition to H. Schönberger 1969, see P. Brennan 1980, for their placement and military intensions.
8. Examples of roads and pathways in the Hungarian Plain were cited in Chapter 5. The situation was common at main points of exchange along the Rhine as well; for example, across from Mainz, Ammianus, 27.10.7. For their initial reception by barbarians, 28.2.6–9.
9. Gregorius Turonensis, *Historiae Francorum,* 2.9, quoting Sulpicius Alexander (bk. 4), a contemporary. It should be noted that Arbogast, like other Roman generals at this time, opted out of the competition

for the emperorship, but without their military backing no man could sit on the imperial throne for long.

10. J. Coulston 1990, 151.
11. With Julian, Ammianus, 20.4.4; the *barritus,* 26.7.17; by 378, Ammianus, 31.16.8.
12. *Codex Theodosianus,* 3.14.1, but it seems directed only at those involved with a Gothic incursion. See H. Sivan 1996.
13. Ammianus, 26.5.7, in which the Alamanni protested Valentinian's reduction of Roman tribute payments. Also, Ammianus, 30.6.2, in which Quadic chiefs tell emperor Valentinian I that they should not be held responsible for bands raiding across the Danube from their area. Further examples of small raids are easily found; for example, 17.13.27; 27.2.1–2. When raiding in *barbaricum,* Romans too broke up into raiding parties, 27.5.4.
14. R. MacMullen 1963. For example, Gothic *asneis,* laborer for hire, and *kalkjo,* a woman companion. On the historical value of the Gothic Bible, see H. Wolfram 1975–76, and especially his book (1988, 112–16 and elsewhere). The 1988 publication is far and away the best treatment of Ulfilas and the Gothic language available in English. Much of the same material is repeated by Wolfram in 1997, 77–79. H. Elton 1996b, 41, on Romans, particularly deserters, living among barbarians in the early fifth century.
15. Ammiaus, 17.1.8, all within ten miles of the Rhine, but 29.4.5, Valentinian burning every Alamannic village with fifty miles of Trier. Obviously the great city attracted more barbarians than normal because of its markets.
16. Ammianus, 16.11.9 (on Julian). Zosimus, 4.11.3 (on Valentinian).
17. *Inscriptiones Latinae Selectae,* 771, dated to 367–75, noting separately and completely that the emperors Valentinian, Valens, and Gratian were each *Germanicus maximus* (conqueror of the Germans), *Alamannicus maximus, Francicus maximus,* and *Gothicus maximus.* In other words, each and together they have pacified all northern barbarians.
18. For Jovian's ceding of five areas (*regiones*) to the east of the Tigris and Roman region, Ammianus, 25.7.9. On Persian-Roman relations, see further R. Blockey 1984; and E. Chrysos 1976. Prior to Valens's reopening of hostilities there had been a long period of calm along the border with Persia, Ammianus, 30.2.1. Petty raids had always been a problem, however; Ammianus, 16.9.1.
19. Ausonius (his teacher), *Grat. Actio,* 2.8.
20. T. Burns 1994, 23–42, with a full discussion of the sources, problems, and secondary bibliography, to which must now be added M. Mackensen 1999. Throughout the current chapter, I have tried to go beyond the narrower chronological and thematic focus of *Barbarians*

within the Gates of Rome: A Study of Roman Military Policy and the Barbarians, ca. 375–425 A.D. in order to provide a broader synthesis. If readers wish greater detail concerning military events and barbarian policies during the five decades covered therein, they are invited to search within *The Gates.*

21. And greater than Scipio's victory over the Carthaginians; Ammianus, 17.1.14. Julian's success was superior for Ammianus, because it was obtained with vastly fewer losses to the legions. It seems that not even Julian claimed to have defeated all Alamanni, just several kingdoms. Like so many other barbarian group names, an author's use of "Alamanni" might imply virtually all barbarians; Ammianus, 20.4.1. The comparative clarity of Ammianus's depiction of the battle at Strasbourg as opposed to that of Adrianople probably derives from his presence at the former and absence at the latter. On the other hand at the strategic level, the events leading up to the battle of Adrianople were much more complex, and they are rather well reported by Ammianus; T. Burns 1994, 23–33.
22. For Alamanni as being exceptionally tall, see Ammianus, 16.12.47. His chapter on the Alans and Huns is surely the most famous and controversial ethnographic description in all of Roman historiography: Ammianus, 31.2; 31.3.8, see also T. Wiedemann 1986.
23. Ammianus, 14.10.1–3. Constantius was able to delegate command, a rare and important quality in this era, but did take the field against the barbarians early in his career (e.g., Ammianus, 14.10.1; 15.4.1–13). As Caesar, the barbarians in neighboring Gaul were Julian's business, but when he needed help, it was dispatched by his emperor Constantius in a timely manner.
24. Zosimus, 3.1–3, written during the fifth century from sources independent of Ammianus, trans. R. Ridley.
25. Ammianus, 16.12.63.
26. Ammianus, 16.3.1 and 4.2.
27. Ammianus, 16.11.4 and 26.5.12–13, with Germans and Alamanni as interchangeable terms. The eyewitness Ammianus was well aware that the *laeti* had a barbarian origin and lived on the Roman side of the Rhine, while some of their relatives stayed on the far bank, 20.8.13.
28. The revolt of Magnentius is not well served by the extant literature. The surviving portions of Ammianus begin just after his death. Zosimus provides a relatively lengthy narrative (2.43–53), noting his heavy use of barbarians (2.51.1) and Constantius's successful efforts to undo the usurper's alliances along the Rhine (2.53.3), but he gives no details except that Magnentius once lived among the *laeti.* Much of

what can be said about this very important usurpation has been assembled from scattered references in later sources and the study of his coinage; see J. Ŝaŝel 1971 and K. Shelton 1981–83.

29. K. Kraft 1978; Constans struck various issues of "hut-type" coinage portraying the *receptio* of barbarians as a Roman soldier leading a barbarian from within a hut and implicitly thus into the empire.
30. Zosimus, 4.16.4, gives as a cause for an invasion by some Sarmatians and Quadi in 374, the breaking of Roman promises and the killing of their king at a banquet (Ammianus, 29.6.5, says the guilty Roman was Marcellinus, *dux Valeriae*). Gothic loyalty to Constantine I and his dynasty resurfaced in support of Procopius, who claimed to be the heir to Constantius, during his revolt in 365 against the newly enthroned Valentinian and Valens: Ammianus, 26.6.11, 26.7.10, and 26.10.3.
31. Ammianus, 15.5.16; also death of supporters, 15.6, revealing that his usurpation attracted supporters of all backgrounds.
32. Ammianus, 16.10.1–3; Zosimus, 3.3. Normal recruitment of barbarians into all units, Ammianus, 31.16.8.
33. On barbarians in the civil wars of Theodosius and his dynasty, see T. Burns 1994, 92–111.
34. Ammianus, districts and regions, 15.4.1, 18.2.15; confederate structure, 16.12.25–26. By the fifth century the Alamanni were under one king, and the various components of the confederacy had established themselves in areas that carried their names throughout the Middle Ages and into modern times: for example, the Brisigavi (Breisgau) and the Raetorvarii (in or near Raetia, settling especially in the Riess area in central Bavaria).
35. Ammianus 17.10.1–10, on the Alamanni; on the Quadi, 17.12.21; on the Sarmatians, 17.12.9–12; on the Amicenses Sarmatians, 17.13.19. On the Goths living in former Dacia, see P. Heather 1991, 97–115; E. Thompson 1966, 43f.; T. Burns 1980, 36–37.
36. Ammianus, 16.12.60, hundreds of personal followers accompanying the king; supplying grain to the Romans by treaty, 17.1.13; providing the Romans with building materials for rebuilding the *limes* forts, 17.10.9; and pledging an annual levy of young men and slaves for the Romans, 17.13.3; territoriality of kings, 17.10.5, Hortarius. The Goths in former Dacia provide us with the best evidence for the internal workings of a barbarian confederacy.
37. Ammianus concerning the Alamanni in A.D. 369, 28.5.9. Kings and nobles at the forefront in battle, 16.12.49; dishonor to survive, 16.12.60; inability to stop or control the scope of the fighting, 16.12.17.
38. Burgundians, Ammianus, 28.5.14; *v. Saba* is translated in P. Heather

and J. Matthews, 1991, 109–17. This volume contains translations of all important martyrologies as well as the Gothic calendar and much else. Elders among the Limigantes, a peculiar group under the Sarmatians, Ammianus, 17.13.21; attempts at collective defense by bringing various units of a confederacy together against Romans; for example, Ammianus, 27.1.1 or 27.10.9–10. The latter reference is also a splendid example of barbarians madly charging Roman infantry, steadfast in their ranks.

39. For example, kin and family among the Sarmatians, Ammianus, 17.13.12. Fighting on foot among Alamannic poor, Ammianus, 16.12.34. So too almost all fighters at Adrianople on both sides were foot soldiers. Philological data from the extant Gothic language supply numerous examples of the importance of family and kindred.

40. The story of Vadomarius runs throughout much of the surviving books of Ammianus; for example, summarized at 18.2.16–18; his pact with Constantius, 16.12.17; and finally as a general against Shapur, 29.1.2. Other Alamannic chiefs were split off by diplomacy as well. See the career of Hortarius, who betrayed his fellow native leaders, 16.12.1, 17.10.5, and 18.2.13.

41. Ammianus, 30.7.11: Valentinian sends Burgundians against Alamanni. Earlier in the century, Constantine I seems to have tried the same tactic with Sarmatians and Goths, but the latter proved too powerful and so he had to commit his own forces; see *Anonymous Valesianus,* 1.31.

42. *Prosopography of the Later Roman Empire,* 1.539.

43. For example, the increasing use of inhumation among elite Alamannic burials seems to have derived from association with the Roman military; see K. Fuchs, 1997, 418–21.

44. Vegetius 2. 5, trans. N. Milner, who suggests, 35, n. 3, that the Christian element was probably added by Vegetius in accordance with the Christian hierarchy rather than actually being a part of the oath. After Theodosius came up against his bishops over his conduct, he became a zealot and would have been careful to make such a distinction between himself and god as we see in this alleged oath. The tenacity of soldiers to the gods of the emperor was a very serious matter, which, as we have seen, could lead to wholesale slaughter and annihilation of units preserving their allegiance to the gods of the old dynasty.

45. On *receptio,* Fritigern, and Adrianople, see T. Burns 1994.

46. *Anonymous Valesianus,* 31–32. On Constantine, T. Burns 1984, 32–33, and, more thoroughly, P. Heather 1991, 107–9, both drawing upon the same source as E. Thompson 1956. On the Roman acknowledgment that they had a duty to protect their clients, Ammianus, 23.2.1.

47. Ammianus, 26.5.7, tribute reassessment; 29.6.2, concern with Valentinian's building projects.
48. Ammianus, 27.5.7.
49. Slavers were encountered on the other side of the Rhine leading their chattels towards Roman markets in the course of one of Valentinian's raids in 372; Ammianus, 29.4.4. Galatian slavers were notorious in ferreting out the best deals, including by selling barbarians. In 362 Constantius allegedly commented that war against the Goths was unworthy and unnecessary. They were better left to the Galatian slavers; Ammianus, 22.7.8. At the end of the century, but with more poetic flair, Claudianus, *In Eutrop.* 1.59, speaks of lines of slaves being offered by the Galatians.
50. Ammianus, 31.4.7; 31.4.11.
51. The nature of barbarian settlement within the empire after 378, and especially after 418, is hotly debated. I have argued my rather traditional view that land in some form was required and provided in T. Burns 1994, 247–79. A radical reinterpretation was offered by W. Goffart 1980 and has won its followers, among them H. Wolfram 1988. The Goffart thesis substitutes land grants with a system of tax credits applied at the local level whereby the share of funds formerly extracted by the central government was redirected to support barbarians settled nearby. Any theory must somehow fit the barbarians into the late Roman tax system and its system of regular reassessment.
52. Ammianus, 29.6.1–11; contraforts on this section of the Danube, see A. Mócsy 1974b; on the watchtower of Hatvan-Gombospustza, lying sixty kilometers beyond the Danube, begun under Constantius, see S. Soproni 1974 and 1978, 81–85.
53. This bifunctionality is sometimes specifically acknowledged in building inscriptions. For example, *Inscriptiones Latinae Selectae,* v. 1, no. 775, ca. 370, commemorating the building of a small fort in Illyricum under Valentinian I: "hunc burgum, cui nomen Commercium, qua causa et factus est." In this case the fort (*burgum*) was named Trade Center (Commercium) and, as the inscription attests, was built and named in keeping with its dual roll along the frontier.
54. Ammianus, 17.13.22–24, provides a convenient example of both the relocation and appointment of a Roman supporter as king with the backing of all concerned. For Julian on the Rhine requisitioning but also realizing that he had good reason not to further invade the lands of those who had submitted, 18.2.3–7; Constantius's considerable difficulty in implementing a successful *receptio,* 19.11.10–13; forced recruitment under Valentinian, 30.6.1–6.
55. Ammianus, 18.2.15; 28.5.11 (Burgundians); 19.11.1 (Limigantes); Free Sarmatians, 17.12.17–20; 29.6.15.

56. Recent studies of the pottery discovered in several of these very lengthy walls in Slovakia and Hungary place them securely in the late Roman era, but hypotheses as to their purpose vary widely. Most scholars suggest some sort of defensive role, often in association with the Roman need to protect Pannonia and ultimately Italy; see T. Kolník 1999, 168–74. The suggestion that some of them may have also demarcated territory in accordance with Rome's designs for its clients is my own. On Athanaric, see Ammianus, 31.3.7: "Taifalorum terras praestringens, muros altius erigebat."
57. A. Cameron and J. Long 1993, 330–33.
58. On Themistius as philosopher, see J. Vanderspoel 1995 and also G. Dagron 1968.
59. See R. Brulet 1996 and E. James 1988. Childeric's burial and its accompanying grave goods together with the decidedly Christian text of Gregory of Tours (2.12 and 18) are marvelous examples of the integration of various elements of the late Roman world in northern Gaul, but they lie chronologically beyond the scope of the present book.
60. The literature on Sutton Hoo is vast and still growing; see R. Bruce-Mitford 1997. On chip carving as a peculiar frontier decorative form, G. Behrens 1930 and S. Hawkes 1961, remain fundamental. There is now a vast number of new finds that confirm their work.
61. H. Bullinger 1969. One of the clearest and most concise discussions of this particular decorative style and its long-term significance available in English is H. Böhme 1981.
62. Ammianus, 17.1.7.
63. K. Pieta and V. Plachá 1999, 183–87; and K. Elschek 1997, 121–23. The only securely identified Roman-style constructions in *barbaricum* found to date lie in Slovakia.
64. For an example of Roman construction materials used along the Main River, note the finds at Frankenwinheim in the valley of the Main, in D. Rosenstock 1984.
65. H. Bender 2001a, 191–92, with bibliography to recent literature for the frontier provinces from Belgica to Carnuntum.
66. On barbarian hilltop fortifications roughly between Mainz and Regensburg, see T. Burns 1994, 129–34; W. Menghin 1990, 50–60; for the area near Lake Constance, H. Steuer 1990; and for the uppermost Rhine valley, B. Overbeck 1973–82 and G. Schneider-Schnekenburger 1980.
67. H. Böhme 1974.
68. T. Burns 1994, 130–45. Some prominent archaeologists, but not all, have accepted the thesis advanced by H. T. Fischer and H. Geisler 1988, whereas others believe that the people with the peculiar cremation pot-

tery, given the heuristic label "Elbgermans" or "Elb-Alamannen," represent the migration of people with similar grave goods found in the area of the Elbe headwaters from much earlier times. As discussed on several occasions, determining a migration archaeologically is extremely difficult.

69. Ammianus, 31.5.10–17. Writing around 392, two years after the formal end of the Gothic wars, he and his audience knew that things had turned out well, but he was nonetheless constrained by the limits of his genre and so was precluded from writing of events of the current emperor. Instead, he inserted this short piece of retrospection as reassurance. He could set the stage for Theodosius's reign and he did. On the east-Germanic or Gothic elements, see especially E. Keller 1986. Regensburg is a particularly interesting example of a site no longer listed as having regular troops in the *Notitia,* but where the presence of Romanized-Germanic troops cannot be doubted. The burial of a man dressed much like a Roman officer at this late date is highly suggestive; see T. Burns 1994, 144–45 with references.
70. H. Bender 2001a, 192, and 2002; and E. Keller 1995–96, 157–58.
71. R. Brulet 1990.
72. Z. Visy 2001, 166–71, also noting that the wheat type, triticum dicocum Schrank, normally found only in *barbaricum,* because its rough qualities were not previously appreciated by Roman troops, now appears for the first time inside Roman camps. The soil in this area does not yield pollen as do bog deposits, but burned seeds found on these sites leave no doubt as to the fact that cereal crops were being consumed in the food supply.
73. Z. Visy 2001, 174–80.
74. For example, *magister militum* (503–20) and consul (520) Vitalian, son of Patriciolus, was apparently a Goth despite the Latin names he and his father bore. He seems to have been very deliberate in naming his sons with non-Latin names, P. Amory 1997, 98, 435. On the use of names in this late period, see also P. Amory 1994. There are quite a few inscriptions from the second half of the fourth century on which some form of Goth occurs as a cognomen (e.g., *CIL* 8.23040).
75. The most famous probably being the ring of Omharus from Apahida in present-day Romania, J. Hampel 1905, I.58, II.42, III.taf.35.
76. A group of four inscriptions from Concordia in Italy dating to ca. 400 (O. Fiebiger and L. Schmidt 1917, no. 291–94) illustrates the straightforward use of Germanic names in the numerus Heruli seniores, a unit of the auxilia palatina, during the last quarter of the fourth century, as well as other units of the army stationed then in Italy, some formerly belonging to the eastern army. On this inscription, see R. Tomlin 1972.

The practice is also attested to in the *Notitia dignitatum, occ.* 5.162, 7.13. Also, O. Fiebiger and L. Schmidt 1917, nos. 316–20, and no. 317, "Adabrandus primerius scutariorum scolae secundae."

77. Ammianus, 31.16.8.
78. W. Schulze 1933, 56–58, has assembled more than examples from the third and fourth centuries. This picture also emerges from the Concordia inscriptions. There are numerous other examples available, to give but two *CIL* 12.2444 and *CIL* 8.23040.
79. *CIL* 6.10951.
80. Sons of veterans getting early promotions, decried in *Codex Theodosianus,* 7.22.1–11; and especially those of officers Sulpicius Severus, *Vita s. Martini,* 2.2. For examples of nonethnic networks within the army, see D. Woods, 1995.
81. This is precisely the response we might anticipate given the isolation and inferior role of most new recruits; see especially the interpretation of this type of restricted display and the problems associated with using archaeology in ethnography in S. Shennan, 1989.
82. Herodian, *Historia,* 4.7.2–3.
83. For the Alamanni, see Ammianus, 16.12.36. On Gothic hair, contrast their language for their hairstyle (*capilli,* cut short) with the scenes of their submission on the obelisk commemorating his victory set up in the hippodrome of Constantinople by Theodosius in 390; see J. Geyssen 1998 and B. Kiilerich 1998. On Vandal hair, see Victor Vitensis, *Historia persecutiones Wandalicae,* 2.8–9.
84. See, for example, "Germans" in S. Thernstrom 1980, 406, 415–16, 422–23.
85. For example, O. Handlin 1946, chs. 6–7, and his 1973, most succinctly, p. 165.
86. This consolidation of *thiudans* in Athanaric's family has been suggested by P. Heather 1991, and H. Wolfram 1988, but certainty is beyond reach given the evidence. The entire question of Gothic identity is reviewed and candidly discussed by P. Heather in Heather 1999, 41–72.
87. Ammianus, 28.5.14.
88. The extremely sparse data that exist are assembled in J. de Vries 1969; but a good place to begin is M. Todd 1992, 104–21.
89. H. Wolfram 1988, 75–85.
90. For a translation of the *v. Saba,* see P. Heather and J. Matthews 1991; on Saba and the persecution, P. Heather 1991, 81–82, 103–6; and in general, M. Todd 1992, 121–24. Much effort has been expended on Saba and the conversion; see most recently A. Schwarcz 1999.
91. D. Riggs 2001, for examples drawn from mainly North Africa but with much wider ramifications. For snow, *v. Saba,* 4.3, but highly selective

weather was routinely associated with special holiness. On divination among the barbarians, see M. Todd, 1992.

92. For examples from Spain, see K. Bowes 2001. The tension between bishops in towns and holy men in the countryside was common throughout the empire and remained so for a long time; for example, that between Saint Nicholas of Sion and Philip, bishop of Myra in sixth-century Lycia (*Life of Saint Nicholas of Sion,* 53–58).
93. The significance and origins of Arianism among the Goths, particularly the Ostrogoths, has been cogently reinterpreted by P. Amory 1997. For the later Visigoths, see especially the various contributions in P. Heather 1999, in which issues of marriage, kinship, family, identity, the economy, and progressive conversion to Catholic orthodoxy among the Visigoths in Spain and southern Gaul are all discussed with the aid of contemporary sources, especially the proceedings of the sixth- and seventh-century church councils and the various legal codes beginning with that of Euric in the late fifth century.

Epilogue

1. In the settlement of 418 Constantius acted as commanding general of the Roman armies in the West for the shadowy emperor Honorius (395–423), in which capacity he had led the western empire since 411. Constantius died within months of his elevation as coemperor in 421. On some of the problems associated with fifth-century settlements, see T. Burns 1994, 247–79.
2. See especially W. Goffart 1988.
3. Ermanaric's suicide is reported in Ammianus Marcellinus, but this was unacceptable by the mid-sixth century, when Jordanes recorded the reworked version. The legend had only just begun its evolution; see C. Brady 1943.
4. On the Gothic Amali and Balthi lines and the myths associated with them, see H. Wolfram 1988, particularly, 30, 393 and 203.
5. There are a great many fine studies available today on the barbarian kingdoms. Among the most accessible not already cited in the notes to this book are E. Thompson 1982; I. Wood 1994; G. Ausenda 1995; R. Collins 1995; and W. Pohl and H. Reimitz 1998.
6. For Gaul, see R. Mathisen 1993.
7. On the role of lists in fashioning needed new identities, see Av. Cameron 1999, 5–8.
8. Priscus of Panion, frag. 39 (ed. L. Dindorf, 1.348); Jordanes, *Getica,* 197–213; 254–64. There is no shortage of work on Attila and the Huns, and the subject continues to fascinate. See E. Thompson 1948; O. Maenchen-Helfen 1973; G. Wirth 1999. On the site and battle of the Catalaunian Fields, see U. Tächholm 1969.

9. *Inscriptiones Latinae Christianae Veteres,* v. 1, no. 1516, p. 290, and O. Fiebiger and L. Schmidt 1917, no. 116.
10. Gregorius of Turonensis, *Historiae Francorum,* 2.30–33, on Clovis and Constantine; and the *Anonymous Valesianus, pars* 2, 95, on Theodoric and Arius.
11. On such "barbarian" brigands, see, for example, J. Ŝaŝel 1979. For Ostrogothic uses of the term barbarian, see the Edictum (ca. A.D. 500), especially 32 ("barbaris, quos certum est reipublicae militare") but note also the Prologue and 34, 89, 107, and 145. On this important source and its ideological significance, see P. Amory 1997, 78–85. The *Edictum* in this regard expressed in legal terms a general feeling also attested to in other sources.
12. R. Sullivan 1960, pp. 47–52.
13. M. McCormick, 2001, 42, noting that the economic infrastructure began to reflect significant change in the first quarter of the fifth century throughout most of the western empire, not just in transportation but as metal production ended at site after site.
14. For example, a certain Evanthius was credited with having made road repairs in Aquitania I in 469. He was probably the provincial governor, *Prosopography of the Later Roman Empire,* 2.403. Praetorian prefects for Gaul are known throughout the century as well, although at some point early in the century their headquarters apparently moved from Trier to Arles.
15. On Flavius Merobaudes, F. Clover 1971. For royal ancestry, *CIL* 13.3682, Trier, ca. 400–425: "Hariulfus protector domesitigus filius Hanhavaldi regalis gentis Burgundionum. . . . Reudilo avunculus ipsius fecit." This is but one of many possible examples chosen here because of the obvious bragging about the rank of the family among the Burgundians.
16. F. Curta 2001.

Bibliography

Primary Sources

Agathias. *Historiae (Historiarum Libri Quinque)*. Edited by R. Keydell. *CFHB*, v. 2. Berlin, 1967.

Ammianus Marcellinus. *Roman History*. Loeb edition. Translated by J. Rolfe. Cambridge, MA, 1935–40.

Anonymous Valesianus. Excerpta Valesiana. In Ammianus Marcellinus, *Roman History*, Loeb edition, v. 3. Translated by J. Rolfe. Cambridge, MA, 1935–40.

Appian (Appianos of Alexandria). *Roman History* (Romaika): *The Surviving Fragments*. Loeb edition. Translated by H. White. Cambridge, MA, 1912.

Aurelianus, Caelius. *On Acute Diseases; and On Chronic Diseases*. Edited and translated by I. Drabkin. Chicago, 1950.

Ausonius, Decimus Magnus. *The Works of Ausonius*. Edited with introduction and commentary by R. P. H. Green. Oxford, 1991.

Caesar, Julius. *Bellum Gallicum*. Loeb edition. Translated by H. Edwards. Cambridge, MA, 1917.

Caesarius Arelatensis. *Opera*. Edited by G. Morin. Turnholti, 1937–42.

Cassius Dio. *Historia Romana*. Loeb edition. Translated by E. Cary. New York, 1914–25.

Cicero. *Opera*, v. 28, *Letters to His Brother Quintus and Others*. Loeb edition. Translated by M. Henderson. Cambridge, MA, 1989.

Claudianus, Claudius. *Carmina*. Loeb edition. Translated by M. Platnauer. Cambridge, MA, 1922.

Codex Theodosianus. Edited by P. Krüger. Berlin, 1923–26.

Corpus inscriptionum graecarum. Edited by A. Boeckhius et al. Berlin, 1828–.

Corpus inscriptionum latinarum consilio et auctoritate Academie litterarum regiae Borussicae editum . . . Berlin, 1862–.

Corpus scriptorum ecclesiasticorum Latinorum. Edited by Hoelder-Pichler-Tempsky. Kaiserl. Akad. der Wissenschaften in Wien. Vienna, 1866–.

Digesta. Digesta seu Pandectae (by Emperor Justinian). Edited by Th. Mommsen. Berlin, 1870.

Diodorus Siculus. *Historicus.* Loeb edition. Translated by F. Walton, Cambridge, MA, 1933.

Edictum Theodorici Regis. Edited by F. Bluhme. In *Monumenta Germaniae Historica, Legum,* v. 5. Hanover, 1875–89.

Florus, Lucius Annaeus. *Epitome rerum romanarum.* Loeb edition. Translated by J. Rolfe. Cambridge, MA, 1929.

Fredegarius. *Chronicon: The Fourth Book of the Chronicle of Fredegar with Its Continuations.* Edited and translated by J. M. Wallace-Hadrill. London, 1960.

Frontinus, Julius. *Strategemata.* Loeb edition. Translated by C. Herschel and M. McElwain. Cambridge, MA, 1980.

Gellius, Aulus. *Noctes Atticae.* Loeb edition. Translated by J. Rolf. Cambridge, MA, 1927.

Gregorius Turonensis. *Historiae Francorum.* Edited and translated by R. Buchner. In *Gregor von Tours: Zehn Bücher Geschichten.* 2d ed. Berlin, 1967.

Herodianus. *Historia.* Loeb edition. Translated by C. R. Whittaker. Cambridge, MA, 1969–70.

Herodotus. *History.* Loeb edition. Translated by A. Godley. Cambridge, MA, 1963–69.

Historia Augusta (Scriptores Historiae Augustae). Loeb edition. Translated by D. Magie. Cambridge, MA, 1921–32.

Inscriptiones Latinae Christianae Veteres. Edited by E. Diehl. Zurich, 1925. Reprint 1967–70.

Inscriptiones Latinae Selectae. 3d ed. Originally edited by H. Dessau. Berlin, 1963.

Jacoby, F. *Die Fragmente der griechischen Historiker.* Berlin, 1923–58.

Jordanes. *Romana et Getica.* Edited by Th. Mommsen. In *Monumenta Germaniae Historica, Auctores Antiquissimi,* v. 5. Berlin, 1882.

The Life of Saint Nicholas of Sion. Edited and translated by I. Ševčenko and N. Patterson Ševčenko. Brookline, 1984.

Livy. *Titi Livi ab urbe condita libri.* Loeb edition. Translated by B. Foster. Cambridge, MA, 1919–59.

Lucian of Samosata (Lucianus Samosatensis Satiricus). *Opera.* Edited by K. Jacobitz. Leipzig, 1836. Reprint 1966.

Museum Veronense, hoc est Antiquarum inscriptionum atque anaglyphorum collectio. Edited by F. Maffei. Verona, 1749.

Notitia dignitatum. Edited by O. Seeck. Frankfurt, 1876.

Orosius, Paulus. *Historiarum adversum paganos libri vii.* Edited by C. Zangemeister. *CSEL,* v. 5. Vienna, 1882.

Panegyrici Latini. In Praise of Later Roman Emperors: The Panegyrici Latini. Introduction, translation, and historical commentary, with the Latin text of R. A. B. Mynors. Translation and comments by C. Nixon and B. Saylor Rogers. Berkeley, 1994.

Panégyriques Latins. Edited and translated by E. Galletier. Collection G. Budé. Paris, 1949–55.

Paulys-Wissowa. Realencyclopädie der klassischen Altertumswissenschaft. Edited by G. Wissowa et al. Stuttgart, 1877–.

Petrus Patricius. *Historiae.* Edited by C. Müller. In *Fragmenta Historicorum Graecorum,* v. 4. Paris, 1883.

Plinius. *Naturalis Historia.* Loeb edition. Translated by H. Rackham and W. Jones. Cambridge, MA, 1938–63.

Plutarchus. *Lives.* Loeb edition. Translated by B. Perrin. Cambridge, MA, 1920.

Polybius. *The Histories.* Loeb edition. Translated by W. R. Paton. Cambridge, MA, 1976–80.

Posidonius. The Fragments. Edited with commentary by L. Edelstein and I. Kidd. Cambridge, 1972–99.

Priscus of Panion. *Fragmenta.* In *Historici Graeci Minores.* Teubner edition. Edited by L. Dindorf. Leipzig, 1870.

Prosopography of the Later Roman Empire. Edited by J. Martindale et al. Cambridge, 1971–92.

Quellen zur Geschichte der Alamannen. Quellen zur Geschichte der Alamannen von Cassius Dio bis Ammianus Marcellinus. Edited and translated by C. Dirlmeier and G. Gottlieb. Kommission für Alamannische Altertumskunde, Schriften v. 1. Sigmaringen, 1976.

Res gestae divi Augusti: The Achievements of the Divine Augustus. Introduction and commentary by P. Brunt and J. Moore. Oxford, 1988.

Roman Imperial Coinage. 1st and 2d eds. Edited by H. Mattingly, E. Sydenham, and since 1966 by R. Carson and C. Sutherland. London, 1923–.

Roman Republican Coinage. Edited by M. Crawford. Cambridge and New York, 1987.

Sallust. *The Histories.* Loeb edition. Translated by J. Rolfe. Cambridge, MA, 1965.

Sextus AureliusVictor. *Liber de Caesaribus.* Translation and introduction by H. Bird. Liverpool, 1994.

———. *Liber de Caesaribus praecedunt Origo gentis Romanae et Liber de viris illustribus urbis Romae subsequitur Epitome de Caesaribus*. Teubner edition. Edited by F. Pichlmayr. Leipzig, 1970.

Strabo. *The Geography*. Loeb edition. Translated by H. Jones. Cambridge, MA, 1923.

Suetonius. *Lives of the Caesars*. Translated with an introduction and notes by C. Edwards. Oxford, 2000.

Sulpicius Severus. *Chronicon*. Edited by C. Halm. *CSEL*, v. 1. Vienna, 1866.

———. *Vie de Saint Martin*. Editions du Cerf. Edited and translated with an introduction by J. Fontaine. Paris, 1967–69.

Tabula Imperii Romani, L-34 Budapest. Amsterdam, 1968.

Tacitus, Cornelius. *The Complete Works of Tacitus*. Translated by M. Hadas. New York, 1942.

———. *Germania*. Loeb edition. Translated by M. Hutton and revised by E. Warmington. Cambridge, MA, 1970.

———. *Opera (Tacitus, in five volumes)*. Loeb edition. Translated by W. Heinemann. Cambridge, MA, 1979–89.

Vegetius (Flavius Vegetius Renatus). *Epitome of Military Science*. Translated by N. Milner. Liverpool texts, v. 16. 1996.

Velleius Paterculus. *Historiae Romanae*. Loeb edition. Translated by F. Shipley. Cambridge, MA, 1924.

Vergil. *The Aenid*. Translated by Robert Fitzgerald. New York, 1983.

———. *Opera*. Loeb edition. Translated by H. Rushton Fairclough. Cambridge, 1916. Revised 1934.

Victor Vitensis. *Historia persecutionis Wandalicae*. Edited by C. Halm. In *Monumenta Germaniae Historica, Auctores Antiquissimi*, 3.1. Berlin, 1879.

Zonaras. *Epitome historiarum*. Edited by T. Büttner-Wobst. In *Corpus Scriptorum Historiae Byzantinae*, v. 50. Bonn, 1897.

Zosimus. *Historia Nova*. Text established and translated by F. Paschoud. Collection G. Budé. Paris, 1971–89.

———. *The New History*. Translation and commentary by R. Ridley. Byzantina Australiensia, v. 2. Sydney, 1982.

Secondary Sources

Adams, W., D. Gerven, and R. Levy. 1978. "The Retreat from Migrationism." *Annual Reviews in Anthropology* 7:483–532.

Alföldi, A. 1932. "The Helmet of Constantine with the Christian Monogram." *Journal of Roman Studies* 22:3–23.

Alföldy, G., B. Dobson, and W. Eck, eds. 2000. *Kaiser, Heer und Gesellschaft in der Römischen Kaiserzeit: Gedenkschrift für Eric Birley*. Stuttgart.

Allen, J. 1975. *Passage through the Garden: Lewis and Clark and the Image of the American Northwest*. Urbana.

Alston, R. 1994a. "Roman Military Pay from Caesar to Diocletian." *Journal of Roman Studies* 84:113–23.

———. 1994b. "Violence and Social Control in Roman Egypt." In *Proceedings of the 20th International Congress of Papyrologists, Copenhagen, 23–29 August 1992*, pp. 517–21. Edited by A. Bülow-Jacobsen. Copenhagen.

Amory, P. 1994. "Names, Ethnic Identity and Community in Fifth- and Sixth-Century Burgundy." *Viator* 25:1–30.

———. 1997. *People and Identity in Ostrogothic Italy, 489–554*. Cambridge.

Ausenda, G., ed. 1995. *After Empire: Towards an Ethnology of Europe's Barbarians*. Woodbridge, England, and Rochester, NY.

Badian, E. 1958. *Foreign Clientelae (264–70 BC)*. Oxford.

Bakker, L. 1993 "Raetia unter Postumus—das Siegesdenkmal einer Juthungenschlacht im Jahre 260 n. Chr. aus Augsburg." *Germania* 71:369–86.

Bálek, M., and O. Ŝedo. 1994. "Neue Forschungsergebnisse in Muŝov (Rettungsgrabungen beim Bau der Autobahn Mikulov-Brno, Juli–November 1993)." In *Markomannenkriege: Ursachen und Wirkungen*, pp. 167–72. Edited by H. Friesinger, J. Tejral, and A. Stuppner. Brno.

Barkóczi, L. 1959. "Transplantations of Sarmatians and Roxolans in the Danube Basin." *Acta Antiqua* 7:443–53.

Barrett, J., A. Fitzpatrick, and L. Macinnes, eds. 1989. *Barbarians and Romans in North-West Europe: From the Later Republic to Late Antiquity*. London.

Barth, F. 1969. *Ethnic Groups and Boundaries: The Social Organization of Culture Difference*. London.

Bastien, P. 1989. *Le Médallion de plomb de Lyon*. Numismatique romaine. Essais, recherches et documents, v. 18. Wetteren.

Beck, H., ed. 1989. *Germanenprobleme in heutiger Sicht*. Berlin.

Behrens, G. 1930. "Spätrömische Kerbschnittschnallen." In *Schumacher-Festschrift*, pp. 285–94. Edited by the Römisch-Germanischen Zentralmuseum Mainz. Mainz.

Bell, M. 1995. "People and Nature in the Celtic World." In *The Celtic World*, pp. 145–58. Edited by M. Green. London.

Bender, H. 2001a. "Archaeological Perspectives on Rural Settlement in Late Antiquity in the Rhine and Danube Areas." In *Urban Centers and Rural Contexts in Late Antiquity*, pp. 185–98. Edited by T. Burns and J. Eadie. East Lansing.

———. 2001b. "Bauliche Gestalt und Struktur römischer Landgüter in den nordwestlichen Provinzen des Imperium Romanum." In *Landwirtschaft im Imperium Romanum*. Edited by P. Herz and G. Waldherr. *Pharos*, 14:1–40. Espelkamp.

———. 2002. *Die römische Siedlung von Weßling-Frauenwiese. Unter-*

suchungen zum ländlichen Siedlungswesen während der Spätantike in Raetien. Passauer Universitätsschriften zur Archäologie 7. Rahden.

Bender, H., and H. Wolff, eds. 1994. *Ländliche Besiedlung und Landwirtschaft in den Rhein-Donau- Provinzen des Römischen Reiches.* Passauer Universitäts Schriften zur Archäologie, v. 2. Espelkamp.

Berger, A. 1953. *Encyclopedic Dictionary of Roman Law.* Philadelphia.

Bichir, G. 1976. *Archaeology and History of the Capri from the Second to the Fourth Century A.D.* BAR, supp. ser. 16. Oxford.

Birley, A. 1987. *Marcus Aurelius: A Biography.* Rev. ed. New Haven and London.

———. 1989. *Septimius Severus: The African Emperor.* New Haven and London.

Blázquez, J. M. 1996. *España romana.* Madrid.

Blockley, R. 1982. "Roman-Barbarian Marriages in the Late Empire." *Florilegium* 4:63–79.

———. 1984. "The Romano-Persian Peace Treaties of A.D. 299 and 363." *Florilegium* 6:28–49.

Böhme, H. 1974. *Zur Chronologie germanischer Grabfunde des 4. bis 5. Jahrhunderts zwischen unterer Elbe und Loire.* Münchner Beiträge zur Vor-u. Frühgeschichte, 19. Munich.

———. 1975. "Archäologische Zeugnisse zur Geschichte der Markomannenkriege (166–180 n. Chr.)." *Jahrbuch des Römisch-Germanischen Zentralmuseum Mainz* 22:153–217.

———. 1981. "Comments on Nordic Animal Style—Background and Origin of Continental Aspects." *Norwegian Archaeological Review* 14:123–31.

Bowersock, G., et al., eds. 1999. *Late Antiquity: A Guide to the Post-Classical World.* Cambridge and London.

Bowes, K. 2001. ". . . Nec sedere in villam; Villa Churches, Rural Piety and the Priscillianist Controversy." In *Urban Centers and Rural Contexts in Late Antiquity,* pp. 323–48. Edited by T. Burns and J. Eadie. East Lansing.

Bowman, A. 1994. *The Vindolanda Writing-Tablets (Tabulae Vindolandensis II).* London.

Brady, C. 1943. *The Legends of Ermanaric.* Los Angeles.

Braudel, F. 1967. *Civilisation matérielle et capitalisme, XVe–XVIIIe siècle.* Paris.

Braund, D. 1984. *Rome and the Friendly King: The Character of the Client Kingship.* London.

Brennan, P. 1980. "Combined Legionary Detachments as Artillery Units in Late Roman Danubian Bridgehead Dispositions." *Chiron* 10:553–67.

Bridget, B. 1981. "The Aeduan Area in the Third Century." In *The Roman*

West in the Third Century, v. 1, pp. 287–315. BAR, int. ser. 109. Edited by A. King and M. Henig. Oxford.

Bruce-Mitford, R. 1997. *The Sutton Hoo Ship Burial: A Handbook.* 3d ed. London.

Brulet, R. 1990. *La Gaule septentrionale au Bas-Empire. Occupation du sol et défense du territoire dans l'arrière-pays du Limes aux IVe et Ve siecle.* Trierer Zeitschrift, Beiheft 11. Trier.

———, ed. 1996. *Die Franken: Wegbereiter Europas vor 1500: König Chlodwig und seine Erben.* Mainz.

Brunner, K., and B. Merta, eds. 1994. *Ethnogenese und Überlieferung: angewandte Methoden der Frühmittelalterforschung.* Vienna.

Brunt, P. 1988. *The Fall of the Roman Republic and Related Essays.* Oxford and New York.

Buckland, W., and A. McNair. 1965. *Roman Law and Common Law: A Comparison in Outline.* Cambridge.

Bullinger, H. 1969. *Spätantike Gürtelbeschläge: Typen, Herstellung, Trageweise und Datierung.* Brugge.

Burnham, B. 1995. "Celts and Romans. Towards a Romano-Celtic Society." In *The Celtic World,* pp. 121–41. Edited by M. Green. London.

Burns, T. 1979. "The Barbarians and the *Scriptores Historiae Augustae.*" *Studies in Latin Literature and Roman History* 1:521–40. Collection Latomus, v. 164. Brussels.

———. 1980. *The Ostrogoths: Kingship and Society. Historia* Einzelschriften, 36. Wiesbaden.

———. 1981. "The Germans and Roman Frontier Policy (ca. A.D. 350–378)." *Arheološki Vestnik* 32:390–404.

———. 1984. *A History of the Ostrogoths.* Bloomington.

———. 1994. *Barbarians within the Gates of Rome: A Study of Roman Military Policy and the Barbarians, ca. 375–425 A.D.* Bloomington.

Burns, T., and J. Eadie, eds. 2001. *Urban Centers and Rural Contexts in Late Antiquity.* East Lansing.

Bursche, A. 1996. *Later Roman-Barbarian Contacts in Central Europe, the Numismatic Evidence. Spätrömische Münzfunde aus Mitteleuropa: ein Beitrage zur Geschichte der Beziehungen zwischen Rom und den Barbaricum im 3. u. 4. Jh. n. Chr.* Berlin.

Cameron, A., and J. Long. with L. Sherry. 1993. *Barbarians and Politics at the Court of Arcadius.* Berkeley.

Cameron, Av. 1993. *The Mediterranean World in Late Antiquity, AD 395–600.* London and New York.

———. 1999. "Remaking the Past." In *Late Antiquity: A Guide to the Postclassical World,* pp. 1–20. Edited by G. Bowersock et al. Cambridge, MA.

Cameron, Av., B. Ward-Perkins, and M. Whitby, eds. 2001. *The Cambridge Ancient History,* v. 14, *Late Antiquity: Empire and Successors, AD 425–600.* 2d ed. Cambridge.

Carney, T. 1970. *A Biography of C. Marius.* Chicago.

Cesa, M. 1994. *Impero tardoantico e barbari: la crisi militare da Adrianopoli al 418.* Como.

Charles-Edwards, T. 1972. "Kinship, Status and the Origins of the Hide." *Past and Present* 56:3- 33.

Chauvot, A. 1998. *Opinions romaines face aux barbares au IVe siècle ap. J.C.* Paris.

Christ, K. 1960. *Antike Münzfunde Südwestdeutschlands.* Heidelberg.

Christlein, R. 1978. *Die Alamannen. Archäologie eines lebendigend Volkes.* 2d ed. Stuttgart.

Chrysos, E. 1973. "Gothia Romana: Zur Rechtlage des Föderatenlandes der Westgoten im 4. Jh." *Dacoromania* 1:52–64.

———. 1976. "Some Aspects of Romano-Persian Legal Relations." *Kleronomia* 8:1–48.

Chrysos, E., and A. Schwarcz, eds. 1989. *Das Reich und die Barbaren.* Vienna and Cologne.

Clover, F. 1971. "An Historical Commentary on and Translation of Flavius Merobaudes." *Transactions of the American Philosophical Society,* 61.1. Philadelphia.

Collins, R. 1995. *Early Medieval Spain: Unity in Diversity, 400–1000.* 2d ed. Basingstoke.

Collis, J. 1984. *Oppida: Earliest Towns North of the Alps.* Sheffield.

———. 1995. "The First Towns." In *The Celtic World,* pp. 159–75. Edited by M. Green. London.

Console, P., and R. Milns. 1983. "Neroian Frontier Policy in the Balkans: The Career of Ti. Plautius Silvanus." *Historia* 32:183–200.

Coulston, J. 1990. "Later Roman Armour, 3rd–6th Centuries A.D." *Journal of Roman Military Equipment Studies* 1:139–59.

Creighton, J., and R. Wilson, eds. 1999. *Roman Germany: Studies in Cultural Interaction. Journal of Roman Archaeology,* supp. ser. 32. Portsmouth, RI.

Crumley, C. 1974. *Celtic Social Structure: The Generation of Archaeologically Testable Hypotheses from Literary Evidence.* Ann Arbor.

Cunliffe, B., and T. Rowley, eds. 1976. *Oppida: The Beginnings of Urbanisation in Barbarian Europe.* BAR, supp. ser. 2. London.

Curchin, L. 1997. "Funerary Customs in Central Spain: The Transition from pre-Roman to Roman Practice." *Historia Antiqua. Revista de historia antiqua* 21:7–34.

Curta, F. 2001. "Peasants as 'Makeshift Soldiers for the Occasion': Sixth-Century Settlement Patterns in the Balkans." In *Urban Centers and Rural*

Contexts in Late Antiquity, pp. 199–217. Edited by T. Burns and J. Eadie. East Lansing.

Dagron, G. 1968. *L'Empire romain d'Orient au IVe siècle et les traditions politiques de l'hellénisme. Le témoignage de Thémistios.* Travaux et Mémoires, 3. Paris.

Dauge, Y. 1981. *Le barbare: Recherches sur la conception romaine de la barbarie et de la civilisation.* Collection Latomus, 176. Brussels.

Demandt, A. 1989. "The Osmosis of Late Roman and Germanic Aristocracies." In *Das Reich und die Barbaren,* pp. 75–86. Edited by E. Chrysos and A. Schwarcz. Vienna.

———. 1990. *Die Spätantike.* Munich.

Demougeot, E. 1978. "L'invasion des Cimbres-Teutons-Ambrons et les Romains." *Latomus* 37: 910–38.

Derks, T. 1998. *Gods, Temples and Religious Practices: The Transformation of Religious Ideas and Values in Roman Gaul.* Amsterdam Archaeological Studies, 2. Amsterdam.

Dietz, K. 1979. *Regensburg zur Römerzeit.* Regensburg.

Dornberg, J. 1992. "The Battle of the Teutoburg Forest." *Archaeology* 45: 26–32.

Drinkwater, J. 1983. *Roman Gaul: The Three Provinces, 58 BC–AD 260.* Ithaca.

———. 1984. "Peasants and Baguadae in Roman Gaul." *Echos du monde classique* 3:349–71.

———. 1987. *The Gallic Empire: Separatism and Continuity in the North-Western Provinces of the Roman Empire, A.D. 260–274.* Historia Einzelschriften, 52. Wiesbaden.

———. 1996. "The 'Germanic Threat on the Rhine Frontier': A Romano-Gallic Artefact?" In *Shifting Frontiers in Late Antiquity: Papers from the First Interdisciplinary Conference on Late Antiquity, the University of Kansas, March, 1995,* pp. 20–30. Edited by R. Mathisen and H. Sivan. Aldershot.

———. 1997. "Julian and the Franks and Valentinian I and the Alamanni: Ammianus on Romano-German Relations." *Francia* 24:1–15.

———. In press. "Maximus to Diocletian and the 'Crisis.'" In *Cambridge Ancient History,* v. 12. Cambridge.

Dumézil, G. 1977. *Les dieux souverains des Indo-Européens.* Paris.

Du Nay, A. 1996. *The Origins of the Rumanians: The Early History of the Rumanian Language.* 2d ed. Toronto and Buffalo.

Dušek, S. 1992. *Römische Handwerker im Germanischen Thüringen, Ergebnisse der Ausgrabungen in Harrhausen, Kreis Arnstadt.* Weimarer Monographien zur Ur- und Frühgeschichte, 27:1–2. Stuttgart.

Duval, P.-M. 1952. *La vie quotidienne en Gaule pendant la paix Romaine.* Rouen.

Dyson, S. 1984. *The Creation of the Roman Frontier.* Princeton.

Eadie, J. 1977. "Civitates and Clients: Roman Frontier Policies in Pannonia and Mauretania Tingitana." In *The Frontier: Comparative Studies,* pp. 57–80. Edited by D. Miller and J. Steffen. Norman, OK.

———. 1980. "Barbarian Invasions and Frontier Politics in the Reign of Gallienius." In *Roman Frontier Studies, 1979: Papers Presented to the 12th International Congress of Roman Frontier Studies,* pp. 1045–50. BAR, int. ser. 71. Edited by W. Hanson and L. Keppie. London.

———. 1996. "One Hundred Years of Rebellion: The Eastern Army in Politics, A.D. 175–272." In *The Roman Army in the East,* pp. 135–51. Edited by D. Kennedy. *Journal of Roman Archaeology,* supp. ser. 18. Ann Arbor.

Eggers, H. 1951. *Der römischen Import im Freien Germanien.* Atlas der Urgeschichte, v. 1. Hamburg.

Eisenstadt, S., and R. Lemarchand. 1981. *Political Clientism, Patronage and Development.* London.

Elliot, J. 1994. *Britain and Spain in America: Colonists and Colonized.* Reading.

Elschek, K. 1997. "Ein römischer Gebäudefund des 4. Jhs. aus Bratislava-Dúbravka." In *Neue Beiträge zur Erforschung der Spätantike im mittleren Donauraum: Materialen der Internationalen Fachkonferenz . . . Kravsko, 17.–20. Mai 1995,* pp. 121–25. Edited by J. Tejral, H. Friesinger, and M. Kazanski. Brno.

Elton, H. 1996a. *Frontiers of the Roman Empire.* Bloomington.

———. 1996b. *Warfare in Roman Europe, AD 350–425.* Oxford.

Evans, D. Ellis. 1967. *Gaulish Personal Names: A Study of Some Continental Celtic Formations.* Oxford.

Fentress, E., ed. 2000. *Romanization and the City: Creation, Transformations, and Failures. Proceedings of a Conference Held at the American Academy in Rome, 14–16 May 1998.* Portsmouth, RI.

Fiebiger, O., and L. Schmidt. 1917. "Inschriftensammlung zur Geschichte der Ostgermanen." *Denkscriften der kaiserlichen Akademie der Wissenschaften in Wien, philosophisch- historische Klasse,* v. 60, Abh. 3 (1917). Continued by Fiebiger alone in v. 70, Abh. 3 (1939) and v. 72 (1944).

Fischer, H., and H. Geisler. 1988. "Herkunft und Stammesbildung der Baiern aus archäologischer Sicht." In *Die Bajuwaren von Severin bis Tassilo 488–788,* pp. 61–68. Edited by H. Dannheimer. Munich.

Fitz, J. 1973. *Gorsium-Herculia-Tác.* Budapest.

Fried, M. 1961. "Warfare, Military Organization, and the Evolution of Society." *Anthropologica* 3:134–47.

———. 1975. *The Notion of Tribe.* Cummings.

Friesinger, H., J. Tejral, and A. Stuppner, eds. 1994. *Markomannenkriege: Ursachen und Wirkungen.* Brno.

Fuchs, K., ed. 1997. *Die Alamannen: Begleitband zur Ausstellung.* Stuttgart.

Fulford, M. 1989. "Roman and Barbarian: The Economy of Roman Frontier Systems." In *Barbarians and Romans in North-West Europe from the Later Republic to Late Antiquity,* pp. 81–95. Edited by J. Barrett. BAR, int. ser. 471. Cambridge.

Gabler, D., ed. 1989. *The Roman fort at Ács-Vaspuszta (Hungary) on the Danubian limes.* BAR, int. ser. 531. Oxford.

———. 1994. "Die landliche Besiedlung Oberpannoniens." In *Ländliche Besiedlung und Landwirtschaft in den Rhein-Donau-Provinzen des Römischen Reiches,* v. 2, pp. 377- 419. Passauer Universitäts Schriften zur Archäologie, 2. Edited by H. Bender and H. Wolff. Espelkamp.

Gabler, D., and A. Vaday. 1986. *Terra sigillata im Barbaricum zwischen Pannonien und Dazien.* Translated by Z. Fülep. Budapest.

Garnsey, P., and C. Whittaker, eds. 1983. *Trade and Famine in Classical Antiquity.* Cambridge.

Gayraud, M. 1981. *Narbonne antique des origines à la origines du IIIe siècle.* Paris.

Geary, P. 1999. "Barbarians and Ethnicity." In *Late Antiquity: A Guide to the Post-Classical World,* pp. 107–29. Edited by G. Bowersock et al. Cambridge and London.

Gerov, B. 1963. "Die gotische Invasion in Mösien und Thrakien unter Decius im Lichte der Hortfunde." *Acta Antiqua Philippopolitana, Studia histor. et philol. Serdicae* 4:127–46.

———. 1977. "Die Einfälle der Nordvölker in den Ostbalkanraum im Lichte der Münzschatzfunde. I. Das II. und III Jahrhundert (101–284)." *Aufstieg und Niedergang der römischen Welt,* II.6:110–81.

Geyssen, J. 1998. "Presentations of Victory on the Theodosian Obelisk Base." *Byzantion* 68:47–55.

Gibbon, E. 1776. *The Decline and Fall of the Roman Empire.* 6th ed., 1912. Edited by J. Bury. London.

Goffart, W. 1980. *Barbarians and Romans (A.D. 418–584): The Techniques of Accomodation.* Princeton.

———. 1988. *The Narrators of Barbarian History (A.D. 550–800).* Princeton.

Goudineau, C., and C. Peyre. 1993. *Bibracte et les Eduens à la découverte d'un peuple gaulois.* Paris.

Green, M., ed. 1995a. *The Celtic World.* London.

———. 1995b. "The Gods and the Supernatural." In *The Celtic World,* pp. 465–88. Edited by M. Green. London.

Hachmann, R. 1971. *The Germanic Peoples.* Translated by J. Hogarth. Geneva.

Hajnóczi, G., T. Mezös, M. Nagy, and Z. Visy, eds. 1998. *Pannonia Hungaria Antiqua.* Budapest.

Hamberg, P. 1945. *Studies in Roman Imperial Art with Special Reference to the State Reliefs of the Second Century.* Uppsala.

Hampel, J. 1905. *Altertümer des frühen Mittelatlters in Ungarn.* Braunschweig. Reprint 1971.

Handlin, O. 1946. *Boston's Immigrants.* Cambridge, MA. Reprint 1969.

———. 1973. *The Uprooted.* 2d ed. Boston.

Harl, K. 1996. *Coinage in the Roman Economy, 300 BC to AD 700.* Baltimore.

Haselgrove, C. 1987. "Culture Process on the Periphery: Belgic Gaul and Rome during the Late Republic and Early Empire." In *Centre and Periphery in the Ancient World,* pp. 104–24. Edited by M. Rowlands et al. Cambridge and New York.

Hawkes, C. 1977. *Pytheas: Europe and the Greek Explorers.* Oxford.

Hawkes, S. 1961. "Soldiers and Settlers in Britain, Fourth to Fifth Century. With a Catalogue of Animal-Ornamented Buckles and Related Belt-Fitings." *Medieval Archaeology* 5:1–71.

Haynes, I. 1993. "The Romanization of Religion in the Auxilia of the Roman Imperial Army from Augustus to Septimius Severus." *Britannia* 24:141–57.

Heather, P. 1991. *Goths and Romans, 332–489.* Oxford.

———. 1996. *The Goths.* Cambridge, MA.

———, ed. 1999. *The Visigoths from the Migration Period to the Seventh Century: An Ethnographic Perspective.* Studies in Historical Archaeoethnology, 4. Suffolk, UK, and Rochester, NY.

———. 2000. "The Late Roman Art of Client Management: Imperial Defense in the Fourth Century West." In *The Transformations of Frontiers from Late Antiquity to the Carolingians,* pp.15–68. Edited by W. Pohl, I. Wood, and H. Reimitz. Leiden, Boston, Cologne.

Heather, P., and J. Matthews. 1991. *The Goths in the Fourth Century.* Translated texts for Historians, 11. Liverpool.

Hedeager, L. 1987. "Empire, Frontier and the Barbarian Hinterland: Rome and Northern Europe from AD 1–400." In *Centre and Periphery in the Ancient World,* pp. 125–40. Edited by M. Rowlands et al. Cambridge and New York.

———. 1992. *Iron-Age Societies: From Tribe to State in Northern Europe, 500 BC to AD 700.* Translated by J. Hines. Oxford.

Hellebrandt, M. 1999. *Celtic Finds from Northern Hungary.* Corpus of Celtic Finds in Hungary, v. 3. Edited by T. Kovács, É. Petres, and M. Szabo. Budapest.

Hildebrandt, H.-J. 1994–99. "Das latènezeitliche Münzsystem im mittleren Europa." *Jahrbuch für Numismatik und Geldgeschichte,* pt. 1, 44 (1994) 35–77; pt. 2, 45 (1995) 7–27; pt. 3 and pt. 4, 48–49 (1998–99) 7–28.

Holder, P. 1980. *Studies in the Auxilia of the Roman Army from Augustus to Trajan.* BAR, int. ser. 70. London.

Horváth, L. 1987. *Transdanubia.* Corpus of Celtic Finds in Hungary, v. 1. Edited by T. Kovács, É. Petres, and M. Szabo. Budapest.

Iluk, J. 1985. "The Export of Gold from the Roman Empire to Barbarian Countries from the 4th to the 6th Centuries." *Münstersche Beiträge zur antiken Handelsgeschichte* 4:79–102.

James, E. 1988. *The Franks.* Oxford.

Jerem, E. 1995. "Celts in Eastern Europe." In *The Celtic World,* pp. 581–602. Edited by M. Green. London.

Jones, A. 1964. *The Later Roman Empire, 284–602: A Social, Economic and Administrative Survey.* Norman, OK.

Jones, S. 1997. *The Archaeology of Ethnicity: Constructing Identities in the Past and Present.* London.

Kajanto, I. 1982. *The Latin Cognomina.* Rome.

Kazanski, M. 1991. *Les Goths: (Ier–VIIe siècles ap. J.-C.).* Paris.

Keller, E. 1986. "Germanenpolitik Roms im bayerischen Teil der Raetia Secunda während des 4. und 5. Jahrhunderts." *Jahrbuch des R. G. Zentralmuseums Mainz* 33:575–92.

———. 1995–96. "Die urnenfelderzeitliche Siedlung und das spätrömische Kalbbrennerviertel in Unterhaching, Lkr. München." *Ber. Bayer. Bodendenkmalpfege* 36–37: 124–68.

Kiilerich, B. 1998. *The Obelisk Base in Constantinople: Court Art and Imperial Ideology.* Rome.

King, A., and M. Henig, eds. 1981. *The Roman West in the Third Century.* BAR, int. ser. 109. Oxford.

Kolník, T. 1999. "Gab es einen Limes Quadorum?—Langwälle in der Südwestslowakei." In *Germanen Beiderseits des Spätantiken Limes: Materialen des X. International Symposiums, "Grundprobleme der frühgeschichtlichen Entwicklung im nördlichen Mitteldonaugebiet, Xanten vom 2.–6. Dezember 1997."* pp. 165–177. Archäologisches Institut der Akademie der Wissenschaften der Tschechischen Republik, Spisy Archeologickeho av cr Brno, 14. Edited by T. Fischer, G. Precht, and J. Tejral. Cologne and Brno.

Kraft, K. 1978. "Die Taten der Kaiser Constans und Constantius II." In *Kleine Schriften,* v. 2, pp. 87–132. Darmstadt.

Krämer, W., gen. ed. 1955–. *Die Ausgrabungen in Manching.* Wiesbaden.

Kunow, J. 1985. "Zum Handel mit römischen Importen in der Germania libera." In *Untersuchungen zu Handel und Verkehr der vor- und frühgeschichtlichen Zeit in Mittel- und Nordeuropa,* pp. 430–50. Edited by K. Düwel et al. Göttingen.

Laffranque, M. 1964. *Poseidonios d'Apamée.* Publications de le faculté des lettres e sciences humaines de Paris, Série "Recherches," v. 13. Paris.

Laser, R., H.-U. Voss, and H. Geisler. 1994–. *Corpus der römischen Funde im europäischen Barbaricum.* Deutschland, v. 1–3, 1994–98. Bonn.

Law, R. 1992. "Warfare on the West African Slave Coast, 1650–1850." In *War in the Tribal Zone: Expanding States and Indigenous Warfare,* pp. 103–26. Edited by R. Ferguson and N. Whitehead. Sante Fe.

Le Bohec, Y. 1994. *The Imperial Roman Army.* London.

Lica, V. 2000. *The Coming of Rome in the Dacian World.* Translated by C. Patac and M. Neagu, revised by A. Birley. Konstanz.

Littman, R., and M. Littman. 1973. "Gallen and the Antonine Plague." *American Journal of Philology* 94:243–55.

Lopez, B. 1986. *Arctic Dreams: Imagination and Desire in a Northern Landscape.* New York.

Luiselli, B. 1992. *Storia culturale dei rapporti tra mondo romano e mondo germanico.* Rome.

Lund, A. 1988. *Germania.* Heidelberg.

Lund-Hanson, U. 1987. *Römischer Import im Norden, Warenaustausch zwischen dem Römischen Reich und dem freien Germanien während der Kaiserzeit unter besonderer Berücksichtigung Nordeuropas.* Copenhagen.

———. 1989. "Beyond the Roman Frontier." In *The Birth of Europe: Archaeology and Social Development in the First Millenium A.D.,* pp. 46–53. Analecta Romana Instituti Danici, supp. 16. Edited by K. Randsborg. Rome.

MacKendrick, P. 1957. "Roman Colonization and the Frontier Hypothesis." In *The Frontier in Perspective,* pp. 3–19. Edited by W. Wyman and C. Kroeber. Madison.

Mackensen, M. 1999. "Late Roman Fortifications and Building Programmes in the Province of Raetia: The Evidence of Recent Excavations and Some New Reflections." In *Roman Germany: Studies in Cultural Interaction,* pp. 109–244. Edited by J. Creighton and R. Wilson. Portsmouth, RI.

MacMullen, R. 1963. "Barbarian Enclaves in the Northern Roman Empire." *Antiquité classique* 32:552–61.

———. 1976. *Roman Government's Response to Crisis, A.D. 235–337.* New Haven.

Maenchen-Helfen, O. 1973. *The World of the Huns: Studies in Their History and Culture.* Berkeley.

Maier, F. 1986. "Vorbericht über die Ausgrabung 1985 in dem spätkeltischen Oppidum von Manching." *Germania* 64:1–43.

Mancini, G. 1933. "Iscrizione sepolcrale di Anversa." In *Atti del Convegno Storico Abruzzese- Molisano, 25–29 marzo 1931,* pp. 449–52. Edited by N. de Arcangelis. Casabordino.

Mathisen, R. 1993. *Roman Aristocrats in Barbarian Gaul: Strategies for Survival in an Age of Transition.* Austin.

Mattern, S. 1999. *Rome and the Enemy: Imperial Strategy in the Principate.* Berkeley.

Matthews, J. 2000. *Laying Down the Law: The Making of the Theodosian Code.* New Haven.

Mattingly, D. 1992. "War and Peace in Roman North Africa: Observations and Models of State-Tribe Interaction." In *War in the Tribal Zone: Expanding States and Indigenous Warfare,* pp. 31–60. Edited by R. Ferguson and N. Whitehead. Sante Fe.

McCormick, M. 2001. *Origins of the European Economy. Communications and Commerce, A.D. 300–900.* Cambridge.

McGrail, S. 1995. "Celtic Seafaring and Transport." In *The Celtic World,* pp. 254–281. Edited by M. Green. London.

Melin, B. 1960. *Die Heimat der Kimbern.* Upsala.

Menghin, W. 1990. *Frühgeschichte Bayerns. Römer und Germanen, Baiern und Schwaben, Franken und Slaven.* Stuttgart.

Mensching, E. 1980. *Caesar und die Germanen im 20. Jahrhundert: Bemerkungen zum Nachleben des Bellum Gallicum in deutschsprachigen Texten.* Göttingen.

Metzler, J., M. Millet, N. Roymans, and J. Slofstra, eds. 1995. *Integration in the Early Roman West.* Luxembourg.

Mócsy, A. 1974a. *Pannonia and Upper Moesia: A History of the Middle Danube Provinces of the Roman Empire.* London.

———. 1974b. "Ein spätantiker Festungstyp am linken Donauufer." In *Roman Frontier Studies, 1969: Proceedings of the Eighth International Congress of Limesforschung,* pp. 191–96. Edited by E. Birley et al. Cardiff.

Montgomery, H. 1972. "Caesar und die Grenzen. Information und Propagand in den Commentarii de bello Gallico." *Symbolae Osloenses* 49:57–92.

Müller-Karpe, A., ed. 1998. *Studien zur Archäologie der Kelten, Römer und Germanen in Mittel- und Westeuropa: Alfred Haffner zum 60. Geburtstag.* Leidorf.

Murray, M. 1993. "The Landscape Survey." In *Settlement, Economy, and Cultural Change at the End of the European Iron Age: Excavations at Kelheim in Bavaria, 1987–91.* Edited by Peter Wells. Ann Arbor.

Nippel, W. 1990. *Griechen, Barbaren und "Wilde": Alte Geschichte und Sozialanthropologie.* Frankfurt.

Norden, E. 1962. *Alt-Germanien. Völker- und namengeschichtlichen Untersuchungen.* 2d ed. Stuttgart.

Okamura, L. 1984. "Alamannia Devicta: Roman-German Conflicts from Caracalla to the First Tetrarchy (A.D. 213–305)." Ph.D. dissertation, University of Michigan.

Overbeck, B. 1973–82. *Das Alpenrheintal in römischer Zeit auf Grund der archäologischen Zeugnisse.* Münchner Beiträge zur Vor- u. Frühgeschichte, 21. Munich.

———. 1987. "Celtic Chronology in South Germany." In *The Coinage of the Roman World in the Late Republic,* pp. 1–12. BAR, int. ser. 326. Edited by A. Burnett and M. Crawford. London.

———. 1996. "Themes on the Fifth- and Sixth-Century Coinage of the Barbarians within the Empire." In *Minorities and Barbarians in Medieval Life and Thought,* pp. 121–140. Sewanee Mediaeval Studies, 7. Edited by S. Ridyard and R. Benson. Sewanee, TN.

———. 2000. *Das Silbermedaillon aus der Münzstätte Ticinum. Ein erstes numismatisches Zeugnis zum Christentum Constantins I.* Iconografica, Fascicolo 3. Milan and Munich.

Page, R. 1987. *Runes.* London.

Palágyi, S. 1981. "Die Römischen Hügelgraber von Inota." *Alba Regia* 19:7–93.

Pauketat, T., and T. Emerson, eds. 1997. *Cahokia: Domination and Ideology in the Mississippian World.* Lincoln.

Petersen, E., A. von Domaszewski, and G. Calderini. 1896. *Die Marcus Säule auf Piazza Colonna in Rom.* Munich.

Petres, E. 1976. "The Late Pre-Roman Age in Hungary with Special Reference to Oppida." In *Oppida: the Beginnings of Urbanisation in Barbarian Europe,* pp. 51–80. Edited by B. Cunliffe and T. Rowley. BAR, supp. ser. 2. London.

Pieta, K., and V. Plachá. 1999. "Die ersten Römer im nördlichen Mittledonauraum im Lichte neuen Grabungen in Devín." In *Germanen Beiderseits des Spätantiken Limes: Materialen des X. International Symposiums, "Grundprobleme der frühgeschichtlichen Entwicklung im nördlichen Mitteldonaugebiet, Xanten vom 2.–6. Dezember 1997."* pp. 179–205. Archäologisches Institut der Akademie der Wissenschaften der Tschechischen Republik, Spisy Archeologickeho av cr Brno, 14. Edited by T. Fischer, G. Precht, and J. Tejral. Cologne and Brno.

Pippidi, D., ed. 1976. *Assimilation et résistance à la culture gréco-romaine dans le monde ancien. Travaux du VIe Congrès International d'Etudes Classiques (Madrid, 1974).* Paris.

Póczy, K. 1977. *Scarbantia: Die Stadt Sopron zur Römerzeit.* Budapest.

Pohl, W., ed. 1997. *Kingdoms of the Empire: The Integration of Barbarians in Late Antiquity.* Leiden, Boston, and Cologne.

Pohl, W., and H. Reimitz, eds. 1998. *Strategies of Distinction: The Construction of Ethnic Communities, 300–800.* Leiden, Boston, and Cologne.

Pohl, W., I. Wood, and H. Reimitz, eds. 2000. *The Transformations of Frontiers from Late Antiquity to the Carolingians.* Leiden, Boston, Cologne.

Potter, D. 1990. *Prophecy and History in the Crisis of the Roman Empire: A Historical Commentary on the Thirteenth Sibylline Oracle.* Oxford.

Rankin, D. 1995. "The Celts through Classical Eyes." In *The Celtic World,* pp. 21–33. Edited by M. Green. London.

Reinhold, M. 1978. *The Golden Age of Augustus.* Toronto.

Reinhold, M., and N. Lewis, eds. 1990. *Roman Civilization: Selected Readings.* 3d ed. New York.

Rieckhoff, S. 1992. "Überlegungen zur Chronologie der Spätlatènezeit im südlichen Mitteleuropa." *Bayerische Vorgeschichtsblätter* 57:103–21.

Rieckhoff-Pauli, S. 1980. "Das Ende der keltischen Welt. Kelten-Römer-Germanen." In *Die Kelten in Mitteleuropa,* pp. 37–47. Edited by L. Pauli. Salzburg.

Riggs, D. 2001. "The Continuity of Paganism between the Cities and Countryside of Late Roman Africa." In *Urban Centers and Rural Contexts in Late Antiquity,* pp. 285–300. Edited by T. Burns and J. Eadie. East Lansing.

Rives, J. 1999. *Germania.* Oxford.

Rivet, A. 1988. *Gallia Narbonensis.* London.

Rosenberger, V. 1992. *Bella et expeditiones: Die antike Terminologie der Kriege.* Stuttgart.

Rosenstock, D. 1984. "Eine prachtvolle römische Emailscheibenfibel und weitere Erzeugnisse römishcen Kunstgewerbes aus der germanischen Siedlung von Frankenwinheim, Landkreis Schweinfurt, Unterfranken." *Das arch. Jahr in Bayern, 1983,* pp. 120–22.

Roth, J. 1998. *The Logistics of the Roman Army at War (264 BC–AD 235).* Leiden and Boston.

Rowlands, M., et al., eds. 1987. *Centre and Periphery in the Ancient World.* Cambridge.

Rugullis, S. 1992. *Die Barbaren in den spätrömischen Gesetzen: Eine Untersuchung des Terminus barbarus.* Frankfurt am Main and New York.

Sacce, C. 1958. *Die Constitutio Antoniniana.* Wiesbaden.

Salmon, E. 1970. *Roman Colonization under the Republic.* Ithaca.

Ŝaŝel, J. 1971. "The Struggle between Magnentius and Constantius II for Italy and Illyricum." *Živa Antika* 2:205–16.

———. 1979. "Antiqui Barbari: Zur Besiedlungsgeschichte Ostnoricums und Pannoniens im 5. und 6. Jahrhundert nach den Schriftenquellen." In *Von der Spätantike zum frühen Mittelalter,* pp. 125–39. Edited by J. Werner and E. Ewig. Sigmaringen.

Schele, L., and D. Freidel. 1990. *A Forest of Kings: The Untold Story of the Ancient Maya.* New York.

Schlüter, W. 1991. *Römer im Osnabrücher Land. Die archäologischen Untersuchungen in der Kalkreiser-Niewedder Senke.* Schriftenreihe Kulturregion Osnabrück des Landschaftsverbandes Osnabrück, v. 4. Bramsche.

———. 1999. "The Battle of the Teutoburg Forest: Archaeological Research at Kalkreis near Osnabrück." In *Roman Germany: Studies in Cul-*

tural Interaction, pp. 125–59. Edited by J. Creighton and R. Wilson. *Journal of Roman Archaeology*, supp. ser. 32. Portsmouth, RI.

Schneider-Schnekenburger, G. 1980. *Churrätien im Frühmittelalter auf Grund der archäologischen Funde.* Münchner Beiträge zur Vor- u. Frühgeschichte, 26. Munich.

Schönbeck, H.-P. 1998. "Augustus als Pater Patriae und Pater Familias im zweiten Tristienbuch des Ovid." *Hermes* 126:454–65.

Schönberger, H. 1969. "The Roman Frontier in Germany: An Archaeological Survey." *Journal of Roman Studies* 59:144–97.

Schulze, W. 1933. *Zur Geschichte lateinischer Eigennamen.* 2d ed. Berlin. Reprint 1966.

Schwarcz, A. 1999. "Cult and Religion among the Tervingi and the Visigoths and the Conversion to Christianity." In *The Visigoths from the Migration Period to the Seventh Century: An Ethnographic Perspective,* pp. 447–59. Studies in Historical Archaeoethnology, v. 4. Edited by P. Heather. Suffolk, UK and Rochester, NY.

Shaffer, L. 1992. *Native Americans before 1492: The Moundbuilding Centers of the Eastern Woodlands.* New York.

Shaw, B. 1984. "Bandits in the Roman Empire." *Past and Present* 105:3–52.

———. 1999. "War and Violence." In *Late Antiquity: A Guide to the Post-Classical World,* pp. 130–69. Edited by G. Bowersock et al. Cambridge, MA, and London.

Shelton, K. 1981–83. "Usurpers' Coins: The Case of Magnentius." *Byzantinische Forschungen* 8:211–35.

Shennan, S. 1989. "Introduction: Archaeological Approaches to Cultural Identity." In *Archaeological Approaches to Cultural Identity,* pp. 1–32. Edited by S. Shennan. London.

Sivan, H. 1996. "Why Not Marry a Barbarian? Marital Frontiers in Late Antiquity (The Example of *CTh* 3.14.1)." In *Shifting Frontiers in Late Antiquity: Papers from the First Interdisciplinary Conference on Late Antiquity, the University of Kansas, March, 1995,* pp.136–45. Edited by R. Mathisen and H. Sivan. Aldershot.

Soproni, S. 1974. "Eine spätrömische Militarstation im sarmatischen Gebiet." In *Roman Frontier Studies, 1969: Proceedings of the Eighth International Congress of Limesforschung,* pp. 197–203. Edited by E. Birley et al. Cardiff.

———. 1978. *Der spätrömische Limes zwischen Esztergom und Szentendre.* Budapest.

Speidel, M. 1975. "The Rise of Ethnic Units in the Roman Imperial Army." *Aufstieg und Niedergang der römischen Welt* II.3:202–231.

———. 1978. *The Religion of Iuppiter Dolichenus in the Roman Army.* Leiden.

———. 1992. "Roman Army Pay Scales." *Journal of Roman Studies* 82:87–106.

Starr, C. 1960. *The Roman Imperial Navy, 31 B.C.–A.D. 324.* 2d ed. New York.

de Ste. Croix, G. 1981. *The Class Struggle in the Ancient Greek World.* London.

Steuer, H. 1990. "Höhensiedlungen des 4. und 5. Jahrhunderts in Südwestdeutschland. Einordnung des Zähringer Burgberges, Gemeinde Gundelfingen, Kreis Breisgau- Hochschwarzwald." In *Archäologie und Geschichte des ersten Jahrtausends in Südwestdeutschland,* pp. 139–205. Edited by H. Nuber, K. Schmid, H. Steuer, and T. Zotz. Sigmaringen.

Stribrny, K. 1989. "Römer rechts des Rhein nach 260 n. Chr. Kartierung, Strukturanalyse und Synope spätrömischer Münzreihen zwischen Koblenz und Regensburg." *Bericht der Römisch-Germanischen Kommission* 70:351–506.

Sullivan, R. 1960. *Heirs of the Roman Empire.* Ithaca.

Suppe, F. 1993. "Continuity of Religious Tradition at Kelheim and the Foundation of Weltenburg Abbey." In *Settlement, Economy, and Cultural Change at the End of the European Iron Age: Excavations at Kelheim in Bavaria, 1987–91,* pp. 156–61. Edited by P. Wells. Ann Arbor.

Szabó, M. 1971. *The Celtic Heritage in Hungary.* Translated by P. Aston. Budapest.

Tächholm, U. 1969. "Aetius and the Catalaunian Fields." *Opuscula Romana* 7:259–76.

Tejral, J. 1994. "Die archäologischen Zeugnisse der Markomannenkriege im Mähren—Probleme der Chronologie und historischen Interpretation." In *Markomannenkriege: Ursachen und Wirkungen,* pp. 299–324. Edited by H. Friesinger, J. Tejral, and A. Stuppner. Brno.

Thernstrom, S., ed. 1980. *Harvard Encyclopedia of American Ethnic Groups.* Cambridge, MA.

Thompson, E. 1948. *A History of Attila and the Huns.* Oxford. Reprint 1996.

———. 1956. "Constantine, Constantius II, and the Lower Danube Frontier." *Hermes* 84:372- 81.

———. 1966. *The Visigoths in the Time of Ulfila.* Oxford.

———. 1982. *Romans and Barbarians: The Decline of the Western Empire.* Madison.

Tierney, J. 1960. "The Celtic Ethnography of Posidonius." *Proceedings of the Royal Irish Academy. Section C.* 60:189–275.

Timpe, D. 1971. "Der römische Verzicht auf die Okkupation Germaniens." *Chiron* 1:267–84.

———. 1995. *Romano-Germanica: Gesammelte Studien zur Germania des Tacitus.* Stuttgart.

Todd, M. 1978. *The Walls of Rome*. London.

———. 1987. *The Northern Barbarians, 100 B.C.– A.D. 300*. 2d ed. Oxford.

———. 1992. *The Early Germans*. Oxford and Cambridge, MA.

Tomlin, R. 1972. "Seniores-Juniores in the Late-Roman Field Army." *American Journal of Philology* 93: 253–78.

Toynbee, J. 1944. *Roman Medallions*. Numismatic Studies, 5. New York.

Untermann, J. 1989. "Sprachvergleichung and Sprachidentität: Methodische Fragen im Zwischenfeld von Keltisch und Germanische." In *Germanenprobleme in heutiger Sicht*, pp. 211–39. Edited by H. Beck. Berlin and New York.

Vallet, F., and M. Kazanski, eds. 1993. *L'armée romaine et les barbares du IIIe au VIIe siècle*. Rouen.

———, eds. 1995. *La noblesse romaine et les chefs barbares du IIIe au VIIe siècle*. Paris.

Vanderspoel, J. 1995. *Themistius and the Imperial Court: Oratory, Civic Duty, and Paideia from Constantius to Theodosius*. Ann Arbor.

Visy, Z. 1977. *Intercisa: Dunaújváros in the Roman Period*. Budapest.

———. 1988. *Der pannonische Limes in Ungarn*. Budapest.

———. 1994. "Die ländliche Besiedlung und Landwirtschaft in Niederpannonien." In *Ländliche Besiedlung und Landwirtschaft in den Rhein-Donau-Provinzen des Römischen Reiches*, v. 2, pp. 421–449. Passauer Universitäts Schriften zur Archäologie, 2. Edited by H. Bender and H. Wolff. Espelkamp.

———. 1997. *Die Wagendarstellungen der pannonischen Grabsteine*. Pécs.

———. 2001. "Towns, Vici and Villae: Late Roman Military Society on the Frontiers of the Province Valeria." In *Urban Centers and Rural Contexts in Late Antiquity*, pp. 163–84. Edited by T. Burns and J. Eadie. East Lansing.

Visy, Z., and D. Planck, eds. 2000. *Von Augustus bis Attila. Leben am Ungarischen Donaulimes*. Stuttgart.

Vittinghof, F. 1952. *Römische Kolonisation und Bürgerrechtspolitik unter Caesar und Augustus*. Wiesbaden.

de Vries, J. 1969. *Altgermanische Religionsgeschichte*. 2d ed. Berlin, 1956.

Wait, G. 1995. "Burial and the Otherworld." In *The Celtic World*, pp. 489–508. Edited by M. Green. London.

Walser, G. 1956. *Caesar und die Germanen; Studien zur politischen Tendenz römischer Feldzugsberichte*. Historia Einzelschriften, 1. Wiesbaden.

Wells, C. 1972. *The German Policy of Augustus: An Examination of the Archaeological Evidence*. Oxford.

———. 1995. "Celts and Germans in the Rhineland." In *The Celtic World*, pp. 603–20. Edited by M. Green. London.

———. 1999. "The German Policy of Augustus: 25 Years On." In *Roman*

Frontier Studies 1997, Proc. 17th International Congress of Roman Frontier Studies, pp. 3–7. Edited by N. Gudea. Zalau, Romania.

Wells, P. 1987. "Industry, Commerce, and Temperate Europe's First Cities: Preliminary Report on 1987 Excavations at Kelheim, Bavaria." *Journal of Field Archaeology* 14:399–412.

———. 1990. "Iron Age Temperate Europe: Some Current Research Issues." *Journal of World Prehistory* 4:437–76.

———, ed. 1993. *Settlement, Economy, and Cultural Change at the End of the European Iron Age: Excavations at Kelheim in Bavaria, 1987–91.* Ann Arbor.

———. 1995a. "Identities, Material Culture, and Change: 'Celts' and 'Germans' in Late-Iron-Age Europe." *Journal of European Archaeology* 3: 169–85.

———. 1995b. "Trade and Exchange." In *The Celtic World,* pp. 230–43. Edited by M. Green. London.

———. 1995c. "Manufactured Objects and the Construction of Identities in Late La Téne Europe." *Eirene* 31:129–50.

———. 1996. "Location, Organization, and Specialization of Craft Production in Late Prehistoric Central Europe." In *Craft Specialization and Social Evolution: In Memory of V. Gordon Childe,* pp. 85–98. Edited by B. Wailes. Philadelphia.

———. 1999. *The Barbarians Speak: How the Conquered Peoples Shaped Roman Europe.* Princeton.

Welwei, K.-W. 1986. "Römische Weltherrschaftsideologie und augusteische Germanienpolitik." *Gymnasium* 93:118–37.

Wenkus, R. 1977. *Stammesbildung und Verfassung. Das Werden der frühmittelalterlichen gentes.* Vienna.

Whatmough, J. 1970. *The Dialects of Ancient Gaul: Prolegomena and Records of the Dialects.* Cambridge, MA.

White, R. 1991. *The Middle Ground: Indians, Empires, and Republics in the Great Lakes Region, 1650–1815.* Cambridge.

Whitehead, N. 1992. "Tribes Make States and States Make Tribes: Warfare and the Creation of Colonial Tribes and States in Northeastern South America." In *War in the Tribal Zone: Expanding States and Indigenous Warfare,* pp. 127–50. Edited by R. Ferguson and N. Whitehead. Sante Fe.

Whittaker, C. 1983. "Trade and Frontiers of the Roman Empire." In *Trade and Famine in Classical Antiquity,* pp. 110–27. Edited by C. Whittaker and P. Garnsey. Cambridge.

———. 1994. *Frontiers of the Roman Empire: A Social and Economic Study.* Baltimore.

Wieczorek, A., U. von Freeden, and U. Koch, eds. 1999. *Völker an Nord- und Ostsee und die Franken: Akten des 48. Sachsensymposiums in Mann-*

heim vom 7. bis 11. September 1997. Mannheimer Geschichtsblätter. Neue Folge. Beihefte, 2. Bonn.

Wiedemann, T. 1986. "Between Man and Beasts. Barbarians in Ammianus Marcellinus." In *Past Perspectives: Studies in Greek and Roman Historical Writing. Papers Presented at a Conference in Leeds, 6–8 April 1983,* pp. 189–211. Edited by I. Moxon, J. Smart, and A. Woodman. Cambridge.

Wilkes, J. 1969. *Dalmatia.* London.

Wirth, G. 1999. *Attila das Hunnenreich und Europas.* Stuttgart.

Witschel, C. 1999. *Krise-Rezession-Stagnation? Der Westen des römischen Reiches im 3. Jh. n. Chr.* Frankfurt am Main.

Wolfram, H. 1975–76. "Gotische Studien II. Die terwingische Stammesverfassung und das Bibelgotische." *Mitteilungen des Instituts für Österreichische Geschichtsforschung,* pt. 1, 83 (1975) 289–324 and pt. 2, 84 (1976) 239–61.

———. 1988. *History of the Goths.* Translated by T. Dunlap. Berkeley.

———. 1997. *The Roman Empire and Its Germanic Peoples.* Translated by T. Dunlap. Berkeley.

Wolfram, H., and W. Pohl, eds. 1990. *Typen der Ethnogenese unter besonderer Berücksichtigung der Bayern: Berichte des Symposions der Kommission für Frühmittelalterforschung, 27. bis 30. Oktober, 1986, Stift Zwettl, Niederösterreich.* Vienna.

Wolters, R. 1990–91. "Zum Waren- und Dienstleistungsaustauch zwischen den Römischen Reich und den Freien Germanien in der Zeit des Principats: Eine Bestandaufnahme." *Münstersche Beiträge zur antiken Handelsgeschichte* 9 (1990) 14–44 and 10 (1991) 78–131.

Wood, I. 1994. *The Merovingian Kingdoms, 450–751.* London and New York.

Woods, D. 1995. "Ammianus Marcellinus and the Deaths of Bonosus and Maximilianus." *Hagiographica* 2:25–55.

Woolf, G. 1998. *Becoming Roman: The Origins of Provincial Civilization in Gaul.* Cambridge.

———. 2000. "Urbanization and Its Discontents in Early Roman Gaul." In *Romanization and the City: Creation, Transformations, and Failures. Proceedings of a Conference Held at the American Academy in Rome, 14–16 May 1998,* pp. 115–32. Edited by E. Fentress. Portsmouth, RI.

Yü, Y. 1967. *Trade and Expansion in Han China: A Study in the Structure of Sino-Barbarian Relations.* Berkeley.

Index

ANCIENT SOCIETY AND HISTORY

The series Ancient Society and History offers books, relatively brief in compass, on selected topics in the history of ancient Greece and Rome, broadly conceived, with a special emphasis on comparative and other nontraditional approaches and methods. The series, which includes both works of synthesis and works of original scholarship, is aimed at the widest possible range of specialist and nonspecialist readers.

Published in the Series:

Eva Cantarella, *Pandora's Daughters*
John E. Stambaugh, *The Ancient Roman City*
Giovanni Comotti, *Music in Greek and Roman Culture*
Mark Golden, *Children and Childhood in Classical Athens*
A. Thomas Cole, *The Origins of Rhetoric in Ancient Greece*
Maurizio Bettini, *Anthropology and Roman Culture: Kinship, Time, Images of the Soul*
Stephen L. Dyson, *Community and Society in Roman Italy*
Suzanne Dixon, *The Roman Family*
Tim G. Parkin, *Demography and Roman Society*
Alison Burford, *Land and Labor in the Greek World*
J. Donald Hughes, *Pan's Travail: Environmental Problems of the Ancient Greeks and Romans*
Steven H. Lonsdale, *Dance and Ritual Play in Greek Religion*
C. R. Whittaker, *Frontiers of the Roman Empire: A Social and Economic Study*
Nancy Demand, *Birth, Death, and Motherhood in Classical Greece*
Pericles Georges, *Barbarian Asia and the Greek Experience: From the Archaic Period to the Age of Xenophon*
Elaine Fantham, *Roman Literary Culture: From Cicero to Apuleius*
Kenneth W. Harl, *Coinage in the Roman Economy, 300 B.C. to 700 A.D.*
Christopher Haas, *Alexandria in Late Antiquity: Topography and Social Conflict*
James C. Anderson, jr., *Roman Architecture and Society*
Matthew R. Christ, *The Litigious Athenian*
Gregory S. Aldrete, *Gestures and Acclamations in Ancient Rome*
H. A. Drake, *Constantine and the Bishops: The Politics of Intolerance*
Tim G. Parkin, *Old Age in the Roman World: A Cultural and Social History*
Thomas S. Burns, *Rome and the Barbarians, 100 B.C.–A.D. 400*